The Gallup Poll

Public Opinion 1982

GEORGE H. GALLUP, founder and chairman of
The Gallup Poll, received a Ph.D. in psychology from
the University of Iowa in 1928. From his undergraduate
days he has had three prime interests: survey research,
public opinion, and politics.
Dr. Gallup is the author of many articles on public
opinion and advertising research and he has published
the following books: *The Pulse of Democracy* (1940);
A Guide Book to Public Opinion Polls (1944); *The Gallup
Political Almanac* (1952); *Secrets of Long Life* (1960);
The Miracle Ahead (1964); *The Sophisticated Poll
Watcher's Guide* (Rev. 1976); *The Gallup Poll,
1935–1971* (1972); *The Gallup Poll: Public Opinion, 1972–1977* (1978);
1978 (1979); *1979* (1980); *1980* (1981); *1981* (1982); *1982* (1983).

Other Gallup Poll Publications Available from Scholarly Resources

The Gallup Poll: Public Opinion, 1981
ISBN 0-8420-2200-7 (1982)

The Gallup Poll: Public Opinion, 1980
ISBN 0-8420-2181-7 (1981)

The Gallup Poll: Public Opinion, 1979
ISBN 0-8420-2170-1 (1980)

The Gallup Poll: Public Opinion, 1978
ISBN 0-8420-2159-0 (1979)

The Gallup Poll: Public Opinion, 1922–1977
2 volumes ISBN 0-8420-2129-9 (1978)

The International Gallup Polls: Public Opinion, 1979
ISBN 0-8420-2180-9 (1981)

The International Gallup Polls: Public Opinion, 1978
ISBN 0-8420-2162-0 (1980)

The Gallup Poll

Public Opinion 1982

Dr. George H. Gallup
Founder and Chairman

SR Scholarly Resources Inc.
Wilmington, Delaware

ACKNOWLEDGMENTS

The preparation of this volume has involved the entire staff of the Gallup Poll and their contributions are gratefully acknowledged. I particularly wish to thank James Shriver, III, managing editor of The Gallup Poll, and Professor Fred L. Israel of the City College of New York, who has been the principal coordinator of this volume and of the nine volumes that preceded it.

G.H.G.

Scholarly Resources Inc.
104 Greenhill Avenue
Wilmington, DE 19805

Library of Congress Catalog Card Number: 79-56557
International Standard Serial Number: 0195-962X
International Standard Book Number: 0-8420-2214-7

CONTENTS

PREFACE

[This introductory essay by Dr. George Gallup is excerpted from a section entitled "How Polls Operate" from his book *The Sophisticated Poll Watcher's Guide.*]

THE CROSS-SECTION

The most puzzling aspect of modern polls to the layman is the cross-section or sample. How, for example, is it possible to interview 1,000 or 2,000 persons out of a present electorate of about 150 million and be sure that the relatively few selected will reflect accurately the attitudes, interests, and behavior of the entire population of voting age?

Unless the poll watcher understands the nature of sampling and the steps that must be taken to assure its representativeness, the whole operation of scientific polling is likely to have little meaning, and even less significance, to him.

With the goal in mind of making the process understandable, and at the risk of being too elementary, I have decided to start with some simple facts about the nature of sampling—a procedure, I might add, that is as old as man himself.

When a housewife wants to test the quality of the soup she is making, she tastes only a teaspoonful or two. She knows that if the soup is thoroughly stirred, one teaspoonful is enough to tell her whether she has the right mixture of ingredients.

In somewhat the same manner, a bacteriologist tests the quality of water in a reservoir by taking a few samples, maybe not more than a few drops from a half-dozen different points. He knows that pollutants of a chemical or bacteriological nature will disperse widely and evenly throughout a body of water. He can be certain that his tiny sample will accurately reflect the presence of harmful bacteria or other pollutants in the whole body of water.

Perhaps a more dramatic example is to be found in the blood tests given routinely in clinics and hospitals. The medical technician requires only a few drops of blood to discover abnormal conditions. He does not have to draw a quart of blood to be sure that his sample is representative.

These examples, of course, deal with the physical world. People are not as much alike as drops of water, or of blood. If they were, then the world of individuals could be sampled by selecting only a half-dozen persons anywhere. People are widely different because their experiences are widely different.

Interestingly, this in itself comes about largely through a sampling process. Every human being gathers his views about people and about life by his own sampling. And, it should be added, he almost invariably ends with a distorted picture because his experience is unique. For example, he draws conclusions about "California" by looking out of his car or airplane window, by observing the people he meets at the airport or on the streets, and by his treatment in restaurants, hotels, and other places. This individual has no hesitancy in telling his friends back home what California is really like—although his views, obviously, are based upon very limited sampling.

The Black man, living his life in the ghetto, working under conditions that are often unpleasant and for wages that are likely to be less than those of the white man who lives in the suburban community, arrives at his own views about racial equality. His sample, likewise, is unrepresentative even though it may be typical of fellow Blacks living under the same conditions. By the same token, well-to-do whites living in the suburbs with the advantages of a college education and travel have equally distorted views of equality. These distortions come about because their sampling, likewise, is based upon atypical experiences.

Although every individual on the face of the earth is completely unique, in the mass he does conform to certain patterns of behavior. No one has expressed this better than A. Conan Doyle, author of the Sherlock Holmes series. He has one of his characters make this observation:

> While the individual man is an insoluble puzzle, in the aggregate he becomes a mathematical certainty. You can never foretell what any one man will do, but you can say with precision what an average number will be up to. Individuals vary, but averages remain constant.

Whenever the range of differences is great—either in nature or man—the sampling process must be conducted with great care to make certain that all major variations or departures from the norm are embraced.

Since some differences that exist may be unknown to the researcher, his best procedure to be sure of representativeness is to select samples from the population by a chance or random process. Only if he follows this procedure can he be reasonably certain that he has covered all major variations that exist.

This principle can be illustrated in the following manner. Suppose that a government agency, such as the Bureau of the Census, maintained an up-to-date alphabetical list of the names of all persons living in the United States eighteen years of age and older. Such a file, at the present time, would include approximately 148 million names.

Now suppose that a survey organization wished to draw a representative sample of this entire group, a sample, say of 10,000 persons. Such a representative sample could be selected by dividing 150,000,000 by 10,000—which produces a figure of 15,000. If the researcher goes systematically through the entire file and records the name of every 15,000th listed, he can be sure that his sample is representative.

The researcher will find that this chance selection, in the manner described, has produced almost the right percentage of Catholics and Protestants, the proper proportion of persons in each age and educational level. The distribution of persons by occupation, sex, race, and income should be broadly representative and consistent with the best available census data. It is important, however, to emphasize the words "broadly representative." The sample—even of 10,000— most likely would not include a single person belonging to the Fox Indian tribe or a single resident of Magnolia, Arkansas. It might not include a single citizen of Afghanistan heritage or a single Zoroastrian.

For the purposes served by polls, a sample normally needs to be only broadly representative. A study could be designed to discover the attitudes of American Indians, in which case the Fox Indians should be properly represented. And a specially designed study of Arkansas would likely embrace interviews with residents of Magnolia.

But for all practical purposes, individuals making up these groups constitute such a small part of the whole population of the United States that their inclusion, or exclusion, makes virtually no difference in reaching conclusions about the total population or even of important segments of the population.

Unfortunately, there is no master file in the United States of persons over the age of eighteen that is available to the researcher. Moreover, even a few weeks after the decennial census such a file would be out of date. Some citizens would have died, some would have moved, and still others would have reached the age of eighteen.

Unlike some European countries, no attempt is made in the United States to keep voter registration lists complete and up to date. Because of this failure to maintain accurate lists of citizens and of registered voters, survey organizations are forced to devise their own systems to select samples that are representative of the population to be surveyed.

Any number of sampling systems can be invented so long as one all-important goal is kept in mind. Whatever the system, the end result of its use must be to give every individual an equal opportunity of being selected. Actually, not every individual will have an equal chance, since some persons will be hospitalized, some in mental or penal institutions, and some in the armed forces in foreign lands. But while these individuals help make up the total United States citizenry, most are disenfranchised by the voting laws of the various states or find difficulty in implementing their opinions at election time. Typically, therefore, they are not included in survey cross-sections.

The Gallup Poll has designed its sample by choosing at random not individuals as described previously, but small districts such as census tracts, census enumeration districts, and townships. A random selection of these small geographical areas provides a good starting point for building a national sample.

The United States population is first arranged by states in geographical order and then within the individual states by districts, also in geographical order. A sampling interval number is determined by dividing the total population of the nation by the number of interviewing locations deemed adequate for a general purpose sample of the population eighteen years of age and older. In the case of the Gallup Poll sample, the number of locations, so selected, is approximately 300.

At the time of this writing, the population of the United States eighteen years and older is approximately 150,000,000. Dividing 150,000,000 by 300 yields a sampling interval of 500,000. A random starting number is then chosen between 1 and 500,000 in order to select the first location. The remaining 299 locations are determined by the simple process of adding 500,000 successively until all 300 locations are chosen throughout the nation.

A geographical sampling unit having been designated, the process of selection is continued by choosing at random a given number of individuals within each unit. Suppose that the sampling unit is a census tract in Scranton, Pennsylvania. Using block statistics, published by the Census Bureau for cities of this size, a block, or a group of blocks, within the tract is chosen by a random method analogous to the procedure used to select the location.

Within a block or groups of blocks so selected, the interviewer is given a random starting point. Proceeding from this point, the interviewer meets his assignment by taking every successive occupied dwelling. Or, as an alternative procedure, he can be instructed to take every third or every fifth or every tenth dwelling unit and to conduct interviews in these designated homes.

In this systematic selection plan, the choice of the dwelling is taken out of the hands of the interviewer. As a reminder to the reader, it should be pointed out that the area or district has been selected by a random procedure; next, the dwelling within the district has been chosen at random. All that now remains is to select, at random, the individual to be interviewed within the household.

This can be done in several ways. A list can be compiled by the interviewer of all persons of voting age residing within each home. From such a household list, he can then select individuals to be interviewed by a random method. Ingenious methods are employed to accomplish this end. One survey organization in Europe, for example, instructs the interviewer to talk to the person in the household whose birthday falls on the nearest date.

Now the process is complete. The district has been selected at random; the dwelling unit within the district has been selected at random; and the individual within the dwelling unit has been selected at random. The end result is that every individual in the nation of voting age has had an equal chance of being selected.

This is the theory. In actual practice, problems arise, particularly in respect to the last stage of the process. The dwelling unit chosen may be vacant, the individual selected within a household may not be at home when the interviewer calls. Of course, the interviewer can return the next day; in fact, he or she can make a half-dozen call backs without finding the person. Each call back adds that much to the cost of the survey and adds, likewise, to the time required to complete the study.

Even with a dozen call backs, some individuals are never found and are never interviewed. They may be in the hospital, visiting relatives, on vacation, on a business trip, not at home except at very late hours, too old or too ill to be interviewed—and a few may even refuse to be interviewed.

Since no nationwide survey has ever reached every person designated by any random selection procedure, special measures must be employed to deal with this situation. In the early 1950s, the Gallup Poll introduced a system called Time-Place interviewing. After an intensive study of the time of day when different members of a household are at home, an interviewing plan was devised that enabled interviewers to reach the highest proportion of persons at the time of their first call.

Since most persons are employed outside the home, interviewing normally must be done in the late afternoon and evening hours, and on weekends. These are the times when men, and especially younger men, are likely to be at home and therefore available to be interviewed.

In various nations, survey organizations are working out new ways to meet this problem of the individual selected for the sample who is not at home. These new procedures may meet more perfectly the ideal requirements of random sampling.

Many ardent advocates of the procedure described as "quota sampling" are still to be found. This, it should be pointed out, was the system generally employed by the leading survey organizations in the pre-1948 era.

The quota system is simplicity itself. If the state of New York has 10% of the total population of the United States, then 10% of all interviews must come from this state. In the case of a national sample of 10,000, this would mean 1,000 interviews.

Going one step further, since New York City contains roughly 40% of the population of the state, then 40% of the 1,000 interviews must be allocated to New York City, or 400. And since Brooklyn has roughly a third of the total population of New York City, a third of the 400 interviews, or 133, must be made in this borough. In similar fashion, all of the 1,000 interviews made in the state of New York can be distributed among the various cities, towns, and rural areas. Other states are dealt with in similar fashion.

Making still further use of census data, the interviews to be made in each city, town, or rural areas can be assigned on an occupational basis: so many white-collar workers, so many blue-collar workers, so many farmers, so many business and professional people, so many retired persons, and so many on the welfare rolls. The allocation can also be made on the basis of rents paid. The interviewer, for example, may be given a "quota" of calls to be made in residential areas with the highest rental values, in areas with medium priced rentals, and in low rental areas.

Typically, in the quota sampling system, the survey organization predetermines the number of men and women and the age, the income, the occupation, and the race of the individuals assigned to each interviewer.

In setting such quotas, however, important factors may be overlooked. In 1960, for example, a quota sample that failed to assign the right proportion of Catholic voters would have miscalculated John Kennedy's political strength. An individual's religious beliefs, obviously, cannot be ascertained by his appearance or by the place where he dwells; this applies to other factors as well.

Not only do theoretical considerations fault the quota system but so do the problems that face the interviewer. When the selection of individuals is left to him, he tends to seek out the easiest-to-interview respondents. He is prone to avoid the worst slum areas, and consequently he turns up with interviews that are likely to be skewed on the high income and educational side. Typically, a quick look at the results of quota sampling will reveal too many persons with a college education, too many persons with average and above average incomes, and in political polls, too many Republicans. Therefore, one of the many advantages of the random procedure is that the selection of respondents is taken out of the hands of the interviewer. In the random method, the interviewer is told exactly where to go and when to go.

Another consideration with cross-sections is keeping them up to date. Although America's population is highly mobile, fortunately for polltakers the basic structure of society changes little. Perhaps the greatest change in America in recent years has been the rising level of education. In 1935, when the Gallup Poll first published poll results, only 7.2% of the adult population had attended college for one year or more. Today that figure is 27%.

How does a research organization know that the sample it has designed meets proper standards? Normally, examination of the socioeconomic data gathered by the interviewer at the end of each interview provides the answer. As the completed interview forms are returned from the field to the Princeton office of the Gallup Poll, the facts from each are punched into IBM cards. In addition to the questions that have dealt with issues and other matters of interest, the interviewer has asked each person to state his occupation, age, how far he went in school, his religious preference, whether he owns or rents his dwelling, and many other questions of a factual nature.

Since the Census Bureau Current Population Surveys provide data on each one of these factors, even a hasty examination will tell whether the cross-section is fairly accurate—that is, whether the important factors line up properly with the known facts, specifically:

—the educational level of those interviewed

—the age level

—the income level

—the proportion of males to females

—the distribution by occupations

—the proportion of whites to nonwhites
—the geographical distribution of cases
—the city-size distribution.

Typically, when the educational level is correct (that is, when the sample has included the right proportion of those who have attended college, high school, grade school, or no school), when the geographical distribution is right and all areas of the nation have been covered in the correct proportion, when the right proportion of those in each income level has been reached, and the right percentages of whites and nonwhites and of men and women are included—then usually other factors tend to fall in line. These include such factors as religious preference, political party preference, and most other factors that bear upon voting behavior, buying behavior, tastes, interests, and the like.

After checking all of the above "controls," it would be unusual to find that every group making up the total population is represented in the sample in the exact percentage that it should be. Some groups may be slightly larger or smaller than they should be. The nonwhite population eighteen years and older, which makes up 11% of the total population, may be found to be less, or more, than this percentage of the returned interviews. Those who have attended high school in the obtained interviews may number 58%, when actually the true figure should be 54%.

Ways have been developed to correct situations such as these that arise out of the over-representation or under-representation of given groups. The sample can be balanced, that is, corrected so that each group is included in the proportion it represents in the total population. When this procedure is followed, the assumption is made that persons within each group who are interviewed are representative of the group in question. But there are obvious limitations to this. If only a few persons are found in a given category, then the danger is always present that they may not be typical or representative of the people who make up this particular group or cell.

On the whole, experience has shown that this process of weighting by the computer actually does produce more accurate samples. Normally, results are changed by only negligible amounts—seldom by more than 1 or 2 percentage points.

A persistent misconception about polling procedures is that a new sample must be designed for measuring each major issue. Actually, Gallup Poll cross-sections are always based upon samples of the entire voting age population. Every citizen has a right to voice his opinion on every issue and to have it recorded. For this reason, all surveys of public opinion seek to reach a representative cross-section of the entire population of voting age.

Some people ask if we go back to the same persons with different polls. The answer, in the case of the Gallup Poll, is "no"; the same person is not interviewed again. Some survey research is based upon fixed cross-sections or "panels." The same persons are reinterviewed from time to time to measure shifts in opinion.

There are certain advantages to this system—it is possible to determine to what extent overall changes cloak individual changes. But a practical disadvantage is that the size of the sample remains fixed. Unless the panel is very large, reliable information cannot be produced for smaller subgroups. In the case of the Gallup Poll, the same question can be placed on any number of surveys and the total sample expanded accordingly, since the same persons are not reinterviewed.

Panels have other limitations. One has to do with determining the level of knowledge. Having asked a citizen what he knows about a certain issue in the first interview, he may very well take the trouble to read about it when he sees an article later in his newspaper or magazine. There is, moreover, a widespread feeling among researchers that the repeated interviewing of the same person tends to make him a "pro" and to render him atypical for this reason. But the evidence is not clear-cut on this point. The greatest weakness, perhaps, is that panels tend to fall apart; persons change their place of residence and cannot be found for a second or subsequent measurement; some refuse to participate more than once and must be replaced by substitutes.

THE SIZE OF SAMPLES

When the subject of public-opinion polls comes up, many people are quick to say that they do not know of anyone who has ever been polled.

The likelihood of any single individual, eighteen years of age or older, being polled in a sample of 1,500 persons is about one chance in 90,000. With samples of this size, and with the frequency that surveys are scheduled by the Gallup Poll, the chance that any single individual will be interviewed—even during a period of two decades—is less than one in 200.

An early experience of mine illustrates dramatically the relative unimportance of numbers in achieving accuracy in polls and the vital importance of reaching a true cross-section of the population sampled.

In the decade preceding the 1936 presidential election, the *Literary Digest* conducted straw polls during elections, with a fair measure of success. The *Literary Digest*'s polling procedure consisted of mailing out millions of postcard ballots to persons whose names were found in telephone directories or on lists of automobile owners.

The system worked so long as voters in average and above-average income groups were as likely to vote Democratic as Republican; and conversely, those in the lower income brackets—the have-nots—were as likely to vote for either party's candidate for the presidency.

With the advent of the New Deal, however, the American electorate became sharply stratified, with many persons in the above average income groups who had been Democrats shifting to the Republican banner, and those below average to the Democratic.

Obviously, a polling system that reached telephone subscribers and automobile owners—the perquisites of the better-off in this era—was certain to overestimate Republican strength in the 1936 election. And that is precisely what did happen. The *Literary Digest*'s final preelection poll showed Landon winning by 57% and Franklin D. Roosevelt losing with 43% of the two-party popular vote.

Landon did not win, as everyone knows. In fact, Roosevelt won by a whopping majority—62.5% to Landon's 37.5%. The error, more than 19 percentage points, was one of the greatest in polling history.

The outcome of the election spelled disaster for the *Literary Digest*'s method of polling, and was a boon to the new type of scientific sampling that was introduced for the first time in that presidential election by my organization, Elmo Roper's, and Archibald Crossley's.

The *Literary Digest* had mailed out 10,000,000 postcard ballots—enough to reach approximately one family in every three at that point in history. A total of 2,376,523 persons took the trouble to mark their postcard ballots and return them.

Experiments with new sampling techniques had been undertaken by my organization as early as 1933. By 1935 the evidence was clear-cut that an important change had come about in the party orientation of voters—that the process of polarization had shifted higher income voters to the right, lower income voters to the left.

When the presidential campaign opened in 1936, it was apparent that the *Literary Digest*'s polling method would produce an inaccurate figure. Tests indicated that a large majority of individuals who were telephone subscribers preferred Landon to FDR, while only 18% of those persons on relief rolls favored Landon.

To warn the public of the likely failure of the *Literary Digest,* I prepared a special newspaper article that was widely printed on July 12, 1936—at the beginning of the campaign. The article stated that the *Literary Digest* would be wrong in its predictions and that it would probably show Landon winning with 56% of the popular vote to 44% for Roosevelt. The reasons why the poll would go wrong were spelled out in detail.

Outraged, the *Literary Digest* editor wrote: "Never before has anyone foretold what our poll was going to show even before it started . . . Our fine statistical friend (George Gallup) should be advised that the Digest would carry on with those old fashioned methods that have produced correct forecasts exactly one hundred percent of the time."

When the election had taken place, our early assessment of what the *Literary Digest* poll would find proved to be almost a perfect prediction of the *Digest*'s final results—actually within 1 percentage point. While this may seem to have been a foolhardy stunt, actually there was little risk. A sample of only 3,000 postcard ballots had been mailed by my office to the same lists of persons who received the

Literary Digest ballot. Because of the workings of the laws of probability, that 3,000 sample should have provided virtually the same result as the *Literary Digest*'s 2,376,523 which, in fact, it did.

Through its own polling, based upon modern sampling procedures, the Gallup Poll, in the 1936 election, reported that the only sure states for Landon were Maine, Vermont, and New Hampshire. The final results showed Roosevelt with 56% of the popular vote to 44% for Landon. The error was 6.8 percentage points, the largest ever made by the Gallup Poll. But because it was on the "right" side, the public gave us full credit, actually more than we deserved.

The *Literary Digest* is not the only poll that has found itself to be on the "wrong" side. All polls, at one time or another, find themselves in this awkward position, including the Gallup Poll in the election of 1948. Ironically, the error in 1936—a deviation of 6.8 percentage points from the true figure—was greater than the error in 1948—5.4 percentage points. But the public's reaction was vastly different.

The failure of polls to have the winning candidate ahead in final results is seldom due to the failure of the poll to include enough persons in its sample. Other factors are likely to prove to be far more important, as will be pointed out later.

Examination of probability tables quickly reveals why polling organizations can use relatively small samples. But first the reader should be reminded that sampling human beings can never produce findings that are *absolutely* accurate except by mere chance, or luck. The aim of the researcher is to come as close as possible to absolute accuracy.

Since money and time are always important considerations in survey operations, the goal is to arrive at sample sizes that will produce results within acceptable margins of error. Fortunately, reasonably accurate findings can be obtained with surprisingly small samples.

Again, it is essential to distinguish between theory and practice. Probability tables are based upon mathematical theory. In actual survey work, these tables provide an important guide, but they can't be applied too literally.

With this qualification in mind, the size of samples to be used in national surveys can now be described. Suppose, for example, that a sample comprises only 600 individuals. What is the theoretical margin of error? If the sample is a perfectly drawn random sample, then the chances are 95 in 100 that the results of a poll of 600 in which those interviewed divide 60% in favor, 40% opposed (or the reverse) will be within 4 percentage points of the true figure; that is, the division in the population is somewhere between 56% and 64% in favor. The odds are even that the error will be less than 2 percentage points—between 58% and 62% in favor, 42% to 38% opposed.

What this means, in the example cited above, is that the odds are 19 to 1 that in repeated samplings the figure for the issue would vary in the case of those favoring the issue from 56% to 64%; the percentage of those opposed would vary between 44% and 36% in repeated samples. So, on the basis of a national sample of only 600 cases, one could say that the odds are great that the addition of many cases—

even millions of cases—would not likely change the majority side to the minority side.

Now, if this sample is doubled in size—from 600 to 1,200—the error factor using the 95 in 100 criterion or confidence level is decreased from 4 percentage points to 2.8 percentage points; if it is doubled again—from 1,200 to 2,400—there is a further decrease—from 2.8 to 2.0, always assuming a mathematically random sample.

Even if a poll were to embrace a total of 2,000,000 individuals, there would still be a chance of error, although tiny. Most survey organizations try to operate within an error range of 4 percentage points at the 95 in 100 confidence level. Accuracy greater than this is not demanded on most issues, nor in most elections, except, of course, those that are extremely close.

Obviously, in many fields an error factor as large as 4 percentage points would be completely unacceptable. In fact, in measuring the rate of unemployment, the government and the press place significance on a change as small as 0.1%. At present, unemployment figures are based upon nationwide samples carried out by the U.S. Bureau of Labor Statistics in the same general manner as polls are conducted. The government bases its findings on samples of some 50,000 persons. But samples even of this size are not sufficient to warrant placing confidence in a change as small as 0.1%. And yet such a change is often headlined on the front pages as indicating a real and significant change in the employment status of the nation.

Even if one were totally unfamiliar with the laws of probability, empirical evidence would suffice to demonstrate that the amassing of thousands of cases does not change results except to a minor extent.

An experiment conducted early in the Gallup Poll's history will illustrate this point. At the time—in the middle 1930s—the National Recovery Act (N.R.A.) was a hotly debated issue. Survey results were tabulated as the ballots from all areas of the United States were returned. The figures below are those actually obtained as each lot of new ballots was tabulated.

NUMBER OF RETURNED BALLOTS	PERCENT VOTING IN FAVOR OF THE N.R.A.
First 500	54.9%
First 1,000	53.9
First 5,000	55.4
First 10,000	55.4
First 30,000	55.5

From these results it can be seen that if only 500 ballots had been received, the figure would have differed little from the final result. In fact the greatest difference found in the whole series is only 1.6 percentage points from the final result.

This example represents a typical experience of researchers in this field. But one precaution needs to be observed. The returns must come from a representative sample of the population being surveyed; otherwise they could be as misleading as trying to project the results of a national election from the vote registered late in the afternoon of election day in a New Hampshire village.

The theoretical error, as noted earlier, can be used only as a guide. The expected errors in most surveys are usually somewhat larger. In actual survey practice, some sample design elements tend to reduce the range of error, as stratification does; some tend to increase the range of error as, for example, clustering. But these are technical matters to be dealt with in textbooks on statistics.

Survey organizations should, on the basis of their intimate knowledge of their sampling procedures and the analysis of their data, draw up their own tables of suggested tolerances to enable laymen to interpret their survey findings intelligently.

The normal sampling unit of the Gallup Poll consists of 1,500 individuals of voting age, that is, eighteen years and over. A sample of this size gives reasonable assurance that the margin of error for results representing the entire country will be less than 3 percentage points based on the factor of size alone.

The margin for sampling error is obviously greater for subgroups. For example, the views of individuals who have attended college are frequently reported. Since about one-fourth of all persons over eighteen years have attended college, the margin of error must be computed on the basis of one-fourth the total sample of 1,500, or 375. Instead of a margin of error of 3 percentage points, the error factor increases to 6 or 7 percentage points in the typical cluster sample.

In dealing with some issues, interest focuses on the views of subgroups such as Blacks, labor union members, Catholics, or young voters—all representing rather small segments of the total population. Significant findings for these subgroups are possible only by building up the size of the total sample.

This can be done in the case of the Gallup Poll by including the same question or questions in successive surveys. Since different, but comparable, persons are interviewed in each study, subgroup samples can be enlarged accordingly. Thus, in a single survey approximately 165 Blacks and other nonwhites would be interviewed in a sample of 1,500, since they constitute 11% of the total voting-age population. On three successive surveys a total of 495 would be reached—enough to provide a reasonably stable base to indicate their views on important political and social issues.

Since much interest before and after elections is directed toward the way different groups in the population vote, it has been the practice of the Gallup Poll to increase the size of its samples during the final month before election day to be in a position to report the political preferences of the many groups that make up the total population—information that cannot be obtained by analyzing the actual election returns. Election results, for example, do not reveal how women voted as opposed to men, how the different age groups voted, how different religious groups voted, how different income levels voted. Many other facts about the public's voting habits can be obtained only through the survey method.

During the heat of election campaigns, critics have asserted on occasion that the Gallup Poll increases its sample size solely to make more certain of being "right." Examination of trend figures effectively answers this criticism. The results reported on the basis of the standard sampling unit have not varied, on the average, more than 1 or 2 percentage points from the first enlarged sample in all of the national elections of the last two decades, and this, of course, is within the margin of error expected.

Persons unfamiliar with the laws of probability invariably assume that the size of the sample must bear a fixed relationship to the size of the "universe" sampled. For example, such individuals are likely to assume that if a polling organization is sampling opinions of the whole United States, a far larger sample is necessary than if the same kind of survey is to be conducted in a single state, or in a single city. Or, to put this in another way, the assumption is that since the population of the United States is roughly ten times that of New York State, then the sample of the United States should be ten times as large.

The laws of probability, however, do not work in this fashion. Whenever the population to be surveyed is many times the size of the sample (which it typically is), the size of samples must be almost the same. If one were conducting a poll in Baton Rouge, Louisiana, on a mayoralty race, the size of the sample should be virtually the same as for the whole United States. The same principle applies to a state.

Two examples, drawn from everyday life, may help to explain this rather mystifying fact. Suppose that a hotel cook has two kinds of soup on the stove—one in a very large pot, another in a small pot. After thoroughly stirring the soup in both pots, the cook need not take a greater number of spoonsful from the large pot or fewer spoonsful from the small pot to taste the quality of the soup, since the quality should be the same.

The second example, taken from the statistician's world, may shed further light on this phenomenon. Assume that 100,000 black and white balls are placed in a large cask. The white balls number 70,000; the black balls, 30,000. Into another cask, a much smaller one, are placed 1,000 balls, divided in exactly the same proportion: 700 white balls, 300 black balls.

Now the balls in each cask are thoroughly mixed and a person, blindfolded, is asked to draw out of each cask exactly 100 balls. The likelihood of drawing 70 white balls and 30 black balls is virtually the same, despite the fact that one cask contains 100 times as many balls as the other.

If this principle were understood then hours of Senate floor time could have been saved in recent years. Senator Albert Gore, of Tennessee, a few years ago, had this to say about the Gallup Poll's sampling unit of 1,500—as reported in the *Congressional Record*:

As a layman I would question that a straw poll of less than 1 per cent of the people could under any reasonable circumstance be regarded as a fair and meaningful cross-section. This would be something more than 500 times as large a sample as Dr. Gallup takes.

In the same discussion on the Senate floor, Senator Russell Long of Lousiana added these remarks:

I believe one reason why the poll information could not be an accurate reflection of what the people are thinking is depicted in this example. Suppose we should try to find how many persons should be polled in a city the size of New Orleans in order to determine how an election should go. In a city that size, about 600,000 people, a number of 1,000 would be an appropriate number to sample to see how the election was likely to go. . . . In my home town of Baton Rouge, Lousiana, I might very well sample perhaps 300 or 400 people and come up with a fairly accurate guess as to how the city or the parish would go, especially if a scientific principle were used. But if I were to sample only a single person or two or three in that entire city, the chances are slim that I would come up with an accurate guess.

If the reader has followed the explanation of the workings of the laws of probability, and of earlier statements about the size of samples, he will be aware of two errors in the senator's reasoning. Since both cities, New Orleans and Baton Rouge, have populations many times the size of the sample he suggested, both require samples of the same size. The second is his assumption that any good researcher would possibly attempt to draw conclusions about either city on the basis of "a single person or two."

The size of the "universe" to be sampled is typically very great in the case of most surveys; in fact, it is usually many times the size of the samples to be obtained. A different principle applies when the "universe" is small. The size of a sample needed to assess opinions of the residents of a community of 1,000 voters is obviously different from that required for a city that is much larger. A sample of 1,000 in such a town would not be a sample; it would be a complete canvass.

DEVELOPING POLL QUESTIONS

Nothing is so difficult, nor so important, as the selection and wording of poll questions. In fact, most of my time and effort in the field of polling has been devoted to this problem.

The questions included in a national survey of public opinion should meet many tests: they must deal with the vital issues of the day, they must be worded in a way to get at the heart of these issues, they must be stated in language understandable to the least well educated, and finally, they must be strictly impartial in presenting the issue.

If any reader thinks this is easy, let him try to word questions on any present-day issue. It is a tough and trying mental task. And even years of experience do not make the problem less onerous.

One rule must always be followed. No question, no matter how simple, must reach the interviewing stage without first having gone through a thorough pretesting procedure. Many tests must be applied to see that each question meets required standards.

Every survey organization has its own methods of testing the wording of questions. Here it will suffice to describe in some detail how the Gallup Poll goes about this task.

Pretesting of questions dealing with complicated issues is carried on in the Interviewing Center maintained in Hopewell, New Jersey, by the Gallup organizations. Formerly, this center was a motion-picture theater. In the early 1950s it was converted into an interviewing center. The town of Hopewell is located in the middle of an area with a total population of 500,000—an area that includes the cities of Trenton and Princeton, suburban communities, small towns, and rural districts. Consequently, people from many walks of life are available for interviewing.

Pretesting procedures normally start with "in-depth" interviews with a dozen or more individuals invited to come to the center. The purpose of these interviews is to find out how much thought each participant has given to the issue under consideration, the level of his or her knowledge about the issue, and the important facets that must be probed. Most of the questions asked in these sessions are "open" questions—that is, questions which ask: "What do you know about the XX problem? What do you think about it? What should the government do about it?" and so forth.

In conversations evoked by questions of this type, it is possible, in an unhurried manner, to discover how much knowledge average persons have of a given issue, the range of views regarding it, and the special aspects of the issue that need to be probed if a series of questions is to be developed.

The next step is to try out the questions, devised at this first stage, on a new group of respondents, to see if the questions are understandable and convey the meaning intended. A simple test for this can be employed. After reading the question, the respondent is asked to "play back" what it says to him. The answer quickly reveals whether the person being interviewed understands the language used and whether he grasps the main point of the question. This approach can also reveal, to the trained interviewer, any unsuspected biases in the wording of the question. When the language in which a question is stated is not clear to the interviewee, his typical reaction is: "Will you read that question again?" If questions have to be repeated, this is unmistakable evidence that they should be worded in a simpler and more understandable manner.

Another procedure that has proved valuable in testing questions is the self-administered interview. The respondent, without the benefit of an interviewer, writes out the answers to the questions. The advantages of this procedure are many. Answers show whether the individual has given real thought to the issue and reveal, also, the degree of his interest. If he has no opinion, he will typically leave the question blank. If he has a keen interest in the issue, he will spell out his views in some detail. And if he is misinformed, this becomes apparent in what he writes.

Self-administered questionnaires can be filled out in one's own home, or privately in an interviewing center. Since the interviewer is not at hand, many issues, such as those dealing with sex, drug addiction, alcoholism, and other personal matters, can be covered in this manner. The interviewer's function is merely to drop off the questionnaire, and pick it up in a sealed envelope the next day—or the respondent can mail it directly to the Princeton office.

Even with all of these precautions, faulty question wordings do sometimes find their way onto the survey interviewing form. Checks for internal consistency, made when the ballots are returned and are tabulated, usually bring to light these shortcomings.

Most important, the reader himself must be the final judge. The Gallup Poll, from its establishment in 1935, has followed the practice of including the exact wording of questions, when this is important, in the report of the poll findings. The reader is thus in a position to decide whether the question is worded impartially and whether the interpretation of the results, based upon the question asked, is fair and objective.

A United States senator has brought up another point about questions:

How do pollsters like yourself determine what questions to ask from time to time? It seems to me that pollsters can affect public opinion simply by asking the question. The results could be pro or anti the president depending upon the questions asked and the president's relation to it.

To be sure, a series of questions could be asked that would prove awkward to the administration, even though worded impartially, and interpreted objectively. But this would be self-defeating because it would soon become apparent to readers and commentators that the survey organization was not engaged solely in fact-finding but was trying to promote a cause.

One way to prevent unintentional biases from creeping into survey operations is to have a staff that is composed of persons representing the different shades of political belief—from right to left. If not only the questions but also the written reports dealing with the results have to run this gamut—as is the practice in the Gallup office—the dangers of unintentional bias are decreased accordingly.

Still one more safeguard in dealing with biases of any type comes about through the financial support of a poll. If sponsors represent all shades of political belief, then economic pressures alone help to keep a poll on the straight and narrow path.

So much for bias in the wording and selection of questions. This still does not answer the question posed by some who wish to know what standards or practices are followed in deciding what issues to present to the public.

Since the chief aim of a modern public opinion poll is to assess public opinion on the important issues of the day and to chart the trend of sentiment, it follows that most subjects chosen for investigation must deal with current national and international issues, and particularly those that have an immediate concern for the typical citizen. Newspapers, magazine, and the broadcast media are all useful sources of ideas for polls. Suggestions for poll subjects come from individuals and institutions—from members of Congress, editors, public officials, and foundations. Every few weeks the public itself is questioned about the most important problems facing the nation, as they see them. Their answers to this question establish priorities, and provide an up-to-date list of areas to explore through polling.

A widely held assumption is that questions can be twisted to get any answer you want. In the words of one publisher: "If you word a question one way you get a result which may differ substantially from the result you get if you word the question in a different way."

It's not that easy. Questions can be worded in a manner to bring confusing and misleading results. But the loaded question is usually self-defeating because it is obvious that it is biased.

Hundreds of experiments with a research procedure known as the split-ballot technique (one-half the cross-section gets Question A, the other half Question B) have proved that even a wide variation in question wordings did not bring substantially different results if the basic meaning or substance of the question remained the same.

Change the basic meaning of the question, add or leave out an essential part, and the results will change accordingly, as they should. Were people insensitive to words—if they were unable to distinguish between one concept and another—then the whole *raison d'être* of polling would vanish.

Often the interpreters of poll findings draw inferences that are not warranted or make assumptions that a close reading of the question does not support. Consider, for example, these two questions:

"Do you feel the United States should have gotten involved in Vietnam in the first place?"

"Do you feel the United States should have helped South Vietnam to defend itself?"

While at first glance these questions seem to deal with the same point—America's involvement—actually they are probing widely different aspects of involvement. In the first case, the respondent can read in that we helped Vietnam "with our own troops"; in the second question, that our help would have been limited to materials. Many polls have shown that the American people are willing to give military supplies to almost any nation in the world that is endangered by the communists, but they are unwilling to send troops.

If the two questions cited above did not bring substantially different results, then all the other poll results dealing with this issue would be misleading.

Questions must be stated in words that everyone understands, and results are likely to be misleading to the extent that the words are not fully understood. Ask people whether they are disturbed about the amount of pornography in their magazines and newspapers and you will get one answer; if you talk about the amount of smut you will get another.

Word specialists may insist that every word in the language conveys a slightly different connotation to every individual. While this may be true, the world (and polls) must operate on the principle that commonly used words convey approximately the same meaning to the vast majority. And this fact can easily be established in the pretesting of questions. When a question is read to a respondent and he is then asked to "play it back" in his own words, it becomes quickly evident whether he has understood the words, and in fact, what they mean to him.

Some questions that pass this test can still be faulty. The sophisticated poll watcher should be on the alert for the "desirable goal" question. This type of question ties together a desirable goal with a proposal for reaching this end. The respondent typically reacts to the goal as well as to the means. Here are some examples of desirable goal questions:

"To win the war quickly in Vietnam, would you favor all-out bombing of North Vietnam?"

"To reduce crime in the cities, would you favor increasing jail and prison sentences?"

"In order to improve the quality of education in the United States, should teachers be paid higher salaries?"

These questions, which present widely accepted goals accompanied by the tacit assumption that the means suggested will bring about the desired end, produce results biased on the favorable side.

The more specific questions are, the better. One of the classic arguments between newspapers and television has centered around a question that asks the public: "Where do you get most of your news about what's going on in the world today—from the newspaper, or radio, or television, or magazines, or talking to people, or where?" The answers show TV ahead of daily newspapers. But when this question is asked in a way to differentiate between international news, and local and state news, TV wins on international news, but the daily newspaper has a big lead on local news. A simple explanation is that the phrase, "What is going on in the *world?*" is interpreted by the average citizen to mean in the faraway places—not his home city.

People are extremely literal minded. A farmer in Ontario, interviewed by the Canadian Gallup Poll, was asked at the close of the interview how long he had lived in the same house; specifically, the length of his residence there. The answer that came back was "Twenty-six feet and six inches."

Whenever it is possible, the questions asked should state both sides of the issue. Realistic alternatives should be offered, or implied.

Looking back through more than four decades of polling, this aspect of question wording warrants the greatest criticism. There is probably little need to state the other side, or offer an alternative, in a question such as this: "Should the voting age be lowered to include those eighteen years of age?" The alternative implied is to leave the situation as it is.

An excellent observation has been made by a political scientist on the faculty of a New England college:

> Somehow more realism must be introduced into polls. . . . People often affirm abstract principles but will not be willing to pay the price of their concrete application. For example, would you be willing to pay more for each box of soap you buy in order to reduce ground pollution—or $200 more for your next car in order to reduce air pollution, etc.?

This type of question is similar to the desirable goal question. The public wants to clear the slums, wants better medical care, improved racial relations, better schools, better housing. The real issue is one of priorities and costs. The role of the public opinion poll in this situation is to shed light on the public's concern about each major problem, establish priorities, and then discover whether the people are willing to foot the bill.

The well-informed person is likely to think of the costs involved by legislation that proposes to deal with these social problems. But to the typical citizen there is no immediate or direct relationship between legislation and the amount he has to pay in taxes. Congress usually tries to disguise costs by failing to tie taxes or costs to large appropriations, leaving John Doe with the impression that someone else will pay the bill.

Still another type of question that is suspect has to do with good intentions. Questions of this type have meaning only when controls are used and when the results are interpreted with a full understanding of their shortcomings.

Examples of questions that fall into this category are those asking people if they "plan to go to church," "read a book," "listen to good music," "vote in the coming election," and so forth.

To the typical American the word "intend" or "plan" connotes many things, such as "Do I think this is a good idea?" "Would I like to do it?" "Would it be good for me?" "Would it be good for other people?" These and similar questions of a prestige nature reveal attitudes, but they are a poor guide to action.

Behavior is always the best guide. The person who attended church last Sunday is likely to go next Sunday, if he says he plans to. The citizen who voted in the last election and whose name is now on the registration books is far more likely to vote than the person who hasn't bothered to vote or to register, even though he insists that he "plans" to do both.

Probably the most difficult of all questions to word is the type that offers the respondent several alternatives. Not only is it hard to find alternatives that are mutually exclusive; it is equally difficult to find a series that covers the entire range of opinions. Added to this is the problem of wording each alternative in a way that doesn't give it a special advantage. And finally, in any series of alternatives that ranges from one extreme of opinion to the other, the typical citizen has a strong inclination to choose one in the middle.

As a working principle it can be stated that the more words included in a question, either by way of explanation or in stating alternatives, the greater the possibilities that the question wording itself will influence answers.

A member of the editorial staff of a newsmagazine voiced a common reaction when he observed:

> On more than a few occasions I have found that I could not, were I asked, answer a poll with a "yes" or "no." More likely my answer would be "yes, but" or "yes, if." I wonder whether pollsters can't or just don't want to measure nuances of feeling.

Obviously it is the desire of a polling organization to produce a full and accurate account of the public's views on any given issue, nuances and all.

First, however, it should be pointed out that there are two main categories of questions serving two different purposes—one to *measure* public opinion, the other to *describe* public opinion. The first category has to do with the "referendum" type of question. Since the early years of polling, heavy emphasis has been placed upon this type of question, which serves in effect as an unofficial national referendum on a given issue, actually providing the same results, within a small margin of error, that an official nationwide referendum would if it were held at the same time and on the same issue.

At some point in the decision process, whether it be concerned with an important issue before Congress, a new law before the state legislature, or a school bond issue in Central City, the time comes for a simple "yes" or "no" vote. Fortunately, or unfortunately, there is no lever on a voting machine that permits the voter to register a "yes, if" or a "yes, but" vote. While discussion can and should proceed at length, the only way to determine majority opinion is by a simple count of noses.

If polling organizations limited themselves to the referendum type of question they would severely restrict their usefulness. They can and should use their machinery to reveal the many facets of public opinion of any issue, and to shed light on the reasons why the people hold the views they do; in short, to explore the "why" behind public opinion.

More and more attention is being paid to this diagnostic approach and the greatest improvements in the field of public opinion research in the future are likely to deal with this aspect of polling.

One of the important developments in question technique was the development in the late 1940s of a new kind of question design that permits the investigation of views on any issue of a complex nature.

This design, developed by the Gallup Poll, has been described as the "quintamensional approach" since it probes five aspects of opinion:

1. the respondent's awareness and general knowledge about it,
2. his overall opinions,
3. the reasons why he holds his views,
4. his specific views on specific aspects of the problem,
5. the intensity with which he hold his opinions.

This question design quickly sorts out those who have no knowledge of a given issue—an important function in successful public opinion polling. And it can even reveal the extent or level of knowledge of the interviewee about the issue.

This is how the system works. The first question put to the person being interviewed (on any problem or issue no matter how complex) is this: "Have you heard or read about the XXX problem (proposal or issue)?"

The person being interviewed can answer either "yes" or "no" to this question, or he can add, "I'm not sure." If he answers in the negative, experience covering many years indicates that he is being entirely truthful. If he answers "yes" or "I'm not sure" he is then asked: "Please tell me in your own words what the debate (or the proposal or issue) is about." At this point the person interviewed must produce evidence that reveals whether he has some knowledge of the problem or issue.

The reader might imagine himself in this interviewing situation. You are called upon by an interviewer and in the course of the interview are asked if you have "heard or read about the Bronson proposal to reorganize the Security Council of the United Nations." The answer is likely to be "no." Possibly you might say: "I seem to have heard about it somewhere." Or suppose that, just to impress the interviewer (something that rarely happens) you fall into the trap of saying "yes."

The next question puts you neatly and delicately on the spot. It asks you to describe in your own words what the Bronson proposal is. You have to admit at this point that you do not know, or come up with an answer that immediately indicates you do not know what it is.

At this stage the questioning can be expanded to discover just how well informed you are. If it is an issue or proposal, then you can be asked to give the main arguments for and the main arguments against the plan or issue. In short, by adding questions at this stage, the *level* of knowledge of the respondent can be determined.

The next question in the design is an "open" question that asks simply: "What do you think should be done about this proposal?" or "How do you think this issue should be resolved?" This type of question permits the person being interviewed to give his views without any specifics being mentioned. Answers, of course, are recorded by the interviewer as nearly as possible in the exact words of the respondent.

The third category of questions seeks to find out the "why" behind the respondent's views. This can be done with a simple question asking: "Why do you feel that way?" or variations of this, along with "nondirective" probes such as "What else?" or "Can you explain that in greater detail?"

The fourth category in the design poses specific issues that can be answered in "yes" or "no" fashion. At this fourth stage it is possible to go back to those who were excluded by the first two questions: those who said they had not heard or read about the issue in question or proved, after the second question, that they were uninformed.

By explaining in neutral language to this group what the problem or issue is and the specific proposals that have been made for dealing with it, the uninformed can voice their opinions, which later can be compared with those of the already informed group.

The fifth category attempts to get at the intensity with which opinions are held. How strongly does each side hold to its views? What action is each individual willing to take to see that his opinion prevails? What chance is there that he may change his mind?

This, then, is the quintamensional approach. And its special merit is that it can quickly sort out the informed from the uninformed. The views of the well informed can be compared not only with the less well informed but with those who are learning about the issue for the first time. Moreover, through cross-tabulations, it is possible to show how special kinds of knowledge are related to certain opinions.

The filtering process may screen out nearly all individuals in the sample because they are uninformed, but it is often of interest and importance to know how the few informed individuals divide on a complex issue. When the best informed individuals favor a proposal or issue, experience indicates that their view tends to be accepted by lower echelons as information and knowledge become more widespread.

But this is not the invariable pattern. In the case of Vietnam, it was the best educated and the best informed who reversed their views as the war went on. The least well educated were always more against the war in Vietnam.

It is now proper to ask why, with all of its obvious merits, this question design is not used more often. The answer is that polling organizations generally avoid technical and complex issues, preferring to deal with those on which the vast majority of Americans have knowledge and opinions. Often the design is shortened to embrace only the filter question that seeks to find out if the individual has read or heard about a given issue, and omits the other questions.

In the field of public opinion research, one finds two schools of thought: one is made up largely of those in academic circles who believe that research on public attitudes should be almost entirely descriptive or diagnostic; the other, made up largely of persons in political life or in journalism or allied fields, who want to know the "score." It is the task of the polling organization to satisfy both groups. And to do this, both categories of questions must be included in the surveys conducted at regular intervals.

The long experience of the Gallup Poll points to the importance of reporting trends of opinion on all the continuing problems, the beliefs, the wishes of the people.

In fact, about four out of every ten questions included in a typical survey are for the purpose of measuring trends. Simple "yes" and "no" questions are far better suited to this purpose than "open-ended" questions, and this accounts chiefly for the high percentage of this type of question in the field of polling.

INTERVIEWERS AND INTERVIEWING PROBLEMS

Since the reliability of poll results depends so much on the integrity of interviewers, polling organizations must go to great lengths to see that interviewers follow instructions conscientiously.

A professor at an Ivy League college sums up the problems that have to do with interviewers in this question: "How do you insure quality control over your interviewers, preventing them from either influencing the answers, mis-recording them, or filling in the forms themselves?"

Before these specific points are dealt with, the reader may wish to know who the interviewers are and how they are selected and trained.

Women make the best interviewers, not only in the United States but in virtually every nation where public opinion survey organizations are established. Generally, they are more conscientious and more likely to follow instructions than men. Perhaps the nature of the work makes interviewing more appealing to them. The fact that the work is part-time is another reason why women prefer it.

Most interviewers are women of middle age, with high-school or college education. Most are married and have children.

Very few interviewers devote full time to this work. In fact, this is not recommended. Interviewing is mentally exhausting and the interviewer who works day after day at this task is likely to lose her zeal, with a consequent drop in the quality of her work.

When an area is drawn for the national cross-section, the interviewing department of the polling organization finds a suitable person to serve as the interviewer in this particular district. All the usual methods of seeking individuals who can meet the requirements are utilized, including such sources as school superintendents, newspaper editors, members of the clergy, and the classified columns of the local press.

Training for this kind of work can be accomplished by means of an instruction manual, by a supervisor, or by training sessions. The best training consists of a kind of trial-by-fire process. The interviewer is given test interviews to do after she has completed her study of the instruction manual. The trial interviews prove whether she can do the work in a satisfactory manner; more important, making these interviews enables the interviewer to discover if she really likes this kind of work. Her interviews are carefully inspected and investigated. Telephone conversations often straighten out procedures and clear up any misunderstandings about them.

Special questions added to the interviewing form and internal checks on consistency can be used to detect dishonesty. Also, a regular program of contacting persons who have been interviewed—to see if they in fact have been interviewed—is commonly employed by the best survey organizations.

It would be foolhardy to insist that every case of dishonesty can be detected in this manner, but awareness of the existence of these many ways of checking honesty removes most if not all of the temptation for the interviewers to fill in the answers themselves.

Experience of many years indicates that the temptation to "fudge" answers is related to the size of the work load given to the interviewer. If too many interviews are required in too short a time, the interviewer may hurry through the assignment, being less careful than she otherwise would be and, on occasion, not above the temptation to fill in a last few details.

To lessen this pressure, the assignment of interviews given to Gallup Poll interviewers has been constantly reduced through the years. At the present time, an assignment consists of only five or six interviews, and assignments come at least a week apart. This policy increases the cost per interview but it also keeps the interviewer from being subjected to too great pressure.

In the case of open questions that require the interviewer to record the exact words of the respondent, the difficulties mount. The interviewer must attempt to record the main thought of the respondent as the respondent is talking, and usually without benefit of shorthand. The addition of "probe" questions to the original open-end questions helps to organize the response in a more meaningful way. In certain circumstances, the use of small tape recorders, carried by the interviewer, is highly recommended.

So much for the interviewer's side of this situation. What about the person being interviewed? How honest is he?

While there is no certain way of telling whether a given individual is answering truthfully, the evidence from thousands of surveys is that people are remarkably honest and frank when asked their views in a situation that is properly structured—that is, when the respondent knows the purpose of the interview and is told that his name will not be attached to any of the things he says, and when the questions are properly worded.

It is important to point out that persons reached in a public opinion survey normally do not know the interviewer personally. For this reason, there is little or no reason to try to impress her. And, contrary to a widely held view, people are not inclined to "sound off" on subjects they know little about. In fact, many persons entitled, on the basis of their knowledge, to hold an opinion about a given problem or issue often hesitate to do so. In the development of the quintamensional procedure, described earlier, it was discovered that the opening question could not be stated: "Have you *followed* the discussion about the XX issue?" Far too many said they hadn't. And for this reason the approach had to be changed to ask: "Have you *heard or read* about the XX issue?"

The interviewer is instructed to read the question exactly as it is worded, and not try to explain it or amplify it. If the interviewee says, "Would you repeat that?" (incidentally, this is always the mark of a bad question), the interviewer repeats the question, and if on the second reading the person does not understand or get the point of the question, the interviewer checks the "no opinion" box and goes on to the next question.

But don't people often change their minds? This is a question often asked of poll-takers. The answer is, "Of course." Interviewed on Saturday, some persons may have a different opinion on Sunday. But this is another instance when the law of averages comes to the rescue. Those who shift their views in one direction will almost certainly be counterbalanced by those who change in the opposite direction. The net result is to show no change in the overall results.

Polls can only reflect people as they are—sometimes inconsistent, often uninformed. Democracy, however, does not require that every individual, every voter, be a philosopher. Democracy requires only that the sum total of individual views—the collective judgment—add up to something that makes sense. Fortunately, there now exists some forty years of polling evidence to prove the soundness of the collective judgment of the people.

How many persons refuse to be interviewed? The percentage is very small, seldom more than 10% of all those contacted. Interestingly, this same figure is found in all the nations where public opinion polls are conducted. Refusals are chiefly a function of lack of interviewing skill. Top interviewers are rarely turned down. This does not mean that a man who must get back to work immediately or a woman who has a cake in the oven will take thirty to forty-five minutes to discuss issues of the day. These situations are to be avoided. And that is why the Time-Place interviewing plan was developed by the Gallup Poll.

Readers may wonder how polls allow for the possible embarrassment or guilty conscience factor that might figure in an interviewee's answers to some questions. For example, while a voter might be prepared to vote for a third-party candidate like George Wallace, he might be uneasy about saying so to a stranger sitting in his living room.

When interviews and the interviewing situation are properly structured, however, this does not happen. In the 1968 election campaign, to follow the same example, the Gallup Poll found Wallace receiving at one point as much as 19% of the total vote. Later his popularity declined. The final poll result showed him with 15% of the vote; he actually received 14%. If there had been any embarrassment about admitting being for Wallace, his vote would obviously have been under-estimated by a sizable amount.

Properly approached, people are not reluctant to discuss even personal matters—their private problems, their religion, sex. By using an interesting technique developed in Sweden, even the most revealing facts about the sex life of an individual can be obtained. And the same type of approach is found to be highly successful in finding out the extent of drug use by college students. Many studies about the religious beliefs of individuals have been conducted by the Gallup Poll without meeting interviewing difficulties.

The desire to have one's voice heard on issues of the day is almost universal. An interviewer called upon an elderly man and found him working in his garden. After he had offered his views on many subjects included in the poll, he called to the interviewer who had started for her car, and said: "You know, two of the most important things in my life have happened this week. First, I was asked to serve on a jury, and now I have been asked to give my views in a public opinion poll."

MEASURING INTENSITY

To the legislator or administrator the intensity with which certain voters or groups of voters hold their opinions has special significance. If people feel strongly enough about a given issue they will likely do something about it—write letters, work for a candidate who holds a contrary view, contribute money to a campaign, try to win other voters to their candidate. To cite an example: Citizens who oppose any kind of gun control laws, though constituting a minority of the public, feel so strongly about this issue that they will do anything they can to defeat such legislation. As a result, they have succeeded in keeping strict gun laws from being adopted in most states and by the federal government.

Since most legislation calls for more money, a practical measure of the intensity of feeling about a given piece of legislation is the willingness to have taxes increased to meet the costs.

One politician made this criticism of polling efforts: "Issue polling often fails to differentiate between hard and soft opinion. If the issue is national health insurance, then the real test is not whether the individual favors it but how much more per year he is willing to pay in taxes for such a program."

This is a merited criticism of polls and, as stated earlier, one that points to the need for greater attention on the part of polling organizations. The action that an individual is willing to take—the sacrifice he is willing to undergo—to see that his side of an issue prevails is one of the best ways of sorting out hard from soft opinion.

Questions put to respondents about "how strongly" they feel, "how important it is to them," and "how much they care" all yield added insights into the intensity of opinions held by the public. The fact, however, that they are used as seldom as they are in the regular polls, here and abroad, indicates that the added information gained does not compensate for the time and the difficulties encountered by the survey interviewer. Most attitude scales are, in fact, better suited to the classroom with students as captive subjects than to the face-to-face interviews undertaken by most survey organizations.

The best hope, in my opinion, lies in the development of new questions that are behavior- or action-oriented. Here, then, is an important area where both academicians and practitioners can work together in the improvement of present research procedures.

The specific complaint mentioned above—that of providing a more realistic presentation of an issue—can probably be dealt with best in the question wording, as noted earlier.

While verbal scales to measure intensity can be usefully employed in many situations, two nonverbal scales have gained wide acceptance and use throughout the world. Since they do not depend upon words, language is no barrier to their use in any nation. Moreover, they can be employed in normal interviewing situations, and on a host of problems.

The scales were devised by Jan Stapel of the Netherlands Institute of Public Opinion and by Hadley Cantril and a colleague, F. P. Kilpatrick. While the scales seem to be similar, each has its own special merits.

The Stapel scale consists of a column of ten boxes. The five at the top are white, the five at the bottom black.

$$
\begin{array}{ll}
\square & +5 \\
\square & +4 \\
\square & +3 \\
\square & +2 \\
\square & +1 \\
\blacksquare & -1 \\
\blacksquare & -2 \\
\blacksquare & -3 \\
\blacksquare & -4 \\
\blacksquare & -5 \\
\end{array}
$$

The boxes are numbered from +5 to −5. The interviewer carries a reproduction of this scale and at the appropriate time in the interview hands it to the respondent. The interviewer explains the scale in these or similar words: "You will notice that the boxes on this card go from the highest position of plus 5—something you like very much—all the way down to the lowest position of minus 5—or something you dislike very much. Now, how far up the scale, or how far down the scale, would you rate the following?"

After this explanation, the interviewer asks the respondent how far up or down the scale he would rate an individual, political party, product, company, proposal, or almost anything at issue. The person is told "put your finger on the box" that best represents his point of view; or, in other situations, to call off the number opposite the box. The interviewer duly records this number on his interviewing form.

One of the merits of the Stapel Scalometer is that it permits the person being interviewed to answer two questions with one response: whether he has a positive or a negative feeling toward the person or party or institution being rated, and at the same time the degree of his liking or disliking. By simply calling off a number he indicates that he has a favorable or unfavorable opinion of the F.B.I., of Jimmy Carter, or of the Equal Rights Amendment, and how much he likes or dislikes each. In actual use, researchers have found the extreme positions on the scale are most indicative and most sensitive to change. These are the $+4$ and $+5$ positions on the favorable side and the -4 and -5 positions on the negative side. Normally these two positions are combined to provide a "highly favorable" or a "highly unfavorable" rating.

Scale ratings thus obtained are remarkably consistent and remarkably reliable in ranking candidates and parties. In fact, the ratings given to the two major-party candidates have paralleled the relative standings of the candidates in elections, especially when the party ratings are averaged with the candidate ratings.

Cantril and Kilpatrick devised the "Self-Anchoring Scale."* Cantril and his associate, Lloyd Free, used this scale to measure the aspirations and fears of people in different nations of the world—both those living in highly developed countries and those in the least developed. They sought "to get an overall picture of the reality worlds in which people lived, a picture expressed by individuals in their own terms and to do this in such a way . . . as to enable meaningful comparisons to be made between different individuals, groups of individuals, and societies."

The Self-Anchoring scale is so simple that it can be used with illiterates and with people without any kind of formal education. A multination survey in which this measuring instrument was employed included nations as diverse in their educational and living standards as Nigeria, India, the United States, West Germany, Cuba, Israel, Japan, Poland, Panama, Yugoslavia, Philippines, Brazil, and the Dominican Republic.

---

*F. P. Kilpatrick and Hadley Cantril, "Self-Anchoring Scale." *Journal of Individual Psychology,* November 1960.

The scale makes use of a ladder device.

```
——— 10 ———
——— 9 ———
——— 8 ———
——— 7 ———
——— 6 ———
——— 5 ———
——— 4 ———
——— 3 ———
——— 2 ———
——— 1 ———
——— 0 ———
```

The person being interviewed describes his own wishes and hopes, the realization of which would constitute the best possible life. This is the top anchoring point of the scale. At the other extreme, the same individual describes his worries and fears embodied in the worst possible life he can imagine. With the use of this device, he is asked where he thinks he stands on the ladder today. Then he is asked where he thinks he stood in the past, and where he thinks he will stand in the future.

This same procedure was used by Albert Cantril and Charles Roll in a survey called *Hopes and Fears of the American People*—a revealing study of the mood of the American people in the spring of 1971.

Use of this scale would be extremely helpful in pursuing the goal set forth by Alvin Toffler in his book *Future Shock*. He writes:

> The time has come for a dramatic reassessment of the directions of change, a reassessment made not by the politicians or the sociologists or the clergy or the elitist revolutionaries, not by technicians or college presidents, but by the people themselves. We need, quite literally, to "go to the people" with a question that is almost never asked of them: "*What kind of a world do you want 10, 20, or 30 years from now?*" We need to initiate, in short, a continuing plebiscite on the future. Toffler points out that "the voter may be polled about specific issues, but not about the general shape of the preferable future."

This is true to a great extent. With the exception of the Cantril-Free studies, this area has been largely overlooked by polling organizations. Toffler advocates a continuing plebiscite in which millions of persons would participate. From a practical point of view, however, sampling offers the best opportunity to discover just what the public's ideas of the future are—and more particularly, the kind of world they want ten years, twenty years, or thirty years from now.

REPORTING AND INTERPRETING POLL FINDINGS

Public opinion polls throughout the world have been sponsored by the media of communication—newspapers, magazines, television, and radio. It is quite proper, therefore, to answer this question: "How well do the various media report and evaluate the results of a given poll?"

Since October 1935, Gallup Poll reports have appeared weekly in American newspapers in virtually all of the major cities. During this period, I am happy to report, no newspaper has changed the wording of poll releases sent to them to make the findings fit the newspaper's editorial or political views. Editors, however, are permitted to write their own headlines because of their own special type and format policies; they can shorten articles or, in fact, omit them if news columns are filled by other and more pressing material.

Since the funds for the Gallup Poll come from this source and since the sponsoring newspapers represent all shades of political belief, the need for strict objectivity in the writing and interpretation of poll results becomes an economic as well as a scientific necessity.

At various stages in the history of the Gallup Poll, charges have been made that the poll has a Republican bias, and at other times, a Democratic bias, largely dependent upon whether the political tide is swinging toward one side or the other. Even a cursory examination of the findings dealing with issues of the day, and of election survey results, will disprove this.

The Gallup Poll is a fact-finding organization, or looked at in another way, a kind of scorekeeper in the political world.

When poll findings are not to the liking of critics there is always a great temptation to try to discredit the poll by claiming that it is "biased," that it makes "secret adjustments" and that it manipulates the figures to suit its fancy, and that it is interfering with "democratic dialogue." Such charges were heard often in earlier years, but time has largely stilled this kind of attack on the poll's integrity.

Limitations of space, in the case of newspapers, and of time in the case of television and radio, impose restrictions on the amount of detail and analysis that can be included in any one report. The news media have a strong preference for "hard" news, the kind that reports the most recent score on candidate or party strength, or the division of opinion on highly controversial subjects. This type of news, it should be added, makes up the bulk of their news budgets.

These space and time requirements do require a different kind of poll report form from one that would be written to satisfy those who prefer a full and detailed description of public opinion.

A political writer for a large metropolitan newspaper has raised this point: "Is it not more accurate to report a point spread instead of a simple single figure? . . . If so, would it not be more responsible to state it that way, even though it would take away some of the sharpness in published reports?"

A degree of error is inherent in all sampling and it is important that this fact be understood by those who follow poll findings. The question is how best to achieve this end. One way, of course, is to educate the public to look at all survey results not as fixed realities or absolutes but as reliable estimates only.

The best examples, as noted earlier, are the monthly figures on unemployment and the cost of living. Should these be published showing a point spread or the margin of error? If they were, then the monthly index of unemployment, based as it is on a sample of 50,000, would read, at a given point in time, not 8.8%, but 8.5% to 9.1%. Reporting the cost of living index in such fashion would almost certainly cause trouble, since many labor contracts are based upon changes as small as 0.1%.

In reporting the trend of opinion, especially on issues, the inclusion of a point spread would make poll reports rather meaningless, particularly if the trend were not a sharp one. The character of the trend curve itself normally offers evidence of the variations due to sample size.

In the case of elections, the reporting of the margin of error can, on occasion, be misleading to the reader. The reason is that polling errors come from many sources, and often the least of these in importance is the size of the sample. Yet, the statistical margin of error relates solely to this one factor.

An example may help to shed light on this point. A telephone poll taken in a mayoralty race in a large eastern city, reported the standings of the candidates and added that they were accurate within "a possible error margin of 3.8%." In short, the newspaper in which the results were published and the polling organization assured readers that the results perforce had to be right within this margin, based upon the laws or probability. Actually, the poll figure was 14 percentage points short on the winning candidate. Factors other than the size of the sample were responsible for this wide deviation.

The best guide to a poll's accuracy is its record. If allowance is to be made for variation in the poll's reported figures, then perhaps the best suggestion, to be reasonably certain that the error will not exceed a stated amount in a national election, is to multiply by 2.5 the average deviation of the poll in its last three or four elections.

Still another way to remind readers and viewers of the presence of some degree of error in all survey findings is to find a word or words that convey this fact. A growing practice among statisticians in dealing with sampling data is to refer to results as "estimates." Unfortunately, this word conveys to some the impression that subjective judgments have entered into the process. A better word needs to be found that removes some of the certainty that is too often attached to poll percentages without, at the same time, erring in the opposite direction. The word "assessment" has been adopted by some survey researchers and it is hoped that it will come into general use in the future.

DESIGN OF THE SAMPLE

The design of the sample used in the Gallup Poll is that of a replicated probability sample down to the block level in the case of urban areas and to segments of townships in the case of rural areas.

After stratifying the nation geographically and by size of community in order to insure conformity of the sample with the latest available estimates by the Census Bureau of the distribution of the adult population, about 350 different sampling locations or areas are selected on a strictly random basis. The interviewers have no choice whatsoever concerning the part of the city or county in which they conduct their interviews.

Interviewers are given maps of the area to which they are assigned, with a starting point indicated, and are required to follow a specified direction. At each occupied dwelling unit, interviewers are instructed to select respondents by following a prescribed systematic method. This procedure is followed until the assigned number of interviews is completed. The standard sample size for most Gallup Polls is 1500 interviews. This is augmented in specific instances where greater survey accuracy is considered desirable.

Since this sampling procedure is designed to produce a sample that approximates the adult civilian population (18 and older) living in private households in the United States (that is, excluding those in prisons and hospitals, hotels, religious institutions, and on military reservations), the survey results can be applied to this population for the purpose of projecting percentages into numbers of people. The manner in which the sample is drawn also produces a sample that approximates the population of private households in the United States. Therefore, survey results also can be projected in terms of numbers of households when appropriate.

SAMPLING TOLERANCES

It should be remembered that all sample surveys are subject to sampling error; that is, the extent to which the results may differ from what would be obtained if the whole population surveyed had been interviewed. The size of such a sampling error depends largely on the number of interviews. Increasing the sample size lessens the magnitude of possible error and vice versa.

The following tables may be used in estimating sampling error. The computed allowances (the standard deviation) have taken into account the effect of the sample design upon sampling error. They may be interpreted as indicating the range (plus or minus the figure shown) within which the results of repeated samplings in the same time period could be expected to vary, 95 percent of the time (or at a confidence level of .5), assuming the same sampling procedure, the same interviewers, and the same questionnaire.

Table A shows how much allowance should be made for the sampling error of a percentage. The table would be used in the following manner: Say a reported percentage is 33 for a group that includes 1500 respondents. Go to the row "percentage near 30" in the table and then to the column headed "1500." The number at this point is three, which means that the 33 percent obtained in the sample is subject to a sampling error of plus or minus 3 points. Another way of saying it is that very probably (95 chances out of 100) the average of repeated samplings would be somewhere between 30 and 36, with the most likely figure being the 33 obtained.

In comparing survey results in two subsamples, such as men and woman, the question arises as to how large must a difference between them be before one can be reasonably sure that it reflects a statistically significant difference. In Table B and C, the number of points that must be allowed for, in such comparisons, is indicated.

For percentages near 20 or 80, use Table B; for those near 50, Table C. For percentages in between, the error to be allowed for is between that shown in the two tables.

Here is an example of how the tables should be used: Say 50 percent of men and 40 percent of women respond the same way to a question—a difference of 10 percentage points. Can it be said with any assurance that the ten-point difference reflects a significant difference between men and women on the question? (Samples, unless otherwise noted, contain approximately 750 men and 750 women.)

Because the percentages are near 50, consult Table C. Since the two samples are about 750 persons each, look for the place in the table where the column and row labeled "750" converge. The number six appears there. This means the allowance for error should be 6 points, and the conclusion that the percentage among men is somewhere between 4 and 16 points higher than the percentage among women would be wrong only about 5 percent of the time. In other words, there is a considerable likelihood that a difference exists in the direction observed and that it amounts to at least 4 percentage points.

If, in another case, male responses amount to 22 percent, and female to 24 percent, consult Table B because these percentages are near 20. The column and row labeled "750" converge on the number five. Obviously, then, the two-point difference is inconclusive.

TABLE A

Recommended Allowance for Sampling Error of a Percentage

In Percentage Points
(at 95 in 100 confidence level)*
Size of the Sample

	3000	1500	1000	750	600	400	200	100
Percentages near 10	2	2	2	3	4	4	5	7
Percentages near 20	2	3	3	4	4	5	7	9
Percentages near 30	2	3	4	4	4	6	8	10
Percentages near 40	3	3	4	4	5	6	9	11
Percentages near 50	3	3	4	4	5	6	9	11
Percentages near 60	3	3	4	4	5	6	9	11
Percentages near 70	2	3	4	4	4	6	8	10
Percentages near 80	2	3	3	4	4	5	7	9
Percentages near 90	2	2	2	3	4	4	5	7

*The chances are 95 in 100 that the sampling error is not larger than the figures shown.

TABLE B

Recommended Allowance for Sampling Error of the Difference Between Two Subsamples

In Percentage Points
(at 95 in 100 confidence level)*

Percentages near 20 or percentages near 80

	1500	750	600	400	200
Size of the Sample					
1500	3				
750	4	5			
600	5	6	6		
400	6	7	7	7	
200	8	8	8	9	10

TABLE C

Percentages near 50

	1500	750	600	400	200
Size of the Sample					
1500	4				
750	5	·6			
600	6	8	8		
400	7	8	8	9	
200	10	10	11	11	13

*The chances are 95 in 100 that the sampling error is not larger than the figures shown.

RECORD OF
GALLUP POLL ACCURACY

Year	Gallup Final Survey*		Election Result*	
1982	55.0%	Democratic	55.8%[1]	Democratic
1980	47.0	Reagan	50.8	Reagan
1978	55.0	Democratic	54.0	Democratic
1976	48.0	Carter	50.0	Carter
1974	60.0	Democratic	58.9	Democratic
1972	62.0	Nixon	61.8	Nixon
1970	53.0	Democratic	54.3	Democratic
1968	43.0	Nixon	43.5	Nixon
1966	52.5	Democratic	51.9	Democratic
1964	64.0	Johnson	61.3	Johnson
1962	55.5	Democratic	52.7	Democratic
1960	51.0	Kennedy	50.1	Kennedy
1958	57.0	Democratic	56.5	Democratic
1956	59.5	Eisenhower	57.8	Eisenhower
1954	51.5	Democratic	52.7	Democratic
1952	51.0	Eisenhower	55.4	Eisenhower
1950	51.0	Democratic	50.3	Democratic
1948	44.5	Truman	49.9	Truman
1946	58.0	Republican	54.3	Republican
1944	51.5	Roosevelt	53.3[2]	Roosevelt
1942	52.0	Democratic	48.0[3]	Democratic
1940	52.0	Roosevelt	55.0	Roosevelt
1938	54.0	Democratic	50.8	Democratic
1936	55.7	Roosevelt	62.5	Roosevelt

*The figure shown is the winner's percentage of the Democratic-Republican vote except in the elections of 1948, 1968, and 1976. Because the Thurmond and Wallace voters in 1948 were largely split-offs from the normally Democratic vote, they were made a part of the final Gallup Poll preelection

[1] Preliminary results.

[2] Civilian vote 53.3, Roosevelt soldier vote 0.5 = 53.8% Roosevelt. Gallup final survey based on civilian vote.

[3] Final report said Democrats would win control of the House, which they did even though the Republicans won a majority of the popular vote.

estimate of the division of the vote. In 1968 Wallace's candidacy was supported by such a large minority that he was clearly a major candidate, and the 1968 percents are based on the total Nixon-Humphrey-Wallace vote. In 1976, because of interest in McCarthy's candidacy and its potential effect on the Carter vote, the final Gallup Poll estimate included Carter, Ford, McCarthy, and all other candidates as a group.

Average Deviation for 24
    National Elections . . . . 2.3 percentage points

Average Deviation for 17
    National Elections
    Since 1950, inclusive . . . . 1.5 percentage points

Trend in Deviation Reduction

Elections	Average Error
1936–48	4.0
1950–58	1.7
1960–68	1.5
1970–82	1.4
1966–82	1.2

CHRONOLOGY

The chronology is provided to enable the reader to relate poll results to specific events or series of events that may have influenced public opinion.

The struggling U.S. economy was the most important domestic issue of 1982. At the start of the year, the recession was officially six months old; by the year's end, it had become the longest business slump since the end of World War II. Unemployment climbed steadily from 8.5% of the work force in January to 10.8% in December—the highest rate in forty-two years. Factories operated at the lowest level of capacity since 1945, and business bankruptcies reached a fifty-year high. Interest rates began to drop during the second half of 1982, but the cost of borrowing money still remained high. Inflation, however, was the exception to an otherwise grim economy. The increase in consumer prices was approximately 6% in 1982, compared with almost 9% in 1981.

1981

December 1   Most U.S. banks lower their prime interest rate to 15¼%.

December 7   The Reagan administration estimates that the federal budget deficit will climb to a record $109 billion in 1982.

December 13   Martial law is declared in Poland, further deteriorating U.S.-Soviet relations.

December 23   The five major American automobile manufacturers claim they have had the worst sales year since 1961.

1982

January 7   President Ronald Reagan decides to continue the registration of young men for possible military conscription.

January 8	The Bureau of Labor Statistics announces that unemployment rose from 8.4% to 8.9% during December. More than 460,000 people were laid off, bringing the total unemployed to 9,462,000. Among blacks, the unemployment figure was 16.1%.
January 26	In his State of the Union message, President Reagan promises to insist on his tax-cut proposals. He also proposes a major "new federalism" plan under which he would give states and cities more control over federal social programs.
January 28	The Reagan administration declares that the United States will increase aid to El Salvador. The president certifies, as required by Congress, that the Salvadoran junta government has made progress in protecting human rights.
February 2	Secretary of State Alexander M. Haig, Jr., pledges that the United States will do whatever is necessary to prevent the overthrow of the Salvadoran junta.
February 6	In his budget message to Congress, President Reagan calls for a decrease in the social responsibilities of the government and an increase in the military strength of the nation.
February 11	The Reagan administration drops its proposal to place the new MX intercontinental missiles in silos reinforced to withstand a nuclear attack.
February 25	The Labor Department reports that the Consumer Price Index for January showed an increase of only 0.3%, the smallest since July 1980. Although the price of food increased, there were declines in the prices of gasoline, new cars, houses, and clothing.
March 3	President Reagan warns Congress that its proposals to rescind part of his tax cuts would result in a continuation of the recession.
March 5	According to the Bureau of Labor Statistics, unemployment rose to 8.8% during February. More than 9.5 million people were without jobs, an increase of 280,000 since January and 1.8 million more than during July 1981.
March 12	Producer prices fell 0.1% in February, the first drop since 1976.

March 22	The space shuttle *Columbia* is lifted into earth's orbit for the third time.
March 28	Salvadorans hold elections and choose the centrist Christian Democrat party led by José Napoleon Duarte.
April 1–10	A rare spring storm hits the United States and generates over eighty tornadoes, abnormally deep snow, floods, and high winds.
April 2	Argentina and Great Britain begin a seventy-four-day war over the right to rule the Falkland Islands.
	The Labor Department announces that unemployment in March rose to 9%. Nearly 9.9 million people were out of work, the highest number since World War II. The unemployment for blacks was a record 18%.
April 9	Union employees of General Motors agree by a narrow margin to a new labor contract, giving up annual pay increases and nine paid holidays as well as postponing three of four quarterly cost-of-living increases. Under the contract, new employees would be hired at 80% of the wage and benefit scales given to current workers.
April 21	The U.S. gross national product for the first quarter of 1982 continues to fall, slowing the rate of inflation.
April 23	As a result of reductions in gasoline, food, and housing costs, the Bureau of Labor Statistics announces that consumer prices declined 0.3% in March, the first drop in almost seventeen years.
May 9	President Reagan proposes an arms reduction plan that calls for the United States and the Soviet Union to reduce one-third of their nuclear warheads on land- and sea-based ballistic missiles.
May 18	Soviet leader Leonid Brezhnev says that the Soviet Union is ready for arms reduction talks but that Reagan's plan is one-sided.
May 31	President Reagan announces that the United States and the Soviet Union will begin negotiations in Geneva on June 29 to

discuss the limitation and reduction of strategic nuclear arms.

June 1   The U.S. Supreme Court rules that police may search automobiles without warrants.

The unemployment rate rose 0.1% in May to 9.5% of the labor force.

June 2   President Reagan arrives in Paris for a nine-day European visit.

June 6   The Israeli army launches a massive invasion into Lebanon, aimed at eliminating the threat of Palestine Liberation Organization (PLO) terrorism on Israel's northern frontier.

June 12   In New York City an estimated 500,000 persons protest against nuclear arms, the largest demonstration in the city's history.

June 14   Argentine troops surrender to Great Britain.

June 21   John Hinckley, Jr., is found not guilty by reason of insanity on all thirteen charges of shooting President Reagan and three others on March 30, 1981.

June 24   The leaders of the fight to ratify the Equal Rights Amendment (ERA) to the Constitution admit defeat. In the ten years since Congress passed the proposed amendment, it has been ratified by only thirty-five states, three short of the three-quarters needed.

June 25   Secretary of State Haig resigns. President Reagan nominates George P. Shultz, former secretary of the treasury, to replace him.

July 2   The U.S. Supreme Court upholds a New York State law prohibiting the use of children in pornographic films, photographs, or performances.

The unemployment rate during June held at 9.5%; among black teen-agers it rose to a record 52.6%.

July 19   The Census Bureau reports that the number of Americans officially classified as poor increased by about 2.2 million (14%) in 1981, giving the country its highest rate since 1967. As established by the government, an income of $9,287 per year for a family of four is considered poverty level.

July 23   The first group of 1,807 Haitian refugees ordered freed by a federal judge in June is released.

August 2   The unemployment rate in July rose to 9.8%, another post-World War II high. An approximate 10,790,000 people were without jobs, and the Bureau of Labor Statistics estimated that another 1.5 million discouraged Americans who have discontinued to job hunt were not included in this figure.

August 17   Enten Eller, a twenty-year-old college student, becomes the first young man to be convicted of failing to register for the draft since mandatory registration was revised in 1980. The government estimates that of the 8.5 million men eligible for registration, 700,000 have failed to do so.

August 19   Both houses of Congress pass President Reagan's $98.3 billion tax bill. More than two-thirds of the revenue raised by this bill over the next three years will come from business, a reversal of the 1981 tax act which had reduced taxes on businesses.

August 20   The Soviet Union accepts the Reagan administration's offer to extend by one year its grain sale agreement.

September 1   The Reagan administration announces that it is prepared to ease sanctions applied against two French companies that had supplied the Soviet Union with natural gas pipeline equipment. The companies had acted in defiance of a U.S. ban.

President Reagan calls for a fresh start in the Middle East peace process and urges full autonomy for Palestinians living in the Gaza Strip under Israeli occupation. He demands a halt to Israeli settlements and asks Jordan to supervise the Palestinians. The plan is unanimously rejected by the Israeli cabinet, claiming it would present a threat to Israel's security.

September 2   The Bureau of Labor Statistics reports that in the week ending August 21 the number of Americans filing initial claims for unemployment benefits rose to 621,000. By mid-August, more than 4 million people had filed for unemployment benefits in 1982.

September 16   Israeli troops seal off the Shatila and Sabra Palestinian refugee camps in West Beirut. In the ensuing two days, hundreds of Palestinian men, women, and children are killed. The massacre followed the September 14 murder of Lebanese president-elect Bashir Gemayel.

October 2   Chicago authorities confirm that the seventh victim of cyanide-tainted Tylenol capsules has died. The bottles of America's best selling over-the-counter pain reliever were all bought on September 29. Johnson & Johnson spends $100 million recalling its product.

October 6   The House of Representatives defeats an administration-backed proposal to amend the Constitution to require a balanced federal budget.

November 11   USSR General Secretary Brezhnev dies at age seventy-five. Yuri Andropov, former head of the Soviet internal security agency (KGB), succeeds him.

November 14   Lech Walesa, leader of the Polish Solidarity Union, returns to his home in Gdansk after eleven months of internment.

November 22   The president announces plans for the "dense pack" deployment near Cheyenne, Wyoming, of the MX missiles in order to modernize U.S. nuclear forces.

November 23   President Reagan agrees to support a $27.5-million program to create jobs by rebuilding the nation's roadways. It will be financed by a federal tax on gasoline.

December 2   Barney Clark becomes the first human to have an artificial polyurethane heart permanently implanted in his chest.

December 3   The jobless rate climbs to 10.8%. In a labor force of approximately 111 million, about 12 million are unemployed.

1

JANUARY 3
PROFESSIONAL FOOTBALL
SPORTSCASTERS

Interviewing Date: 11/13–16/81
Survey #185-G

> *Just about how many times, if any, have you, yourself, watched professional football on television since the season started ten weeks ago? Count each Sunday as one time, and each Monday as one time.*

None	42%
1–5 times	22
6–10 times	15
11–15 times	6
16–19 times	3
20 or more times	10
Don't know	2

By Sex
Male

None	29%
1–5 times	23
6–10 times	19
11–15 times	8
16–19 times	4
20 or more	15
Don't know	2

Female

None	54%
1–5 times	21
6–10 times	12
11–15 times	4

16–19 times	1
20 or more times	6
Don't know	2

By Race
White

None	43%
1–5 times	22
6–10 times	14
11–15 times	6
16–19 times	3
20 or more times	10
Don't know	2

Black

None	35%
1–5 times	23
6–10 times	18
11–15 times	7
16–19 times	2
20 or more times	11
Don't know	4

By Education
College

None	32%
1–5 times	30
6–10 times	17
11–15 times	7
16–19 times	1
20 or more times	11
Don't know	2

High School

None	42%
1–5 times	20
6–10 times	16
11–15 times	5
16–19 times	3
20 or more times	12
Don't know	2

Grade School

None	62%
1–5 times	19
6–10 times	9

11–15 times	3
16–19 times	1
20 or more times	4
Don't know	2

By Age
18–29 Years

None	31%
1–5 times	29
6–10 times	16
11–15 times	8
16–19 times	3
20 or more times	10
Don't know	3

30–49 Years

None	41%
1–5 times	22
6–10 times	14
11–15 times	6
16–19 times	4
20 or more times	11
Don't know	2

50 Years and Over

None	51%
1–5 times	17
6–10 times	15
11–15 times	3
16–19 times	2
20 or more times	10
Don't know	2

Asked of the 56% of the sample who have watched professional football at least once during the previous ten weeks: As I read off the names of some professional football announcers, one at a time, would you indicate how much you enjoy that person's football commentary. [Respondents were handed a card.] The more you enjoy an announcer's commentary on television, the higher the number you should pick; the less you enjoy his commentary, the lower the number you should pick:

Don Meredith?

Highly enjoyable	45%
Moderately enjoyable	37
	82%*

Frank Gifford?

Highly enjoyable	39%
Moderately enjoyable	43
	82%*

Pat Summerall?

Highly enjoyable	27%
Moderately enjoyable	50
	77%*

Fran Tarkenton?

Highly enjoyable	34%
Moderately enjoyable	41
	75%*

Bryant Gumbel?

Highly enjoyable	31%
Moderately enjoyable	42
	73%*

Dick Enberg?

Highly enjoyable	17%
Moderately enjoyable	48
	65%*

Vin Scully?

Highly enjoyable	20%
Moderately enjoyable	44
	64%*

Tom Brookshier?

Highly enjoyable	16%
Moderately enjoyable	45
	61%*

John Madden?

Highly enjoyable	18%
Moderately enjoyable	41
	59%*

Len Dawson?

Highly enjoyable 10%
Moderately enjoyable 49
                                              59%*

John Brodie?

Highly enjoyable 15%
Moderately enjoyable 42
                                              57%*

Howard Cosell?

Highly enjoyable 20%
Moderately enjoyable 20
                                              40%*

*Total enjoyable

Note: In a nationwide Gallup Sports Survey respondents were asked to rate sportscasters on a ten-point scale to indicate how much they enjoyed an announcer's commentary on television. The list contained the twelve most active announcers—four from each of the three major networks broadcasting pro football—of the approximately twenty men currently covering this sport. Ratings are based on the 56% of the adult population that have viewed pro football games at least once during the first ten weeks of the season, projecting to nearly 88 million adults. And as many as 10% or 16 million adults watched pro football on every possible occasion during this period, that is, on every Sunday and Monday night.

The recent survey findings of U.S. adults show Don Meredith and Frank Gifford tied for the most popular pro football sportscaster, followed closely in third, fourth, and fifth places by Pat Summerall, Fran Tarkenton, and Bryant Gumbel, respectively. The remaining sportscasters, in order, include Dick Enberg, Vin Scully, Tom Brookshier, John Madden, Len Dawson, John Brodie, and Howard Cosell. The lower enjoyment ratings assigned these men result largely from a high percentage of neutral ratings rather than from negative scores, which average only about 8%.

Significantly, Cosell, along with Meredith, is the highest rated of any of the commentators among black Americans. More than three in four blacks (76%) say they find Cosell enjoyable to watch, with 20% saying they enjoy watching him a great deal. This represents the greatest highly enjoyable rating recorded for any of the twelve commentators among any group in the population. To a lesser extent, Cosell is also rated relatively more enjoyable to watch by a larger percentage of women than are the other football commentators.

John Madden, like Cosell, one of the more outspoken commentators, rates toward the bottom of the list. Those who rate him as enjoyable to watch, however, tend to rate him as very enjoyable, particularly pro football addicts, or those who watch twenty or more games. With this group more than one-third gave Madden a highly enjoyable rating, behind only Meredith, Gifford, and Tarkenton.

JANUARY 7
SATISFACTION INDEX

Interviewing Date: 12/11–14/81
Survey #187-G

In general are you satisfied or dissatisfied with the way things are going in the United States at this time?

Satisfied............................ 27%
Dissatisfied 67
No opinion 6

By Sex
Male

Satisfied............................ 26%
Dissatisfied 68
No opinion 6

Female

Satisfied............................ 27%
Dissatisfied 67
No opinion 6

By Race
White

Satisfied............................29%
Dissatisfied........................65
No opinion 6

Nonwhite

Satisfied............................17%
Dissatisfied........................79
No opinion 4

By Education
College

Satisfied............................29%
Dissatisfied........................66
No opinion 5

High School

Satisfied............................26%
Dissatisfied........................68
No opinion 6

Grade School

Satisfied............................25%
Dissatisfied........................67
No opinion 8

By Region
East

Satisfied............................26%
Dissatisfied........................66
No opinion 8

Midwest

Satisfied............................20%
Dissatisfied........................74
No opinion 6

South

Satisfied............................34%
Dissatisfied........................60
No opinion 6

West

Satisfied............................25%
Dissatisfied........................70
No opinion 5

By Age
18–29 Years

Satisfied............................31%
Dissatisfied........................63
No opinion 6

30–49 Years

Satisfied............................23%
Dissatisfied........................71
No opinion 6

50 Years and Over

Satisfied............................27%
Dissatisfied........................67
No opinion 6

*In general, are you satisfied or dissatis-
fied with the way things are going in your
own personal life?*

Satisfied............................81%
Dissatisfied........................17
No opinion 2

By Sex
Male

Satisfied............................80%
Dissatisfied........................18
No opinion 2

Female

Satisfied............................81%
Dissatisfied........................17
No opinion 2

By Race
White

Satisfied............................84%
Dissatisfied........................14
No opinion 2

Nonwhite

Satisfied............................62%
Dissatisfied.........................36
No opinion 2

By Education
College

Satisfied............................85%
Dissatisfied.........................13
No opinion 2

High School

Satisfied............................78%
Dissatisfied.........................20
No opinion 2

Grade School

Satisfied............................81%
Dissatisfied.........................17
No opinion 2

By Region
East

Satisfied............................78%
Dissatisfied.........................18
No opinion 4

Midwest

Satisfied............................81%
Dissatisfied.........................16
No opinion 3

South

Satisfied............................80%
Dissatisfied.........................19
No opinion 1

West

Satisfied............................83%
Dissatisfied.........................16
No opinion 1

By Age
18–29 Years

Satisfied............................78%
Dissatisfied.........................19
No opinion 3

30–49 Years

Satisfied............................81%
Dissatisfied.........................18
No opinion 1

50 Years and Over

Satisfied............................82%
Dissatisfied.........................16
No opinion 2

Note: The mood of the American public is slightly more pessimistic today than last June—67% express dissatisfaction with the way things are going in the nation—but considerably brighter than one year ago. In the latest survey 27% of persons interviewed say they are satisfied with the national outlook, compared to 17% who expressed this view at the beginning of 1981.

The higher level of satisfaction with developments in the country is found among most major population groups with the notable exception of nonwhites. Here is the comparison with the early 1981 survey:

	Dec. 1982	Jan. 1981
National	27%	17%
White	29	18
Nonwhite	17	18

Although only about three in ten Americans express satisfaction with the way things are going in the nation, as many as eight in ten of all adults interviewed say they are satisfied with the way things are going in their personal lives, the same proportion found one year ago.

While considerable fluctuation has been recorded over the last two and one-half years in views of the state of the nation, remarkable stability has been found in the public's views on their personal lives. Again sharp differences are noted on the basis of race, with 84% of whites expressing satisfaction with the way things are going in their personal lives, compared to 62% among nonwhites.

National Trend of Attitude Toward Nation

	Satisfied	Dissatisfied	No opinion
June 1981	33%	61%	6%
January 1981	17	78	5
November 1979	19	77	4
August 1979	12	84	4
February 1979	26	69	5

National Trend of Attitude Toward Personal Life

	Satisfied	Dissatisfied	No opinion
June 1981	81%	16%	3%
January 1981	81	17	2
November 1979	79	19	2
August 1979	73	23	4
February 1979	77	21	2

JANUARY 10
PRESIDENT REAGAN

Interviewing Date: 12/11–14/81
Survey #187-G

Do you approve or disapprove of the way Ronald Reagan is handling his job as president?

Approve............................49%
Disapprove 41
No opinion 10

By Sex
Male

Approve............................51%
Disapprove 42
No opinion 7

Female

Approve............................46%
Disapprove 41
No opinion 13

By Race
White

Approve............................55%
Disapprove 35
No opinion 10

Black

Approve............................17%
Disapprove 74
No opinion 9

By Education
College

Approve............................52%
Disapprove 40
No opinion 8

High School

Approve............................50%
Disapprove 41
No opinion 9

Grade School

Approve............................36%
Disapprove 46
No opinion 18

By Region
East

Approve............................45%
Disapprove 45
No opinion 10

Midwest

Approve............................51%
Disapprove 39
No opinion 10

South

Approve............................48%
Disapprove 42
No opinion 10

West

Approve............................51%
Disapprove 39
No opinion 10

By Age
18–29 Years

Approve............................49%
Disapprove 43
No opinion 8

30–49 Years

Approve............................48%
Disapprove 41
No opinion 11

50 Years and Over

Approve............................49%
Disapprove 41
No opinion 10

By Income
$25,000 and Over

Approve............................65%
Disapprove 29
No opinion 6

$20,000–$24,999

Approve............................56%
Disapprove 35
No opinion 9

$15,000–$19,999

Approve............................52%
Disapprove 40
No opinion 8

$10,000–$14,999

Approve............................41%
Disapprove 47
No opinion 12

$5,000–$9,999

Approve............................34%
Disapprove 53
No opinion 13

Under $5,000

Approve............................27%
Disapprove 55
No opinion 18

By Politics
Republicans

Approve............................81%
Disapprove 13
No opinion 6

Democrats

Approve............................29%
Disapprove 62
No opinion 9

Independents

Approve............................50%
Disapprove 38
No opinion 12

Note: President Ronald Reagan's final 1981 job performance rating of 49% approval is his lowest to date, down 19 points from the high point of 68% in May and 9 points below his first-year average approval rating of 58%.

The table below shows the average approval ratings and the high and low points in approval in the first year of Reagan and his four elected predecessors:

Presidential Approval Ratings

	Average approval	High	Low
Ronald Reagan—1981	58%	68%	49%
Jimmy Carter—1977	62	75	51
Richard Nixon—1969	62	67	56
John Kennedy—1961	75	83	71
Dwight Eisenhower—1953	69	75	61

The sharpest decline in approval between Reagan's high point (68%) and low point (49%), due in considerable measure to growing pessimism regarding the economy, has occurred among Democrats (down 22 points) and independents (down 20). As might be expected, support has been firmer among Republicans, with the drop off in approval somewhat less (down 16 points) than in the case of Democrats and independents.

The decline in Reagan's approval ratings has been about equal for men and women, by educational background, and by other demographic groups, as shown in the following table:

Reagan Approval Ratings

	High point (May 8–11)	Low point (Dec. 11–14)	Point change
National	68%	49%	−19
By Sex			
Male	70%	51%	−19
Female	65	46	−19
By Race			
White	73%	55%	−18
Black	27	12	−15
By Education			
College	72%	52%	−20
High school	68	50	−18
Grade school	55	36	−19
By Region			
East	64%	45%	−19
Midwest	70	51	−19
South	69	48	−21
West	68	51	−17
By Age			
18–29 years	65%	49%	−16
30–49 years	72	48	−24
50 years and over	65	49	−16
By Politics			
Republicans	92%	81%	−11
Democrats	51	29	−22
Independents	70	50	−20

JANUARY 13
STATEHOOD FOR PUERTO RICO

Interviewing Date: 9/28–10/1/79
Survey #139-G

If a majority of the people of Puerto Rico vote in favor of becoming the fifty-first U.S. state, would you favor or oppose having Puerto Rico admitted as a state in the Union?

Favor 59%
Oppose 25
No opinion 16

By Education
College

Favor 68%
Oppose 24
No opinion 8

High School

Favor 59%
Oppose 25
No opinion 16

Grade School

Favor 42%
Oppose 25
No opinion 33

By Age
18–29 Years

Favor 65%
Oppose 24
No opinion 11

30–49 Years

Favor 65%
Oppose 23
No opinion 12

50 Years and Over

Favor 49%
Oppose 27
No opinion 24

If a majority of the people of Puerto Rico vote in favor of becoming a separate and independent nation, should the United States grant Puerto Rico its independence or not?

Should 67%
Should not 17
No opinion 16

By Education
College

Should 77%
Should not 17
No opinion 6

High School

Should 67%
Should not 18
No opinion 15

Grade School

Should 49%
Should not 17
No opinion 34

By Age
18–29 Years

Should 74%
Should not 15
No opinion 11

30–49 Years

Should 71%
Should not 17
No opinion 12

50 Years and Over

Should 58%
Should not 19
No opinion 23

Note: President Ronald Reagan's announcement on January 12 that he would support statehood for Puerto Rico "should the people of that island choose it in a free and democratic election" comes against a backdrop of public opinion in the United States that is favorable to such a move.

A 1979 Gallup survey showed that statehood, if the islanders want it, has the backing of 59% of Americans. In fact, the U.S. public is prepared to give Puerto Rico its complete independence if that is the wish of Puerto Rican citizens.

JANUARY 14
SOCIAL CHANGES

Interviewing Date: 12/11–14/81
Survey #187-G

Here are some social changes which might occur in coming years. [Respondents were handed a card listing seven items.] Would you welcome these or not welcome them:

More emphasis on traditional family ties?

Welcome 92%
Not welcome 5
Don't know 3

By Sex
Male

Welcome 91%
Not welcome 6
Don't know 3

Female

Welcome 93%
Not welcome 3
Don't know 4

By Race
White

Welcome 93%
Not welcome 4
Don't know 3

Nonwhite

Welcome............................89%
Not welcome........................ 7
Don't know........................ 4

By Education
College

Welcome............................92%
Not welcome........................ 5
Don't know........................ 3

High School

Welcome............................92%
Not welcome........................ 4
Don't know........................ 4

Grade School

Welcome............................93%
Not welcome........................ 4
Don't know........................ 3

By Age
18–29 Years

Welcome............................89%
Not welcome........................ 7
Don't know........................ 4

30–49 Years

Welcome............................91%
Not welcome........................ 5
Don't know........................ 4

50 Years and Over

Welcome............................96%
Not welcome........................ 2
Don't know........................ 2

By Importance of Religion
Very Important

Welcome............................96%
Not welcome........................ 3
Don't know........................ 1

Fairly Important

Welcome............................91%
Not welcome........................ 5
Don't know........................ 4

Not Very Important

Welcome............................81%
Not welcome........................ 9
Don't know........................10

More respect for authority?

Welcome............................89%
Not welcome........................ 6
Don't know........................ 5

By Sex
Male

Welcome............................89%
Not welcome........................ 7
Don't know........................ 4

Female

Welcome............................89%
Not welcome........................ 6
Don't know........................ 5

By Race
White

Welcome............................89%
Not welcome........................ 6
Don't know........................ 5

Nonwhite

Welcome............................88%
Not welcome........................ 7
Don't know........................ 5

By Education
College

Welcome............................82%
Not welcome........................13
Don't know........................ 5

High School

Welcome.............................91%
Not welcome........................ 4
Don't know 5

Grade School

Welcome.............................95%
Not welcome........................ 3
Don't know 2

By Age
18–29 Years

Welcome.............................83%
Not welcome........................10
Don't know 7

30–49 Years

Welcome.............................90%
Not welcome........................ 6
Don't know 4

50 Years and Over

Welcome.............................93%
Not welcome........................ 4
Don't know 3

By Importance of Religion
Very Important

Welcome.............................93%
Not welcome........................ 4
Don't know 3

Fairly Important

Welcome.............................90%
Not welcome........................ 7
Don't know 3

Not Very Important

Welcome.............................76%
Not welcome........................13
Don't know 11

Religious beliefs playing a greater role in people's lives?

Welcome.............................76%
Not welcome........................13
Don't know 11

By Sex
Male

Welcome.............................70%
Not welcome........................16
Don't know 14

Female

Welcome.............................81%
Not welcome........................10
Don't know 9

By Race
White

Welcome.............................75%
Not welcome........................13
Don't know 12

Nonwhite

Welcome.............................81%
Not welcome........................11
Don't know 8

By Education
College

Welcome.............................66%
Not welcome........................18
Don't know 16

High School

Welcome.............................79%
Not welcome........................11
Don't know 10

Grade School

Welcome.............................83%
Not welcome........................ 9
Don't know 8

By Age
18–29 Years

Welcome........................69%
Not welcome....................14
Don't know.....................17

30–49 Years

Welcome........................73%
Not welcome....................15
Don't know.....................12

50 Years and Over

Welcome........................84%
Not welcome.....................9
Don't know......................7

By Importance of Religion
Very Important

Welcome........................93%
Not welcome.....................4
Don't know......................3

Fairly Important

Welcome........................69%
Not welcome....................15
Don't know.....................16

Not Very Important

Welcome........................31%
Not welcome....................37
Don't know.....................32

Less emphasis on money?

Welcome........................71%
Not welcome....................21
Don't know......................8

By Sex
Male

Welcome........................74%
Not welcome....................19
Don't know......................7

Female

Welcome........................68%
Not welcome....................23
Don't know......................9

By Race
White

Welcome........................75%
Not welcome....................17
Don't know......................8

Nonwhite

Welcome........................54%
Not welcome....................38
Don't know......................8

By Education
College

Welcome........................81%
Not welcome....................16
Don't know......................3

High School

Welcome........................69%
Not welcome....................22
Don't know......................9

Grade School

Welcome........................60%
Not welcome....................26
Don't know.....................14

By Age
18–29 Years

Welcome........................69%
Not welcome....................24
Don't know......................7

30–49 Years

Welcome........................77%
Not welcome....................18
Don't know......................5

50 Years and Over

Welcome 68%
Not welcome 21
Don't know 11

By Importance of Religion
Very Important

Welcome 73%
Not welcome 20
Don't know 7

Fairly Important

Welcome 69%
Not welcome 23
Don't know 8

Not Very Important

Welcome 70%
Not welcome 19
Don't know 11

Less emphasis on working hard?

Welcome 28%
Not welcome 66
Don't know 6

By Sex
Male

Welcome 28%
Not welcome 66
Don't know 6

Female

Welcome 28%
Not welcome 65
Don't know 7

By Race
White

Welcome 26%
Not welcome 68
Don't know 6

Nonwhite

Welcome 38%
Not welcome 53
Don't know 9

By Education
College

Welcome 25%
Not welcome 71
Don't know 4

High School

Welcome 29%
Not welcome 64
Don't know 7

Grade School

Welcome 30%
Not welcome 60
Don't know 10

By Age
18–29 Years

Welcome 30%
Not welcome 62
Don't know 8

30–49 Years

Welcome 31%
Not welcome 65
Don't know 4

50 Years and Over

Welcome 23%
Not welcome 70
Don't know 7

By Importance of Religion
Very Important

Welcome 27%
Not welcome 67
Don't know 6

Fairly Important

Welcome............................31%
Not welcome........................65
Don't know......................... 4

Not Very Important

Welcome............................23%
Not welcome........................63
Don't know.........................14

More acceptance of sexual freedom?

Welcome............................25%
Not welcome........................67
Don't know......................... 8

By Sex
Male

Welcome............................31%
Not welcome........................60
Don't know......................... 9

Female

Welcome............................19%
Not welcome........................73
Don't know......................... 8

By Race
White

Welcome............................23%
Not welcome........................69
Don't know......................... 8

Nonwhite

Welcome............................33%
Not welcome........................56
Don't know.........................11

By Education
College

Welcome............................35%
Not welcome........................57
Don't know......................... 8

High School

Welcome............................23%
Not welcome........................68
Don't know......................... 9

Grade School

Welcome............................13%
Not welcome........................81
Don't know......................... 6

By Age
18–29 Years

Welcome............................46%
Not welcome........................44
Don't know.........................10

30–49 Years

Welcome............................24%
Not welcome........................67
Don't know......................... 9

50 Years and Over

Welcome............................10%
Not welcome........................83
Don't know......................... 7

By Importance of Religion
Very Important

Welcome............................15%
Not welcome........................80
Don't know......................... 5

Fairly Important

Welcome............................33%
Not welcome........................57
Don't know.........................10

Not Very Important

Welcome............................46%
Not welcome........................39
Don't know.........................15

More acceptance of marijuana usage?

Welcome 13%
Not welcome 82
Don't know 5

By Sex
Male

Welcome 15%
Not welcome 78
Don't know 7

Female

Welcome 12%
Not welcome 84
Don't know 4

By Race
White

Welcome 13%
Not welcome 82
Don't know 5

Nonwhite

Welcome 14%
Not welcome 80
Don't know 6

By Education
College

Welcome 21%
Not welcome 72
Don't know 7

High School

Welcome 12%
Not welcome 83
Don't know 5

Grade School

Welcome 1%
Not welcome 97
Don't know 2

By Age
18–29 Years

Welcome 28%
Not welcome 64
Don't know 8

30–49 Years

Welcome 12%
Not welcome 83
Don't know 5

50 Years and Over

Welcome 3%
Not welcome 93
Don't know 4

By Importance of Religion
Very Important

Welcome 8%
Not welcome 90
Don't know 2

Fairly Important

Welcome 14%
Not welcome 80
Don't know 6

Not Very Important

Welcome 33%
Not welcome 52
Don't know 15

Note: According to the latest Gallup survey, most Americans cling to conservative social values, mirroring the political policies now being carried out by the Reagan administration. The survey finds the public willing to give at least lip service to seven social changes, reflecting a return to traditional values.

Younger adults and those with a college background tend to be more liberal in their outlook about social changes, particularly those related to morals, with young people far more likely than their elders to say they would welcome both more acceptance of marijuana and more sexual freedom.

Persons in the survey who say that religion is very important in their lives tend to have more conservative attitudes toward social change than do those for whom religion is less important. This difference is especially striking with regard to attitudes about sexual freedom, marijuana use, and, understandably, about religion's role in people's lives. For example, 15% of those whose religious beliefs are very strong say they would welcome more sexual freedom, compared to 33% of those whose beliefs are fairly important and 46% of persons who claim religion is not very important to them.

The opinions of men and women are quite similar, with two exceptions: men are much more likely to say they would welcome more sexual freedom (31%) than are women (19%), while women (81%) are more apt than men (70%) to want to see religion play a larger part in American society.

JANUARY 17
SATISFACTION INDEX

Interviewing Date: 12/11–14/81
Survey #187-G

Now, here are some questions concerning how satisfied or dissatisfied you are with various things about your life. To indicate this, would you use this card. [Respondents were handed a card with "extremely satisfied" at 10 down to "extremely dissatisfied" at 0.] If you are extremely satisfied with something, you would call off the highest number, 10. If you are extremely dissatisfied, you would mention the lowest number, 0. If you are neither extremely satisfied nor extremely dissatisfied you would mention some number in between 0 and 10—the higher the number, the more satisfied; the lower the number, the more dissatisfied. Considering everything, how satisfied or dissatisfied are you with:

Your relations with your children?*

	Highly satisfied**
National	81%

By Sex

Male	80%
Female	83

By Race

White	84%
Black	69

By Education

College	81%
High school	79
Grade school	80

By Age

18–29 years	76%
30–49 years	80
50–64 years	83
65 years and over	81

Your family life?

	Highly satisfied**
National	79%

By Sex

Male	78%
Female	80

By Race

White	81%
Black	69

By Education

College	81%
High school	79
Grade school	76

By Age

18–29 years	74%
30–49 years	81

50–64 years. 80
65 years and over. 81

Your relations with other people?

Highly
satisfied**

National 79%

By Sex

Male. 76%
Female. 80

By Race

White. 79%
Black 70

By Education

College. 84%
High school. 76
Grade school. 75

By Age

18–29 years 73%
30–49 years. 79
50–64 years. 79
65 years and over. 84

Your marriage?*

Highly
satisfied**

National 78%

By Sex

Male. 82%
Female. 76

By Race

White. 82%
Black 58

By Education

College. 81%
High school. 77
Grade school. 81

By Age

18–29 years 70%
30–49 years. 81
50–64 years. 82
65 years and over. 81

Your health today?

Highly
satisfied**

National 70%

By Sex

Male. 71%
Female. 69

By Race

White. 71%
Black 64

By Education

College. 79%
High school. 69
Grade school. 52

By Age

18–29 years 80%
30–49 years. 78
50–64 years. 59
65 years and over. 50

Your present housing?

Highly
satisfied**

National 69%

By Sex

Male. 69%
Female. 68

By Race

White. 72%
Black 49

By Education

College............................70%
High school.........................68
Grade school........................68

By Age

18–29 years 56%
30–49 years.........................67
50–64 years.........................78
65 years and over....................80

The way things are going in your personal life?

	Highly satisfied**
National	67%

By Sex

Male...............................65%
Female.............................68

By Race

White...............................71%
Black 51

By Education

College............................73%
High school.........................67
Grade school........................60

By Age

18–29 years 65%
30–49 years.........................68
50–64 years.........................66
65 years and over....................74

Your community as a place to live?

	Highly satisfied**
National	66%

By Sex

Male...............................64%
Female.............................69

By Race

White...............................68%
Black 57

By Education

College............................64%
High school.........................65
Grade school........................78

By Age

18–29 years 54%
30–49 years.........................66
50–64 years.........................72
65 years and over....................83

*Your job/the work you do?**

	Highly satisfied**
National	64%

By Sex

Male...............................61%
Female.............................65

By Race

White...............................64%
Black 46

By Education

College............................73%
High school.........................52
Grade school........................58

By Age

18–29 years 53%
30–49 years.........................67
50–64 years.........................69
65 years and over....................66

Your standard of living?

	Highly satisfied**
National	57%

By Sex

Male	56%
Female	57

By Race

White	58%
Black	44

By Education

College	59%
High school	56
Grade school	53

By Age

18–29 years	45%
30–49 years	57
50–64 years	61
65 years and over	71

Your free time—the time when you are not working at your job?

	Highly satisfied**
National	56%

By Sex

Male	56%
Female	57

By Race

White	57%
Black	53

By Education

College	52%
High school	58
Grade school	53

By Age

18–29 years	52%
30–49 years	54
50–64 years	59
65 years and over	66

The work you do—that is, doing housework or household chores?***

	Highly satisfied**
National	54%

Your household income?

	Highly satisfied**
National	43%

By Sex

Male	43%
Female	42

By Race

White	46%
Black	29

By Education

College	48%
High school	41
Grade school	41

By Age

18–29 years	34%
30–49 years	41
50–64 years	53
65 years and over	49

*Responses of applicable groups (parents, married persons, those who have jobs, housewives).
**Top three positions on ten-point scale.
***Asked of housewives only. Further breakdowns are not possible because of limited sample.

Note: Despite mounting concern about the economy and rising unemployment, the American public expresses a high degree of satisfaction with most of the important dimensions of their lives. In fact, a comparison of the results of the latest Gallup Poll with one taken in another recession period (1974) shows there is greater satisfaction now with most of the items included in both surveys.

Currently, 81% of parents give their relations with their children one of the top three ratings on a ten-point scale, indicating a high level of satisfaction with this quality of life, the highest rated category of the thirteen included in the study. Other aspects given very high ratings by the public are family life (79%), relations with other people (79%), marriage (78%), health (70%), housing (69%), personal life (67%), and community as a place to live (66%).

Somewhat lower ratings are accorded their job (64%), standard of living (57%), the way in which free time is spent (56%), housework (54% from housewives), and household income (43%). For example, 55% of blacks give all thirteen aspects a highly satisfactory rating on average, compared to 69% of whites holding these views. While this difference may not seem extreme, on some individual items a far greater disparity is noted. Thus, while 72% of whites indicate they are highly satisfied with their housing, only 49% of blacks have the same outlook. Similarly, 29% of blacks report great satisfaction with their household income, while 46% of whites share this opinion.

Satisfaction Index
(Percent highly satisfied)

	Average of 13 categories
National	66%

By Sex

Male*	66%
Female	67

By Race

White	69%
Black	55

By Education

College	75%
High school	66
Grade school	64

*Twelve categories

By Age

18–29 years	67%
30–49 years	67
50 years and over	70

By Income

$15,000 and over	71%
Under $15,000	60

JANUARY 21
INTOLERANCE

Interviewing Date: 12/11–14/81
Survey #187-G

On this list are various groups of people. [Respondents were handed a card listing nine groups.] Could you please sort out any that you would not like to have as neighbors?

	Not wanted as neighbors
Members of minority religious cults or sects	30%
Cuban refugees	25
Hispanics (Mexicans, Puerto Ricans, Cubans)	18
Vietnamese refugees	17
Unmarried single people living together	14
Religious fundamentalists	11
Jews	2
Catholics	1
Protestants	1

By Sex
Male

Cults; sects	29%
Cuban refugees	26
Hispanics	20
Vietnamese refugees	20
Unmarried living together	14
Fundamentalists	12
Jews	2
Catholics	1
Protestants	1

Female

Cults; sects	31%
Cuban refugees	23
Hispanics	16
Vietnamese refugees	13
Unmarried living together	15
Fundamentalists	10
Jews	2
Catholics	1
Protestants	1

By Race
White

Cults; sects	34%
Cuban refugees	26
Hispanics	19
Vietnamese refugees	17
Unmarried living together	15
Fundamentalists	12
Jews	1
Catholics	1
Protestants	1

Nonwhite

Cults; sects	10%
Cuban refugees	19
Hispanics	10
Vietnamese refugees	14
Unmarried living together	10
Fundamentalists	4
Jews	5
Catholics	4
Protestants	1

By Education
College

Cults; sects	30%
Cuban refugees	21
Hispanics	12
Vietnamese refugees	13
Unmarried living together	9
Fundamentalists	15
Jews	1
Catholics	1
Protestants	*

High School

Cults; sects	32%
Cuban refugees	27
Hispanics	19
Vietnamese refugees	17
Unmarried living together	15
Fundamentalists	9
Jews	2
Catholics	2
Protestants	1

Grade School

Cults; sects	22%
Cuban refugees	23
Hispanics	24
Vietnamese refugees	23
Unmarried living together	21
Fundamentalists	8
Jews	5
Catholics	1
Protestants	1

By Age
18–29 Years

Cults; sects	27%
Cuban refugees	25
Hispanics	15
Vietnamese refugees	16
Unmarried living together	5
Fundamentalists	8
Jews	2
Catholics	2
Protestants	1

30–49 Years

Cults; sects	32%
Cuban refugees	23
Hispanics	12
Vietnamese refugees	16
Unmarried living together	13
Fundamentalists	9
Jews	2
Catholics	1
Protestants	1

50 Years and Over

Cults; sects	31%
Cuban refugees	26
Hispanics	24
Vietnamese refugees	18
Unmarried living together	22
Fundamentalists	13
Jews	2
Catholics	1
Protestants	1

By Religion

Protestants

Cults; sects	31%
Cuban refugees	27
Hispanics	19
Vietnamese refugees	17
Unmarried living together	19
Fundamentalists	10
Jews	2
Catholics	2
Protestants	1

Catholics

Cults; sects	33%
Cuban refugees	22
Hispanics	16
Vietnamese refugees	18
Unmarried living together	9
Fundamentalists	10
Jews	3
Catholics	*
Protestants	1

*Less than 1%

Note: While better educated Americans tend to be more tolerant than those with less education about persons of different nationalities, races, and life-styles, they are less so when it comes to religious fundamentalists. The college trained, for example, are more willing to have Cuban and Vietnamese refugees and Hispanics as neighbors but less likely to welcome persons belonging to fundamentalist religions.

While persons with a college background tend to hold attitudes similar to those with less formal education toward members of sects and cults, they reveal considerably more tolerance toward other groups tested in the survey. The college trained are also less inclined than the noncollege group to reject singles as neighbors, although differences in attitudes toward this group appear to be largely a function of age.

Views of other demographic groups show that in general southerners are more inclined than persons living outside the South to say they would not welcome the various groups tested. By age, young adults tend to be more tolerant than their elders. And while Protestants and Catholics hold similar views toward most of the nine groups, Protestants tend to be less tolerant than Catholics of unmarried people living together.

JANUARY 24
MORAL MAJORITY

Interviewing Date: 12/11–14/81
Survey #187-G

Have you heard or read about the organization called the Moral Majority?

Yes	55%*
No	45

*In a November 1980 survey 40% had heard or read about the Moral Majority.

Asked of those who responded in the affirmative: Generally speaking, do you have a favorable or an unfavorable opinion of this organization?

Favorable	12%
Unfavorable	28
No opinion	15
	55%*

By Sex

Male

Favorable	13%
Unfavorable	31
No opinion	16
	60%*

Female

Favorable 11%
Unfavorable 25
No opinion 15
                                   51%*

By Race
White

Favorable 14%
Unfavorable 31
No opinion 15
                                   60%*

Nonwhite

Favorable 5%
Unfavorable 12
No opinion 12
                                   29%*

By Education
College

Favorable 14%
Unfavorable 50
No opinion 16
                                   80%*

High School

Favorable 13%
Unfavorable 20
No opinion 16
                                   49%*

Grade School

Favorable 6%
Unfavorable 11
No opinion 12
                                   29%*

By Region
East

Favorable 9%
Unfavorable 27
No opinion 13
                                   49%*

Midwest

Favorable 15%
Unfavorable 26
No opinion 20
                                   61%*

South

Favorable 13%
Unfavorable 24
No opinion 14
                                   51%*

West

Favorable 12%
Unfavorable 37
No opinion 13
                                   62%*

By Age
18–29 Years

Favorable 11%
Unfavorable 30
No opinion 17
                                   58%*

30–49 Years

Favorable 13%
Unfavorable 31
No opinion 15
                                   59%*

50–64 Years

Favorable 13%
Unfavorable 27
No opinion 16
                                   56%*

65 Years and Over

Favorable 12%
Unfavorable 18
No opinion 13
                                   43%*

By Income

$15,000 and Over

Favorable 15%
Unfavorable 36
No opinion 17
                                   68%*

Under $15,000

Favorable 10%
Unfavorable 17
No opinion 13
                                   40%*

By Politics

Republicans

Favorable 21%
Unfavorable 27
No opinion 17
                                   65%*

Democrats

Favorable 8%
Unfavorable 26
No opinion 13
                                   47%*

Independents

Favorable 12%
Unfavorable 31
No opinion 18
                                   61%*

By Religion

Protestants

Favorable 15%
Unfavorable 25
No opinion 16
                                   56%*

Catholics

Favorable 10%
Unfavorable 25
No opinion 15
                                   50%*

Liberal in Religious Beliefs

Favorable 6%
Unfavorable 49
No opinion 12
                                   67%*

Middle of the Road in Religious Beliefs

Favorable 11%
Unfavorable 26
No opinion 18
                                   55%*

Conservative in Religious Beliefs

Favorable 21%
Unfavorable 21
No opinion 15
                                   57%*

By Occupation

Professional and Business

Favorable 15%
Unfavorable 54
No opinion 14
                                   83%*

Clerical and Sales

Favorable 15%
Unfavorable 30
No opinion 17
                                   62%*

Manual Workers

Favorable 13%
Unfavorable 21
No opinion 16
                                   50%*

Nonlabor Force

Favorable 11%
Unfavorable 20
No opinion 14
                                   45%*

*Those who have heard or read about the Moral Majority.

Also asked of those who had heard or read about the Moral Majority: If you were asked to do so, do you think you would be willing to belong to this organization, or not?

Would be (or are already members)..... 5%
Would not be 41
Not sure........................... 9
$\overline{\hspace{2em}55\%}$

Note: Although public awareness of the Moral Majority has increased from 40% to 55% during the past year, unfavorable attitudes continue to outweigh favorable views by about a 2-to-1 ratio. Overall opinion of this fundamentalist political movement, founded by the Reverend Jerry Falwell, is far more negative than positive, but sharp differences are recorded on the basis of background characteristics and on whether survey respondents consider themselves conservative or liberal in their religious beliefs.

Among those who place themselves toward the liberal end of a ten-point scale, unfavorable attitudes outweigh favorable by 8 to 1. Among those with middle-of-the-road religious beliefs, the division is about 2 to 1 negative. Among those who place themselves on the conservative end of the scale, however, opinions are evenly divided.

Some political observers hold the Moral Majority responsible for the defeat of key members of Congress in the 1980 elections. The Moral Majority, which at the time claimed it had registered 4 million new fundamentalist voters nationally, gave candidates "morality ratings," according to their stand on issues ranging from abortion to SALT II.

Most likely to indicate a willingness to join the Moral Majority are southerners (9%), Protestants (7%), Republicans (9%), and those who say their religious beliefs are conservative (10%).

Interviewing Date: 6/19–22/81
Survey #175-G

You will notice that the ten boxes on this card go from the highest position of +5 for someone you have a very favorable opinion of all the way down to the lowest position of −5 for someone you have a very unfavorable opinion of. How far up the scale or how far down the scale would you rate Jerry Falwell?

Highly favorable (+5, +4)............. 7%
Moderately favorable (+3, +2, +1)..... 28
Moderately unfavorable (−1, −2, −3)... 14
Highly unfavorable (−4, −5)........... 15
Don't know; unable to identify......... 36

JANUARY 28
PERSONAL ASSETS AND MATERIAL POSSESSIONS

Interviewing Date: 12/11–14/81
Survey #187-G

Using this card, please tell me how important you feel each of these is to you. [Respondents were handed a card with positions ranging from ten to zero.] If you think something is extremely important, you would call off the highest number, 10. If you think something is extremely unimportant, you would mention the lowest number, 0. If you think something is neither extremely important nor extremely unimportant you would mention some number between 0 and 10—the higher the number, the more important you think it is; the lower the number, the less important.

Having a good family life?

	Very important
National	82%

By Race

White	83%
Black	76

By Age

18–29 years	78%
30–49 years	81
50 years and over	85

Being in good physical health?

	Very important
National	81%

By Race

White	81%
Black	83

By Age

18–29 years	78%
30–49 years	82
50 years and over	83

Having a good self-image or self-respect?

	Very important
National	79%

By Race

White	81%
Black	75

By Age

18–29 years	77%
30–49 years	79
50 years and over	81

Personal satisfaction or happiness?

	Very important
National	77%

By Race

White	78%
Black	75

By Age

18–29 years	79%
30–49 years	78
50 years and over	75

Freedom of choice to do what I want?

	Very important
National	73%

By Race

White	74%
Black	65

By Age

18–29 years	72%
30–49 years	75
50 years and over	70

Living up to my full potential?

	Very important
National	71%

By Race

White	73%
Black	67

By Age

18–29 years	75%
30–49 years	71
50 years and over	70

Having an interesting and enjoyable job?

	Very important
National	69%

By Race

White	69%
Black	66

By Age

18–29 years	75%
30–49 years	66
50 years and over	65

Having a sense of accomplishment and lasting contribution?

	Very important
National	63%

By Race

White	64%
Black	59

By Age

18–29 years	63%
30–49 years	65
50 years and over	62

Following God's will?

	Very important
National	61%

By Race

White	60%
Black	69

By Age

18–29 years	48%
30–49 years	59
50 years and over	74

Having many friends?

	Very important
National	54%

By Race

White	55%
Black	51

By Age

18–29 years	50%
30–49 years	50
50 years and over	61

Giving time to helping people in need?

	Very important
National	54%

By Race

White	52%
Black	62

By Age

18–29 years	50%
30–49 years	52
50 years and over	59

Working for the betterment of American society?

	Very important
National	51%

By Race

White	51%
Black	55

By Age

18–29 years	45%
30–49 years	50
50 years and over	56

Having an exciting, stimulating life?

	Very important
National	51%

By Race

White	51%
Black	59

By Age

18–29 years	59%
30–49 years	53
50 years and over	44

Following a strict moral code?

	Very important
National	47%

By Race

White	47%
Black	50

By Age

18–29 years	29%
30–49 years	47
50 years and over	62

Taking part in church or synagogue related activities?

	Very important
National	40%

By Race

White	38%
Black	52

By Age

18–29 years	29%
30–49 years	38
50 years and over	49

Having a nice home, car, and other belongings?

	Very important
National	39%

By Race

White	35%
Black	63

By Age

18–29 years	36%
30–49 years	39
50 years and over	43

Having a high income?

	Very important
National	37%

By Race

White	32%
Black	64

By Age

18–29 years	38%
30–49 years	40
50 years and over	34

Having enough leisure time?

	Very important
National	36%

By Race

White	34%
Black	44

By Age

18–29 years	36%
30–49 years	36
50 years and over	36

Social recognition?

	Very important
National	22%

By Race

White	21%
Black	34

By Age

18–29 years	19%
30–49 years	22
50 years and over	24

Note: In a recent Gallup survey a high percentage of the American people considered the personal aspects of their lives—family (82%), health (81%), and self-respect (79%), for example—to be far more important than the possession of material goods. Blacks and whites share this general assessment, but the principal difference observed is that blacks are much more likely than whites to value material possessions and status-related goals, which undoubtedly is a reflection of their generally lower income level. For instance, twice the proportion of blacks (64%) as whites (32%) assign more importance to having a large income. Similarly, blacks are more inclined than whites to esteem a nice home, car, and other personal belongings as well as social recognition.

While there is greater similarity than disparity in the views of both races, blacks attach greater importance than whites to the religion-related values: following God's will and taking part in church activities, although there is no significant difference in the proportions of each race who give very important ratings to following a strict moral code in their lives.

While there is general agreement among various age groups about the relative significance of the personal assets measured in the survey, there are some notable exceptions. For example, 62% of Americans aged fifty and older consider following a strict moral code extremely important, but the figures drop to 47% among thirty to forty-nine year olds and only 29% for those eighteen to twenty-nine.

There is other evidence that younger people place less importance on religiously oriented values. Far fewer younger than older persons consider following God's will and being active in church or synagogue affairs to be very important in their lives. In contrast, men and women under thirty are more inclined to place a high degree of importance on having an exciting, stimulating life and an interesting job than are persons thirty and over.

Women in the survey attach more importance to religious, ethical, and altruistic values than do men. For instance, 60% of women considered helping the needy very important, while merely 47% of men shared this view. By the same token, two out of three women (69%), compared to roughly half the male sample (53%), believe that following God's will is very important.

JANUARY 31
CONGRESSIONAL ELECTIONS*

With President Ronald Reagan's job performance rating on a long slide (19 points) since last May, speculation is mounting about the likely effect of his rating on the congressional races this fall. While events on the domestic and international fronts can of course change the pattern, the Gallup record over a thirty-two year

*This Gallup analysis was written by Andrew Kohut, president of the Gallup Organization Inc.

period, encompassing eight off-year congressional elections, shows that a president's job performance rating almost invariably declines between the beginning of the year and just prior to the fall elections. The average decline for eight elections has been 11 percentage points.

Examination of the relationship between presidential popularity and gains or losses in House seats shows that when a president's popularity dips into the low 40s or 30s at the time of the November elections, it can spell trouble for the party in power and bring about a greater than normal seat loss. Traditionally, the party in control of the White House has lost seats in off-year elections. The average loss for the party in power has been 30 seats in off-year elections since 1946.

Not since 1934 has a party that has just won the White House made gains in the House at mid-term. Typically, a "political bounceback" develops, which aids the party not in power. In 1934, the one exception in two generations, President Franklin Roosevelt's New Deal, was still gaining momentum and the Democrats registered gains in that fall's congressional elections.

An example of the relationship between the last presidential popularity rating prior to the congressional elections and a greater than average seat loss can be found in the 1946 congressional elections when President Harry Truman had a 32% approval score. The 54-seat loss for Democratic congressmen that year greatly exceeded the average. And President Lyndon Johnson's preelection approval rating just before the 1966 House races was 44% and his party lost 48 seats.

While a low presidential popularity rating historically has been accompanied by a greater than expected seat loss for the party in the White House, a strong popularity rating—in the high 50s or 60s—has tended to hold this party in good stead at the congressional level. President John Kennedy, for example, enjoyed an approval rating of 61% shortly before the 1962 congressional elections, and the Democrats lost only 5 seats that November. President Richard Nixon had a 58% rating on the eve of the 1970 elections, and the GOP suffered a loss of only 8 seats.

Events can distort what otherwise appears to be a fairly close correlation between presidential popularity ratings and losses in congressional seats. For example, President Dwight Eisenhower had a rating of 58% prior to the 1958 congressional elections, but his party suffered a greater than normal loss (47 seats), undoubtedly due in considerable measure to the recession that year.

The year 1950 is another good example of the impact of events on a congressional campaign. President Truman's low popularity rating of 39% approval, recorded in October, should have contributed to a larger than normal seat loss in that fall's elections. The loss for the Democrats of 29 seats, however, was just about the norm for off-year elections. A likely explanation lies in the fact that the 1950 elections took place only a few days after a series of military victories in the Korean War, culminating in General Douglas MacArthur's successful drive to the Manchurian border. Hopes were high that the war was nearing an end and U.S. troops would be home by Christmas.

Presidential Popularity and Congressional Seat Change*

	Start of year†	Final before elections†	Seat Change Republicans	Seat Change Democrats
1978				
Carter	55%	49%	+14	−16
1970				
Nixon	61	58	−8	+11
1966				
Johnson	59	44	+47	−48
1962				
Kennedy	78	61	+ 3	− 5

*Figures for 1974 are not given because of the change of administrations in August.
† Percent approving of job performance.

1958				
Eisenhower	60	58	−47	+51
1954				
Eisenhower	71	61	−18	+21
1950				
Truman	45	39	+28	−29
1946				
Truman	63	32	+55	−54

FEBRUARY 4
PRESIDENT REAGAN

Interviewing Date: 1/8–11/82
Survey #188-G

Do you approve or disapprove of the way Ronald Reagan is handling his job as president?

Approve............................49%
Disapprove 40
No opinion 11

National Trend

	Approve	Disapprove	No opinion
1981			
December	49%	41%	10%
November	54	37	9
August	60	29	11
June	59	29	12
April	67	18	15
February	55	18	27

Now let me ask you about specific foreign and domestic problems. As I read off each problem, one at a time, would you tell me whether you approve or disapprove of the way President Reagan is handling that problem:

Economic conditions in this country?

Approve............................41%
Disapprove 51
No opinion 8

National Trend

	Approve	Disapprove	No opinion
1981			
December	41%	50%	9%
November	40	50	10
October	44	47	9
August	53	35	12
May	58	31	11
March	56	32	12

Inflation?

Approve. 37%
Disapprove 53
No opinion 10

National Trend

	Approve	Disapprove	No opinion
1981			
November	42%	45%	13%
October	42	48	10
August	53	35	12
May	56	30	14
March	56	30	14

Unemployment?

Approve. 26%
Disapprove 63
No opinion 11

National Trend

	Approve	Disapprove	No opinion
1981			
November	32%	49%	19%
October	33	53	14
August	39	38	23
May	42	34	24
March	40	37	23

Relations with the Soviet Union?

Approve. 47%
Disapprove 33
No opinion . . . .-.'. 20

	Approve	Disapprove	No opinion
1981			
December	53%	29%	18%
October	53	25	22
May	53	23	24
March	58	19	23

Do you approve or disapprove of the way President Reagan is dealing with the situation in Poland?*

Approve. 52%
Disapprove 25
No opinion 23

By Politics
Republicans

Approve. 68%
Disapprove 16
No opinion 16

Democrats

Approve. 44%
Disapprove 30
No opinion 26

Independents

Approve. 49%
Disapprove 28
No opinion 23

*This question was asked for the first time on the current survey.

Note: As President Ronald Reagan embarks on his second year in office, his overall job performance rating and the public's assessment of his handling of four important national problems are at a low point. Specifically, 49% of Americans now approve of Reagan's handling of his presidential duties; 41%, the way he is dealing with economic conditions; 37%, his handling of inflation; 26%, his dealing with unemployment; and 47%, our relations with the Soviet Union. At no time since these Gallup measurements were initiated has there been significantly lower approval ratings and in two instances—Reagan's handling of inflation and unemployment—his current ratings are lower than any recorded to date for him. However, on the brighter side from the president's point of view, twice as many Americans approve (52%) as disapprove (25%) of his handling of the Polish situation.

The nation's economic news in January was mixed. The good news that the rate of inflation had returned to single digits was offset by a worsening in the unemployment rate. There was also the disquieting prospect of a $100-billion deficit for the 1982 fiscal year.

One person in eight nationwide (13%) expresses unqualified approval of Reagan, giving him a vote of confidence for his overall performance in office and for all five specific issues tested. Slightly fewer, 10%, express unqualified disapproval. Most inclined to do so are blacks, with almost three in ten (28%) giving consistently negative responses.

FEBRUARY 7
MOST IMPORTANT PROBLEM

Interviewing Date: 1/8–11/82
Survey #188-G

What do you think is the most important problem facing this country today?

High cost of living; inflation	49%
Unemployment; recession	28
Reagan budget cuts	7
International problems	6
Crime	5
Fear of war	5
Moral decline in society	4
Excessive government spending	3
All other responses	8
No opinion	2
	117%*

*Total adds to more than 100% due to multiple responses.

The following shows the key breakdowns among the respondents who mentioned inflation and unemployment as the most important problem:

	Inflation	Unem-ployment
National	49%	28%

By Race

White	50%	27%
Black	43	33

By Education

College	57%	25%
High school	48	28
Grade school	38	32

By Region

East	51%	29%
Midwest	51	35
South	47	24
West	48	21

By Age

18–29 years	48%	31%
30–49 years	55	24
50 years and over	45	28

By Occupation

Professional and business	57%	24%
Clerical and sales	52	25
Manual workers	45	34
Nonlabor force	46	28

Asked of those who named a problem: Which political party do you think can do a better job of handling the problem you have just mentioned——the Republican party or the Democratic party?

Republican	30%
Democratic	34
No difference (volunteered)	26
No opinion	10

Party Better Able to Handle Inflation and Unemployment

	Inflation	Unem-ployment
Republican	36%	21%
Democratic..............	31	43
No difference (volunteered)	26	27
No opinion	7	9

Note: The top concern of the American public continues to be inflation and the high cost of living, but more people today than at any other time during the last five years name unemployment as the number one problem. Moreover, with the exception of a brief period in 1976–77, the current figure on joblessness is higher than it has been since these measurements began in 1939. In that year 36% cited unemployment as the most important problem facing the nation; keeping out of war received about the same number of responses. The high point of 39% was recorded in 1977.

In the latest survey 49% names the high cost of living and 28% unemployment as the nation's most urgent problem. The proportion citing unemployment has grown from 8% one year ago, to 17% last fall, to the current figure. After the high cost of living and unemployment, the Reagan budget cuts, international problems, crime, and fear of war are named most often.

Little difference is noted in the proportions of people from different regions of the nation naming the high cost of living, but unemployment is less often mentioned in the Sun Belt states in the South and West. Black Americans are more apt to cite unemployment than are whites, but inflation is the dominant concern of both races. In addition, far more blacks (21%) than whites (7%) name the Reagan budget cuts as the most important national problem.

The Democratic party holds a slight edge as the party voters see as better able to deal with the problem they consider uppermost, with 34% naming the Democrats, 30% the Republicans, and 26% saying there is no difference between the parties or not expressing an opinion. These findings represent a turnabout from those recorded in October, when 29% named the

Democrats, 32% the GOP, and 39% were uncommitted. One year ago the Republican party held a nineteen-point advantage over the Democrats, the widest lead ever enjoyed by the GOP in this assessment.

For almost forty years the Gallup Poll has asked Americans what they consider to be the most important problem facing the nation and which political party they think can better deal with this problem. This Gallup Poll issue barometer has proved to be a key predictor of the outcome of national elections. In sixty-seven Gallup Poll measurements the GOP has been named more often than the Democratic party only thirteen times as being better able to deal with the national problem considered most important at the time. However, as in 1975, the Democratic margin has been as wide as 28 percentage points.

The Democrats owe their slight lead on the current Gallup Poll issue barometer to the wide advantage they have with voters on the issue of unemployment. Twice as many people who think unemployment is the major problem credit the Democrats as being the party better able to deal with this problem. On the other hand, the GOP leads as the party better able to handle inflation. The margin between the parties, however, is smaller than in the case of unemployment.

FEBRUARY 11
INFLATION AND UNEMPLOYMENT

Interviewing Date: 1/8–11/82
Survey #188-G

The inflation rate during 1981 was about 9%. By the end of 1982 what do you think the inflation rate will be?

15% or more	11%
14%	1
13%	3
12%	12
11%	12
10%	14
9% or less	36
Don't know........................	11

Median estimate: 10.2%

Comparison Table: March 1981*

15% or more	35%
14%	10
13%	6
12%	15
11%	4
10%	12
9% or less	7
Don't know	11

Median estimate: 13.5%

*Question asked what inflation rate will be at the end of 1981.

The current unemployment rate is now 8.4%. By the end of 1982 what do you think the unemployment rate will be?

10% or more	44%
9%	18
8%	11
7%	9
6%	7
5% or less	2
Don't know	9

Median estimate: 9.4%

Comparison Table: March 1981*

10% or more	28%
9%	13
8%	17
7%	15
6%	11
5% or less	7
Don't know	9

Median estimate: 8.2%

*Question asked what unemployment rate will be at the end of 1981.

Note: The public predicts an improvement in the nation's inflation rate by the end of the year but a further deterioration in the unemployment situation. In the latest Gallup survey, Americans' median estimate of the year-end inflation rate now stands at 10.2%, compared to their estimates of 13.5% last March and 13.6% in November 1980. In contrast, the public's median estimate of the unemployment rate by the end of 1982 is now 9.4%, compared to the 8.2% and 7.1% estimates for 1981 covered in the two previous surveys. It is interesting to note that the public's median estimates for both the inflation and unemployment rates are marginally higher than the latest government estimates.

The misery index, the sum of the public's forecasts of both the inflation and unemployment rates, is now 20%, statistically indistinguishable from the 22% and 21% obtained in the two earlier surveys, with the current lower inflation forecast offset by the higher unemployment prediction.

A dramatic contrast between the current and previous unemployment predictions is found by comparing the proportions saying the jobless rate will be 9% or over by the end of 1981 and 1982, respectively. In the November 1980 survey 24% of the public foresaw an unemployment rate of this magnitude; by March 1981 the figure had grown to 41%; in the current survey the comparable number is 62%.

The public's improved perceptions of the inflation picture are equally striking: in the 1980 survey 41% thought the inflation rate would be 14% or higher by the end of 1980; the figure grew to 45% in the 1981 survey; and merely 12% think inflation will be 14% or more by the end of this year.

The misery index was created in 1976 by presidential candidate Jimmy Carter to dramatize the failure of the Ford administration to improve the economy. Candidate Ronald Reagan, in turn, found the index an effective political weapon to use against President Carter during the 1980 campaign.

President Reagan's economic program, assisted by stable oil prices and high interest rates, has succeeded in reducing inflation but at the price of the current recession. The government figure of 8.5% unemployment for January was down from the adjusted 8.8% December figure, but government statisticians reported no increase in employment in January. The explanation given is that many persons who have been out of work for a long time have simply given up looking for jobs and, by the government's definition, are not counted as unemployed.

FEBRUARY 12
POLITICAL DIFFERENCES BETWEEN MEN AND WOMEN INCREASE*

Over a decade ago the reemerging feminist movement attempted to raise the political consciousness of women. For a long time the polls were unable to detect the results of their efforts. However, surveys of public opinion are now showing substantial differences between men and women on almost all political indicators and on many key issues. Ironically, Gallup and other surveys indicate that feminist issues are not the ones that now divide men and women. In fact, there is generally more agreement between the sexes on feminist issues than there is on most other public questions.

The most striking political difference between men and women is their reaction to the Reagan administration and its policies. Men gave much greater support than women to Ronald Reagan in the 1980 election, and men have since expressed more backing for his administration. In the most recent Gallup Poll men were approving rather than disapproving of Reagan by a margin of 53% to 37%. On the other hand, women were divided about equally—45% approved and almost as many (43%) disapproved. Overall, men and women have had more divergent views about the Reagan stewardship than has been the case with previous administrations.

During the campaign, Reagan's "problem with women" was thought to center on the peace issue. Women were more likely than men to believe that a Reagan presidency might lead to war. Even today women express much less support than men for Reagan's foreign policy. A January *Newsweek* Poll found 63% of men approving of Reagan's dealing with the Soviet Union, compared to only 47% of women, and it also found women much more critical than men of the administration's defense spending policies.

However, differences in opinion by sex about the Reagan presidency extend beyond foreign

policy and defense spending. Women are much less likely to express faith in Reaganomics and are more critical of federal budget cuts overall as well as on a program-by-program basis. By almost 2 to 1 (61% to 33%) men supported the Reagan budget cuts in the January *Newsweek* Poll, compared to a 49% to 41% support division among women.

Political differences between the sexes are not limited to views on the Reagan administration. The Democratic party is generally enjoying more support among women than men. Throughout the past decade there were no significant differences in party affiliation between men and women, but in 1981 the Democrats enjoyed a 19 percentage-point edge among women in party identification, compared to 12 percentage points among men.

Congressional voting intentions also show a similar pattern. Democrats hold a 24 percentage-point margin over Republicans among women, compared to a 9 percentage-point margin among men. The following table illustrates that difference:

Congressional Preference*

	Republicans	Democrats	Democrats (advantage)
National	38%	55%	+17
By Sex			
Male	43	52	+ 9
Female	34	58	+24

Historically, women take a softer line on foreign policy issues and express greater concern about war and peace. Youthful demonstrators aside, women, especially older women, were the group most critical of U.S. involvement in Vietnam during the early stages. Women today still express the greatest concern about nuclear war and are more disturbed about American involvement in El Salvador.

Differences in opinion between the sexes, however, are found on a wide range of issues. Women show greater opposition than men to

*This Gallup analysis was written by Andrew Kohut, president of the Gallup Organization Inc.

*Gallup Poll, November 1981

easing environmental standards, express more support for gun control, are more in favor of bringing prayer back into the schools, and show less support than men for the death penalty. A major exception to this is on feminist issues. Men and women do not differ significantly on the ERA or, for that matter, on abortion. The sexes are equally divided on abortion, and both show support for the ERA, in principle.

The political and socioeconomic opinions between men and women take on greater importance because of changes in the composition of the voting public. According to the U.S. census, in each election a progressively larger percentage of the electorate is female. The census studies of self-reported voting show that for the first time in history equal proportions of men and women voted in the 1980 election. As a consequence, women now represent a majority of the voting public. It is not easy to pinpoint why women are voting at relatively greater rates or to determine whether the differences in political opinion by sex will endure. Perhaps the redefinition of sexual roles and the women's movement in general are related factors, but polls provide little evidence that feminist issues are at the core of women's political beliefs.

Opinion about the Reagan administration appears to have brought to a head the divergent political views of men and women. Men have more basic faith and confidence in Reagan's foreign policy and economic program. Women's traditionally greater concerns about peace, coupled with their generally more liberal social views, have led them to a harsher evaluation of Reagan and to a decidedly more Democratic stance, at least for the present.

FEBRUARY 13
RELIGION

The 1981 figures on religious preference are based on accumulated samples totaling more than 30,000 interviews. The 1981 figures on church attendance and membership are based on national surveys conducted during five selected weeks during the year.

How many times did you happen to attend church or synagogue in the last thirty days? Those who responded not at all were asked: Have you attended the church or synagogue of your choice in the past six months, apart from weddings, funerals, or special holidays such as Christmas, Easter, or Yom Kippur?

Within last seven days 41%
    More than weekly 17
    Weekly 14
    Less than every week* 10
More than seven days to thirty days 16
More than thirty days to six months 15
More than six months 28

*Attended church or synagogue within the last seven days but did not attend every week within the last thirty days.

Did you, yourself, happen to attend church or synagogue in the last seven days?

                                     Yes
National 41%

National Trend
(Church/Synagogue Attendance)

1980................................ 40%
1979................................ 40
1977................................ 41
1967................................ 43
1958................................ 49
1957................................ 47
1955................................ 49
1954................................ 46
1950................................ 39
1940................................ 37
1939................................ 41

Do you happen to be a member of a church or synagogue?

                                     Yes
National 69%

National Trend
(Church/Synagogue Membership)

1980	69%
1978	68
1976	71
1965	73
1952	73
1947	76
1942	75
1937	73

What is your religious preference—Protestant, Roman Catholic, Jewish, or an Orthodox church such as the Greek or Russian Orthodox Church?

Protestant	59%
Catholic	28
Jewish	2
Eastern Orthodox	*
Other	3
None	8

*Less than 1%

The table below shows the change between 1947 and 1981 in the proportions claiming a preference for each of the three major religious groups in the country:

Change in Religious Preference

	1981	1947	Point change	Proportional change
Catholics	28%	20%	+ 8	+40%
Protestants	59	69	−10	−15
Jews	2	5	− 3	−60

Note: Churchgoing has remained remarkably constant since 1969, after having suffered a decline from the high points of 49% recorded in 1955 and 1958. Attendance has not varied by more than 2 percentage points since 1969. Similarly, the proportion who say they are church members has changed little in recent years, with about seven out of ten Americans (69%) now claiming membership in a church or synagogue. The largest proportion of church members (76%) was found in 1947, close to the 73% noted in the first Gallup audit in 1937.

More than nine in ten in the latest survey state a specific religious preference, with 59% saying they are Protestants, 28% Catholics, and 2% Jews. The remainder express a preference for another church or religion (3%), while 8% claim no religious preference.

Between 1947 and 1981 the proportion of Catholics in the population grew dramatically— from 20% in 1947 to 28% in recent years— while Protestants declined from 69% to 59%. The proportion of Jews fell from 5% in 1947 to 2% in 1981. In each of these shifts the most pronounced changes occurred during the 1947–74 period.

The proportion of adult church or synagogue members declined in the period between the mid-1940s and the late 1970s. In 1980, however, the percentage leveled out at 69%, where it remained in 1981. It is important to bear in mind that the membership figures reported here are *self-classifications,* representing the proportion of people who say they are members of a church or synagogue and thus may include some who are not actually on the rolls of a local church. It also should be stressed that adherents of certain churches—for example, the Roman Catholic and Eastern Orthodox churches—are considered members at birth.

FEBRUARY 18
DEMOCRATIC PRESIDENTIAL CANDIDATES

Interviewing Date: 1/22–25/82
Survey #189-G

Asked of Democrats and independents: Suppose the choice for president in the Democratic convention in 1984 narrows down to Jimmy Carter and Edward Kennedy. Which one would you prefer to have the Democratic convention select?

Total Democrats

Carter	31%
Kennedy	52
Undecided	17

Northern Democrats

Carter............................24%
Kennedy 57
Undecided.........................19

Southern Democrats

Carter............................45%
Kennedy 41
Undecided.........................14

Independents

Carter............................26%
Kennedy 46
Undecided.........................28

Asked of Democrats and independents: Suppose the choice for president in the Democratic convention in 1984 narrows down to Walter Mondale and Edward Kennedy. Which one would you prefer to have the Democratic convention select?

Total Democrats

Mondale 31%
Kennedy 54
Undecided.........................15

Northern Democrats

Mondale 30%
Kennedy 56
Undecided.........................14

Southern Democrats

Mondale 35%
Kennedy 48
Undecided.........................17

Independents

Mondale 35%
Kennedy 41
Undecided.........................24

Note: Senator Edward Kennedy is a strong early favorite over two potential rivals for the 1984 Democratic presidential nomination. The Massachusetts senator has a 5-to-3 edge over both former President Jimmy Carter and former Vice-President Walter Mondale among Democratic voters to be their party's standard-bearer. In separate head-to-head matches Kennedy tops Carter 52% to 31% and bests Mondale by an almost identical 54% to 31%.

Among political independents, who may vote in Democratic primaries in some states, Mondale fares better against Kennedy than does Carter. Kennedy is the choice of 41% of independents to 35% for Mondale, while Kennedy leads Carter among this group 46% to 26%. As is typical in these Gallup nomination tests, a far larger proportion of independents than Democrats are uncommitted.

As might be expected Carter performs much better against Kennedy among southern Democrats, while Kennedy's margin over the former president among northern Democrats tops 2 to 1.

In eleven Gallup nomination showdown tests from early 1979 into November of that year, Kennedy was the decisive choice of Democrats for the 1980 nomination—at times by margins approaching 3 to 1. After the Iranian hostage crisis erupted in November, Democrats rallied behind President Carter, and Kennedy never again represented a serious threat to Carter for the 1980 nomination. By way of comparison, Carter was a 36-point underdog to Kennedy in July 1979; one year later Carter led Kennedy by 26 points.

Other factors contributed to Kennedy's loss of support for the 1980 nomination, although the hostage situation was undoubtedly paramount. The Chappaquiddick incident of 1969 and consequent doubts about Kennedy's character were revived. Kennedy also made remarks about the former Shah of Iran and the Iranian terrorists that many voters at the time considered injudicious.

Kennedy seems certain to retain his Senate seat in this fall's election, but some observers believe that Chappaquiddick again may become an issue if he decides to run for the presidency in 1984. His liberalism and belief in a large federal government also may run counter to the mood of the electorate, which now espouses less, rather than more, centralization of political power in

Washington. On the other hand, if the public's concern that President Reagan's economic program unfairly penalizes the needy continues to grow, Kennedy-style liberalism may become more politically attractive.

FEBRUARY 21
JOB SECURITY

Interviewing Date: 1/22–25/82
Survey #189-G

Asked of employed persons: Thinking about the next twelve months, how likely do you think it is that you will lose your job or be laid off—very likely, fairly likely, not too likely, or not at all likely?

Very likely. 5%
Fairly likely. 10
Not too likely 25
Not at all likely. 57
Don't know 3

Asked of the entire sample: Which do you think the federal government should give greater attention to—trying to curb inflation or trying to reduce unemployment?

Curb inflation 44%
Reduce unemployment 49
No opinion 7

National Trend

	October 1980	February 1975
Curb inflation	33%	46%
Reduce unemployment	61	44
No opinion	6	10

Note: The latest unemployment rate of 8.5% is one of the highest since World War II. According to the current Gallup survey, an additional 15% of persons presently employed in either full-time or part-time positions think it is at least fairly likely they will lose their jobs within the next twelve months. Fear of unemployment is highest among workers whose annual family income is less than $15,000 (24% say their jobs

may be in jeopardy), blacks (22%), members of labor union families (22%), manual workers (21%), Democrats (19%), midwesterners (19%), and workers under thirty years of age (18%).

As reported recently, Americans continue to cite inflation as the nation's top problem, although more people today than at any time during the last five years name unemployment as the most important problem. However, public opinion leans toward the view that the federal government should give greater priority to reducing unemployment than to curbing inflation. A key reason for this apparent contradiction is found in recent survey results showing that the public predicts an improvement in the nation's inflation rate by year-end but a further deterioration in the unemployment situation.

FEBRUARY 25
NATIONAL SERVICE AND
DRAFT REGISTRATION

Interviewing Date: 1/22–25/82
Survey #189-G

One European nation requires every physically able young man at the age of twenty to spend seventeen weeks in military training. Afterwards he must devote three weeks a year for the next eight years to this military training. Would you favor or oppose having the U.S. adopt such a plan?

Favor. 51%
Oppose. 41
No opinion 8

By Age
18–24 Years

Favor. 46%
Oppose. 49
No opinion 5

25–29 Years

Favor. 38%
Oppose. 53
No opinion 9

30–49 Years

Favor..............................53%
Oppose..............................39
No opinion 8

50 Years and Over

Favor..............................54%
Oppose..............................36
No opinion 10

Do you favor or oppose continuing to register young men so that in the case of an emergency the time needed to call up men for a draft would be reduced?

Favor..............................71%
Oppose..............................23
No opinion 6

By Age
18–24 Years

Favor..............................61%
Oppose..............................35
No opinion 4

25–29 Years

Favor..............................66%
Oppose..............................32
No opinion 2

30–49 Years

Favor..............................72%
Oppose..............................23
No opinion 5

50 Years and Over

Favor..............................76%
Oppose..............................16
No opinion 8

National Trend

	July 1980	February 1980	1979
Favor	80%	83%	76%
Oppose	15	13	17
No opinion	5	4	7

Interviewing Date: 6/5–8/81
Survey #174-G

Would you favor or oppose requiring all young men to give one year of service to the nation—either in the military forces or in nonmilitary work here or abroad, such as work in hospitals or with elderly people?

Favor..............................71%
Oppose..............................24
No opinion 5

By Age
18–24 Years

Favor..............................58%
Oppose..............................37
No opinion 5

25–29 Years

Favor..............................64%
Oppose..............................34
No opinion 2

30–49 Years

Favor..............................75%
Oppose..............................21
No opinion 4

50 Years and Over

Favor..............................76%
Oppose..............................18
No opinion 6

National Trend

	1979	1976	1973	1969
Favor	60%	62%	64%	79%
Oppose	33	33	29	16
No opinion	7	5	7	5

Note: President Jimmy Carter reinstated draft registration after the Soviet Union's invasion of Afghanistan in December 1979. Although he originally opposed the move, President Ronald Reagan decided last month to continue registration and named February 28 as the final day for men born from 1960 to 1963 to comply with the registration law. Now with the president's "grace period" for eligible young men to register for the draft expiring, Americans broadly endorse continuing the registration program.

In the latest Gallup survey 71% of the public favor continuing to register young men so that the time needed to call up men for a draft in the case of an emergency would be reduced, while 23% are opposed and 6% uncommitted. The present 3-to-1 level of support for registration, however, is somewhat lower than that found in surveys conducted in 1979 and 1980.

The revival of draft registration has spurred debate on alternate programs for military and nonmilitary service. One plan studied in the current survey is the present military service system in Switzerland, which requires every physically able young man to spend seventeen weeks in military training when he becomes twenty years old. After completing this training Swiss males must devote three weeks a year for the next eight years to the armed forces. The American people lean in support of this plan, with 51% in favor and 41% opposed.

A broader program of compulsory national service for young men and women has even wider support. Under this plan, young people would have their choice of service, either in the military forces or in nonmilitary work, here or abroad, such as work in hospitals or with the elderly.

FEBRUARY 28
PRESIDENT REAGAN

Interviewing Date: 2/5–8/82
Survey #190-G

Do you approve or disapprove of the way Ronald Reagan is handling his job as president?

Approve.............................47%
Disapprove 43
No opinion 10

The following are ratings given the five most recently elected presidents in February of their second year in office:

Presidential Approval Ratings

	Approve
Ronald Reagan	47%
Jimmy Carter	49
Richard Nixon	60
John Kennedy	78
Dwight Eisenhower	69

Apart from whether you approve or disapprove of the way Reagan is handling his job as president, what do you think of Reagan as a person? Would you say you approve or disapprove of him?

Approve.............................70%
Disapprove 20
No opinion 10

By Politics
Republicans

Approve.............................92%
Disapprove 3
No opinion 5

Democrats

Approve.............................59%
Disapprove 30
No opinion 11

Independents

Approve.............................72%
Disapprove 17
No opinion 11

Those Who Disapprove of Way Reagan Is Handling His Job As President

Approve.............................48%
Disapprove 40
No opinion 12

Now let me ask you about specific foreign and domestic problems. As I read off each problem, one at a time, would you tell me whether you approve or disapprove of the way President Reagan is handling that problem:

Economic conditions in this country?

Approve............................38%
Disapprove 53
No opinion 9

Inflation?

Approve............................37%
Disapprove 53
No opinion 10

Unemployment?

Approve............................27%
Disapprove 63
No opinion 10

National defense?

Approve............................55%
Disapprove 34
No opinion 11

Relations with the Soviet Union?

Approve............................49%
Disapprove 33
No opinion 18

Foreign policy?

Approve............................44%
Disapprove 38
No opinion 18

Note: Despite the deepening recession, President Ronald Reagan's popularity has leveled off, with 47% in the latest survey approving of his job performance, not a significant change from his approval ratings since early December.

Three key factors may have helped stabilize the president's overall popularity rating in recent weeks from the much higher levels of last summer:

1) There is continuing high public regard for President Reagan as a person. Seventy percent of Americans now approve of Reagan, the man, which is close to the 74% recorded in November and not far below the 78% favorable assessment in the first Gallup test last July.

2) Reagan receives relatively high marks for his handling of national defense and U.S. relations with the Soviet Union: 55% now approve of the president's handling of the national defense, while 49% approve of his conduct of our relations with the Soviets.

3) Although Reagan's ratings for dealing with the nation's economy, inflation, and unemployment are far below his earlier scores, the precipitous declines suffered since last summer have leveled out.

MARCH 4
REAGANOMICS

Interviewing Date: 2/5–8/82
Survey #190-G

Now let's talk about the Reagan administration's economic policies. What effect do you think these policies will have on your own and your family's financial situation? Do you feel your financial situation will be much better, somewhat better, somewhat worse, or much worse as a result of the Reagan economic policies?

Much better.......................... 4%
Somewhat better.....................27
Somewhat worse 30
Much worse.........................14
Same; no opinion 25

National Trend

	November 1981	May 1981
Much better................	6%	7%
Somewhat better............	29	41
Somewhat worse............	28	29
Much worse................	21	8
Same; no opinion	16	15

How about the nation? What effect do you think the Reagan administration's economic policies will have on the nation's economic situation? Do you feel the nation's economic situation will be much better, somewhat better, somewhat worse, or much worse as a result of the Reagan economic policies?

Much better.	7%
Somewhat better.	33
Somewhat worse	28
Much worse.	16
Same; no opinion	16

National Trend

	November 1981	October 1981
Much better	9%	9%
Somewhat better.	35	44
Somewhat worse	27	24
Much worse	15	13
Same; no opinion	14	10

We are interested in how people's financial situation may have changed. Would you say that you are financially better off now than you were a year ago or are you financially worse off now?

Better	28%
Worse.	47
Same (volunteered)	24
Don't know	1

By Sex
Male

Better	30%
Worse.	44
Same (volunteered)	25
Don't know	1

Female

Better	26%
Worse.	49
Same (volunteered)	24
Don't know	1

By Race
White

Better	30%
Worse.	43
Same (volunteered)	26
Don't know	1

Nonwhite

Better	13%
Worse.	67
Same (volunteered)	17
Don't know	3

By Education
College

Better	39%
Worse.	36
Same (volunteered)	25
Don't know	*

High School

Better	27%
Worse.	50
Same (volunteered)	22
Don't know	1

Grade School

Better	11%
Worse.	56
Same (volunteered)	22
Don't know	1

By Region
East

Better	27%
Worse.	45
Same (volunteered)	28
Don't know	*

Midwest

Better	27%
Worse.	50
Same (volunteered)	22
Don't know	1

South

Better	30%
Worse.	47
Same (volunteered)	22
Don't know	1

West

Better	28%
Worse	44
Same (volunteered)	26
Don't know	2

By Age
18–29 Years

Better	39%
Worse	45
Same (volunteered)	15
Don't know	1

30–49 Years

Better	30%
Worse	48
Same (volunteered)	21
Don't know	1

50–64 Years

Better	22%
Worse	47
Same (volunteered)	31
Don't know	*

65 Years and Over

Better	15%
Worse	46
Same (volunteered)	38
Don't know	1

By Income
$25,000 and Over

Better	39%
Worse	36
Same (volunteered)	24
Don't know	1

$15,000–$24,999

Better	36%
Worse	39
Same (volunteered)	25
Don't know	*

*Less than 1%

Under $15,000

Better	17%
Worse	58
Same (volunteered)	24
Don't know	1

National Trend

	October 1981	June 1981
Better	28%	33%
Worse	43	35
Same (volunteered)	28	30
Don't know	1	2

Now looking ahead, do you expect that at this time next year you will be financially better off than now or worse off than now?

Better	42%
Worse	31
Same (volunteered)	21
Don't know	6

National Trend

	October 1981	June 1981
Better	40%	44%
Worse	31	25
Same (volunteered)	21	23
Don't know	8	8

Note: Despite a further loss of public confidence in the Reagan administration's economic program, there is a persistent feeling among Americans that their financial condition will eventually improve. However, at the present time the public continues to believe that their family's financial situation will worsen rather than improve as a result of Reaganomics.

In November 1981, 35% of those surveyed thought that their finances would be improved by the Reagan program, while 49% held the opposite viewpoint. The latest findings show almost exactly the same ratio of positive to negative appraisals but with an increase in those who are uncommitted. And by contrast in August 1981, 48% were optimistic about the effect of Reaganomics on their personal financial situation, while only 36% were pessimistic.

Wide differences of opinion are found among population groups regarding their viewpoints on the effect of Reagan's program, the most striking of which is found among those who approve or disapprove of the president's overall performance in office. Fifty-three percent of those who approve of Reagan believe that his economic policies will improve their financial condition, while 21% think it will have the opposite effect. On the other hand, merely 12% of those who disapprove are optimistic about Reaganomics, compared to 70% who say that their financial situation will worsen. These findings underscore the strong link that surveys have found between President Reagan's popularity and the public's perceptions of the effectiveness of his economic policies.

MARCH 7
PARTY BETTER FOR PEACE AND PROSPERITY

Interviewing Date: 2/5–8/82
Survey #190-G

Which political party do you think would be more likely to keep the United States out of World War III—the Republican party or the Democratic party?

Republican 24%
Democratic 41
No difference 23
No opinion 12

National Trend

	Republican	Democratic	No difference	No opinion
Oct. 1981	29%	34%	22%	15%
Apr. 1981	26	39	22	13
1980	28	32	24	16
1978	25	31	27	17
1974	24	33	19	24
1970	28	22	36	14

Which political party—the Republican party or the Democratic party—do you think will do a better job of keeping the country prosperous?

Republican 32%
Democratic 42
No difference 17
No opinion 9

National Trend

	Republican	Democratic	No difference	No opinion
Oct. 1981	40%	31%	14%	14%
Apr. 1981	41	28	18	13
1980	31	37	20	12
1978	23	41	23	13
1974	19	49	14	18
1970	25	40	23	12

Note: Peace and prosperity historically have been the key issues in national elections, with the political party on top on both having a distinct advantage at election time. However, the Republican party's political fortunes have taken a turn for the worse; it has lost its lead over the Democrats as the party voters think will do a better job of keeping the United States prosperous. The GOP also has slipped further behind the Democrats as the party voters see more likely to keep the nation at peace.

Currently, 42% of the public name the Democratic party and 32% the Republicans as better able to keep the country prosperous. Last April the Democrats, who had virtually owned the prosperity issue since these Gallup measurements began three decades ago, relinquished their lead to the Republicans for the first time. As recently as October 1981 the GOP was cited more often than the Democrats, 40% to 31%.

The GOP's edge over the Democrats, however, was short-lived, persisting only as long as Americans were bullish about the Reagan administration's economic program. As reported last week, 31% of the public now believe their family's financial situation will improve as a result of Reaganomics, while 44% think their finances will worsen.

The Democratic party currently holds a 17 percentage point advantage over the GOP as the party voters perceive as better able to keep the country out of war, with 41% of the public naming the Democrats and 24% the Republicans as superior in this respect. In October the Democrats led the GOP by only 5 points, 34% to 29%.

MARCH 11
CRIME

Interviewing Date: 1/22–25/82
Survey #189-G

Is there any area right around here—that is, within a mile—where you would be afraid to walk alone at night?

Yes.................................48%
No..................................52
No answer........................... *

By Community Size
One Million and Over

Yes.................................57%
No..................................42
No answer........................... 1

500,000–999,999

Yes.................................54%
No..................................45
No answer........................... 1

50,000–499,999

Yes.................................53%
No..................................47
No answer........................... *

2,500–49,999

Yes.................................50%
No..................................50
No answer........................... *

Under 2,500; Rural

Yes.................................31%
No..................................68
No answer........................... 1

National Trend

	1981	1977	1972	1965
Yes	45%	45%	42%	34%
No	54	54	58	63
No answer	1	1	*	3

*Less than 1%

Have you heard or read about a community program called crime watch (or neighborhood watch)?

Yes.................................73%
No..................................27

Asked of those who responded in the affirmative: Do you happen to know if there is a crime-watch program in your own neighborhood?

Yes.................................12%
No..................................44
Not sure............................17
                                    ____
                                    73%*

By Region
East

Yes.................................12%
No..................................39
Not sure............................13
                                    ____
                                    64%*

Midwest

Yes.................................11%
No..................................45
Not sure............................13
                                    ____
                                    69%*

South

Yes.................................12%
No..................................50
Not sure............................16
                                    ____
                                    78%*

West

Yes	12%
No	39
Not sure	31
	82%*

By Type of Community
Central Cities

Yes	18%
No	35
Not sure	21
	74%*

Suburbs

Yes	11%
No	37
Not sure	24
	72%*

Nonmetro Areas

Yes	8%
No	55
Not sure	9
	72%*

*Percent of those who have heard or read about the crime-watch program.

Asked of those who have heard or read about crime watch but who do not have crime-watch programs in their own neighborhoods: Would you like to see such a program in your neighborhood, or not?

	Yes
National	82%

By Type of Community

Central cities	86%
Suburbs	89
Nonmetro areas	77

Also asked of those who have heard or read about crime watch but who do not have crime-watch programs in their own neighborhoods: Would you, yourself, be interested in joining such a program, or not?

	Yes
National	67%

By Type of Community

Central cities	68%
Suburbs	70
Nonmetro areas	64

Note: About half of all Americans (48%) say there are areas in their immediate neighborhood where they would be afraid to walk alone at night. This is the highest figure recorded since this measurement began in 1965.

As the fear of crime becomes endemic, many Americans are turning to neighborhood crime-watch programs as a partial solution, and many more find the idea appealing.

One person in six nationally (17%) reports that his or her community now has some kind of organized, volunteer anticrime program. The survey shows that as many as eight in ten Americans who do not presently have a crime-watch program in their neighborhood would like to see one established. A large majority also say they themselves would be interested in joining a crime-watch program.

With crime levels increasing sharply in many areas of the nation, the concept of citizen participation in crime prevention has taken hold over the last decade. Crime-watch programs, using tactics such as walking patrols and encouraging the reporting of suspicious activities, are viewed by most experts as helpful in preventing crime. Officials of the Law Enforcement Assistance Administration note that crime has decreased by more than 50% in some communities that have neighborhood crime-watch programs.

Most programs are aimed specifically at burglary or vandalism since burglary accounts for a substantial portion of crime and can be effectively resisted. Other activities of crime-watch groups include keeping a lookout for unfamiliar vehicles, making home security checks, improving street lighting, and distributing safety tips throughout the neighborhood.

MARCH 14
NEW FEDERALISM

Interviewing Date: 2/5–8/82
Survey #190-G

Have you heard or read about the Reagan administration's New Federalism proposal?

Yes................................ 49%
No................................. 51

Those who answered affirmatively were then asked to describe the New Federalism program. The 42% who were both aware of and could describe the program were considered to be the informed group.

Asked of the informed group: Under the New Federalism program, many of the present responsibilities of the federal government would be turned over to the individual states and local communities. To begin with, the federal government would provide the necessary money to pay for those social programs, but gradually the states would take over the payments for their own programs by local taxation. Does this New Federalism sound like a good idea or a poor idea to you?

Good idea........................... 54%
Poor idea........................... 39
Not sure............................ 7

By Region
East

Good idea........................... 47%
Poor idea........................... 47
Not sure............................ 6

Midwest

Good idea........................... 55%
Poor idea........................... 37
Not sure............................ 8

South

Good idea........................... 56%
Poor idea........................... 37
Not sure............................ 7

West

Good idea........................... 61%
Poor idea........................... 28
Not sure............................ 11

By Type of Community
Center Cities

Good idea........................... 43%
Poor idea........................... 48
Not sure............................ 9

Suburbs

Good idea........................... 53%
Poor idea........................... 40
Not sure............................ 7

Nonmetro Areas

Good idea........................... 65%
Poor idea........................... 29
Not sure............................ 6

By Income
$15,000 and Over

Good idea........................... 59%
Poor idea........................... 34
Not sure............................ 7

Under $15,000

Good idea........................... 44%
Poor idea........................... 48
Not sure............................ 8

By Politics
Republicans

Good idea........................... 83%
Poor idea........................... 13
Not sure............................ 4

Democrats

Good idea........................... 35%
Poor idea........................... 57
Not sure............................ 8

Independents

Good idea 54%
Poor idea 37
Not sure 9

Also asked of the informed group: Under the New Federalism program, do you feel the states will take care of the needs of the poor and needy as well as the federal government, better than the federal government, or not as well as the federal government?

Federal government better 43%
State government better............... 28
State and federal equal (volunteered) 24
No opinion 5

Also asked of the informed group: Under the New Federalism program, do you think the total taxes paid by your family—that is, state and federal combined—will go up, go down, or stay about the same?

Will go up.......................... 64%
Will go down........................ 9
Will stay the same 23
No opinion 4

Note: Although most Americans endorse the principles underlying President Ronald Reagan's New Federalism program, many are concerned about certain possible consequences. Despite these specific concerns, the public's overall favorable appraisal of the New Federalism tends to reflect the basic findings of a Gallup survey conducted last fall in which the public leaned strongly toward the principles behind the New Federalism—that is, the individual states are closer than the federal government to the people and therefore are better able to minister to their needs.*

Under President Reagan's New Federalism proposals, which, if enacted, would begin October 1, 1983, there would be a gradual shift of

*See October 18, 1981 release, *The Gallup Poll: Public Opinion, 1981* (Wilmington, DE, 1982), pp. 235–36.

responsibility to the states for many of the programs now funded and run by the federal government. As a first step, the federal government would assume the entire administrative and financial burden of Medicaid, the most expensive welfare program, while the states would take over the Aid to Families with Dependent Children and food stamp programs, both now shared by the states and Washington.

The second major provision of the New Federalism calls for the establishment of a transitional federal trust fund that would help the states and localities finance more than forty education, highway, and community programs. This fund, to be financed by federal excise taxes, would be phased out by 1991, when state and local governments would shoulder the full financial responsibility.

Backers of the New Federalism hail it as the most effective way of reducing the size and power of the federal government. Its detractors fear the states will not distribute benefits equitably, with some predicting a migration of the needy from poor to rich states.

MARCH 18
COST OF LIVING

Interviewing Date: 1/22–25; 2/5–8/82
Survey #189-G; 190-G

On the average, about how much does your family spend on food, including milk, each week?

	Median average
National	$70*

By Region

East	$74
Midwest	$60
South	$65
West	$74

*Farm families were excluded from the survey because many farmers raise their own food.

By Type of Community

Center cities.........................$71
Suburbs..............................$74
Nonmetro areas......................$64

By Income

$15,000 and over $75
Under $15,000 ....$52

By Size of Household

Single person $43
Two-person family $56
Three-person family $74
Four-person family $80
Five-person-or-more family...........$100

National Trend

	Median average
1982	$70
1981	$62
1980	$59
1977	$48
1975	$47
1973	$37
1969	$33
1959	$29
1949	$25
1937	$11

Note: If it now costs your family more to put food on the table than it did at this time last year, you are right in step with most other Americans. The 1982 Gallup survey of weekly food expenditures shows the median amount spent by a representative (nonfarm) U.S. household is now $70 per week, the highest figure since the Gallup Poll began charting food expenditures in 1937 and more than six times the $11 recorded in the initial audit. The latest figure represents an $8 increase over the $62 median amount reported last year.

During the twenty-year period between 1949 and 1969, the figure grew from $25 per week to $33 per week, an increase of only 32%. However from 1970 to the present—a span of only thirteen years—the increase has been a whopping 106%, from $34 per week to $70.

Persons in the survey whose annual family income is over $15,000 report spending half again as much on food as do those with lower incomes. However, food costs represent a larger portion of total expenditures of families in the lower-income category than is true of upper-income households. And, as in the past, food costs take a smaller portion out of the family budget of midwesterners than those living elsewhere in the nation.

MARCH 21
COST OF LIVING

Interviewing Date: 1/22–25; 2/5–8/82
Survey #189-G; 190-G

What is the smallest amount of money a family of four (husband, wife, and two children) needs each week to get along in this community?

	Median average
National	$296*

By Region

East..............................$297
Midwest $252
South.............................$261
West $306

By Type of Community

Central cities $297
Suburban areas $307
Nonmetro areas....................$250

*Farm families were excluded from the survey because many farmers raise their own food.

National Trend

	Median average
1982	$296
1981	$277
1980	$250
1977	$199
1975	$161
1973	$149

1969	$120
1959	$ 79
1947	$ 43
1937	$ 30

What is the smallest amount of money your family needs each week to get along in this community?

By Size of Household

	Median average
Single person	$150
Two-person family	$201
Three-person family	$250
Four-person family	$300
Five-person-or-more family	$300

Note: These annual cost-of-living audits have corresponded closely to the U.S. Bureau of Labor Statistics' Consumer Price Index (CPI). For example, the latest Gallup Poll figure of $296 per week for a husband, wife, and two children to make ends meet is about 7% higher than the estimate of $277 for 1981. During the period from January 1981 to January 1982, the cost of living rose 8.4% according to the CPI. Similarly, the public's 1981 estimate of the minimum amount needed by a four-person family was almost 11% higher than the $250 recorded in 1980, while the CPI rose 12.5%.

In 1937, when the Gallup Poll first surveyed the public's perception of weekly living costs for a family of four, the median response was $30, or one-tenth the current amount. In 1947 the figure climbed to $43, but it did not hit three-digit proportions until 1967 when the median average was $101.

MARCH 25
PARTY BETTER ABLE TO HANDLE KEY NATIONAL PROBLEMS

Interviewing Date: 2/5–8/82
Survey #190-G

Which political party—the Republican or the Democratic—do you think would do a better job of dealing with:

Economic conditions in this country?

Republican	34%
Democratic	43
No difference	16
No opinion	7

Inflation?

Republican	37%
Democratic	39
No difference	15
No opinion	9

Unemployment?

Republican	22%
Democratic	56
No difference	15
No opinion	7

Foreign affairs?

Republican	34%
Democratic	37
No difference	18
No opinion	11

Relations with the Soviet Union?

Republican	34%
Democratic	36
No difference	19
No opinion	11

National defense?

Republican	44%
Democratic	33
No difference	14
No opinion	9

Energy situation?

Republican	25%
Democratic	41
No difference	22
No opinion	12

Environmental issues?

Republican	19%
Democratic	50

No difference 20
No opinion 11

Note: With the congressional elections now less than eight months away, the Republican party is losing ground to the Democratic party in what might be called the "battle of the issues," with the GOP coming off distinctly second best as the party Americans perceive as better able to deal with most of the key problems facing the nation. In fact, on only one of eight issues tested in the latest Gallup survey—handling our national defense—does the GOP enjoy a clear-cut (44% to 33%) margin of superiority over the Democrats.

The Republican party is about even with its Democratic rivals on the issue of handling U.S. relations with the Soviet Union, with 36% of the public naming the Democratic party and 34% the GOP as better in this respect. The vote is also close on the ability of the parties to deal with foreign affairs in general, with the Democrats the choice of 37% of Americans and the Republicans of 34%.

Despite a sharp decline in the rate of inflation during the Reagan administration's tenure, the best the Republicans can manage is a statistical tie with the Democrats as the party better able to deal with this problem, with 37% naming the GOP and 39% the Democrats.

On the four other issues tested the voters credit the Democratic party as being superior to the GOP, with a 41% to 25% advantage on the energy situation and 43% to 34% on coping with economic conditions. Further, the Republican party is perceived by only about one American in five as better able to deal with environmental issues (19%) and unemployment (22%), while 50% and 56% give the edge to the Democratic party on each of these problems, respectively.

Since Democrats in the survey outnumber Republicans by almost a 2-to-1 ratio (47% to 25%), a critical test of party strength is the proportion of nominal Democrats and Republicans who believe that the rival party would do a better job of dealing with the issues tested.

On a Republican party weak front—dealing with unemployment—75% of Democrats say their own party would better handle this problem, while 8% cite the GOP. On the other hand, 55% of Republicans in the survey name their own party but as many as one in four (27%) cites the Democratic party as superior in this respect.

The same pattern is found in the party perceived as better able to handle environmental issues, with 27% of Republicans crossing party lines to vote for the Democrats as better for these problems. And the Republican party gains a share of Democratic defectors on the issues of foreign affairs, dealing with the Soviet Union, and handling national defense. On the latter, 25% of Democrats choose the Republican party as better qualified than their own.

MARCH 28
CONGRESSIONAL ELECTIONS

Interviewing Date: 1/8–11; 22–25; 2/5–8/82
Surveys #188-G; #189-G; #190-G

Asked of registered voters: If the elections for Congress were being held today, which party would you like to see win in this congressional district—the Republican party or the Democratic party? [Those who said they were undecided or who voted for a different party were asked: As of today do you lean more to the Republican party or to the Democratic party?]

Republican 43%
Democratic 57

By Region
South

Republican 44%
Democratic 56

Non-South

Republican 43%
Democratic 57

*The above percentages represent the projected vote for Congress based on the choices of registered voters in the three most recent surveys.

When allowance is made for voter turnout based on the results of the 1970, 1974, and 1978 off-year congressional elections, the projected vote is:

Republican 46%
Democratic 54

By Region
South

Republican 41%
Democratic 59

Non-South

Republican 47%
Democratic 53

Note: Unless there is a sharp upturn in the economy between now and November, the Republicans face severe losses in the elections for the House of Representatives. The Democrats now have a 51-seat majority. This could reach 100 seats unless the political mood of the nation changes.

In the latest Gallup congressional test elections, the Democrats have a strong 54% to 46% lead over the Republicans in the popular vote for House seats. In addition, the tide of public opinion has swung against the GOP in a variety of ways. As reported earlier, the Democratic party is perceived by voters as better able than the Republican party to deal with the key problems facing the nation. In fact, the public is evenly divided on which party is more competent to handle inflation, one issue on which the Reagan administration has a solid record of accomplishment. (On only one of eight issues tested—dealing with the nation's defense—does the GOP enjoy a clear-cut margin of superiority over the Democratic party.)

Other factors pointing to a reduction in the number of Republican congressional seats in this fall's elections include:

1) The public's confidence in the Reagan administration's economic program continues to decline, with only 31% in the latest Gallup survey believing their family's financial situation will improve because of Reaganomics, while 44% hold the opposite point of view.

2) The GOP's short-lived lead over the Democrats as the party voters think will do a better job of keeping the United States prosperous has vanished, and to make matters worse from the Republican point of view, the GOP has slipped further behind the Democrats as the party more likely to keep the nation at peace.

3) President Reagan may be more of a liability than an asset for many incumbent and aspiring Republican congressmen. The president now receives less than majority public support for his performance in office.

4) Historical precedent is working against Republican aspirants. Only twice in the last fifty years—in 1946 and again in 1952—has the Republican party won more seats in the lower house than the Democrats.

5) The party that holds the presidency has lost House seats in every off-year election since 1946. In nine such elections from 1946 to 1978 inclusive, the loss has ranged from 5 seats (in 1962) to 54 (in 1946), with an average loss of 31 seats.

MARCH 28
SHARP DISTINCTIONS FOUND IN PUBLIC OPINION ON EL SALVADOR AND VIETNAM*

Opinion polls consistently show American unwillingness to become deeply involved in the conflict in El Salvador. The latest polls confirm what the first Gallup Polls on the subject revealed more than a year ago—stay out of that conflict. When these surveys are contrasted to the early polls on Vietnam, they say a lot about how American response to this type of foreign policy issue has changed.

The most striking difference between the opinions of 1965/66 and 1981/82 is that now

*This Gallup analysis was written by Andrew Kohut, president of the Gallup Organization, Inc.

the public can disassociate more easily their overall opinions of a president from their views on his handling a specific foreign policy issue. When the first polls on El Salvador were taken, newly elected Ronald Reagan's overall approval rating stood at 60%, yet only 44% approved of his handling of the situation in El Salvador and about as many disapproved.

In 1965, on the other hand, there was a much higher correlation between approval of President Lyndon B. Johnson overall and approval of his handling U.S. involvement in Vietnam. In late 1965, Johnson's popularity rating was in the mid-60s, while on Vietnam his approval rating was nearly as high (57%).

The single most frequently mentioned reason for approving of Johnson's Vietnam buildup policies in June 1965 was that "he knows the situation . . . he is doing his best." It is inconceivable in the post-Vietnam and post-Watergate years that large numbers of Americans would voice support for a foreign involvement on the basis of a "president-knows-best" sentiment. Trust in presidents has fallen to such an extent that a *Washington Post*/ABC News Poll found the public divided on whether the Reagan administration is even telling the truth when it pledges not to send troops to El Salvador.

As faith in the president and his popularity are no longer sufficient to mobilize public opinion in support of foreign involvement, neither are appeals to Americans' concerns about Leftist aggression or the domino theory. A recent Roper Poll found 71% of Americans opposed to sending U.S. troops to El Salvador even if that were the only way to prevent the government from falling to Leftist guerrillas. The results take on added significance because the question was asked after Roper had informed respondents that guerrillas were reportedly receiving support from Cuba.

In the early stages of Vietnam, halting the spread of communism held great sway with the American public. In February 1967, 55% of Americans believed we did the right thing in sending troops in order to prevent Communist expansion, while 35% thought the United States

should not have become involved in the internal affairs of another nation. In contrast, the current Roper results testify to the extent to which stopping the spread of communism in Third World countries by armed force has lost currency with the public.

This is not to say that Americans in 1982 are unconcerned about the spread of Leftist subversion in Central America. The *Newsweek* Poll found that more than eight in ten Americans thought it likely that if rebel forces were to win in El Salvador the same kind of thing will happen in other countries in Latin America. The difference between now and then is that concern about the spread of revolution is not as scary to the average citizen as reliving Vietnam.

A February *Newsweek* Poll on El Salvador indicates that there is only a slight correlation between the public believing that the United States should support the Duarte regime and thinking the regime's fall will lead to further instability in that region. In fact, among those who say a rebel victory will lead to revolutions elsewhere, 55% want to stay out of El Salvador altogether. On the other hand, the same survey shows a strong correlation between thinking El Salvador is another Vietnam and opposing involvement.

There is little evidence in the polls to suggest that public reluctance to become involved in El Salvador reflects a softer line on communism or lack of concern for our national security. On the contrary, surveys show Americans favoring a tougher line toward the Soviet Union and approval of the largest military buildup in peacetime history.

Public opinion on El Salvador and similar situations are a by-product of America's Vietnam experience. As a consequence, Americans differ with their leaders about possible military involvement even when those leaders command general respect and respect with regard to foreign policy in particular. Americans also are more hesitant than in the past to commit resources and military forces to conflicts for the sake of geopolitical theories, especially in regions of the world they regard as unstable and undemocratic.

APRIL 1
PRESIDENT REAGAN

Interviewing Date: 3/12–15/82
Survey #191-G

Do you approve or disapprove of the way Ronald Reagan is handling his job as president?

Approve............................46%
Disapprove 45
No opinion 9

By Sex
Male

Approve............................52%
Disapprove 40
No opinion 8

Female

Approve............................41%
Disapprove 49
No opinion 10

By Race
White

Approve............................51%
Disapprove 40
No opinion 9

Nonwhite

Approve............................13%
Disapprove 76
No opinion 11

By Education
College

Approve............................54%
Disapprove 42
No opinion 4

High School

Approve............................46%
Disapprove 44
No opinion 10

Grade School

Approve............................30%
Disapprove 54
No opinion 16

By Region
East

Approve............................46%
Disapprove 45
No opinion 9

Midwest

Approve............................48%
Disapprove 44
No opinion 8

South

Approve............................47%
Disapprove 42
No opinion 11

West

Approve............................44%
Disapprove 49
No opinion 7

By Age
18–24 Years

Approve............................47%
Disapprove 45
No opinion 8

25–29 Years

Approve............................42%
Disapprove 46
No opinion 12

30–49 Years

Approve............................50%
Disapprove 43
No opinion 7

50–64 Years

Approve............................45%
Disapprove 46
No opinion 9

65 Years and Over

Approve............................43%
Disapprove 46
No opinion 11

By Income
$25,000 and Over

Approve............................61%
Disapprove 34
No opinion 5

$15,000 and Over

Approve............................54%
Disapprove 39
No opinion 7

Under $15,000

Approve............................35%
Disapprove 53
No opinion 12

By Politics
Republicans

Approve............................84%
Disapprove 10
No opinion 6

Democrats

Approve............................26%
Disapprove 66
No opinion 8

Independents

Approve............................47%
Disapprove 43
No opinion 10

By Religion
Protestants

Approve............................48%
Disapprove 43
No opinion 9

Catholics

Approve............................46%
Disapprove 45
No opinion 9

By Occupation
Professional and Business

Approve............................62%
Disapprove 34
No opinion 4

Clerical and Sales

Approve............................46%
Disapprove 36
No opinion 18

Manual Workers

Approve............................40%
Disapprove 50
No opinion 10

Nonlabor Force

Approve............................41%
Disapprove 49
No opinion 10

By Community Size
One Million and Over

Approve............................40%
Disapprove 50
No opinion 10

500,000–999,999

Approve............................49%
Disapprove 48
No opinion 3

50,000–499,999

Approve............................43%
Disapprove 49
No opinion 8

2,500–49,000

Approve............................47%
Disapprove 47
No opinion 6

Under 2,500; Rural

Approve............................52%
Disapprove 34
No opinion 14

Labor Union Members Only

Approve............................40%
Disapprove 52
No opinion 8

Nonlabor Union Members Only

Approve............................49%
Disapprove 42
No opinion 9

The following is a comparison of presidential approval ratings in mid-March of the second year in office:

	Approve	Dis-approve	No opinion
Carter..............	50%	35%	15%
Nixon..............	53	30	17
Kennedy	79	12	9
Eisenhower	65	22	13

Now let me ask you about specific foreign and domestic problems. As I read off each problem, one at a time, would you tell me whether you approve or disapprove of the way President Reagan is handling that problem:

Economic conditions in this country?

Approve............................38%
Disapprove 54
No opinion 8

By Sex
Male

Approve............................43%
Disapprove 50
No opinion 7

Female

Approve............................33%
Disapprove 59
No opinion 8

By Race
White

Approve............................41%
Disapprove 51
No opinion 8

Nonwhite

Approve............................ 8%
Disapprove 81
No opinion 11

By Education
College

Approve............................46%
Disapprove 51
No opinion 3

High School

Approve............................37%
Disapprove 55
No opinion 8

Grade School

Approve............................22%
Disapprove 61
No opinion 17

By Region
East

Approve............................37%
Disapprove 54
No opinion 9

Midwest

Approve............................38%
Disapprove 55
No opinion 7

South

Approve............................38%
Disapprove 52
No opinion 10

West

Approve............................37%
Disapprove 57
No opinion 6

By Age
18–29 Years

Approve............................35%
Disapprove 58
No opinion 7

30–49 Years

Approve............................39%
Disapprove 54
No opinion 7

50 Years and Over

Approve............................38%
Disapprove 52
No opinion 10

By Income
$25,000 and Over

Approve............................52%
Disapprove 44
No opinion 4

$15,000 and Over

Approve............................46%
Disapprove 48
No opinion 6

Under $15,000

Approve............................25%
Disapprove 64
No opinion 11

By Occupation
Professional and Business

Approve............................52%
Disapprove 46
No opinion 2

Clerical and Sales

Approve............................33%
Disapprove 59
No opinion 8

Manual Workers

Approve............................32%
Disapprove 59
No opinion 9

Nonlabor Force

Approve............................35%
Disapprove 52
No opinion 13

Labor Union Members Only

Approve............................32%
Disapprove 60
No opinion 8

Nonlabor Union Members Only

Approve............................40%
Disapprove 52
No opinion 8

Inflation?

Approve............................37%
Disapprove 54
No opinion 9

By Sex
Male

Approve............................45%
Disapprove 49
No opinion 6

Female

Approve. 30%
Disapprove 58
No opinion 12

By Race
White

Approve. 41%
Disapprove 50
No opinion 9

Nonwhite

Approve. 7%
Disapprove 84
No opinion 9

By Education
College

Approve. 49%
Disapprove 47
No opinion 4

High School

Approve. 34%
Disapprove 56
No opinion 10

Grade School

Approve. 23%
Disapprove 61
No opinion 16

By Region
East

Approve. 36%
Disapprove 54
No opinion 10

Midwest

Approve. 40%
Disapprove 52
No opinion 8

South

Approve. 38%
Disapprove 54
No opinion 8

West

Approve. 34%
Disapprove 55
No opinion 11

By Age
18–29 Years

Approve. 33%
Disapprove 60
No opinion 7

30–49 Years

Approve. 41%
Disapprove 52
No opinion 7

50 Years and Over

Approve. 37%
Disapprove 50
No opinion 13

By Income
$25,000 and Over

Approve. 51%
Disapprove 43
No opinion 6

$15,000 and Over

Approve. 45%
Disapprove 48
No opinion 7

Under $15,000

Approve. 26%
Disapprove 62
No opinion 12

By Occupation
Professional and Business
Approve...........................51%
Disapprove 45
No opinion 4

Clerical and Sales
Approve...........................40%
Disapprove 52
No opinion 8

Manual Workers
Approve...........................32%
Disapprove 60
No opinion 8

Nonlabor Force
Approve...........................31%
Disapprove 52
No opinion 17

Labor Union Members Only
Approve...........................33%
Disapprove 60
No opinion 7

Nonlabor Union Members Only
Approve...........................39%
Disapprove 51
No opinion 10

Unemployment?
Approve...........................25%
Disapprove 64
No opinion 11

By Sex
Male
Approve...........................27%
Disapprove 64
No opinion 9

Female
Approve...........................24%
Disapprove 65
No opinion 11

By Race
White
Approve...........................28%
Disapprove 61
No opinion 11

Nonwhite
Approve........................... 5%
Disapprove 86
No opinion 9

By Education
College
Approve...........................30%
Disapprove 62
No opinion 8

High School
Approve...........................25%
Disapprove 65
No opinion 10

Grade School
Approve...........................18%
Disapprove 66
No opinion 16

By Region
East
Approve...........................26%
Disapprove 63
No opinion 11

Midwest
Approve...........................24%
Disapprove 67
No opinion 9

South
Approve...........................28%
Disapprove 61
No opinion 11

West

Approve..............................22%
Disapprove 67
No opinion 11

By Age
18–29 Years

Approve..............................19%
Disapprove 73
No opinion 8

30–49 Years

Approve..............................28%
Disapprove 62
No opinion 10

50 Years and Over

Approve..............................27%
Disapprove 61
No opinion 12

By Income
$25,000 and Over

Approve..............................36%
Disapprove 55
No opinion 9

$15,000 and Over

Approve..............................32%
Disapprove 58
No opinion 10

Under $15,000

Approve..............................17%
Disapprove 72
No opinion 11

By Occupation
Professional and Business

Approve..............................34%
Disapprove 60
No opinion 6

Clerical and Sales

Approve..............................22%
Disapprove 69
No opinion 9

Manual Workers

Approve..............................21%
Disapprove 71
No opinion 8

Nonlabor Force

Approve..............................26%
Disapprove 60
No opinion 14

Labor Union Members Only

Approve..............................19%
Disapprove 71
No opinion 10

Nonlabor Union Members Only

Approve..............................27%
Disapprove 62
No opinion 11

National defense?

Approve..............................51%
Disapprove 36
No opinion 13

By Sex
Male

Approve..............................60%
Disapprove 34
No opinion 6

Female

Approve..............................43%
Disapprove 38
No opinion 19

By Race
White

Approve..............................54%
Disapprove 34
No opinion 12

Nonwhite

Approve...............................27%
Disapprove 55
No opinion 18

By Education
College

Approve...............................53%
Disapprove 42
No opinion 5

High School

Approve...............................52%
Disapprove 33
No opinion 15

Grade School

Approve...............................42%
Disapprove 36
No opinion 22

By Region
East

Approve...............................47%
Disapprove 40
No opinion 13

Midwest

Approve...............................52%
Disapprove 37
No opinion 11

South

Approve...............................53%
Disapprove 31
No opinion 16

West

Approve...............................52%
Disapprove 37
No opinion 11

By Age
18–29 Years

Approve...............................50%
Disapprove 40
No opinion 10

30–49 Years

Approve...............................52%
Disapprove 34
No opinion 14

50 Years and Over

Approve...............................50%
Disapprove 36
No opinion 14

By Income
$25,000 and Over

Approve...............................62%
Disapprove 32
No opinion 6

$15,000 and Over

Approve...............................58%
Disapprove 34
No opinion 8

Under $15,000

Approve...............................41%
Disapprove 40
No opinion 19

By Occupation
Professional and Business

Approve...............................56%
Disapprove 41
No opinion 3

Clerical and Sales

Approve...............................50%
Disapprove 33
No opinion 17

Manual Workers

Approve...........................53%
Disapprove 36
No opinion 11

Nonlabor Force

Approve...........................48%
Disapprove 35
No opinion 17

Labor Union Members Only

Approve...........................51%
Disapprove 39
No opinion 10

Nonlabor Union Members Only

Approve...........................51%
Disapprove 35
No opinion 14

Foreign affairs?

Approve...........................36%
Disapprove 44
No opinion 20

By Sex
Male

Approve...........................40%
Disapprove 44
No opinion 16

Female

Approve...........................33%
Disapprove 44
No opinion 23

By Race
White

Approve...........................39%
Disapprove 41
No opinion 20

Nonwhite

Approve...........................16%
Disapprove 62
No opinion 22

By Education
College

Approve...........................44%
Disapprove 44
No opinion 12

High School

Approve...........................36%
Disapprove 42
No opinion 22

Grade School

Approve...........................22%
Disapprove 48
No opinion 30

By Region
East

Approve...........................36%
Disapprove 43
No opinion 21

Midwest

Approve...........................38%
Disapprove 47
No opinion 15

South

Approve...........................37%
Disapprove 39
No opinion 24

West

Approve...........................32%
Disapprove 49
No opinion 19

By Age
18–29 Years

Approve...........................38%
Disapprove 47
No opinion 15

30–49 Years

Approve. 37%
Disapprove 43
No opinion 20

50 Years and Over

Approve. 34%
Disapprove 42
No opinion 24

By Income
$25,000 and Over

Approve. 47%
Disapprove 38
No opinion 15

$15,000 and Over

Approve. 43%
Disapprove 41
No opinion 16

Under $15,000

Approve. 27%
Disapprove 48
No opinion 25

By Occupation
Professional and Business

Approve. 48%
Disapprove 39
No opinion 13

Clerical and Sales

Approve. 38%
Disapprove 44
No opinion 18

Manual Workers

Approve. 37%
Disapprove 47
No opinion 16

Nonlabor Force

Approve. 30%
Disapprove 44
No opinion 26

Labor Union Members Only

Approve. 37%
Disapprove 47
No opinion 16

Nonlabor Union Members Only

Approve. 36%
Disapprove 43
No opinion 21

Relations with the Soviet Union?

Approve. 41%
Disapprove 36
No opinion 23

By Sex
Male

Approve. 49%
Disapprove 32
No opinion 19

Female

Approve. 34%
Disapprove 39
No opinion 27

By Race
White

Approve. 44%
Disapprove 34
No opinion 22

Nonwhite

Approve. 18%
Disapprove 52
No opinion 30

By Education

College

Approve.............................52%
Disapprove 32
No opinion 16

High School

Approve.............................38%
Disapprove 38
No opinion 24

Grade School

Approve.............................32%
Disapprove 36
No opinion 22

By Region

East

Approve.............................41%
Disapprove 37
No opinion 22

Midwest

Approve.............................45%
Disapprove 34
No opinion 21

South

Approve.............................39%
Disapprove 33
No opinion 28

West

Approve.............................39%
Disapprove 41
No opinion 20

By Age

18–29 Years

Approve.............................39%
Disapprove 39
No opinion 22

30–49 Years

Approve.............................44%
Disapprove 34
No opinion 22

50 Years and Over

Approve.............................40%
Disapprove 35
No opinion 25

By Income

$25,000 and Over

Approve.............................53%
Disapprove 30
No opinion 17

$15,000 and Over

Approve.............................48%
Disapprove 34
No opinion 18

Under $15,000

Approve.............................31%
Disapprove 40
No opinion 29

By Occupation

Professional and Business

Approve.............................56%
Disapprove 32
No opinion 12

Clerical and Sales

Approve.............................36%
Disapprove 37
No opinion 27

Manual Workers

Approve.............................38%
Disapprove 40
No opinion 22

Nonlabor Force

Approve..............................38%
Disapprove 35
No opinion 27

Labor Union Members Only

Approve..............................39%
Disapprove 40
No opinion 21

Nonlabor Union Members Only

Approve..............................42%
Disapprove 34
No opinion 24

The situation in El Salvador?

Approve..............................22%
Disapprove 50
No opinion 28

By Sex
Male

Approve..............................27%
Disapprove 48
No opinion 25

Female

Approve..............................18%
Disapprove 51
No opinion 31

By Race
White

Approve..............................24%
Disapprove 48
No opinion 28

Nonwhite

Approve..............................11%
Disapprove 65
No opinion 24

By Education
College

Approve..............................25%
Disapprove 54
No opinion 21

High School

Approve..............................23%
Disapprove 48
No opinion 29

Grade School

Approve..............................18%
Disapprove 45
No opinion 37

By Region
East

Approve..............................25%
Disapprove 49
No opinion 26

Midwest

Approve..............................21%
Disapprove 51
No opinion 28

South

Approve..............................24%
Disapprove 43
No opinion 33

West

Approve..............................19%
Disapprove 57
No opinion 24

By Age
18–29 Years

Approve..............................21%
Disapprove 56
No opinion 23

30–49 Years

Approve............................23%
Disapprove 52
No opinion 25

50 Years and Over

Approve............................24%
Disapprove 43
No opinion 33

By Income
$25,000 and Over

Approve............................31%
Disapprove 45
No opinion 24

$15,000 and Over

Approve............................26%
Disapprove 48
No opinion 26

Under $15,000

Approve............................17%
Disapprove 52
No opinion 31

By Occupation
Professional and Business

Approve............................27%
Disapprove 56
No opinion 17

Clerical and Sales

Approve............................19%
Disapprove 54
No opinion 27

Manual Workers

Approve............................24%
Disapprove 49
No opinion 27

Nonlabor Force

Approve............................20%
Disapprove 47
No opinion 33

Labor Union Members Only

Approve............................24%
Disapprove 50
No opinion 26

Nonlabor Union Members Only

Approve............................22%
Disapprove 49
No opinion 29

Note: For the first time since President Ronald Reagan took office fourteen months ago, as many Americans disapprove (45%) as approve (46%) of his performance in office, a statistically insignificant difference.

President Reagan is far off the pace set by his elected predecessors at comparable points during their second year. At this time in 1978, for example, 50% approved of Jimmy Carter's performance in office, while 35% disapproved. Richard Nixon, John Kennedy, and Dwight Eisenhower had still better approval to disapproval ratios.

President Reagan's latest ratings for his handling of specific problem areas show no improvement on economic issues, at a low ebb to begin with, and deterioration on issues relating to defense and foreign affairs. Only 22% of the public, for example, now approve of the way the president is handling the situation in El Salvador, compared to 36% who had a favorable opinion one year ago.

As has been the case in every Gallup survey conducted during Reagan's tenure, more men (52%) than women (41%) now approve of Reagan's job performance. Other population groups in which substantially greater support for the president is found include: Republicans (84%), whites (51%), college educated (54%), and persons with family incomes of $15,000 or more (54%). Conversely, lower approval scores are recorded among blacks (12%), Democrats

(26%), persons with only a grade-school education (30%), those whose annual income is less than $15,000 (35%), and members of labor union families (40%).

APRIL 4
PRISON REFORM

Interviewing Date: 1/22–25/82
Survey #189-G

In your opinion, does your state need more prisons, or not?

Yes...............................57%
No................................30
Don't know........................13

By Sex
Male

Yes...............................60%
No................................30
Don't know........................10

Female

Yes...............................53%
No................................31
Don't know........................16

By Race
White

Yes...............................57%
No................................30
Don't know........................13

Nonwhite

Yes...............................51%
No................................33
Don't know........................16

By Education
College

Yes...............................56%
No................................31
Don't know........................13

High School

Yes...............................59%
No................................30
Don't know........................11

Grade School

Yes...............................51%
No................................31
Don't know........................18

By Region
East

Yes...............................60%
No................................27
Don't know........................13

Midwest

Yes...............................50%
No................................37
Don't know........................13

South

Yes...............................58%
No................................29
Don't know........................13

West

Yes...............................58%
No................................29
Don't know........................13

By Age
18–29 Years

Yes...............................53%
No................................33
Don't know........................14

30–49 Years

Yes...............................56%
No................................31
Don't know........................13

50 Years and Over

Yes................................59%
No.................................28
Don't know.........................13

By Income
$25,000 and Over

Yes................................58%
No.................................31
Don't know.........................11

$15,000 and Over

Yes................................56%
No.................................32
Don't know.........................12

Under $15,000

Yes................................57%
No.................................29
Don't know.........................14

If more prisons were needed in your state, would you be willing to pay more taxes to help build these prisons, or not?

Yes................................49%
No.................................44
Don't know......................... 7

By Sex
Male

Yes................................51%
No.................................43
Don't know......................... 6

Female

Yes................................46%
No.................................46
Don't know......................... 8

By Race
White

Yes................................51%
No.................................43
Don't know......................... 6

Nonwhite

Yes................................36%
No.................................56
Don't know......................... 8

By Education
College

Yes................................59%
No.................................36
Don't know......................... 5

High School

Yes................................47%
No.................................46
Don't know......................... 7

Grade School

Yes................................33%
No.................................57
Don't know.........................10

By Region
East

Yes................................43%
No.................................49
Don't know......................... 8

Midwest

Yes................................41%
No.................................52
Don't know......................... 7

South

Yes................................56%
No.................................37
Don't know......................... 7

West

Yes................................57%
No.................................40
Don't know......................... 3

By Age
18–29 Years

Yes...............................48%
No.................................45
Don't know.........................7

30–49 Years

Yes...............................51%
No.................................43
Don't know.........................6

50 Years and Over

Yes...............................47%
No.................................46
Don't know.........................7

By Income
$25,000 and Over

Yes...............................56%
No.................................39
Don't know.........................5

$15,000 and Over

Yes...............................52%
No.................................44
Don't know.........................4

Under $15,000

Yes...............................45%
No.................................46
Don't know.........................9

Those Who Say State Needs More Prisons

Yes...............................66%
No.................................29
Don't know.........................5

Those Who Say State Does Not Need More Prisons

Yes...............................21%
No.................................75
Don't know.........................4

It has been proposed that army bases not now being used be converted into prisons. Does this sound like a good idea to you or a poor idea?

Good idea.........................76%
Poor idea.........................18
No opinion.........................6

By Region
East

Good idea.........................78%
Poor idea.........................18
No opinion.........................4

Midwest

Good idea.........................77%
Poor idea.........................17
No opinion.........................6

South

Good idea.........................74%
Poor idea.........................19
No opinion.........................7

West

Good idea.........................77%
Poor idea.........................18
No opinion.........................5

Do you think it would be a good idea or a poor idea to establish two kinds of prisons: one for first offenders who have not committed serious crimes, and one for those who have committed serious crimes?

Good idea.........................88%
Poor idea..........................8
No opinion.........................4

By Region
East

Good idea.........................90%
Poor idea..........................6
No opinion.........................4

Midwest

Good idea 88%
Poor idea 8
No opinion 4

South

Good idea 86%
Poor idea 10
No opinion 4

West

Good idea 89%
Poor idea 9
No opinion 2

Note: The American people are clearly ready for innovative and far-reaching prison reform. The first report in a two-part series shows a majority calling for more prisons in their state, a willingness to pay more taxes to build prison facilities, in favor of converting army bases into prisons, and fully behind a proposal to build separate prisons for first offenders who have not committed serious crimes and those who have. These views are recorded at a time when the public is increasingly fearful of crime. A record 48% are now afraid of venturing out alone after dark in their own neighborhood.

The problem of prison overcrowding in state and federal correctional institutions is of considerable urgency today because some states are under court order to relieve crowded jail conditions. Local officials are also concerned that early release of inmates to ease crowding poses a threat to public safety by putting dangerous persons back on the streets. Critics further state that the nation's current prison facilities are outdated, understaffed, and are not rehabilitating criminals.

As one way to ease crowded prison conditions, presidential counselor Edwin Meese III has indicated that the Reagan administration hopes to turn over facilities on unused military bases to state governments to be converted into prisons. Such a proposal, put to the public in the current survey, meets with widespread support in all regions of the nation. A total of 76% of survey respondents, nationwide, think this would be a good idea, while 18% say a poor idea, and 6% are undecided.

APRIL 5
PRISON REFORM

Interviewing Date: 1/22–25/82
Survey #189-G

In dealing with men who are in prison, do you think it is more important to punish them for their crimes, or more important to get them started on the right road?

Punish them 30%
Start on right road 59
No opinion 11

By Sex
Male

Punish them 30%
Start on right road 60
No opinion 10

Female

Punish them 30%
Start on right road 59
No opinion 11

By Race
White

Punish them 28%
Start on right road 61
No opinion 11

Nonwhite

Punish them 42%
Start on right road 49
No opinion 9

By Education
College

Punish them 23%
Start on right road 64
No opinion 13

High School

Punish them 32%
Start on right road 58
No opinion 10

Grade School

Punish them 37%
Start on right road 55
No opinion 8

By Region

East

Punish them 30%
Start on right road 61
No opinion 9

Midwest

Punish them 25%
Start on right road 64
No opinion 11

South

Punish them 34%
Start on right road 54
No opinion 12

West

Punish them 31%
Start on right road 58
No opinion 11

By Age

18–29 Years

Punish them 31%
Start on right road 58
No opinion 11

30–49 Years

Punish them 26%
Start on right road 62
No opinion 12

50 Years and Over

Punish them 32%
Start on right road 59
No opinion 9

By Income

$25,000 and Over

Punish them 24%
Start on right road 64
No opinion 12

$15,000 and Over

Punish them 27%
Start on right road 62
No opinion 11

Under $15,000

Punish them 33%
Start on right road 57
No opinion 10

I am going to read you some proposals that have been made to improve prisons and to reduce crime. Please tell me whether you think the proposal is a good idea or a poor idea:

Require prisoners to have a skill or learn a trade to fit them for a job before they are released from a prison?

Good idea 94%
Poor idea 4
No opinion 2

By Region

East

Good idea 95%
Poor idea 4
No opinion 1

Midwest

Good idea 94%
Poor idea 4
No opinion 2

South

Good idea 94%
Poor idea 3
No opinion 3

West

Good idea 96%
Poor idea 3
No opinion 1

Require every prisoner to be able to read and write before he or she is released from prison?

Good idea 89%
Poor idea 8
No opinion 3

By Region
East

Good idea 93%
Poor idea 5
No opinion 2

Midwest

Good idea 86%
Poor idea 9
No opinion 5

South

Good idea 88%
Poor idea 8
No opinion 4

West

Good idea 90%
Poor idea 9
No opinion 1

Keep prisoners constructing buildings, making products, or performing services that the state would have to hire other people to do?

Good idea 83%
Poor idea 13
No opinion 4

By Region
East

Good idea 81%
Poor idea 15
No opinion 4

Midwest

Good idea 83%
Poor idea 13
No opinion 4

South

Good idea 83%
Poor idea 12
No opinion 5

West

Good idea 84%
Poor idea 13
No opinion 3

Manual Workers Only

Good idea 82%
Poor idea 14
No opinion 4

Labor Union Members Only

Good idea 82%
Poor idea 14
No opinion 4

Pay prisoners for their work but require them to return two-thirds of this amount to their victims or to the state for the cost of maintaining the prison?

Good idea 81%
Poor idea 15
No opinion 4

By Region
East

Good idea 81%
Poor idea 14
No opinion 5

Midwest

Good idea 84%
Poor idea 13
No opinion 3

South

Good idea 77%
Poor idea 18
No opinion 5

West

Good idea 83%
Poor idea 13
No opinion 4

Permit wives to spend some weekends each year with their husbands in special weekend guest houses within the prison grounds?

Good idea 61%
Poor idea 31
No opinion 8

By Sex
Male

Good idea 63%
Poor idea 30
No opinion 7

Female

Good idea 58%
Poor idea 33
No opinion 9

By Race
White

Good idea 59%
Poor idea 33
No opinion 8

Nonwhite

Good idea 71%
Poor idea 19
No opinion 10

By Education
College

Good idea 71%
Poor idea 25
No opinion 4

High School

Good idea 59%
Poor idea 33
No opinion 8

Grade School

Good idea 45%
Poor idea 40
No opinion 15

By Region
East

Good idea 58%
Poor idea 36
No opinion 6

Midwest

Good idea 61%
Poor idea 31
No opinion 8

South

Good idea 59%
Poor idea 31
No opinion 10

West

Good idea 66%
Poor idea 27
No opinion 7

By Age
18–29 Years

Good idea 71%
Poor idea 23
No opinion 6

30–49 Years

Good idea 68%
Poor idea 26
No opinion 6

50 Years and Over

Good idea 46%
Poor idea 43
No opinion 11

By Income
$25,000 and Over

Good idea 65%
Poor idea 30
No opinion 5

$15,000 and Over

Good idea 64%
Poor idea 31
No opinion 5

Under $15,000

Good idea 57%
Poor idea 32
No opinion 11

Refuse parole to any prisoner who has been paroled before for a serious crime?

Good idea 80%
Poor idea 14
No opinion 6

By Region
East

Good idea 82%
Poor idea 13
No opinion 5

Midwest

Good idea 79%
Poor idea 14
No opinion 7

South

Good idea 82%
Poor idea 12
No opinion 6

West

Good idea 75%
Poor idea 20
No opinion 5

Appoint more judges in order to reduce the time between arrest and trial to a maximum of two months?

Good idea 74%
Poor idea 18
No opinion 8

By Region
East

Good idea 80%
Poor idea 16
No opinion 4

Midwest

Good idea 71%
Poor idea 22
No opinion 7

South

Good idea 71%
Poor idea 16
No opinion 13

West

Good idea 75%
Poor idea 17
No opinion 8

Note: Despite the widespread fear of crime in the United States today and the high level of victimization, the American people by a 2-to-1 margin believe it is more important to get prisoners started on the right road than it is to punish them for their crimes. In fact, the public overwhelmingly supports a wide range of proposals that have been suggested as ways of rehabilitating criminals and reducing crime.

While the public clearly backs proposals to help criminals find their way into useful roles in society, they take a harder line in terms of such matters as parole, with 80% saying it would be a good idea to refuse parole to any prisoner who has been paroled before for a serious crime.

APRIL 7
NATIONAL DEFENSE

Interviewing Date: 3/12–15/82
Survey #191-G

At the present time which nation do you feel is stronger in terms of military power— the United States or the Soviet Union— or do you think they are about equal, militarily?

United States 22%
Soviet Union........................ 43
About equal......................... 28
No opinion 7

By Sex
Male

United States 21%
Soviet Union........................ 46
About equal......................... 29
No opinion 4

Female

United States 23%
Soviet Union........................ 41
About equal......................... 27
No opinion 9

By Race
White

United States 22%
Soviet Union........................ 45
About equal......................... 27
No opinion 6

Nonwhite

United States 23%
Soviet Union........................ 33
About equal......................... 34
No opinion 10

By Education
College

United States 18%
Soviet Union........................ 48
About equal......................... 31
No opinion 3

High School

United States 22%
Soviet Union........................ 44
About equal......................... 28
No opinion 6

Grade School

United States 30%
Soviet Union........................ 35
About equal......................... 21
No opinion 14

By Region
East

United States 24%
Soviet Union........................ 41
About equal......................... 27
No opinion 8

Midwest

United States 18%
Soviet Union........................ 49
About equal......................... 28
No opinion 5

South

United States 23%
Soviet Union........................ 37
About equal......................... 31
No opinion 9

West

United States	22%
Soviet Union	49
About equal	25
No opinion	4

By Age
18–29 Years

United States	21%
Soviet Union	45
About equal	31
No opinion	3

30–49 Years

United States	23%
Soviet Union	41
About equal	31
No opinion	5

50 Years and Over

United States	21%
Soviet Union	45
About equal	24
No opinion	10

By Politics
Republicans

United States	23%
Soviet Union	50
About equal	22
No opinion	5

Democrats

United States	23%
Soviet Union	40
About equal	30
No opinion	7

Independents

United States	20%
Soviet Union	45
About equal	30
No opinion	5

Note: When this question was first asked two years ago, the two superpowers were at parity in the eyes of the public, with 33% saying the United States was superior, 32% naming the Soviet Union, and 26% saying they were military equals.

There is much discussion as to the amount of money the government in Washington should spend for national defense and military purposes. How do you feel about this? Do you think we are spending too little, too much, or about the right amount?

Too little	19%
Too much	36
About right	36
No opinion	9

By Region
East

Too little	15%
Too much	41
About right	38
No opinion	6

Midwest

Too little	19%
Too much	33
About right	40
No opinion	8

South

Too little	25%
Too much	32
About right	31
No opinion	12

West

Too little	19%
Too much	38
About right	35
No opinion	8

By Politics

Republicans

Too little 27%
Too much 18
About right 46
No opinion 9

Democrats

Too little 16%
Too much 43
About right 32
No opinion 9

Independents

Too little 18%
Too much 39
About right 36
No opinion 7

Views on Military Superiority of Those Who Replied Too Little

United States stronger................ 16%
Soviet Union stronger 62
About equal.......................... 17
No opinion 5

Views on Military Superiority of Those Who Replied Too Much

United States stronger................ 23%
Soviet Union stronger 37
About equal.......................... 34
No opinion 6

Views on Military Superiority of Those Who Replied About Right

United States stronger................ 24%
Soviet Union stronger 43
About equal.......................... 29
No opinion 4

Views on Military Superiority of Those Who Replied No Opinion

United States stronger................ 23%
Soviet Union stronger 30
About equal.......................... 25
No opinion 22

The following table shows a sharp change in the public's views:

National Trend

	Too little	Too much	About right	No opinion
1981	51%	15%	22%	12%
1976	22	36	32	10
1973	13	46	30	11
1969	8	52	31	9
1960	21	18	45	16
1953	22	20	45	13

Note: Whether President Ronald Reagan was correct or incorrect in his assertion on March 30 that the Soviet Union had achieved military superiority over the United States, that perception is shared by a plurality of the American people. Asked which nation is stronger in terms of military power, 43% in the latest Gallup survey named the Soviet Union, while one-half that proportion, 22%, said the United States. The remaining 35% thought the nations were about equally strong (28%) or were uncommitted (7%).

At the same time, however, the weight of public opinion has clearly swung toward the view that the amount of money budgeted by Washington for defense and military purposes is too much (36%) or about the right amount (36%), rather than too little (19%). A year ago, at the start of the Reagan administration, a 51% majority thought too little was spent on defense.

President Reagan has argued that the United States has a "window of vulnerability"—a period when the Soviets could mount a nuclear attack on the United States without fear of effective retaliation—as his main justification for a greatly expanded defense capability. The huge budget deficit projected for fiscal 1983, however, has caused many voters to believe that the defense budget, together with spending for other programs, will have to be reduced.

Understandably, the 19% minority of survey respondents who believe the amount budgeted for defense is too little are overwhelmingly (4 to 1) of the opinion that the Soviet Union is militarily stronger than the United States. However, among those who say that the U.S. defense budget is adequate (36% of the total), the 2-to-1 view is that the USSR is stronger. And even among the 36% who think too much is spent on defense, the weight of opinion is that the Soviets have a military advantage.

At his televised news conference on March 30, Reagan said, in response to a question, "the truth of the matter is that, on balance, the Soviet Union does have a definite margin of superiority." The president's remarks set off a torrent of conflicting statements, endorsing and criticizing his contention that the USSR could launch a nuclear strike, survive an American retaliatory attack, and strike again. This was the first time any president had claimed a clear-cut nuclear superiority for the Soviet Union. Critics have long argued that both sides possess the capability of destruction great enough to make the concept of military superiority meaningless.

As might be expected, there is a strong political coloration to public opinion on the adequacy of U.S. military spending. A preponderance of Republicans, for instance, believes the amount being spent is sufficient (46%) or too little (27%), while only 18% think it is too much. Democrats, on the other hand, criticize our defense expenditures as being too much (43%), 32% say it is about right, and 16% that not enough is budgeted. However, public opinion on the power of the United States and the Soviet Union is relatively apolitical, with roughly equivalent proportions of Democrats, Republicans, and independents saying the USSR possesses greater military strength.

APRIL 11
CRIME

Interviewing Date: 1/22–25/82
Survey #189-G

During the last twelve months, have any of these happened to you? [Respondents were handed a card listing crimes.]

Yes

Money, property stolen	14%
Property vandalized	11
Burglary or attempt	7
Robbery, assault	3
Car stolen	2
One or more incidents	25

By Sex
Male

Money, property stolen	13%
Property vandalized	12
Burglary or attempt	7
Robbery, assault	2
Car stolen	2
One or more incidents	26

Female

Money, property stolen	14%
Property vandalized	10
Burglary or attempt	8
Robbery, assault	1
Car stolen	1
One or more incidents	24

By Race
White

Money, property stolen	14%
Property vandalized	12
Burglary or attempt	7
Robbery, assault	1
Car stolen	2
One or more incidents	25

Nonwhite

Money, property stolen	14%
Property vandalized	7
Burglary or attempt	8
Robbery, assault	2
Car stolen	1
One or more incidents	20

By Education
College

Money, property stolen	16%
Property vandalized	16

Burglary or attempt 10
Robbery, assault. 3
Car stolen 3
One or more incidents 30

High School

Money, property stolen. 13%
Property vandalized. 10
Burglary or attempt 7
Robbery, assault. 1
Car stolen 2
One or more incidents 24

Grade School

Money, property stolen. 10%
Property vandalized. 8
Burglary or attempt 3
Robbery, assault. . . . . *
Car stolen . . . . *
One or more incidents 16

By Region

East

Money, property stolen. 12%
Property vandalized. 13
Burglary or attempt 6
Robbery, assault. 2
Car stolen 2
One or more incidents 27

Midwest

Money, property stolen. 14%
Property vandalized. 10
Burglary or attempt 5
Robbery, assault. 1
Car stolen 1
One or more incidents 20

South

Money, property stolen. 14%
Property vandalized. 9
Burglary or attempt 8
Robbery, assault. 1
Car stolen 1
One or more incidents 22

West

Money, property stolen. 15%
Property vandalized. 14
Burglary or attempt 11
Robbery, assault. 2
Car stolen 4
One or more incidents 33

By Age
18–29 Years

Money, property stolen. 20%
Property vandalized. 18
Burglary or attempt 10
Robbery, assault. 2
Car stolen 2
One or more incidents 34

30–49 Years

Money, property stolen. 13%
Property vandalized. 11
Burglary or attempt 7
Robbery, assault. 1
Car stolen 2
One or more incidents 24

50 Years and Over

Money, property stolen. 9%
Property vandalized. 6
Burglary or attempt 5
Robbery, assault. 1
Car stolen 1
One or more incidents 18

By Income
$25,000 and Over

Money, property stolen. 13%
Property vandalized. 13
Burglary or attempt 7
Robbery, assault. 1
Car stolen 3
One or more incidents 26

$15,000 and Over

Money, property stolen. 13%
Property vandalized. 11

Burglary or attempt 6
Robbery, assault. 1
Car stolen 2
One or more incidents 25

Under $15,000

Money, property stolen 15%
Property vandalized 11
Burglary or attempt 9
Robbery, assault. 2
Car stolen 1
One or more incidents 25

*Less than 1%

National Trend

	1981	1979	1977
Money, property stolen	11%	11%	8%
Property vandalized	11	10	11
Burglary or attempt	7	7	5
Robbery, assault	3	3	3
Car stolen	2	2	1
One or more incidents	23	22	23

Asked of those who experienced a crime: Did you happen to report this to the police, or not?

	Crime incidence	Reported to police
Money, property stolen	14%	9%
Property vandalized	11	7
Burglary or attempt	7	5
Robbery, assault	2	2
Car stolen	2	1
One or more incidents	25	17

Is there any area right around here—that is, within a mile—where you would be afraid to walk alone at night?

	Yes
National	48%

By Sex

Male	31%
Female	64

By Race

White	47%
Nonwhite	55

By Region

East	45%
Midwest	41
South	50
West	58

By Age

18–29 years	44%
30–49 years	40
50–64 years	51
65 years and over	65

By Income

$15,000 and over	45%
Under $15,000	52

By Community Size

One million and over	57%
500,000–999,999	54
50,000–499,999	53
2,500–49,999	50
Under 2,500; rural	31

Center cities	62%
Suburbs	46
Nonmetro areas	38

The following is a selected nationwide trend, showing the percentage of those who are fearful in their neighborhood:

1981	45%
1979	42
1977	45
1972	42
1965	34

Note: The latest Gallup Poll crime victimization audit shows that as many as one-fourth of U.S. households were victimized by crimes during 1981. These were crimes either against property (money or property stolen or vandalized) or against persons (robberies or assaults). As has been the case since these surveys started, many crime victims did not report these incidents to the police, indicating that the U.S. Justice Department's figures underestimate the extensiveness of crime.

Along with a continuing high crime rate has come an increasing fear of crime. About one-half (48%) of survey respondents say they are afraid to walk alone at night in their neighborhood, the highest figure recorded since this measurement began in 1965. The proportion approaches two in three (64%) in the case of women, persons sixty-five years of age and older (65%), and residents of the nation's center cities (62%).

APRIL 15
REAGANOMICS

Interviewing Date: 3/12–15/82
Survey #191-G

What effect do you think the Reagan administration's economic policies will have on the nation's economic situation? Do you feel the nation's economic situation will be much better, somewhat better, somewhat worse, or much worse as a result of the Reagan economic policies?

Better 40%
Worse 48
Same (volunteered) 5
No opinion 7

By Sex
Male

Better 40%
Worse 48
Same (volunteered) 5
No opinion 7

Female

Better 44%
Worse 45
Same (volunteered) 5
No opinion 6

By Race
White

Better 44%
Worse 45

Same (volunteered) 5
No opinion 6

Nonwhite

Better 12%
Worse 73
Same (volunteered) 5
No opinion 10

By Age
18–29 Years

Better 41%
Worse 49
Same (volunteered) 4
No opinion 6

30–49 Years

Better 43%
Worse 46
Same (volunteered) 5
No opinion 6

50 Years and Over

Better 38%
Worse 49
Same (volunteered) 5
No opinion 8

By Income
$25,000 and Over

Better 54%
Worse 40
Same (volunteered) 2
No opinion 4

$15,000 and Over

Better 48%
Worse 44
Same (volunteered) 3
No opinion 5

Under $15,000

Better 29%
Worse 54

Same (volunteered) 7
No opinion 10

By Politics
Republicans
Better 72%
Worse 18
Same (volunteered) 6
No opinion 4

Democrats
Better 23%
Worse 66
Same (volunteered) 3
No opinion 8

Independents
Better 41%
Worse 48
Same (volunteered) 5
No opinion 6

Those Who Approve of President Reagan
Better 72%
Worse 19
Same (volunteered) 5
No opinion 4

Those Who Disapprove of President Reagan
Better 11%
Worse 82
Same (volunteered) 2
No opinion 5

National Trend

	Better	Worse	Same; no opinion
February 1982	40%	44%	16%
November 1981	44	42	14
October 1981	53	37	10

How about a year from now? Do you feel the nation's economic situation will be better or worse as a result of the Reagan economic policies?

Better 42%
Worse 40
Same (volunteered) 9
No opinion 9

Those Who Approve of President Reagan
Better 74%
Worse 13
Same (volunteered) 8
No opinion 5

Those Who Disapprove of President Reagan
Better 12%
Worse 70
Same (volunteered) 9
No opinion 9

How about over the long run? Do you feel the nation's economic situation will be better or worse because of the Reagan economic policies?

Better 49%
Worse 34
Same (volunteered) 6
No opinion 11

Those Who Approve of President Reagan
Better 81%
Worse 9
Same (volunteered) 4
No opinion 6

Those Who Disapprove of President Reagan
Better 18%
Worse 63
Same (volunteered) 7
No opinion 12

What effect do you think these policies will have on your own and your family's financial situation? Do you feel your financial situation will be much better, somewhat better, somewhat worse, or much worse as a result of the Reagan economic policies?

Better 28%
Worse 51

Same (volunteered) 15
No opinion 6

By Sex
Male

Better. 31%
Worse. 48
Same (volunteered) 14
No opinion 7

Female

Better. 25%
Worse. 54
Same (volunteered) 15
No opinion 6

By Race
White

Better. 30%
Worse. 48
Same (volunteered) 16
No opinion 6

Nonwhite

Better. 9%
Worse. 75
Same (volunteered) 6
No opinion 10

By Age
18–29 Years

Better. 28%
Worse. 51
Same (volunteered) 15
No opinion 6

30–49 Years

Better. 31%
Worse. 52
Same (volunteered) 11
No opinion 6

50 Years and Over

Better. 26%
Worse. 50

Same (volunteered) 17
No opinion 7

By Income
$25,000 and Over

Better. 41%
Worse. 40
Same (volunteered) 14
No opinion 5

$15,000 and Over

Better. 35%
Worse. 45
Same (volunteered) 15
No opinion 5

Under $15,000

Better. 19%
Worse. 59
Same (volunteered) 14
No opinion 8

By Politics
Republicans

Better. 50%
Worse. 24
Same (volunteered) 21
No opinion 5

Democrats

Better. 16%
Worse. 67
Same (volunteered) 11
No opinion 6

Independents

Better. 28%
Worse. 51
Same (volunteered) 14
No opinion 7

Those Who Approve of President Reagan

Better. 51%
Worse. 25

Same (volunteered) 18
No opinion 6

Those Who Disapprove of President Reagan

Better............................. 7%
Worse.............................. 81
Same (volunteered) 9
No opinion 3

National Trend

	Better	Worse	Same; no opinion
February 1982	31%	44%	25%
November 1981	35	49	16
August 1981	48	36	16

Note: The public's confidence in the Reagan administration's economic program continues to slide. In the latest Gallup survey, only four persons in ten (40%) think Reaganomics will improve the national economy, while 48% hold the opposite opinion. Yet over the long term, optimism about its effectiveness outweighs pessimism by a 3-to-2 ratio.

The public consistently has been less sanguine about the effect of Reaganomics on their own economic health than on the nation, suggesting a willingness to undergo personal sacrifice if it means the United States as a whole will benefit. And, although positive assessments of Reaganomics' impact on the nation have eroded, along with diminished personal expectations, the rate of decline has not been so steep in the case of the nation.

Americans' evaluation of Reaganomics is very closely linked to their general appraisal of President Ronald Reagan's performance in office. Among those who approve of Reagan's overall handling of his presidential duties (46% of the total), there is a much greater tendency to believe Reaganomics will improve the nation's financial situation (72%) than is true of the 45% who disapprove of Reagan, only 11% of whom have a positive outlook. Similarly, an overwhelming 81% majority of Reagan backers think Reaganomics will benefit the nation over the long run, while only 18% of the president's detractors feel the same way. Even among the

latter, however, long-term appraisals of Reaganomics are more favorable than short-term.

APRIL 16
FALKLAND ISLANDS CRISIS

The following questions were asked in Great Britain and South America by the Gallup Organization's affiliates in those countries.

Interviewing Date: 4/10–13/81*
Great Britain

The government has been criticized for being caught off guard by the Argentinians' invasion of the Falkland Islands. Do you think this criticism is justified or not?

Justified............................78%
Not justified 14
Don't know 8

Do you approve or disapprove of the decision to send a British fleet to the Falkland Islands?

Approve.............................78%
Disapprove 16
Don't know 6

Do you approve or disapprove of the government's action in general, following the invasion of the Falkland Islands?

Approve.............................67%
Disapprove 24
Don't know 9

In order to regain the Falkland Islands, would you approve or disapprove of:

Attacking the Argentine ships and troops guarding the Falkland Islands?

Approve.............................61%
Disapprove 32
Don't know 7

Attacking mainland Argentina itself?

Approve...............................24%
Disapprove..........................68
Don't know.......................... 8

Cutting off all trade with Argentina?

Approve...............................86%
Disapprove.......................... 9
Don't know.......................... 5

*The British Gallup Poll is based on in-person interviews conducted nationwide.

Interviewing Date: 4/5–10/82*
South America

You may know that a serious incident between Argentina and Great Britain has taken place in the Malvinas Islands. Who do you believe owns the islands based on historical, geographic, and legal reasons? Argentina or Great Britain?

Brazil

Argentina 39%
Great Britain........................40
Other; no opinion....................21

Ecuador

Argentina 78%
Great Britain........................15
Other; no opinion.................... 7

Peru

Argentina 93%
Great Britain........................ 4
Other; no opinion.................... 3

Uruguay

Argentina 84%
Great Britain........................11
Other; no opinion.................... 5

*The South American Poll is conducted by personal interviews in urban centers of Brazil, Ecuador, Peru, and Uruguay.

Argentina occupied the islands militarily and evicted the British forces. Do you believe that military procedure was correct or should there have been peaceful negotiations?

Brazil

Correct, militarily 13%
Peaceful negotiations.................81
No opinion 6

Ecuador

Correct, militarily 23%
Peaceful negotiations.................77
No opinion........................... *

Peru

Correct, militarily 43%
Peaceful negotiations.................55
No opinion 2

Uruguay

Correct, militarily 35%
Peaceful negotiations.................64
No opinion........................... **

*No opinion results have been omitted.
**Less than 1%

The United Nations is demanding that Argentina immediately remove the forces that occupy the Malvinas Islands and is exhorting both countries to hold peaceful negotiations. Do you believe Argentina should remove its troops or should not remove its troops?

Brazil

Should...............................71%
Should not...........................23
No opinion 6

Ecuador

Should...............................41%
Should not...........................59
No opinion........................... *

Peru

Should 16%
Should not 77
No opinion 7

Uruguay

Should 47%
Should not 52
No opinion . . . . **

*No opinion results have been omitted.
**Less than 1%

What do you think Great Britain will do? Will they try to regain the islands by force or negotiate peacefully for them?

Brazil

Regain by force 35%
Negotiate 55
No opinion 10

Ecuador

Regain by force 54%
Negotiate 46
No opinion . . . . *

Peru

Regain by force 54%
Negotiate 41
No opinion 5

Uruguay

Regain by force 40%
Negotiate 58
No opinion 2

*No opinion results have been omitted.

If Great Britain decides to take the islands by force, do you believe Argentina will or will not fight?

Brazil

Will 87%
Will not 8
No opinion 5

Ecuador

Will 99%
Will not 1
No opinion . . . . *

Peru

Will 95%
Will not 4
No opinion 1

Uruguay

Will 85%
Will not 14
No opinion 1

*No opinion results have been omitted.

In the case of an armed conflict, which of the two countries do you believe will win the war? Great Britain or Argentina?

Brazil

Argentina 14%
Great Britain 53
No opinion 33

Ecuador

Argentina 11%
Great Britain 89
No opinion . . . . *

Peru

Argentina 34%
Great Britain 41
No opinion 25

Uruguay

Argentina 25%
Great Britain 64
No opinion 10

*No opinion results have been omitted.

Do you believe this town (country) is on the side of Argentina or Great Britain in this dispute?

Brazil

Argentina 41%
Great Britain. 20
No opinion 39

Ecuador

Argentina 98%
Great Britain. 2
No opinion. . . . . *

Peru

Argentina 94%
Great Britain. 1
No opinion 5

Uruguay

Argentina 74%
Great Britain. 14
No opinion 11

*No opinion results have been omitted.

There are those who think the occupation by Argentina was motivated to distract the country from its serious political and economic problems. Others think not, that it is the recovery of a historic right closed until now. Which of these two explanations is closer to your way of thinking?

Brazil

Political purpose 40%
Historic right. 39
No opinion 21

Ecuador

Political purpose 42%
Historic right. 58
No opinion. . . . . *

Peru

Political purpose 14%
Historic right. 79
No opinion 7

Uruguay

Political purpose 62%
Historic right. 34
No opinion 4

*No opinion results have been omitted.

President Reagan has offered to mediate in the conflict between Argentina and England provoked by the occupation of the Malvinas Islands. Do you consider Reagan a good or a bad mediator in this conflict?

Brazil

Good mediator. 48%
Bad mediator. 34
No opinion 18

Ecuador

Good mediator. 35%
Bad mediator. 65
No opinion. . . . . *

Peru

Good mediator. 40%
Bad mediator. 44
No opinion 16

Uruguay

Good mediator. 46%
Bad mediator. 49
No opinion 5

*No opinion results have been omitted.

Note: A just completed Gallup survey in Great Britain reveals that the British public strongly supports the sending of their fleet to the Falklands and the use of military force, if necessary, to regain the islands. Parallel Gallup surveys in four South American countries, however, show the public in three of these nations against an immediate withdrawal of Argentine forces from the Falkland Islands, although opinion in all four holds that the Argentinians were wrong in taking the Falklands by military force. The publics in three of the four nations also believe that the Argentinians are the rightful possessors of these islands.

The survey in Great Britain, based on interviews with 874 British adults, found 78% approving the decision to send a fleet to the South Atlantic and 67% generally approving the government's actions since the invasion. At the same time, however, almost eight in ten agree with those who criticize the government for being caught off guard by Argentina's takeover of the islands.

A 61% majority of the British surveyed would approve of attacking Argentinian ships and troops guarding the Falklands in order to gain control of the islands and 32% would disapprove. And as many as 24% would approve of British forces attacking the Argentine mainland itself, but 68% disapprove.

In each of the four South American countries surveyed, majorities believe Argentina should have attempted to negotiate the situation rather than resort to military force. In Brazil, 71% think Argentina should now withdraw its forces, as has been requested by the United Nations. However, majorities of Ecuadorians, Peruvians, and Uruguayans are opposed to an Argentine withdrawal. Similarly, majorities in Ecuador (78%), Peru (93%), and Uruguay (84%) hold the opinion that Argentina has rights to the islands. Basic sympathies in the dispute follow this same pattern with almost universal public support for Argentina in each country except Brazil, where sympathies divide more closely.

No consensus is found in the South American countries as to the Argentine government's motives for the invasion. Brazilians are divided as to whether it was launched for the sake of internal political purposes (40%) or because of beliefs about Argentina's historic right to the Falklands (39%). A majority of Uruguayans (62%) think the invasion is politically motivated, while in Ecuador and Peru majorities believe the invasion was not launched for political purposes.

Greater agreement among these countries is found in terms of what will happen if Argentina and Great Britain engage in armed conflict. By a margin of 53% to 14%, Brazilians see the British

prevailing. In Ecuador, 89% agree, as do 64% in Uruguay. Opinion is more equally divided in Peru, with 34% thinking Argentina would win; Great Britain, 41%. However, nine in ten respondents say that the Argentinians will put up a fight if the British attempt to take the Falklands by force.

Opinion regarding the Reagan administration as a mediator in the dispute is mixed. In Brazil, 48% believe that the United States is a good intermediary for this conflict, while 34% do not. On the other hand, two-thirds of Ecuadorians view the Reagan administration as a bad mediator; in Peru and Uruguay the publics are about equally divided.

APRIL 18
PRESIDENT REAGAN

Interviewing Date: 3/12–15/82
Survey #191-G

Would you like to see Ronald Reagan run for president in 1984, or not?

Would 35%
Would not 52
No opinion 13

By Politics
Republicans

Would 68%
Would not 20
No opinion 12

Democrats

Would 19%
Would not 72
No opinion 9

Independents

Would 33%
Would not 52
No opinion 15

Regardless of whether or not you would like to see him run, do you think Reagan will run for president in 1984, or not?

Will 59%
Will not 30
No opinion 11

By Politics
Republicans

Will 62%
Will not 27
No opinion 11

Democrats

Will 56%
Will not 34
No opinion 10

Independents

Will 62%
Will not 29
No opinion 9

Note: Amid speculation about President Ronald Reagan's plans to run in 1984, a recent Gallup Poll shows 52% of the public leaning toward the view that Reagan should not seek reelection. Even among the president's own party members, as many as 20% say they would not like to see the seventy-one-year-old chief executive enter the 1984 contest.

While the weight of public sentiment at present is against the president's seeking reelection, it is important to bear in mind that Reagan held substantial leads over three potential Democratic rivals in early test elections. Late last fall, when his approval rating was in the low 50s, he led former President Jimmy Carter, 54% to 35%; Senator Edward Kennedy, 56% to 35%; and former Vice-President Walter Mondale, 54% to 37%.

Undoubtedly a key factor in current attitudes toward the president's seeking reelection is growing concern over the economy. Opinion is 51% to 28% that Reaganomics, at least in the short term, will worsen rather than improve individuals' financial situation. Even among Republicans, as many as one-fourth (24%) say their financial situation is likely to get worse rather than better (50%) as a result of the president's economic program, while 26% express uncertainty.

APRIL 22
DRINKING AND DRIVING

Interviewing Date: 3/12–15/82
Survey #191-G

Do you think there should or should not be stricter laws regarding drinking and driving?

Should 89%
Should not 9
No opinion 2

By Region
East

Should 90%
Should not 7
No opinion 3

Midwest

Should 91%
Should not 8
No opinion 1

South

Should 87%
Should not 11
No opinion 2

West

Should 86%
Should not 12
No opinion 2

By Age

18–29 Years

Should 83%
Should not 15
No opinion 2

30–49 Years

Should 90%
Should not 8
No opinion 2

50 Years and Over

Should 93%
Should not 5
No opinion 2

In some states drunk drivers convicted of a first offense are required to serve a mandatory two-day jail sentence. Would you like to see such a law in this state, or not?

Would 77%
Would not 21
No opinion 2

By Region

East

Would 75%
Would not 23
No opinion 2

Midwest

Would 78%
Would not 19
No opinion 3

South

Would 74%
Would not 24
No opinion 2

West

Would 81%
Would not 17
No opinion 2

By Age

18–29 Years

Would 74%
Would not 23
No opinion 3

30–49 Years

Would 78%
Would not 20
No opinion 2

50 Years and Over

Would 78%
Would not 19
No opinion 3

Do you favor or oppose police stopping motorists at random—that is, making spot checks to give them a test such as a breath alcohol or coordination test, even though they may not have committed an offense?

Favor 36%
Oppose 62
No opinion 2

By Region

East

Favor 38%
Oppose 57
No opinion 5

Midwest

Favor 35%
Oppose 63
No opinion 2

South

Favor 38%
Oppose 61
No opinion 1

West

Favor 31%
Oppose 67
No opinion 2

By Age

18–29 Years

Favor............................29%
Oppose...........................70
No opinion 1

30–49 Years

Favor............................36%
Oppose...........................62
No opinion 2

50 Years and Over

Favor............................43%
Oppose...........................54
No opinion 3

Note: President Ronald Reagan's decision to launch a highway safety campaign to reduce drunken driving is applauded by the American people who demand tougher laws on drinking and driving. A large and growing majority nationwide, as well as heavy majorities in each of the four major regions, want stricter drinking/driving laws in general. In addition, eight in ten endorse a mandatory two-day jail sentence for drunk drivers convicted of a first offense. Although supporting tougher laws, 62% are opposed to police stopping motorists at random to administer an alcohol-level test, even though they may have not committed an offense.

The current survey also reveals that four out of every ten drivers say they have operated a vehicle after drinking, while as many as one in six admits to have driven after drinking too much to drive safely. And in a Gallup Youth Survey, one teen-ager in ten admits to having driven while under the influence.

Recently President Reagan established a thirty-member commission to work with state and local governments on drinking/driving problems. The panel is charged with heightening public awareness of the problem, urging states to deal with drunken driving in a more organized and systematic manner, encouraging the use of the latest techniques for solving the problem, and generating local support for better enforcement of laws against drunken driving.

Each year drunken driving is blamed for about one-half the country's 50,000 automobile fatalities, an estimated 800,000 auto accidents, 750,000 serious injuries, and $5 billion in economic losses. Federal studies have shown that on weekend nights one in ten motorists is intoxicated and only one in 2,000 is arrested.

APRIL 25
CONGRESSIONAL ELECTIONS

Interviewing Date: 4/2–5/82
Survey #192-G

Asked of registered voters: If the elections for Congress were being held today, which party would you like to see win in this congressional district—the Democratic party or the Republican party? [Those who said they were undecided or who voted for a different party were asked: As of today, do you lean more to the Republican party or to the Democratic party?]

Republican 34%
Democratic 54
Other; undecided 12

By Politics
Republicans

Republican 85%
Democratic 11
Other; undecided 4

Democrats

Republican 8%
Democratic 88
Other; undecided 4

Independents

Republican 34%
Democratic 36
Other; undecided 30

Those Who Approve of President Reagan

Republican 61%
Democratic 27
Other; undecided 12

Those Who Disapprove of President Reagan

Republican 9%
Democratic 83
Other; undecided 8

Those Who Approve of President Reagan's Handling of the Economy

Republican 64%
Democratic 25
Other; undecided 11

Those Who Disapprove of President Reagan's Handling of the Economy

Republican 14%
Democratic 76
Other; undecided 10

National Trend

	Republican	Democratic	Other; undecided
1982			
Feb. 5–8	36%	55%	9%
Jan. 22–25	39	52	9
1981			
Oct. 2–5	41	51	8
June 19–22	45	49	6

Note: With the elections less than eight months away, the Democratic party enjoys a huge 20-percentage point lead over the Republican party in the popular vote for seats in the U.S. House of Representatives. This is the largest margin recorded in eight Gallup test elections since June 1981 and suggests that a Democratic landslide may be in the making.

In the latest measurement, the Democrats are the choice of 54% of registered voters to 34% for the Republicans. The current GOP shortfall represents the culmination of a steady downtrend since January, when the Republicans trailed the Democrats by only 8 points— 42% to 50%. The public's disaffection with President Ronald Reagan and his handling of the nation's economy go far toward explaining the relatively poor showing of Republicans in the current congressional test election.

At present, Americans are evenly divided in their assessment of Reagan's performance in office, with 46% approving and 45% disapproving. He fares less well in the public's judgment of his competency on the economic front, with 38% giving him positive ratings and 54%, negative.

The difficulty facing Republican candidates for the House in November is not only that their party has just half as many rank-and-file members as the Democratic party but also that even among voters who approve of Reagan's overall performance and those who think he is doing a good job of dealing with the economy, as many as one person in four says he would vote for the local Democratic candidate in his district if the House elections were being held today.

A comparison of the current relationship between attitudes toward President Reagan and congressional preference with the situation four years ago suggests that the 1982 House elections may be a much greater test of Reagan's popularity than 1978 was of President Jimmy Carter. As shown in the table below, those who approved of Carter's handling of the presidency in April 1978 were more inclined to vote for Democratic candidates for Congress than is now the case with Reagan and Republican candidates. Even more importantly, a substantial 43% minority of those who disapproved of Carter's job performance nevertheless backed his party's congressional candidates, compared to merely 9% of Reagan's detractors who now vote for Republicans:

National Trend

	April 1982	April 1978
Vote for president's party	34%	55%
Vote for opposition party	54	33
Vote for other party; undecided	12	12

Approve of President

	April 1982	April 1978
Vote for president's party	61%	70%
Vote for opposition party	27	19
Vote for other party; undecided	12	11

Disapprove of President

	April 1982	April 1978
Vote for president's party	9%	43%
Vote for opposition party	83	47
Vote for other party; undecided	8	10

The outcome of the 1978 elections was that Democratic candidates won about 55% of the popular vote and lost 16 seats in the House of Representatives, approximately one-half the normal attrition in off-year elections.

APRIL 28
NUCLEAR FREEZE MOVEMENT*

Despite the emotional appeal and political potential of the nuclear freeze movement, recent polls show the American public is as wary of the Soviet Union as they are favorably disposed to nuclear disarmament. At first glance, public reaction to the idea of a nuclear freeze is over-whelmingly positive, but the polls also have shown significant public reservations about a freeze if it means the Soviets will maintain a nuclear advantage or that the United States must take the first step toward disarmament without the Soviet Union's compliance.

A March *Newsweek* Poll showed 60% of respondents favoring the freeze position, when it was described as the belief that the United States and Soviet Union have enough weapons to destroy each other, and as such there should be a ban on all testing, production, and deployment of nuclear weapons. But majority support gave way to majority opposition, with 61%

*This Gallup analysis was written by Andrew Kohut, president of the Gallup Organization Inc.

saying they opposed a freeze if it meant the Soviet Union would maintain a nuclear advantage in some areas.

A March NBC/AP Poll showed the same pattern—74% favored a freeze on the production of nuclear weapons in both the United States and Soviet Union, but only 14% thought the United States should move toward disarmament on its own. And 50% thought we should disarm only if the Soviets do so as well. Similarly, the *Los Angeles Times* Poll indicated general support for the freeze but even stronger opposition to unilateral nuclear disarmament.

Verification is another stumbling block to public approval on a nuclear freeze. In measuring its importance in a nuclear arms agreement, *Newsweek* found only 25% in favor of reducing the U.S. nuclear arsenal if we cannot be sure the other side is doing so as well.

Despite these concerns and reservations, the public holds many views that are sympathetic to those of the nuclear disarmament movement:

1) It rejects the notion of a limited nuclear war, with only about one in four saying a confrontation with the Soviets could be limited to the use of tactical nuclear weapons. (*Newsweek*)

2) A majority of Americans are opposed to using tactical nuclear weapons to prevent the fall of Western Europe to conventional Soviet forces (*Newsweek*), but a 49% plurality think the Reagan administration would favor the use of nuclear weapons in such a case. (*Los Angeles Times*)

3) Few Americans (7%) believe we are ahead of the Soviets in nuclear weaponry. Opinion divides equally (41%) between those who say we are behind and those who feel the United States is at parity. Nonetheless, 50% think the United States has enough weapons to destroy its enemies, while only 31% think we need more. (*Los Angeles Times*)

There is little question that the nuclear freeze movement has made a major political impact in the United States, and it has the potential to make an even greater one. But the outer bounds on the movement are U.S. attitudes toward the Soviet Union. American opinion of the Soviet Union generally mirrors the trend in U.S.-Soviet relations. In a 1953 Gallup Poll, 1% of the public held a favorable view of the Soviets. In 1973, in an era of détente, it rose to 45%; today 20% hold a positive view of the USSR.

For the freeze movement to succeed in achieving majority support, it must either raise nuclear concern to such a level that it overwhelms mistrust of the Soviet Union or its proposals must address that mistrust.

APRIL 19
LEGAL DRINKING AGE

Interviewing Date: 3/12–15/82
Survey #191-G

Do you think the legal drinking age in this state should be raised, lowered, or kept where it is?

In states where legal age is now eighteen or nineteen?

Raised	58%
Lowered	2
Kept as is	37
No opinion	3

By Age
18–24 Years

Raised	34%
Lowered	4
Kept as is	59
No opinion	3

25–29 Years

Raised	51%
Lowered	5
Kept as is	44
No opinion	*

30–49 Years

Raised	61%
Lowered	1
Kept as is	36
No opinion	2

50–64 Years

Raised	63%
Lowered	1
Kept as is	33
No opinion	3

65 Years and Over

Raised	70%
Lowered	2
Kept as is	24
No opinion	5

In states where legal age is now twenty or twenty-one?

Raised	10%
Lowered	13
Kept as is	75
No opinion	2

By Age
18–24 Years

Raised	6%
Lowered	20
Kept as is	72
No opinion	2

25–29 Years

Raised	8%
Lowered	18
Kept as is	76
No opinion	*

30–49 Years

Raised	14%
Lowered	10
Kept as is	76
No opinion	*

50–64 Years

Raised	9%
Lowered	13
Kept as is	76
No opinion	2

65 Years and Over

Raised 17%
Lowered........................... 2
Kept as is......................... 80
No opinion 1

*Less than 1%

Note: President Ronald Reagan's announcement of a major drive to reduce drunken driving comes at a time when a majority of adults living in states where eighteen or nineteen year olds can legally purchase alcoholic beverages believe the legal age should be raised. In these twenty states, 58% of residents favor raising the legal age to twenty or twenty-one years, while 37% think the present minimum age limits should be retained. And in the thirty states where the law provides for legal purchases at age twenty or twenty-one, the overwhelming public sentiment is that the drinking age should be kept where it is now, with 75% of residents expressing this view.

When the 26th Amendment giving eighteen year olds the right to vote was ratified in 1971, many states lowered their legal drinking age, reflecting the belief that if teen-agers are old enough to vote, marry, and serve in the Armed Forces, they are mature enough to drink alcoholic beverages responsibly. However, some states that lowered their drinking age have experienced an increase in problem drinking by teen-agers, including a rise in the number of young drivers convicted of driving while intoxicated. Consequently, states such as Massachusetts, New Jersey, and Connecticut are now returning to higher age limits. In New Jersey, which raised its legal age from eighteen to nineteen in 1980, newly elected Governor Thomas Kean has pledged his support to further increase the minimum age to twenty-one if he believes this will have a positive effect. One of the principal arguments for raising the legal age is that it would help prevent high-school seniors, many of whom are now of legal age, from buying alcoholic beverages for their younger schoolmates.

Comparing the latest adult findings with those recorded in a Gallup Youth Survey of thirteen to eighteen year olds conducted last year, far fewer teen-agers living in states with lower drinking ages favored raising the legal age, while in states with higher limits many more expressed a preference for lowering the drinking age. There is a widespread feeling among teen-agers that the legal drinking age is almost academic, since they can readily obtain alcoholic beverages regardless of their age.

It has been estimated that there are 3.3 million American teen-agers with serious drinking problems; 8,000 young people are killed each year in alcohol-related traffic accidents, while another 40,000 are disfigured. Including vandalism and other crimes, in addition to drunk driving, alcohol-related arrests in the last seven years have doubled for boys under eighteen and tripled for girls.

MAY 2
MOST IMPORTANT PROBLEM

Interviewing Date: 4/2–5/82
Survey #192-G

What do you think is the most important problem facing this country today?

Unemployment; recession 44%
High cost of living; inflation 24
Economy (general)................... 11
Reagan budget cuts 7
High interest rates 7
Fear of war 5
Excessive government spending........ 4
International problems 3
Crime.............................. 3
Moral decline 3
Defense; security 3
Others 7
Don't know 2
_____
123%*

*Total adds to more than 100% due to multiple responses.

Most Important Problem

	Unemployment	Inflation
National..........	44%	24%

By Region

East..............	45%	24%
Midwest	54	20
South	38	30
West..............	38	23

As you know, the economy is now in a recession, with employment and productivity far below what they were a year ago. What's your best guess: Do you think the recession will become worse during the next three months, or do you think the economy will begin to recover?

Become worse........................50%
Begin to recover 30
Stay the same (volunteered)...........16
No opinion 4

By Race
White

Become worse........................47%
Begin to recover 34
Stay the same (volunteered)...........16
No opinion 3

Nonwhite

Become worse........................62%
Begin to recover 13
Stay the same (volunteered)...........15
No opinion 10

By Education
College

Become worse........................46%
Begin to recover 39
Stay the same (volunteered)...........13
No opinion 2

High School

Become worse........................49%
Begin to recover 28

Stay the same (volunteered)...........18
No opinion 5

Grade School

Become worse........................58%
Begin to recover 23
Stay the same (volunteered)...........13
No opinion 6

By Region
East

Become worse........................54%
Begin to recover 26
Stay the same (volunteered)...........18
No opinion 2

Midwest

Become worse........................48%
Begin to recover 29
Stay the same (volunteered)...........19
No opinion 4

South

Become worse........................47%
Begin to recover 33
Stay the same (volunteered)...........14
No opinion 6

West

Become worse........................50%
Begin to recover 36
Stay the same (volunteered)...........10
No opinion 4

By Income
$15,000 and Over

Become worse........................46%
Begin to recover 35
Stay the same (volunteered)...........16
No opinion 3

Under $15,000

Become worse........................54%
Begin to recover 24

Stay the same (volunteered) 16
No opinion 6

Labor Union Households Only

Become worse 54%
Begin to recover 26
Stay the same (volunteered) 16
No opinion 4

Nonlabor Union Households Only

Become worse 48%
Begin to recover 32
Stay the same (volunteered) 16
No opinion 4

Asked of employed persons: If you were to lose the job you now have, do you think it would be easy to get another job as good, or would it be difficult?

Easy 20%
Difficult 77
Not sure 3

By Race
White

Easy 22%
Difficult 77
Not sure 1

Nonwhite

Easy 10%
Difficult 86
Not sure 4

By Education
College

Easy 38%
Difficult 61
Not sure 1

High School

Easy 29%
Difficult 68
Not sure 3

Grade School

Easy 12%
Difficult 85
Not sure 3

By Region
East

Easy 24%
Difficult 74
Not sure 2

Midwest

Easy 24%
Difficult 74
Not sure 2

South

Easy 38%
Difficult 58
Not sure 4

West

Easy 37%
Difficult 62
Not sure 1

By Income
$15,000 and Over

Easy 33%
Difficult 66
Not sure 1

Under $15,000

Easy 25%
Difficult 71
Not sure 4

Labor Union Households Only

Easy 23%
Difficult 76
Not sure 1

Nonlabor Union Households Only

Easy 33%
Difficult 64
Not sure 3

Asked of employed persons: Would you be prepared to accept less money or lower status to get another job?

Yes 67%
No 23
Depends (volunteered) 8
Not sure 2

Asked of employed persons: Suppose you were faced with the choice of losing the job you now have, or taking a pay cut of 10%—which would you do?

Lose job 11%
Take 10% pay cut 85
Not sure 4

Note: While the Reagan administration is taking credit for reducing the rate of inflation to its lowest level since 1965, worry over unemployment is mounting fast and is now the most urgent concern of Americans in every region of the nation. Those naming unemployment as the nation's top problem outnumber, by a 2-to-1 ratio, those citing inflation or the high cost of living. Nor are most Americans expecting relief, at least in the short term. By a 5-to-3 ratio, people think the recession will worsen during the next three months rather than the economy begin to recover.

These survey findings bring cold comfort to Republican candidates in the coming congressional elections. The latest Gallup Poll figures on the national popular vote in the race for the House shows the Democrats currently leading the GOP among registered voters by a lopsided 54% to 34% margin.

The dimensions of concern over unemployment are reflected in other survey findings that show worry about joblessness is both widespread and deep-seated. Not only is the unemployment rate at a high level, but a recent Gallup survey also showed that one person in seven among those presently employed thinks his job is in jeopardy. Moreover, fully three-fourths (77%) of employed persons say that if they were to lose their present job, it would be difficult to get another as good. These findings represent a dramatic change from those recorded in 1979, when only 51% expressed this view.

MAY 6
FALKLAND ISLANDS CRISIS

Interviewing Date: 4/16–24/82
Special Telephone Survey

Have you heard or read about the dispute between Argentina and Great Britain over the Falkland Islands?

Yes 90%
No 10

Asked of those who replied in the affirmative: Do you think the United States should help Argentina, help Great Britain, or stay completely out of this situation?

Argentina 2%
Great Britain 17
Stay completely out 65
No opinion 16

Also asked of those who replied in the affirmative: In the Falkland Islands dispute, are your sympathies more with Argentina or more with Great Britain?

Argentina 15%
Great Britain 50
Both sides equally (volunteered) 21
No opinion; neither 14

Note: As fighting between Argentina and Great Britain broke out last week, both nations had solid public opinion backing for their governments' actions.

In Britain, as recently reported by the British Gallup Poll, the public emphatically sided with their government but were critical of it for allowing the situation to reach crisis proportions. In Argentina, the public's intransigence was so strong that they voted down any proposals for mediating the crisis.

Here is the status of public opinion in Argentina just before the fighting began but after the United States indicated it sided with Great Britain:*

1) Ninety percent of Argentines supported their government's decision to defend the Malvinas (as the Falkland Islands are known there) against British attempts to retake the islands by force.

2) Almost as many Argentines (86%) rejected a British proposal to return to the status quo that prevailed before Argentina's April 2 takeover, with the ultimate sovereignty of the islands to be negotiated between Argentina and Great Britain and through the self-determination of the islanders.

3) By better than a 5-to-1 ratio, the Argentine public opposed any negotiations at all over the sovereignty of the islands.

4) Having the United Nations administer the islands while their future is decided by the two belligerent nations did not fare much better, with the weight of Argentine public opinion 3 to 1 in opposition.

The determined mood of the Argentine public is further clarified by additional survey findings:

1) Seventy-six percent picked Argentina to win an armed conflict in the islands, with only 3% naming Great Britain and 21% undecided.

2) By an 8-to-1 margin, the United States was thought to have been a poor, rather than a good, mediator in the dispute.

3) The Argentine people overwhelmingly—by 84% in its military efforts and by 88% in its diplomatic sphere—back their government's moves in the crisis.

A British Gallup Poll taken in mid-April showed the public strongly supporting the sending of their fleet to the Falklands and the use of military force to regain the islands. Specifically, 78% approved the decision to send the fleet to

*The Argentine results are based on interviews conducted on April 29–30, 1982.

the South Atlantic. At the same time, however, an equal number criticized the government for being caught off guard by Argentina's takeover of the islands.

A 61% majority of the British surveyed approved of attacking the Argentinian ships and troops guarding the Falklands in order to regain control of the islands, while 32% disapproved. And as many as 24% would approve of British forces attacking the Argentine mainland, but 68% disapproved.

MAY 9
YOUTH EMPLOYMENT

Interviewing Date: 1/22–25/82
Survey #189-G

One European nation has dealt with the problem of unemployed youth this way: Employers are required to hire a certain number of sixteen to eighteen year olds, based on the total number of their full-time employees. Young people so employed spend three days each week learning a trade or business on the job and the other two days in school. Would you favor or oppose having the United States adopt such a plan?

Favor 62%
Oppose 30
No opinion 8

By Sex
Male

Favor 58%
Oppose 35
No opinion 7

Female

Favor 66%
Oppose 26
No opinion 8

By Education

College

Favor 56%
Oppose 37
No opinion 7

High School

Favor 64%
Oppose 29
No opinion 7

Grade School

Favor 68%
Oppose . . . . ? 20
No opinion 12

By Age

18–24 Years

Favor 69%
Oppose 25
No opinion 6

25–29 Years

Favor 63%
Oppose 30
No opinion 7

30–49 Years

Favor 58%
Oppose 35
No opinion 7

50 Years and Over

Favor 63%
Oppose 29
No opinion 8

By Politics

Republicans

Favor 59%
Oppose 34
No opinion 7

Democrats

Favor 62%
Oppose 31
No opinion 7

Independents

Favor 65%
Oppose 27
No opinion 8

By Occupation

Professional and Business

Favor 57%
Oppose 37
No opinion 6

Clerical and Sales

Favor 66%
Oppose 28
No opinion 6

Manual Workers

Favor 70%
Oppose 26
No opinion 4

Labor Union Families Only

Favor 67%
Oppose 29
No opinion 4

Nonlabor Union Families Only

Favor 61%
Oppose 31
No opinion 8

Note: As the Reagan administration ponders how to deal with the seemingly intractable problem of youth unemployment, widespread public support, by a 2-to-1 vote, is found for a proposal requiring business firms to provide on-the-job training for sixteen to eighteen year olds, with the number hired prorated to the size of a company's fulltime staff. Young people so employed would spend three days each week learning a trade or business on the job and the other two days in school.

Proponents of such a plan see three major advantages: 1) it would almost eliminate unemployment among youth, 2) it would develop salable skills in young people, and 3) it would provide not only practical job skills but also theoretical knowledge. On the other hand, critics believe the cost might be prohibitive and question how the proposed program would be funded, whether by the government, employers, or some combination thereof.

Joblessness among youth is presently at a very high level, and in the case of some minorities, as many as one-half of all youths are unemployed. Most social observers believe that job training and placement are of vital importance to the nation, since chronically high unemployment contributes to a high crime rate, drug abuse, and other social ills.

During the past twenty years the federal government has spent large sums in developing plans to deal with youth unemployment—a reported $53 billion since 1975 alone. These efforts thus far have not met with great success.

MAY 13
PRESIDENTIAL TRIAL HEATS

Interviewing Date: 4/23–26/82
Survey #193-G

Asked of registered voters: Suppose the presidential election were being held today. If President Ronald Reagan were the Republican candidate and former President Jimmy Carter were the Democratic candidate, which would you like to see win? [Those who named another candidate or who were undecided were asked: As of today, do you lean more to Reagan, the Republican, or to Carter, the Democrat?]

Reagan............................50%
Carter..............................42
Other; undecided 8

By Politics
Republicans

Reagan............................92%
Carter.............................. 5
Other; undecided 3

Democrats

Reagan............................19%
Carter..............................74
Other; undecided 7

Independents

Reagan............................58%
Carter..............................30
Other; undecided 12

Asked of registered voters: Suppose the presidential election were being held today. If President Ronald Reagan were the Republican candidate and former Vice-President Walter Mondale were the Democratic candidate, which would you like to see win? [Those who named another candidate or who were undecided were asked: As of today, do you lean more to Reagan, the Republican, or to Mondale, the Democrat?]

Reagan............................46%
Mondale............................46
Other; undecided 8

By Politics
Republicans

Reagan............................90%
Mondale............................ 7
Other; undecided 3

Democrats

Reagan............................17%
Mondale............................74
Other; undecided 9

Independents

Reagan............................49%
Mondale............................37
Other; undecided 14

Asked of registered voters: Suppose the presidential election were being held today. If President Ronald Reagan were the Republican candidate and Senator Edward Kennedy were the Democratic candidate, which would you like to see win? [Those who named another candidate or who were undecided were asked: As of today, do you lean more to Reagan, the Republican, or to Kennedy, the Democrat?]

Reagan............................45%
Kennedy 51
Other; undecided 4

By Politics
Republicans

Reagan............................87%
Kennedy 11
Other; undecided 2

Democrats

Reagan............................14%
Kennedy 83
Other; undecided 3

Independents

Reagan............................49%
Kennedy 43
Other; undecided 8

Asked of registered voters: Suppose the presidential election were being held today. If Vice-President George Bush were the Republican candidate and former Vice-President Walter Mondale were the Democratic candidate, which would you like to see win? [Those who named another candidate or who were undecided were asked: As of today, do you lean more to Bush, the Republican, or to Mondale, the Democrat?]

Bush..............................40%
Mondale...........................48
Other; undecided 12

By Politics
Republicans

Bush..............................83%
Mondale...........................12
Other; undecided 5

Democrats

Bush..............................14%
Mondale...........................74
Other; undecided 12

Independents

Bush..............................38%
Mondale...........................44
Other; undecided 18

Asked of registered voters: Suppose the presidential election were being held today. If Vice-President George Bush were the Republican candidate and Senator Edward Kennedy were the Democratic candidate, which would you like to see win? [Those who named another candidate or who were undecided were asked: As of today, do you lean more to Bush, the Republican, or to Kennedy, the Democrat?]

Bush..............................41%
Kennedy 52
Other; undecided 7

By Politics
Republicans

Bush..............................80%
Kennedy 18
Other; undecided 2

Democrats

Bush..............................16%
Kennedy 79
Other; undecided 5

Independents

Bush..............................41%
Kennedy 47
Other; undecided 12

Note: Senator Edward Kennedy, the early favorite among the nation's Democrats to be their 1984 standard-bearer, has made dramatic gains in recent months and now leads President Ronald Reagan 51% to 45% in a test election for the presidency. In an earlier Gallup test, Kennedy also easily beat fellow Democrats Jimmy Carter 52% to 31% and Walter Mondale 54% to 31% for the nomination.

In a similar contest last October, the president was able to decisively beat Kennedy by holding 92% of the Republican vote, scoring a lopsided 62% to 24% victory among independents and causing almost one-third (31%) of Democrats to cross party lines and vote for Reagan. The result was a 56% to 35% Reagan victory over Kennedy. And presently the president fares better against Carter, considered a long shot for the 1984 Democratic nomination, beating him 50% to 42%. However, Reagan manages only a tie against Mondale, with each man receiving 46% of the vote.

An important element in President Reagan's current relatively poor showing against Kennedy is the steady erosion of Reagan's popularity. Since January less than a majority of Americans have approved of the way Reagan has carried out his presidential duties. For the first time disapproval of the president's performance in office outweighs approval, with 43% of the public now giving him positive marks and 47% negative. Last October, 56% approved of Reagan's handling of his duties and 35% disapproved. Reagan's detractors are particularly critical of his economic program, with 51% saying they are financially worse off now than they were a year ago, compared to 28% who say they are better off.

President Reagan and other Republican hopefuls, should Reagan choose not to seek reelection, also must cope with their party's minority status. Currently, 28% of registered voters claim affiliation with the GOP, compared to 45% who say they are Democrats and 27% of independents. For the Republicans to have a winner in test or actual elections, their candidate must attract large numbers of Democratic and independent votes.

In the current contest the president has only one crucial element working for him: he holds his own party members, with 87% of Republicans voting for him. However, there is very little of the cross-over vote found in the earlier contests, as 83% of Democrats now vote for Kennedy. Finally, independents are fairly evenly divided, with 49% choosing Reagan and 43% Kennedy.

In the event that President Reagan decides not to run in 1984, the Republican mentioned most often as the GOP's nominee is Vice-President George Bush. Paired against Kennedy, Bush comes out on the short end of a 52% to 41% vote. And, in a contest against Walter Mondale, Bush is the choice of 40% of registered voters to 48% for Mondale.

MAY 16
DEMOCRATIC PRESIDENTIAL CANDIDATES

Interviewing Date: 4/23–26/82
Survey #193-G

Asked of Democrats: Would you please look over this list [respondents were handed a card listing fifteen names] and tell me which of these persons, if any, you have heard something about? Those who replied in the affirmative were asked: Can you tell me something about these persons?

	Heard something	Know something
Jimmy Carter	98%	87%
Edward Kennedy	98	84
Walter Mondale..........	90	60
Edmund (Jerry) Brown, Jr.	83	57
John Glenn	74	50
Jay Rockefeller	58	25
Daniel (Pat) Moynihan....	52	25
Robert Strauss	41	15
Bill Bradley..............	35	14
Alan Cranston	35	15
John Y. Brown...........	31	14
Reubin Askew	22	8

Gary Hart	21	7
Ernest Hollings	14	5
Bruce Babbitt	12	4

Asked of Democrats: Which one of these persons [respondents were handed a card listing fifteen names and titles of possible nominees] would you like to see nominated as the Democratic party's candidate for president in 1984? And who would be your second and third choices?

First Choices of Democrats*

Kennedy 45%
Mondale..............................12
Carter...................................11
Brown (Jerry) 6
Glenn.................................... 6

*All others on the list each received 2% or less of the vote of survey respondents.

First, Second, and Third Choices of Democrats*

Kennedy 70%
Mondale.............................42
Carter................................36
Brown (Jerry) 24
Glenn................................24
Rockefeller 10
Moynihan 7
Bradley 5

*All others on the list each received less than 5% of the vote of survey respondents.

Note: Senator Edward Kennedy far outstrips his potential rivals at this early stage in the race for the 1984 Democratic presidential nomination. The Massachusetts senator is the top choice of Democrats of fifteen persons mentioned as possible contenders. At this point in each of the four previous presidential campaigns Kennedy either led or was in a virtual tie for the lead.

Although the current figures show that many Democratic hopefuls have a long way to go before they are known to a majority of the electorate, they can take encouragement from the dramatic example of Jimmy Carter, who two years before the 1976 primaries was known to few people outside his native Georgia. In fact, it was not until mid-1975 that as many as one Democrat in four had heard of Carter. At that time he was the choice of merely 1% of Democrats to be their party's standard-bearer in the 1976 presidential race.

MAY 20
PRESIDENT REAGAN

Interviewing Date: 4/30–5/3/82
Survey #194-G

Do you approve or disapprove of the way Ronald Reagan is handling his job as president?

Approve..............................44%
Disapprove 46
No opinion 10

You will notice that the ten boxes on this scale go from the highest position of +5 for someone you have a very favorable opinion of all the way down to the lowest position of −5 for someone you have a very unfavorable opinion of. How far up or down the scale would you rate Ronald Reagan?

Highly favorable (+5, +4)............25%
Mildly favorable (+3, +2, +1)........44
Mildly unfavorable (−1, −2, −3)......13
Highly unfavorable (−4, −5)..........15
No opinion 3

By Sex
Male

Total favorable......................73%
Total unfavorable....................25
No opinion 2

Female

Total favorable......................66%
Total unfavorable....................32
No opinion 2

By Sex
White

Total favorable......................74%
Total unfavorable....................24
No opinion 2

Nonwhite

Total favorable......................41%
Total unfavorable....................54
No opinion 5

By Education
College

Total favorable......................76%
Total unfavorable....................22
No opinion 2

High School

Total favorable......................68%
Total unfavorable....................30
No opinion 2

Grade School

Total favorable......................59%
Total unfavorable....................36
No opinion 5

By Region
East

Total favorable......................69%
Total unfavorable....................29
No opinion 2

Midwest

Total favorable......................70%
Total unfavorable....................26
No opinion 4

South

Total favorable......................70%
Total unfavorable....................28
No opinion 2

West

Total favorable......................67%
Total unfavorable....................32
No opinion 1

By Age
18–29 Years

Total favorable......................71%
Total unfavorable....................27
No opinion 2

30–49 Years

Total favorable......................71%
Total unfavorable....................27
No opinion 2

50 Years and Over

Total favorable......................66%
Total unfavorable....................31
No opinion 3

By Income
$25,000 and Over

Total favorable......................78%
Total unfavorable....................21
No opinion 1

$15,000 and Over

Total favorable......................76%
Total unfavorable....................22
No opinion 2

Under $15,000

Total favorable......................61%
Total unfavorable....................36
No opinion 3

By Politics
Republicans

Total favorable......................92%
Total unfavorable.................... 7
No opinion 1

Democrats

Total favorable........................55%
Total unfavorable.....................43
No opinion 2

Independents

Total favorable........................72%
Total unfavorable.....................26
No opinion 2

Apart from whether you approve or disapprove of the way Reagan is handling his job as president, what do you think of Reagan as a person? Would you say you approve or disapprove of him?

Approve.............................69%
Disapprove 19
No opinion 12

Note: Despite the deepening recession, President Ronald Reagan's job approval ratings have held up remarkably well, as has his personal popularity. In the latest Gallup survey, 44% approve of the way Reagan is handling his presidential duties, just 5 percentage points below the 49% of the public who gave a positive evaluation in January. Also, 69% now approve of Reagan as a person, statistically indistinguishable from the 70% who made the same assessment early this year.

Although there is no doubt that most Americans like President Reagan as a person—evidenced by the 25-point spread between his personality and job performance ratings—a special Gallup analysis shows that, contrary to a widely held belief, Reagan's personal popularity is not disproportionately greater than his predecessors.

The following table shows that when their job performance scores were at roughly the same level as Reagan's current rating, Presidents Ford, Carter, and Johnson had personality ratings as high or higher than Reagan's. The most comparable data available during the Eisenhower, Nixon, and Kennedy presidencies show a similar wide spread between job approval and personal appeal.

Comparison of Personal and Job Performance Ratings

	Job approval	Personality rating
Eisenhower—July 1958	52%	84%
Kennedy—May 1963	64	86
Johnson—April 1967	48	80
Nixon—June 1970	55	78
Ford—October 1975	44	69
Carter—Mar.–Apr. 1978	48	72
Reagan—Apr.–May 1982	44	69

MAY 23
VIOLENCE ON TELEVISION

Interviewing Date: 3/12–15/82
Survey #191-G

There has been a good deal of discussion lately about television programs that show violence—that is, gunplay, fistfights, and the like. Do you think there is a relationship between violence on television and the rising crime rate in the United States, or not?

Yes................................66%
No.................................30
Not sure........................... 4

By Sex
Male

Yes................................59%
No.................................37
Not sure........................... 4

Female

Yes................................72%
No.................................24
Not sure........................... 4

By Race
White

Yes................................67%
No.................................29
Not sure........................... 4

Nonwhite

Yes.................................56%
No..................................38
Not sure............................ 6

By Age
13–18 Years*

Yes.................................67%
No..................................31
Not sure............................ 2

19–29 Years

Yes.................................63%
No..................................35
Not sure............................ 2

30–49 Years

Yes.................................61%
No..................................36
Not sure............................ 3

50–64 Years

Yes.................................68%
No..................................28
Not sure............................ 4

65 Years and Over

Yes.................................76%
No..................................16
Not sure............................ 8

Parents Only

Yes.................................62%
No..................................35
Not sure............................ 3

Nonparents Only

Yes.................................69%
No..................................27
Not sure............................ 4

*Teen-agers' responses were taken from a November 1981 Gallup Youth Survey.

It has been proposed that all television programs with violence be shown only after 10 o'clock at night, after most children's bedtime. Would you favor or oppose this?

Favor...............................67%
Oppose..............................27
Not sure............................ 6

By Sex
Male

Favor...............................62%
Oppose..............................32
Not sure............................ 6

Female

Favor...............................73%
Oppose..............................21
Not sure............................ 6

By Race
White

Favor...............................68%
Oppose..............................26
Not sure............................ 6

Nonwhite

Favor...............................64%
Oppose..............................32
Not sure............................ 4

By Age
18–29 Years

Favor...............................66%
Oppose..............................31
Not sure............................ 3

30–49 Years

Favor...............................61%
Oppose..............................31
Not sure............................ 8

50–64 Years

Favor...............................67%
Oppose..............................25
Not sure............................ 8

65 Years and Over

Favor............................81%
Oppose..........................14
Not sure......................... 5

Parents Only

Favor............................65%
Oppose..........................29
Not sure......................... 6

Nonparents Only

Favor............................69%
Oppose..........................25
Not sure......................... 6

Those Who See Violence/Crime Link

Favor............................80%
Oppose..........................16
Not sure......................... 4

Those Who Do Not See Violence/Crime Link

Favor............................41%
Oppose..........................50
Not sure......................... 9

It has been proposed that all television programs which show violence be taken off television entirely. Would you favor or oppose this?

Favor............................34%
Oppose..........................60
Not sure......................... 6

By Sex
Male

Favor............................28%
Oppose..........................66
Not sure......................... 6

Female

Favor............................39%
Oppose..........................56
Not sure......................... 5

By Race
White

Favor............................34%
Oppose..........................61
Not sure......................... 5

Nonwhite

Favor............................37%
Oppose..........................55
Not sure......................... 8

By Age
13–18 Years*

Favor............................20%
Oppose..........................76
Not sure......................... 4

19–29 Years

Favor............................21%
Oppose..........................76
Not sure......................... 3

30–49 Years

Favor............................27%
Oppose..........................66
Not sure......................... 7

50–64 Years

Favor............................42%
Oppose..........................50
Not sure......................... 8

65 Years and Over

Favor............................57%
Oppose..........................38
Not sure......................... 5

Parents Only

Favor............................26%
Oppose..........................67
Not sure......................... 7

*Teen-agers' responses were taken from a November 1981 Gallup Youth Survey.

Nonparents Only

Favor............................39%
Oppose...........................56
Not sure........................ 5

Those Who See Violence/Crime Link

Favor............................47%
Oppose...........................49
Not sure........................ 4

Those Who Do Not See Violence/Crime Link

Favor............................ 7%
Oppose...........................87
Not sure........................ 6

Note: According to a recent Gallup Poll, two out of three Americans (66%) believe there is a relationship between violence shown on television programs and the nation's high crime rate. This survey finding parallels the conclusions of the National Institute of Mental Health, which recently reported finding "overwhelming evidence" that violence on television leads to aggressive behavior among children and teen-agers.

Although parents of school-age children and nonparents share the view that television programs featuring gunplay, fistfights, and the like induce criminal behavior, they reject a proposal for completely taking this type of show off the air. However, by a better than 2-to-1 ratio they support a curfew on violent television programs until after 10 PM when most young children have gone to bed. Among parents of children under eighteen, 62% perceive a relationship between television violence and crime, while 69% of nonparents share this perception. This apparent paradox is primarily a function of age, since parents of younger children tend themselves to be younger. Significantly fewer persons under fifty than over this age think there is a link between television violence and crime.

A proposal to eliminate violent television shows is favored by one-third of the public (34%) and opposed by 60%. Again, the age of survey respondents is an important factor, with a 57% majority of persons aged sixty-five years and over approving of the proposal, while a 67%

majority of those under age sixty-five disapprove. And heavy majorities in all population groups endorse a ban on televising violent programs until 10 PM.

Since the infancy of the medium in the 1950s, murder and mayhem on television have been held at least partly responsible by the public for the nation's burgeoning crime rate, with many critics believing that youngsters brought up on a constant diet of brutality and criminality will emulate this kind of behavior as they mature. The issue gained currency earlier this year when an organization called Coalition for Better Television threatened to boycott products advertised on television shows with an excessive amount of violence, sex, and profanity. Such boycotts have not been successful in the past and earlier Gallup surveys have found the public unreceptive to them. In a 1977 study, for example, 55% of respondents said it was a bad idea rather than a good idea (35%) to boycott products made by sponsors of violent television shows.

More recently, the National Institute of Mental Health published a summary of a decade's research on the behavioral effects of television viewing, concluding that violence on television leads to aggressive behavior by children and teen-agers who watch these programs. According to the report, "in magnitude, television violence is as strongly correlated with aggressive behavior as any other behavioral variable that has been measured." The report was based on about 2,500 studies and publications issued since 1970.

MAY 27
MIDDLE EAST SITUATION

Interviewing Date: 4/30–5/3/82
Survey #194-G

Have you heard or read about the situation in the Middle East?

Yes................................81%
No................................19

Asked of those who replied in the affirmative: In the Middle East situation, are your sympathies more with Israel or more with the Arab nations?

Israel	51%
Arab nations	12
Neither	26
No opinion	11

By Sex
Male

Israel	53%
Arab nations	14
Neither	25
No opinion	8

Female

Israel	49%
Arab nations	10
Neither	28
No opinion	13

By Race
White

Israel	52%
Arab nations	11
Neither	26
No opinion	11

Nonwhite

Israel	40%
Arab nations	24
Neither	28
No opinion	8

Black

Israel	41%
Arab nations	25
Neither	26
No opinion	8

By Education
College

Israel	56%
Arab nations	12

Neither	26
No opinion	6

High School

Israel	48%
Arab nations	13
Neither	28
No opinion	11

Grade School

Israel	50%
Arab nations	8
Neither	21
No opinion	21

By Region
East

Israel	50%
Arab nations	12
Neither	27
No opinion	11

Midwest

Israel	49%
Arab nations	12
Neither	29
No opinion	10

South

Israel	52%
Arab nations	12
Neither	22
No opinion	14

West

Israel	53%
Arab nations	14
Neither	27
No opinion	6

By Age
18–29 Years

Israel	49%
Arab nations	12

Neither...........................29
No opinion 10

30–49 Years

Israel 55%
Arab nations 11
Neither...........................25
No opinion 9

50 Years and Over

Israel 49%
Arab nations 13
Neither...........................25
No opinion 13

By Income
$25,000 and Over

Israel 56%
Arab nations 15
Neither...........................22
No opinion 7

$15,000 and Over

Israel 53%
Arab nations 14
Neither...........................24
No opinion 9

Under $15,000

Israel 49%
Arab nations 10
Neither...........................29
No opinion 12

By Politics
Republicans

Israel 56%
Arab nations 13
Neither...........................23
No opinion 8

Democrats

Israel 47%
Arab nations 13

Neither...........................30
No opinion 10

Independents

Israel 54%
Arab nations 11
Neither...........................24
No opinion 11

By Religion
Protestants

Israel 54%
Arab nations 13
Neither...........................22
No opinion 11

Catholics

Israel 44%
Arab nations 12
Neither...........................35
No opinion 9

National Trend*

	Israel	Arab nations	Neither	No opinion
Jan. 1982	49%	14%	23%	14%
1981	44	11	34	11
1979	40	14	31	15
1978	44	10	33	13
1975	44	8	22	26
1973	50	7	25	18
1970	44	3	32	21
1969	50	5	28	17
1967	56	4	25	15

*Percentages based on those who have heard or read about the Middle East situation.

Also asked of the aware group: As part of the Camp David agreements, Israel returned the Sinai territory to Egypt last week. Do you feel this will increase the chances for a lasting peace between Israel and the Arab nations, decrease the chances for peace, or won't it make much difference in relations between Israel and the Arab nations?

Increase chances 35%
Decrease chances. 9
No difference 47
No opinion 9

By Sex
Male

Increase chances 38%
Decrease chances. 10
No difference 47
No opinion 5

Female

Increase chances 33%
Decrease chances. 8
No difference 48
No opinion 11

By Race
White

Increase chances 34%
Decrease chances. 9
No difference 49
No opinion 8

Nonwhite

Increase chances 44%
Decrease chances. 8
No difference 35
No opinion 13

Black

Increase chances 43%
Decrease chances. 8
No difference 35
No opinion 14

By Education
College

Increase chances 40%
Decrease chances. 9
No difference 47
No opinion 4

High School

Increase chances 33%
Decrease chances. 9
No difference 49
No opinion 9

Grade School

Increase chances 32%
Decrease chances. 10
No difference 39
No opinion 19

By Politics
Republicans

Increase chances 41%
Decrease chances. 9
No difference 44
No opinion 6

Democrats

Increase chances 35%
Decrease chances. 10
No difference 44
No opinion 11

Independents

Increase chances 31%
Decrease chances. 9
No difference 54
No opinion 6

Note: Israel's April 25 withdrawal from the occupied Sinai Peninsula came at a time when there was greater American sympathy for the Jewish state than had existed for almost a decade. In the latest Gallup survey, 51% of Americans aware of the Middle East situation (81% of the total) said they sympathized more with Israel, 12% backed the Arab nations, and 26% took neither side. The last time there was a comparable level of American sympathy for Israel (54%) was in 1973 shortly after the Yom Kippur War.

Also, in the current survey 35% of the aware group expressed the view that Israel's return of the Sinai territory to Egypt would enhance the long-term chances for peace between Israel and the Arab nations. The weight of public opinion, however, was that this act of compliance with the Camp David accords would not have any appreciable effect on Arab-Israeli relations (47%), or that it would even decrease (9%) the prospects for peace in the region.

The American public's current assessment of the likely impact of Israel's withdrawal from the Sinai is strikingly similar to that recorded when the agreement was signed by Egypt and Israel three years ago. In March 1979, 32% of the informed public said they thought it would lead to peace between Israel and the Arab nations, while 56% held the opposite opinion.

Some observers have characterized Israel's return of the Sinai to Egypt as an easy first step in the far more difficult process of forging a lasting peace in the Middle East. Many problems remain to be solved, including the question of a homeland for the Palestinian Arabs and the disposition of Jerusalem and the Israeli-occupied West Bank and Gaza Strip. The depth and complexity of these still unresolved issues may partly account for Americans' skepticism about the long-term outlook for peace.

It is interesting to note that the current upsurge in sympathy for Israel has not been accompanied by a comparable downturn in pro-Arab sentiment. The 7-point increase in Israel's favor (from 44% last year to 51% today) is traceable to a sizable decrease (from 34% to 26%) in the proportion unwilling to take either side.

MAY 30
PRESIDENT REAGAN

Interviewing Date: 4/30–5/3/82
Survey #194-G

Do you approve or disapprove of the way Ronald Reagan is handling his job as president?

Approve. 44%
Disapprove 46
No opinion 10

By Politics
Republicans

Approve. 81%
Disapprove 14
No opinion 5

Democrats

Approve. 24%
Disapprove 67
No opinion 9

Independents

Approve. 45%
Disapprove 42
No opinion 13

Now let me ask you about specific foreign and domestic problems. As I read off each problem, one at a time, would you tell me whether you approve or disapprove of the way President Reagan is handling that problem:

Economic conditions in this country?

Approve. 37%
Disapprove 55
No opinion 8

By Politics
Republicans

Approve. 72%
Disapprove 21
No opinion 7

Democrats

Approve. 17%
Disapprove 76
No opinion 7

Independents

Approve. 38%
Disapprove 54
No opinion 8

Inflation?

Approve........................... 36%
Disapprove 57
No opinion 7

By Politics
Republicans

Approve........................... 67%
Disapprove 26
No opinion 7

Democrats

Approve........................... 19%
Disapprove 75
No opinion 6

Independents

Approve........................... 36%
Disapprove 58
No opinion 6

Unemployment?

Approve........................... 23%
Disapprove 67
No opinion 10

By Politics
Republicans

Approve........................... 51%
Disapprove 38
No opinion 11

Democrats

Approve........................... 9%
Disapprove 84
No opinion 7

Independents

Approve........................... 23%
Disapprove 67
No opinion 10

National defense?

Approve........................... 49%
Disapprove 38
No opinion 13

By Politics
Republicans

Approve........................... 68%
Disapprove 25
No opinion 7

Democrats

Approve........................... 38%
Disapprove 47
No opinion 15

Independents

Approve........................... 51%
Disapprove 36
No opinion 13

Foreign policy?

Approve........................... 42%
Disapprove 38
No opinion 20

By Politics
Republicans

Approve........................... 65%
Disapprove 18
No opinion 17

Democrats

Approve........................... 32%
Disapprove 47
No opinion 21

Independents

Approve........................... 41%
Disapprove 39
No opinion 20

Relations with the Soviet Union?

Approve........................... 45%
Disapprove 32
No opinion 23

By Politics
Republicans

Approve............................65%
Disapprove........................17
No opinion........................18

Democrats

Approve............................34%
Disapprove........................42
No opinion........................24

Independents

Approve............................47%
Disapprove........................30
No opinion........................23

Note: To an unusual degree President Ronald Reagan must rely mainly on solid bedrock support from his own party members to uphold his leadership and the programs he is trying to put into place. For while he has intensely loyal Republican support, Reagan enjoys less backing from Democrats than did either of his two Republican predecessors, Gerald Ford and Richard Nixon, at comparable periods in their presidencies.

Reagan's standing with the American people has plummeted in the last year, from 67% approval last April to 44% today, a drop of 23 percentage points. Among Republican voters, however, Reagan's job performance rating slid merely 6 points, from 87% approval in 1981 to 81% at present. In the same period approval of Reagan's stewardship by Democrats and independents fell 28 and 24 points, respectively.

Reagan Job Approval Ratings

	April 1982	April 1981	Point change
Overall job performance			
National	44%	67%	−23
Republicans	81	87	− 6
Democrats	24	52	−28
Independents	45	69	−24

Economic conditions			
National	37%	60%	−23
Republicans	72	86	−14
Democrats	17	43	−26
Independents	38	61	−23

Inflation			
National	36%	58%	−22
Republicans	67	82	−15
Democrats	19	42	−23
Independents	23	43	−20

Unemployment			
National	23%	43%	−20
Republicans	51	62	−11
Democrats	9	30	−21
Independents	23	43	−20

National defense			
National	49%	64%*	−15
Republicans	68	83	−15
Democrats	38	54	−16
Independents	51	63	−12

Foreign policy			
National	43%	53%*	−10
Republicans	65	74	− 9
Democrats	32	40	− 8
Independents	41	51	−10

Relations with Soviet Union			
National	45%	56%	−11
Republicans	65	72	− 7
Democrats	34	49	−15
Independents	47	53	− 6

*March 1981

Examination of the records of President Reagan's three immediate predecessors at comparable points in their administrations reveals Reagan's political support to be much less broadly based—more restricted to members of his own party with less rival party backing—than were the bases of Presidents Carter, Ford, and Nixon. The main drawback to Reagan's narrow support base lies in the numerical minority of Republican party members. In the current survey, 26% of respondents claim affiliation with the Republican party, while 45% say they are Democrats and 29%, independents.

Presidential Approval Ratings After Fifteen Months in Office

Ronald Reagan
(April–May 1982)

National 44%
    Republicans 81
    Democrats 24
    Independents 45

Jimmy Carter
(April–May 1978)

National 41%
    Republicans 21
    Democrats 56
    Independents 35

Gerald Ford
(November 1975)

National 41%
    Republicans 60
    Democrats 30
    Independents 42

Richard Nixon
(April 1970)

National 56%
    Republicans 80
    Democrats 42
    Independents 56

President Reagan's fellow Republicans also are more steadfast in their assessment of his handling of specific problems. As shown in the table below, there has been far less GOP defection in the past year than there has been by Democrats and independents. The loss of approval has been particularly acute on the president's handling of the economy in general and, specifically, on inflation and unemployment. The declines in approval of Reagan's handling of foreign policy, national defense, and U.S. relations with the Soviet Union have been less

severe, and in the case of the first two, have occurred about equally among Republicans, Democrats, and independents.

JUNE 3
SATISFACTION INDEX

Interviewing Date: 4/2–5/82
Survey #192-G

In general, are you satisfied or dissatisfied with the way things are going in the United States at this time?

Satisfied............................ 25%
Dissatisfied 71
No opinion 4

By Sex
Male

Satisfied............................ 27%
Dissatisfied 70
No opinion 3

Female

Satisfied............................ 22%
Dissatisfied 73
No opinion 5

By Race
White

Satisfied............................ 28%
Dissatisfied 68
No opinion 4

Nonwhite

Satisfied............................ 8%
Dissatisfied 87
No opinion 5

Black

Satisfied............................ 5%
Dissatisfied 89
No opinion 6

By Education
College

Satisfied 33%
Dissatisfied 65
No opinion 2

High School

Satisfied 23%
Dissatisfied 73
No opinion 4

Grade School

Satisfied 13%
Dissatisfied 81
No opinion 6

By Income
$25,000 and Over

Satisfied 30%
Dissatisfied 67
No opinion 3

$15,000 and Over

Satisfied 29%
Dissatisfied 68
No opinion 3

Under $15,000

Satisfied 20%
Dissatisfied 75
No opinion 5

National Trend

	Satisfied	Dis-satisfied	No opinion
December 1981	27%	67%	6%
June 1981	33	61	6
January 1981	17	78	5
July 1979	12	84	4
February 1979	26	69	5

In general, are you satisfied or dissatisfied with the way things are going in your own personal life?

Satisfied 76%
Dissatisfied 22
No opinion 2

By Sex
Male

Satisfied 78%
Dissatisfied 20
No opinion 2

Female

Satisfied 74%
Dissatisfied 23
No opinion 3

By Race
White

Satisfied 80%
Dissatisfied 18
No opinion 2

Nonwhite

Satisfied 52%
Dissatisfied 44
No opinion 4

Black

Satisfied 49%
Dissatisfied 47
No opinion 4

By Education
College

Satisfied 85%
Dissatisfied 14
No opinion 1

High School

Satisfied 72%
Dissatisfied 25
No opinion 3

Grade School

Satisfied	70%
Dissatisfied	26
No opinion	4

By Income
$20,000 and Over

Satisfied	87%
Dissatisfied	11
No opinion	2

$15,000 and Over

Satisfied	85%
Dissatisfied	14
No opinion	1

Under $15,000

Satisfied	65%
Dissatisfied	31
No opinion	4

National Trend

	Satisfied	Dis-satisfied	No opinion
December 1981	81%	17%	2%
June 1981	81	16	3
January 1981	81	17	2
July 1979	73	23	4
February 1979	77	21	2

Note: The mood of the American people is considerably less optimistic than it was a year ago, with fewer now than last June expressing satisfaction with the state of the nation and with their personal lives. In a recent Gallup survey, 25% of persons interviewed said they were satisfied with the way things are going in the United States, about the same as the 27% recorded last December but 8 percentage points below the peak assessment of 33% last June. In that survey, 61% expressed dissatisfaction with the state of the nation; today the figure is 71%.

A decline in the proportion who are satisfied with the way things are going in the country is found in every major population group, but the sharpest drop has occurred among blacks. In the latest survey, only 5% of blacks say they are satisfied with the national status quo, down by two-thirds from the 15% recorded in June 1981. There is ample evidence that satisfaction with the state of the nation is related to material well-being. In the current study the greatest degree of satisfaction is expressed by the college educated, whites, persons from upper-income families, and those employed in business and the professions.

Although only one-fourth of Americans say they are satisfied with the nation, three in four (76%) express satisfaction with their personal lives, down from the 81% who felt this way a year ago. Among whites the satisfaction figure is 80%; among blacks it is 49%. In the June 1981 survey the comparable figures for whites and blacks were 84% and 59%, representing a ten-point loss of satisfaction on the part of blacks, compared to 4 points for whites on an absolute basis, and a far greater proportional decline for blacks.

JUNE 6
PRESIDENT REAGAN

Interviewing Date: 5/14–17/82
Survey #195-G

> *Here is a list of terms—shown as pairs of opposites—that have been used to describe Ronald Reagan. From each pair of opposites, would you select the term which you feel best describes Reagan?*

Reagan's Perceived Personal Characteristics

Bright, intelligent	70%
Not too bright	22
No opinion	8

Likable person	65%
Not likable	26
No opinion	9

High moral principles	69%
Not moral	21
No opinion	10

Displays good judgment in crisis 54%
Might panic in crisis 21
No opinion 25

Strong leadership qualities 60%
Lacks strong leadership qualities 31
No opinion 9

Religious person 51%
Not religious 35
No opinion 14

Reagan's Perceived Job-Related Characteristics

Can get job done 56%
Cannot get job done 33
No opinion 11

Has clear understanding of issues 46%
Does not understand issues 45
No opinion 9

Has well thought out solutions to
  national problems 40%
Has simple solutions to national
  problems 48
No opinion 12

Has modern, up-to-date solutions to
  national problems 36%
Has old-fashioned solutions to
  national problems 51
No opinion 13

Reagan's Perceived Concern for Needs and Problems of Different Population Groups

Upper-income, wealthy people
  Cares 75%
  Does not care 14
  No opinion 11

Middle-income people
  Cares 41%
  Does not care 49
  No opinion 10

Poor people
  Cares 34%
  Does not care 65
  No opinion 11

Women
  Cares 42%
  Does not care 42
  No opinion 16

Elderly
  Cares 41%
  Does not care 48
  No opinion 11

Blacks
  Cares 37%
  Does not care 50
  No opinion 13

Average citizen
  Cares 28%
  Does not care 61
  No opinion 11

People like yourself
  Cares 39%
  Does not care 51
  No opinion 10

Note: During a two-year period in which President Ronald Reagan has been in the forefront of the American political scene, most of the positive personal attributes that made him an attractive candidate have been reinforced. On the other hand, far fewer Americans now say Reagan is sympathetic to the problems of the poor or that he sides with the average citizen.

Comparison of the latest Gallup survey with a June 1980 study shows that President Reagan rates higher than candidate Reagan in the public's perception of him as bright and intelligent, likable, a man of high moral principles, a religious person, and as having strong leadership abilities. At the same time, however, there has been a 15 percentage-point drop in the proportion of Americans who believe Reagan sides with the average citizen, from 43% in 1980 to 28% today, and a decline from 41% to 34% in those who think he is sympathetic to poor people's problems.

In characteristics measured for the first time in the new survey, Reagan does best as the kind of person who can get the job done, while roughly equal proportions think he has or does not have a clear understanding of the issues facing the country. He fares less well, with negative public attitudes outweighing positive, as having well thought out and modern, up-to-date solutions to national problems.

In terms of caring about the needs and problems of different population groups, President Reagan is thought by a majority of the public to favor upper-income or wealthy people. Attitudes are predominantly negative about Reagan's caring for middle income, poor people, the elderly, or blacks. Those who say the president cares about women's problems and needs are equal in number to those who think he does not.

On two dichotomies where neither side clearly can be considered positive or negative, 40% of the public said Reagan was adaptable and willing to compromise on his positions, while 47% claimed he was inflexible and unwilling to compromise. Similarly, the beliefs that Reagan takes moderate, middle-of-the-road positions and that he is an extremist each received the vote of 43%.

JUNE 10
PRAYER IN PUBLIC SCHOOLS

Interviewing Date: 5/14–17/82
Survey #195-G

Have you heard or read about a proposed amendment to the U.S. Constitution that would allow voluntary prayer in public schools?

Yes................................ 82%
No................................. 18

Asked of those who replied in the affirmative: What would you say are the arguments in favor of such an amendment?

People should have the opportunity to
pray when they wish to do so 23%
It is a good idea; no reason to be
against it........................... 13
A good idea, if voluntary; should
not be forced 12
Prayer is a good thing; can do no harm... 11
Would improve morals, teach values,
increase respect for teachers, build
character.......................... 11
One way for children to get religion if
they do not get it at home........... 7
The United States was founded on the
basis of a belief in God............. 4
Schools used to have prayers in the past ... 4
Other responses 6
None; no opinion 18
109%*

*Total adds to more than 100% due to multiple responses.

Also asked of those who heard or read about the proposed prayer amendment: And what would you say are the arguments against such an amendment?

Constitutional reasons; separation of
church and state 14%
Concern that such an amendment could
lead to mandatory or required prayer... 14
Concern that such an amendment might
lead to one religion being forced on
persons of different religions 12
Concern that such an amendment would
offend people who are atheists 10
Other responses 5
None; no opinion 48
103%*

*Total adds to more than 100% due to multiple responses.

The 75% of the sample who both heard or read about the amendment and were able to offer arguments pro and con were then asked: Do you favor or oppose this proposed amendment?

Favor............................79%
Oppose...........................16
No opinion 5

By Sex
Male

Favor............................76%
Oppose...........................19
No opinion 5

Female

Favor............................81%
Oppose...........................13
No opinion 6

By Race
White

Favor............................79%
Oppose...........................16
No opinion 5

Nonwhite

Favor............................78%
Oppose...........................15
No opinion 7

By Education
College

Favor............................68%
Oppose...........................26
No opinion 6

High School

Favor............................84%
Oppose...........................10
No opinion 6

Grade School

Favor............................87%
Oppose...........................11
No opinion 2

By Age
18–29 Years

Favor............................71%
Oppose...........................19
No opinion 10

30–49 Years

Favor............................81%
Oppose...........................14
No opinion 5

50–64 Years

Favor............................81%
Oppose...........................16
No opinion 3

65 Years and Over

Favor............................84%
Oppose...........................13
No opinion 3

By Religion
Protestants

Favor............................82%
Oppose...........................13
No opinion 5

Catholics

Favor............................82%
Oppose...........................11
No opinion 7

Church Members

Favor............................83%
Oppose...........................13
No opinion 4

Nonchurch Members

Favor............................68%
Oppose...........................24
No opinion 8

Attend Church Regularly

Favor 86%
Oppose. 9
No opinion 5

Do Not Attend Church Regularly

Favor 73%
Oppose. 21
No opinion 6

Asked of the entire sample: Which one of the following do you think is the most important in the religious and spiritual development of a child—the home, school, or the church?

Home. 86%
School 2
Church 10
No opinion 2

By Sex
Male

Home. 85%
School 3
Church 10
No opinion 2

Female

Home. 87%
School 2
Church 9
No opinion 2

By Race
White

Home. 88%
School 2
Church 9
No opinion 1

Nonwhite

Home. 78%
School 5
Church 13
No opinion 4

By Education
College

Home. 90%
School 3
Church 6
No opinion 1

High School

Home. 86%
School 1
Church 12
No opinion 1

Grade School

Home. 81%
School 6
Church 9
No opinion 4

By Age
18–29 Years

Home. 81%
School 3
Church 15
No opinion 1

30–49 Years

Home. 89%
School 3
Church 6
No opinion 2

50–64 Years

Home. 89%
School 2
Church 8
No opinion 1

65 Years and Over

Home. 87%
School 2
Church 8
No opinion 3

By Religion

Protestants

Home	85%
School	2
Church	11
No opinion	2

Catholics

Home	88%
School	3
Church	7
No opinion	2

Church Members

Home	87%
School	2
Church	9
No opinion	2

Nonchurch Members

Home	85%
School	2
Church	11
No opinion	2

Attend Church Regularly

Home	88%
School	2
Church	9
No opinion	1

Do Not Attend Church Regularly

Home	86%
School	3
Church	9
No opinion	2

Note: Americans who have followed the pros and cons of the debate over prayer in public schools come down heavily in favor of President Ronald Reagan's recent proposal for a constitutional amendment permitting voluntary group prayer in public schools. Nationally, the vote is 79% in favor, with 16% opposed. Majority support is found in every region of the nation and among all major population groups as well as among both church members and nonmembers.

Although the public overwhelmingly favors permitting voluntary prayer in schools, the prevailing opinion among all groups and faiths is that the home is more important than either the church or schools in the religious training of children. Currently, 86% say the home is most important in the religious and spiritual development of a child, while 10% name the church and only 2% the schools. This view has gained in popularity since a 1979 survey, when 75% said the home, 16% the church, and 3% the schools.

President Reagan recently proposed a constitutional amendment permitting organized prayer in public schools. (Organized group prayer in public schools effectively came to an end in 1962 after the U.S. Supreme Court ruled it was not permissible under the First Amendment.) The president's proposed amendment states that "nothing in this Constitution shall be construed to prohibit individual or group prayer in public schools or other public institutions. No person shall be required by the United States or by any state to participate in prayer." The congressional outlook for this amendment is unclear. Congress has rejected such proposed amendments several times over the past twenty years since the Court's decision.

Some religious-oriented groups oppose the amendment because they believe that it is impossible to devise a meaningful prayer acceptable to all groups. They also argue that religion should remain in the domain of the family and churches. Other groups opposed to prayer in public schools express concern that, in allowing voluntary prayer, some states might be led to require children to participate in prayer, which might offend children and parents who prefer private prayer.

JUNE 13
BALANCED BUDGET AMENDMENT

Interviewing Date: 5/14–17/82
Survey #195-G

Have you heard or read about the proposal for a constitutional amendment which would require the federal government to balance the national budget each year?

Yes.................................66%
No..................................34

Asked of those who replied in the affirmative: A proposed amendment to the Constitution would require Congress to approve a balanced federal budget each year. Government spending would have to be limited to no more than expected revenues, unless a three-fifths majority of Congress voted to spend more than expected revenue. Would you favor or oppose this amendment to the Constitution?

Favor...............................74%
Oppose..............................17
No opinion 9

By Sex
Male

Favor...............................76%
Oppose..............................19
No opinion 5

Female

Favor...............................72%
Oppose..............................16
No opinion 12

By Race
White

Favor...............................76%
Oppose..............................17
No opinion 7

Nonwhite

Favor...............................59%
Oppose..............................24
No opinion 17

By Education
College

Favor...............................75%
Oppose..............................19
No opinion 6

High School

Favor...............................74%
Oppose..............................15
No opinion 11

Grade School

Favor...............................70%
Oppose..............................23
No opinion 7

By Age
18–29 Years

Favor...............................73%
Oppose..............................19
No opinion 8

30–49 Years

Favor...............................76%
Oppose..............................17
No opinion 7

50–64 Years

Favor...............................77%
Oppose..............................14
No opinion 9

65 Years and Over

Favor...............................65%
Oppose..............................22
No opinion 13

By Income
$25,000 and Over

Favor...............................78%
Oppose..............................17
No opinion 5

$15,000 and Over

Favor...............................78%
Oppose..............................16
No opinion 6

Under $15,000

Favor.............................66%
Oppose............................20
No opinion 14

By Politics
Republicans

Favor.............................83%
Oppose............................12
No opinion 5

Democrats

Favor.............................67%
Oppose............................21
No opinion 12

Independents

Favor.............................76%
Oppose............................18
No opinion 6

Those Who Approve of Reagan

Favor.............................81%
Oppose............................14
No opinion 5

Those Who Disapprove of Reagan

Favor.............................66%
Oppose............................22
No opinion 12

Asked of the entire sample: Which of these do you favor as ways of reducing the federal budget deficit:

Reduce military spending?

Favor.............................43%
Oppose............................47
No opinion 10

By Politics
Republicans

Favor.............................36%
Oppose............................57
No opinion 7

Democrats

Favor.............................44%
Oppose............................43
No opinion 13

Independents

Favor.............................48%
Oppose............................46
No opinion 6

Those Who Approve of Reagan

Favor.............................35%
Oppose............................57
No opinion 8

Those Who Disapprove of Reagan

Favor.............................52%
Oppose............................36
No opinion 12

Reduce spending for social programs?

Favor.............................40%
Oppose............................51
No opinion 9

By Politics
Republicans

Favor.............................59%
Oppose............................34
No opinion 7

Democrats

Favor.............................30%
Oppose............................59
No opinion 11

Independents

Favor.............................41%
Oppose............................53
No opinion 5

Those Who Approve of Reagan

Favor.............................57%
Oppose............................37
No opinion 6

Those Who Disapprove of Reagan

Favor 25%
Oppose 64
No opinion 11

Postpone the tax cuts scheduled for this year and next year?

Favor 44%
Oppose 41
No opinion 15

By Politics
Republicans

Favor 40%
Oppose 47
No opinion 13

Democrats

Favor 44%
Oppose 41
No opinion 15

Independents

Favor 48%
Oppose 40
No opinion 12

Those Who Approve of Reagan

Favor 42%
Oppose 45
No opinion 13

Those Who Disapprove of Reagan

Favor 45%
Oppose 38
No opinion 17

Increase the tax on gasoline?

Favor 19%
Oppose 73
No opinion 8

By Politics
Republicans

Favor 22%
Oppose 70
No opinion 8

Democrats

Favor 17%
Oppose 74
No opinion 9

Independents

Favor 18%
Oppose 78
No opinion 4

Those Who Approve of Reagan

Favor 21%
Oppose 72
No opinion 7

Those Who Disapprove of Reagan

Favor 19%
Oppose 74
No opinion 7

Increase the tax on cigarettes and liquor?

Favor 70%
Oppose 23
No opinion 7

By Politics
Republicans

Favor 76%
Oppose 18
No opinion 6

Democrats

Favor 67%
Oppose 27
No opinion 6

Independents

Favor 73%
Oppose 22
No opinion 5

Those Who Approve of Reagan

Favor 74%
Oppose 19
No opinion 7

Those Who Disapprove of Reagan

Favor 64%
Oppose 28
No opinion 8

Note: While Congress tosses around the unresolved 1983 federal budget, the electorate is unequivocal in its support for an amendment to the U.S. Constitution that would mandate a balanced federal budget each year. In the latest Gallup survey, 74% of Americans who are familiar with the proposal favor a constitutional amendment requiring Congress to spend no more than expected revenues unless overridden by a three-fifths majority of its members. Opposition to the amendment is expressed by only one person in six (17%).

The survey, conducted two weeks after President Ronald Reagan announced his backing for such an amendment, finds majority support in every population group including Democrats. Republicans vote for the proposal by an overwhelming 7-to-1 margin.

President Reagan undoubtedly expressed the mood of the electorate when he said, in urging the enactment of a balanced budget amendment, "government will have to do what each of us does with our own family budgets—spend no more than we can afford." The president added that "only a constitutional amendment will do the trick. We've tried the carrot and it failed. With the stick of a balanced budget amendment, we can stop government's squandering, overtaxing ways and save our economy."

Increasing taxes on cigarettes and liquor is the choice of 70% of the public as a way of reducing the prospective budget deficit, followed by postponing the tax cuts scheduled for this year and next year (44%), decreasing military spending (43%), and reducing spending for social programs (40%). Little backing is found for increased taxes on gasoline, favored by only 19%.

There is a strong political cast to the relative appeal of these deficit-reducing measures, with further cuts in social programs far more palatable to Republicans (59%) than to Democrats (30%). On the other hand, cuts in defense spending are more attractive to Democrats (44%) than to Republicans (36%).

JUNE 17
KEY REAGAN ADVISERS

Interviewing Date: 4/30–5/3/82
Survey #194-G

You will note that the ten boxes on this scale go from the highest position of +5 for someone you have a very favorable opinion of all the way down to the lowest position of −5 for someone you have a very unfavorable opinion of. How far up or down the scale would you rate the following people:

Vice-President George Bush?

Highly favorable (+5, +4) 14%
Mildly favorable (+3, +2, +1) 54
Mildly unfavorable (−1, −2, −3) 14
Highly unfavorable (−4, −5) 10
No opinion; unable to rate 8

By Education
College

Highly favorable (+5, +4) 13%
Mildly favorable (+3, +2, +1) 61
Mildly unfavorable (−1, −2, −3) 15
Highly unfavorable (−4, −5) 6
No opinion; unable to rate 5

*It is important to keep in mind that these percentages reflect personal and not job performance ratings for each man.

High School

Highly favorable (+5, +4)............13%
Mildly favorable (+3, +2, +1)........52
Mildly unfavorable (−1, −2, −3).......15
Highly unfavorable (−4, −5)...........11
No opinion; unable to rate 9

Grade School

Highly favorable (+5, +4)............15%
Mildly favorable (+3, +2, +1)........48
Mildly unfavorable (−1, −2, −3)......13
Highly unfavorable (−4, −5)...........13
No opinion; unable to rate 11

By Politics
Republicans

Highly favorable (+5, +4)............25%
Mildly favorable (+3, +2, +1)........62
Mildly unfavorable (−1, −2, −3).......5
Highly unfavorable (−4, −5)........... 1
No opinion; unable to rate 7

Democrats

Highly favorable (+5, +4)............ 9%
Mildly favorable (+3, +2, +1)........46
Mildly unfavorable (−1, −2, −3).......22
Highly unfavorable (−4, −5)...........16
No opinion; unable to rate 7

Independents

Highly favorable (+5, +4)............13%
Mildly favorable (+3, +2, +1)........59
Mildly unfavorable (−1, −2, −3)......11
Highly unfavorable (−4, −5)........... 8
No opinion; unable to rate 9

Secretary of Defense Caspar Weinberger?

Highly favorable (+5, +4)............11%
Mildly favorable (+3, +2, +1)........51
Mildly unfavorable (−1, −2, −3).......16
Highly unfavorable (−4, −5)........... 6
No opinion; unable to rate 16

By Education
College

Highly favorable (+5, +4)............. 9%
Mildly favorable (+3, +2, +1)........55
Mildly unfavorable (−1, −2, −3).......18
Highly unfavorable (−4, −5)........... 9
No opinion; unable to rate 9

High School

Highly favorable (+5, +4).............10%
Mildly favorable (+3, +2, +1)........51
Mildly unfavorable (−1, −2, −3)......18
Highly unfavorable (−4, −5)........... 6
No opinion; unable to rate 15

Grade School

Highly favorable (+5, +4).............19%
Mildly favorable (+3, +2, +1)........40
Mildly unfavorable (−1, −2, −3)....... 7
Highly unfavorable (−4, −5)........... 4
No opinion; unable to rate 30

By Politics
Republicans

Highly favorable (+5, +4).............19%
Mildly favorable (+3, +2, +1)........61
Mildly unfavorable (−1, −2, −3)...... 8
Highly unfavorable (−4, −5)........... 1
No opinion; unable to rate 11

Democrats

Highly favorable (+5, +4)............. 9%
Mildly favorable (+3, +2, +1)........43
Mildly unfavorable (−1, −2, −3)......19
Highly unfavorable (−4, −5)........... 9
No opinion; unable to rate 20

Independents

Highly favorable (+5, +4)............. 8%
Mildly favorable (+3, +2, +1)........54
Mildly unfavorable (−1, −2, −3)......18
Highly unfavorable (−4, −5)........... 6
No opinion; unable to rate 14

Secretary of the Treasury Donald Regan?

Highly favorable (+5, +4)............. 9%
Mildly favorable (+3, +2, +1)........ 50
Mildly unfavorable (−1, −2, −3)...... 15
Highly unfavorable (−4, −5).......... 8
No opinion; unable to rate 18

By Education
College

Highly favorable (+5, +4)............. 8%
Mildly favorable (+3, +2, +1)........ 56
Mildly unfavorable (−1, −2, −3)...... 17
Highly unfavorable (−4, −5).......... 6
No opinion; unable to rate 13

High School

Highly favorable (+5, +4)............. 10%
Mildly favorable (+3, +2, +1)........ 49
Mildly unfavorable (−1, −2, −3)...... 15
Highly unfavorable (−4, −5).......... 9
No opinion; unable to rate 17

Grade School

Highly favorable (+5, +4)............. 12%
Mildly favorable (+3, +2, +1)........ 37
Mildly unfavorable (−1, −2, −3)...... 12
Highly unfavorable (−4, −5).......... 7
No opinion; unable to rate 30

By Politics
Republicans

Highly favorable (+5, +4)............. 19%
Mildly favorable (+3, +2, +1)........ 61
Mildly unfavorable (−1, −2, −3)...... 5
Highly unfavorable (−4, −5).......... 2
No opinion; unable to rate 13

Democrats

Highly favorable (+5, +4)............. 7%
Mildly favorable (+3, +2, +1)........ 42
Mildly unfavorable (−1, −2, −3)...... 21
Highly unfavorable (−4, −5).......... 12
No opinion; unable to rate 18

Independents

Highly favorable (+5, +4)............. 7%
Mildly favorable (+3, +2, +1)........ 51
Mildly unfavorable (−1, −2, −3)...... 16
Highly unfavorable (−4, −5).......... 8
No opinion; unable to rate 18

Secretary of State Alexander Haig?

Highly favorable (+5, +4)............. 19%
Mildly favorable (+3, +2, +1)........ 44
Mildly unfavorable (−1, −2, −3)...... 17
Highly unfavorable (−4, −5).......... 13
No opinion; unable to rate 7

By Education
College

Highly favorable (+5, +4)............. 16%
Mildly favorable (+3, +2, +1)........ 48
Mildly unfavorable (−1, −2, −3)...... 19
Highly unfavorable (−4, −5).......... 13
No opinion; unable to rate 4

High School

Highly favorable (+5, +4)............. 18%
Mildly favorable (+3, +2, +1)........ 44
Mildly unfavorable (−1, −2, −3)...... 18
Highly unfavorable (−4, −5).......... 12
No opinion; unable to rate 8

Grade School

Highly favorable (+5, +4)............. 25%
Mildly favorable (+3, +2, +1)........ 41
Mildly unfavorable (−1, −2, −3)...... 10
Highly unfavorable (−4, −5).......... 11
No opinion; unable to rate 13

By Politics
Republicans

Highly favorable (+5, +4)............. 26%
Mildly favorable (+3, +2, +1)........ 53
Mildly unfavorable (−1, −2, −3)...... 12
Highly unfavorable (−4, −5).......... 5
No opinion; unable to rate 4

Democrats

Highly favorable (+5, +4)............ 16%
Mildly favorable (+3, +2, +1)........ 40
Mildly unfavorable (−1, −2, −3)...... 20
Highly unfavorable (−4, −5).......... 17
No opinion; unable to rate 7

Independents

Highly favorable (+5, +4)............ 18%
Mildly favorable (+3, +2, +1)........ 45
Mildly unfavorable (−1, −2, −3)...... 18
Highly unfavorable (−4, −5).......... 13
No opinion; unable to rate 6

Secretary of the Interior James Watt?

Highly favorable (+5, +4)............ 7%
Mildly favorable (+3, +2, +1)........ 42
Mildly unfavorable (−1, −2, −3)...... 15
Highly unfavorable (−4, −5).......... 15
No opinion; unable to rate 21

By Education
College

Highly favorable (+5, +4)............ 5%
Mildly favorable (+3, +2, +1)........ 41
Mildly unfavorable (−1, −2, −3)...... 19
Highly unfavorable (−4, −5).......... 23
No opinion; unable to rate 12

High School

Highly favorable (+5, +4)............ 7%
Mildly favorable (+3, +2, +1)........ 37
Mildly unfavorable (−1, −2, −3)...... 7
Highly unfavorable (−4, −5).......... 12
No opinion; unable to rate 37

Grade School

Highly favorable (+5, +4)............ 7%
Mildly favorable (+3, +2, +1)........ 37
Mildly unfavorable (−1, −2, −3)...... 7
Highly unfavorable (−4, −5).......... 12
No opinion; unable to rate 37

By Politics
Republicans

Highly favorable (+5, +4)............ 11%
Mildly favorable (+3, +2, +1)........ 57
Mildly unfavorable (−1, −2, −3)...... 13
Highly unfavorable (−4, −5).......... 7
No opinion; unable to rate 12

Democrats

Highly favorable (+5, +4)............ 5%
Mildly favorable (+3, +2, +1)........ 36
Mildly unfavorable (−1, −2, −3)...... 17
Highly unfavorable (−4, −5).......... 18
No opinion; unable to rate 24

Independents

Highly favorable (+5, +4)............ 5%
Mildly favorable (+3, +2, +1)........ 42
Mildly unfavorable (−1, −2, −3)...... 16
Highly unfavorable (−4, −5).......... 19
No opinion; unable to rate 18

Note: Voters in this fall's congressional elections will be basing their decision not only on party loyalty and issues but also on their opinion of key people in President Ronald Reagan's cabinet.

In a recent Gallup survey, a cross-section of adults, eighteen and older, were asked whether they have a favorable or unfavorable opinion of the members of the cabinet who have figured prominently in the news in recent months. The poll also sought to determine the percentage of persons surveyed who state they know each of the men tested well enough to offer a rating. The table below shows the respondents' awareness levels for each of the following presidential cabinet members:

Know Enough About Person To Rate Him

Haig.................................. 93%
Bush.................................. 92
Weinberger 84
Regan................................. 82
Watt.................................. 79

JUNE 20
CONGRESSIONAL ELECTIONS

Interviewing Date: 4/30–5/3; 5/14–17/82
Survey #194-G, #195-G

*Asked of registered voters: If the elections for Congress were being held today, which party would you like to see win this congressional district, the Democratic party or the Republican party? [Those who said they were undecided or who named a different party were asked: As of today, do you lean more to the Republican party or to the Democratic party?]**

Republican 38%
Democratic 53
Other; undecided 9

By Sex
Male

Republican 41%
Democratic 50
Other; undecided 9

Female

Republican 35%
Democratic 56
Other; undecided 9

By Race
White

Republican 43%
Democratic 48
Other; undecided 9

*These findings are based on two successive in-person surveys with 3,141 adults, of whom 2,282 are registered voters eighteen years and older. For results based on a combined sample of this size, one can say with 95% confidence that the error attributable to sampling and other random effects could be 2 percentage points in either direction.

Nonwhite

Republican 7%
Democratic 87
Other; undecided 6

By Education
College

Republican 49%
Democratic 42
Other; undecided 9

High School

Republican 35%
Democratic 56
Other; undecided 9

Grade School

Republican 23%
Democratic 68
Other; undecided 9

By Region
East

Republican 35%
Democratic 56
Other; undecided 9

Midwest

Republican 40%
Democratic 50
Other; undecided 10

South

Republican 36%
Democratic 59
Other; undecided 5

West

Republican 41%
Democratic 45
Other; undecided 14

By Age

18–24 Years

Republican 37%
Democratic 55
Other; undecided 8

25–29 Years

Republican 44%
Democratic 45
Other; undecided 11

30–49 Years

Republican 36%
Democratic 54
Other; undecided 10

50 Years and Over

Republican 39%
Democratic 54
Other; undecided 7

By Income

$15,000 and Over

Republican 44%
Democratic 47
Other; undecided 9

Under $15,000

Republican 28%
Democratic 63
Other; undecided 9

By Politics

Republicans

Republican 90%
Democratic 6
Other; undecided 4

Democrats

Republican 7%
Democratic 90
Other; undecided 3

Southern Democrats Only

Republican 8%
Democratic 89
Other; undecided 3

Northern Democrats Only

Republican 7%
Democratic 90
Other; undecided 3

Independents

Republican 37%
Democratic 40
Other; undecided 23

By Religion

Protestants

Republican 41%
Democratic 51
Other; undecided 8

Catholics

Republican 33%
Democratic 59
Other; undecided 8

By Occupation

Professional and Business

Republican 48%
Democratic 42
Other; undecided 10

Clerical and Sales

Republican 41%
Democratic 51
Other; undecided 8

Manual Labor

Republican 32%
Democratic 60
Other; undecided 8

Skilled Labor Only

Republican 36%
Democratic 56
Other; undecided 8

Unskilled Labor Only

Republican 27%
Democratic 65
Other; undecided 8

Labor Union Households Only

Republican 27%
Democratic 62
Other; undecided 11

Nonunion Households Only

Republican 41%
Democratic 51
Other; undecided 8

On a two-way basis, the current figures are 58% Democratic and 42% Republican. By way of comparison, the following is the division of the vote for Congress in May of each congressional year since 1958:

National Trend Toward Congressional Election Preferences

	Republican	Democratic
1982	42%	58%
1978	41	59
1974	36	64
1970	41	59
1966	47	53
1962	42	58
1958	42	58

Note: With the congressional elections less than five months away, the Democratic party enjoys a lead of landslide proportions over the Republican party in the popular vote for seats in the House of Representatives. In the latest survey, the Democrats are the choice of 53% of registered voters to 38% of the Republicans. In the 1978 congressional elections, Democratic candidates won about 55% of the popular vote and the seat division was 276 for the Democrats and 157 for the Republicans.

While the current findings look anything but hopeful for the Republicans this fall in terms of the overall division of House seats, GOP strength has remained constant in recent weeks after a steady decline between June 1981 and April 1982. Significantly, this steadiness in GOP support in the congressional races parallels a leveling out in the downtrend in President Reagan's job performance rating.

At this point in time, however, the GOP appears headed for greater than normal seat losses for the party holding the White House, losses that have averaged about 30 seats in off-year elections during the last thirty-five years.

JUNE 24
HANDGUN LAWS

Interviewing Date: 4/2–5/82
Survey #192-G

Do you favor or oppose the registration of all handguns?

Favor 66%
Oppose 30
No opinion 4

By Sex
Male

Favor 63%
Oppose 34
No opinion 3

Female

Favor 69%
Oppose 26
No opinion 5

By Race
White

Favor 65%
Oppose 31
No opinion 4

Nonwhite

Favor 68%
Oppose 27
No opinion 5

By Education

College

Favor............................72%
Oppose...........................26
No opinion 2

High School

Favor............................64%
Oppose...........................32
No opinion 4

Grade School

Favor............................60%
Oppose...........................32
No opinion 8

By Region

East

Favor............................74%
Oppose...........................23
No opinion 3

Midwest

Favor............................67%
Oppose...........................30
No opinion 3

South

Favor............................59%
Oppose...........................35
No opinion 6

West

Favor............................64%
Oppose...........................32
No opinion 4

By Age

18–29 Years

Favor............................71%
Oppose...........................26
No opinion 3

30–49 Years

Favor............................65%
Oppose...........................31
No opinion 4

50 Years and Over

Favor............................63%
Oppose...........................32
No opinion 5

Interviewing Date: 4/3–6/81
Survey #171-G

In general, do you feel that the laws covering the sale of handguns should be made more strict, less strict, or kept as they are now?

More strict 65%
Less strict 3
Kept same 30
Don't know 2

Do you think there should or should not be a law which would forbid the possession of handguns except by the police or other authorized persons?

Should 39%
Should not.......................58
No opinion 3

Note: Californians will have the opportunity to vote this fall on a unique statewide ballot initiative that, if passed, would place stringent controls on the purchase and possession of handguns. The initiative would require the registration of handguns, prohibit their sale through the mails, mandate a six-month jail sentence for anyone carrying an unregistered handgun, and restrict the future sale of this type of weapon to law enforcement personnel.

Each year in this country, 20,000 Americans are killed by handguns. It has been estimated that someone is murdered with a handgun in the United States every fifty minutes. Advocates of stronger laws dealing with handguns point out that, during the seven peak years of the Vietnam War, 40,000 Americans were killed in combat, while during this same period 50,000 Americans were killed with handguns on the domestic front.

Those who oppose a ban on handguns believe such a move would violate their constitutional rights and that a prohibition would not reduce the number of crimes committed, because a person who will violate laws against rape, robbery, or murder will not obey a gun law. Supporters of a ban, however, counter that a large majority of the nation's gun victims (70% in some estimates) are shot not by burglars or other criminals but by people they know, who in a moment of passion or anger reach for a handgun rather than use some less deadly outlet for their aggression.

JUNE 27
MOST IMPORTANT PROBLEM

Interviewing Date: 6/11–14/82
Survey #196-G

What do you think is the most important problem facing this country today?

Unemployment; recession 41%*
Inflation; high cost of living 25
Economy (general). 11
High interest rates 10
Fear of war 10
Excessive government spending. 6
Reagan budget cuts 5
Moral decline in society 4
International problems 3
Crime. 3
All others. 8
Don't know 3
                                                    129%**

*Among all major population groups unemployment is cited more frequently than the high cost of living but is considered particularly urgent by women, blacks, those with a less formal education, persons thirty to forty-nine years old, Democrats, and residents of the East and Midwest.

**Toal adds to more than 100% due to multiple responses.

All persons who named a problem were then asked: Which political party do you think can do a better job of handling the problem you have just mentioned—the Republican party or the Democratic party?

Republican 28%
Democratic 35
No difference 25
No opinion 12

By Sex
Male

Republican 30%
Democratic 34
No difference 25
No opinion 11

Female

Republican 41%
Democratic 23
No difference 23
No opinion 13

By Race
White

Republican 32%
Democratic 31
No difference 25
No opinion 12

Black

Republican 62%
Democratic 6
No difference 18
No opinion 14

By Education
College

Republican 30%
Democratic 37
No difference 21
No opinion 12

High School

Republican 36%
Democratic 24
No difference 28
No opinion 12

Grade School

Republican 47%
Democratic 22
No difference 19
No opinion 12

By Region
East

Republican 37%
Democratic 24
No difference 27
No opinion 12

Midwest

Republican 34%
Democratic 27
No difference 28
No opinion 11

South

Republican 37%
Democratic 32
No difference 20
No opinion 11

West

Republican 33%
Democratic 29
No difference 22
No opinion 16

By Income
$20,000 and Over

Republican 28%
Democratic 35
No difference 25
No opinion 12

Under $20,000

Republican 41%
Democratic 23
No difference 23
No opinion 13

By Politics
Republicans

Republican 5%
Democratic 71
No difference 17
No opinion 7

Democrats

Republican 65%
Democratic 5
No difference 20
No opinion 10

Independents

Republican 21%
Democratic 24
No difference 37
No opinion 18

By political affiliation the following are the results of those citing unemployment and inflation as the nation's dominant concerns:

	Unemployment	Inflation	Other problems
Republican	23%	27%	28%
Democratic	40	37	35
No difference	24	25	25
No opinion	13	11	12

Note: With the congressional elements now less than five months away, substantially more Americans believe that the Democratic party rather than the Republican party can better deal with the nation's most urgent problems— unemployment and inflation. In the latest Gallup survey, 41% name unemployment as the most important issue facing the country, while 25% cite inflation or the high cost of living. These percentages are similar to those found in an April survey, when 44% named unemployment and 24% inflation as the most pressing problems.

The Democratic party now enjoys a 7 percentage-point advantage as the party voters see as better able to deal with the problem they consider uppermost, with 35% naming the Democrats, 28% the GOP, and 37% saying there is no difference between the parties or not expressing an opinion.

In January the Democratic party's lead was only 4 percentage points—34% to 30% for the Republican party. In that survey, as in the current one, the Democrats held a wide margin over the GOP as better able to handle the paramount problem of unemployment. However, in the earlier survey the Republican party (36%) was thought to be more qualified than the Democrats (31%) to deal with inflation, an advantage it no longer holds.

JULY 1
EQUAL RIGHTS AMENDMENT

Interviewing Date: 6/11–14/82
Survey #196-G

> *Have you heard or read about the Equal Rights Amendment to the U.S. Constitution which would prohibit discrimination on the basis of sex?*

Yes................................. 90%
No.................................. 10

> *Asked of those who responded in the affirmative: Do you favor or oppose this amendment?*

Favor............................. 56%
Oppose............................ 34
No opinion 10

By Sex
Male

Favor............................. 55%
Oppose............................ 36
No opinion 9

Female

Favor............................. 57%
Oppose............................ 33
No opinion 10

By Race
White

Favor............................. 54%
Oppose............................ 36
No opinion 10

Nonwhite

Favor............................. 77%
Oppose............................ 16
No opinion 7

By Education
College

Favor............................. 61%
Oppose............................ 32
No opinion 7

High School

Favor............................. 56%
Oppose............................ 34
No opinion 10

Grade School

Favor............................. 44%
Oppose............................ 42
No opinion 14

By Region
East

Favor............................. 67%
Oppose............................ 24
No opinion 9

Midwest

Favor............................. 52%
Oppose............................ 38
No opinion 10

South

Favor....................................51%
Oppose...................................40
No opinion 9

West

Favor....................................56%
Oppose...................................32
No opinion 12

By Age
18–24 Years

Favor....................................66%
Oppose...................................27
No opinion 7

25–29 Years

Favor....................................66%
Oppose...................................23
No opinion 11

30–49 Years

Favor....................................56%
Oppose...................................35
No opinion 9

50–64 Years

Favor....................................51%
Oppose...................................39
No opinion 10

65 Years and Over

Favor....................................45%
Oppose...................................41
No opinion 14

By Income
$25,000 and Over

Favor....................................56%
Oppose...................................37
No opinion 7

$15,000 and Over

Favor....................................57%
Oppose...................................35
No opinion 8

Under $15,000

Favor....................................55%
Oppose...................................32
No opinion 13

By Politics
Republicans

Favor....................................44%
Oppose...................................46
No opinion 10

Democrats

Favor....................................64%
Oppose...................................27
No opinion 9

Independents

Favor....................................56%
Oppose...................................33
No opinion 11

By Religion
Protestants

Favor....................................53%
Oppose...................................36
No opinion 11

Catholics

Favor....................................58%
Oppose...................................36
No opinion 6

By Occupation
Professional and Business

Favor....................................62%
Oppose...................................31
No opinion 7

Clerical and Sales

Favor............................63%
Oppose...........................31
No opinion 6

Manual Workers

Favor............................61%
Oppose...........................29
No opinion 10

Nonlabor Force

Favor............................47%
Oppose...........................41
No opinion 12

By Marital Status
Married

Favor............................51%
Oppose...........................39
No opinion 10

Single

Favor............................71%
Oppose...........................22
No opinion 7

Widowed

Favor............................50%
Oppose...........................39
No opinion 11

National Trend

	Favor	Oppose	No opinion
1982	56%	34%	10%
1981	63	32	5
1980	58	31	11
1978	58	31	11
1976	57	24	19
1975	58	24	18

Also asked of the aware group: As you may know, the deadline for ratification of the Equal Rights Amendment runs out at the end of this month. Would you favor or oppose having this measure reoffered so that the states could have another chance to vote on it?

Favor............................56%
Oppose...........................37
No opinion 7

By Sex
Male

Favor............................51%
Oppose...........................43
No opinion 6

Female

Favor............................61%
Oppose...........................32
No opinion 7

By Race
White

Favor............................54%
Oppose...........................40
No opinion 6

Nonwhite

Favor............................75%
Oppose...........................14
No opinion 11

By Education
College

Favor............................55%
Oppose...........................40
No opinion 5

High School

Favor............................58%
Oppose...........................36
No opinion 6

Grade School

Favor............................51%
Oppose...........................36
No opinion 13

By Region
East
Favor.............................62%
Oppose............................30
No opinion 8

Midwest
Favor.............................54%
Oppose............................40
No opinion 6

South
Favor.............................52%
Oppose............................42
No opinion 6

West
Favor.............................57%
Oppose............................37
No opinion 6

By Age
18–24 Years
Favor.............................64%
Oppose............................30
No opinion 6

25–29 Years
Favor.............................65%
Oppose............................34
No opinion 1

30–49 Years
Favor.............................55%
Oppose............................38
No opinion 7

50–64 Years
Favor.............................53%
Oppose............................41
No opinion 6

65 Years and Over
Favor.............................49%
Oppose............................42
No opinion 9

By Income
$25,000 and Over
Favor.............................55%
Oppose............................42
No opinion 3

$15,000 and Over
Favor.............................55%
Oppose............................40
No opinion 5

Under $15,000
Favor.............................59%
Oppose............................33
No opinion 8

By Politics
Republicans
Favor.............................42%
Oppose............................52
No opinion 6

Democrats
Favor.............................65%
Oppose............................29
No opinion 6

Independents
Favor.............................57%
Oppose............................37
No opinion 6

By Religion
Protestants
Favor.............................54%
Oppose............................40
No opinion 6

Catholics

Favor...................................59%
Oppose..................................36
No opinion 5

By Occupation
Professional and Business

Favor...................................53%
Oppose..................................41
No opinion 6

Clerical and Sales

Favor...................................66%
Oppose..................................27
No opinion 7

Manual Workers

Favor...................................59%
Oppose..................................35
No opinion 6

Nonlabor Force

Favor...................................49%
Oppose..................................43
No opinion 8

By Marital Status
Married

Favor...................................51%
Oppose..................................43
No opinion 6

Single

Favor...................................66%
Oppose..................................28
No opinion 6

Widowed

Favor...................................60%
Oppose..................................33
No opinion 7

Those Who Favor ERA

Favor...................................85%
Oppose..................................11
No opinion 4

Those Who Oppose ERA

Favor...................................15%
Oppose..................................82
No opinion 3

Also asked of the aware group: Just your best guess, if the Equal Rights Amendment is reoffered, do you think it will or will not be passed by the required thirty-eight state legislatures?

Will pass...............................33%
Will not pass...........................54
No opinion 13

Those Who Favor ERA

Will pass...............................45%
Will not pass...........................41
No opinion 14

Those Who Oppose ERA

Will pass...............................13%
Will not pass...........................79
No opinion 8

Those Who Favor Reoffering ERA

Will pass...............................46%
Will not pass...........................39
No opinion 15

Those Who Oppose Reoffering ERA

Will pass...............................14%
Will not pass...........................80
No opinion 6

Note: The proposed Equal Rights Amendment to the U.S. Constitution states: "Equality of rights under the law shall not be denied or abridged by the United States or by any state on account of sex." When time ran out on the ratification process, thirty-five states out of a required thirty-eight had voted in favor. Strong last-minute fights were waged in the fifteen states that had not ratified, none of them successful.

Opposition to the ERA centered around the beliefs that ratification would mean increased competition between men and women for jobs and that de facto equality between the sexes already exists. A small minority of those opposed to the amendment contends that "a woman's place is in the home," and still fewer associate ratification with making women eligible for the military draft.

The amendment had the solid support of the American people, as had been the case throughout its stormy ten-year course through the ratification process. The extent of the public's backing is indicated by the fact that a majority favors having the amendment introduced, though skepticism outweighs optimism on its future passage. In its final referendum on the measure, the Gallup Poll found 56% of persons who had heard or read about it (90% of the total) favoring ratification of the ERA, with 34% opposed, a level of public support similar to that found in Gallup surveys conducted since 1975.

Proponents of the amendment have vowed to reintroduce the measure in Congress, a move supported by 56% of the aware public and opposed by 37%. However, even among those in the survey who favor reintroduction of the measure, opinion is closely divided about its chances for ratification, with 46% believing it will be passed and 39% that it will not. And among those who oppose reoffering the amendment, 80% believe it will fail.

Strong support for the ERA is found in all major population groups except Republicans, among whom opinion is evenly divided, with 44% in favor and 46% opposed. Republican backing has dropped 11 percentage points from the 1981 survey, when 55% had expressed support. On the other hand, Democrats are almost as steadfast in this latest survey as they had been earlier, with 64% today compared to 67% last year. Substantially fewer Republicans (42%) than either Democrats (65%) or independents (57%) favor reintroduction of the amendment.

While roughly equal proportions of men (55%) and women (57%) lean toward ratification of the ERA, women (61%) are more inclined than men (51%) to favor reoffering the measure.

JULY 4
MIDDLE EAST SITUATION

Interviewing Date: 6/11–14/82
Survey #196-G

Have you heard or read about the situation in the Middle East?

Yes 92%
No 8

Asked of those who replied in the affirmative: In the Middle East situation, are your sympathies more with Israel or more with the Arab nations?

Israel 52%
Arab nations 10
Neither (volunteered) 29
No opinion 9

By Sex
Male

Israel 54%
Arab nations 10
Neither (volunteered) 28
No opinion 8

Female

Israel 49%
Arab nations 10
Neither (volunteered) 30
No opinion 11

By Race
White

Israel 54%
Arab nations 9
Neither (volunteered) 28
No opinion 9

Nonwhite

Israel 35%
Arab nations 16
Neither (volunteered) 35
No opinion 14

West

Israel 53%
Arab nations 13
Neither (volunteered) 26
No opinion 8

By Education
College

Israel 60%
Arab nations 13
Neither (volunteered) 21
No opinion 6

By Age
18–29 Years

Israel 54%
Arab nations 12
Neither (volunteered) 28
No opinion 6

High School

Israel 49%
Arab nations 9
Neither (volunteered) 31
No opinion 11

30–49 Years

Israel 57%
Arab nations 8
Neither (volunteered) 26
No opinion 9

Grade School

Israel 38%
Arab nations 8
Neither (volunteered) 40
No opinion 14

50 Years and Over

Israel 45%
Arab nations 10
Neither (volunteered) 33
No opinion 12

By Region
East

Israel 51%
Arab nations 10
Neither (volunteered) 33
No opinion 6

By Income
$25,000 and Over

Israel 58%
Arab nations 10
Neither (volunteered) 25
No opinion 7

Midwest

Israel 48%
Arab nations 10
Neither (volunteered) 33
No opinion 9

$15,000 and Over

Israel 57%
Arab nations 10
Neither (volunteered) 27
No opinion 6

South

Israel 55%
Arab nations 9
Neither (volunteered) 23
No opinion 13

Under $15,000

Israel 44%
Arab nations 10
Neither (volunteered) 33
No opinion 13

By Politics

Republicans

Israel	55%
Arab nations	8
Neither (volunteered)	27
No opinion	10

Democrats

Israel	51%
Arab nations	10
Neither (volunteered)	29
No opinion	10

Independents

Israel	49%
Arab nations	11
Neither (volunteered)	32
No opinion	8

By Religion

Protestants

Israel	51%
Arab nations	8
Neither (volunteered)	30
No opinion	11

Catholics

Israel	54%
Arab nations	10
Neither (volunteered)	30
No opinion	6

National Trend

	Israel	Arab nations	Neither	No opinion
June 1982	52%	10%	29%	9%
April–May 1982	51	12	26	11
January 1982	49	14	23	14
1981	44	11	34	11
1979	40	14	31	15
1975	44	8	22	26
1973	50	7	25	18
1970	44	3	32	21
1967	56	4	25	15

Also asked of the aware group: Israel recently began military operations in southern Lebanon to stop Palestinian artillery attacks on settlements in Israel. Do you approve or disapprove of this action by Israel?*

Approve	40%
Disapprove	35
No opinion	25

By Sex

Male

Approve	46%
Disapprove	34
No opinion	20

Female

Approve	34%
Disapprove	37
No opinion	29

By Race

White

Approve	42%
Disapprove	35
No opinion	23

Nonwhite

Approve	26%
Disapprove	36
No opinion	38

By Education

College

Approve	46%
Disapprove	38
No opinion	16

*In an analogous situation last summer, a *Newsweek* Poll conducted by the Gallup Organization found that American reaction toward Israel's bombing of PLO positions in Beirut was more critical, with 50% believing the bombing was not justified and 31% saying it was. However, that survey found no change in Americans' basic sympathies in the area.

High School

Approve..............................39%
Disapprove 33
No opinion 28

Grade School

Approve..............................30%
Disapprove 36
No opinion 34

By Region
East

Approve..............................31%
Disapprove 36
No opinion 33

Midwest

Approve..............................38%
Disapprove 33
No opinion 29

South

Approve..............................47%
Disapprove 33
No opinion 20

West

Approve..............................45%
Disapprove 40
No opinion 15

By Age
18–29 Years

Approve..............................40%
Disapprove 35
No opinion 25

30–49 Years

Approve..............................45%
Disapprove 34
No opinion 21

50 Years and Over

Approve..............................35%
Disapprove 37
No opinion 28

By Income
$25,000 and Over

Approve..............................43%
Disapprove 38
No opinion 19

$15,000 and Over

Approve..............................44%
Disapprove 36
No opinion 20

Under $15,000

Approve..............................35%
Disapprove 33
No opinion 32

By Politics
Republicans

Approve..............................40%
Disapprove 34
No opinion 26

Democrats

Approve..............................38%
Disapprove 37
No opinion 25

Independents

Approve..............................44%
Disapprove 34
No opinion 22

By Religion
Protestants

Approve..............................39%
Disapprove 35
No opinion 26

Catholics

Approve. 43%
Disapprove 36
No opinion 21

Asked of the entire sample: You will notice that the ten boxes on this scale go from the highest position of +5 for someone you have a very favorable opinion of all the way down to the lowest position of −5 for someone you have a very unfavorable opinion of. How far up or down the scale would you rate Menachem Begin?

Highly favorable (+5, +4). 9%
Favorable (+3, +2, +1). 43
Unfavorable (−1, −2, −3). 21
Highly unfavorable (−4, −5). 13
No opinion 14

National Trend

	Highly favorable	Total favorable
1981	10%	54%
1978, after Camp David	11	59
1978, before Camp David . . .	8	39

Note: Although almost as many Americans disapprove as approve of Israel's June 6 incursion into Lebanon, the Israeli action appears not to have altered Americans' basic loyalties in the Middle East. In a Gallup survey completed a week after Israel's move to stop Palestinian attacks on Israeli settlements, 40% of Americans who had followed the Middle East situation (92% of the total) approved of the Israeli action, while 35% disapproved and 25% had no opinion.

At the same time, 52% of the survey respondents said their sympathies in the region lay with Israel, while 10% sided with the Arab nations and 29% claimed no allegiance to either side. Nearly identical figures were recorded in April at the time of Israel's return to Egypt of the captured Sinai territory, representing the highest level of pro-Israeli sentiment since 1973, the year of the Yom Kippur War.

This same 52% majority of the American public that takes Israel's part in the Middle East situation strongly endorses Israel's action in Lebanon, with 60% in favor and 23% opposed. On the other hand, those with pro-Arab sympathies overwhelmingly denounce Israel's action, 73% to 14%. Among the three Americans in ten who say their sympathies lie with neither Israel nor the Arab nations, the weight of opinion is 2 to 1 against Israel's Lebanese operation.

JULY 8
PRESIDENT REAGAN

Despite his recent European trip, the outbreak of war in the Middle East, and the continuing recession, President Ronald Reagan's job performance rating remains on dead center, with 45% of Americans approving and 45% disapproving. This remarkable stability, noted in Reagan's ratings since the beginning of the year, shows that many people already have developed strong convictions about the president and either strongly approve or disapprove of his job performance; relatively few are found in the middle ground.

Further evidence of this polarization is seen in the fact that sharply divergent views about Reagan are found among population groups, particularly between men and women and between whites and nonwhites.

The combination of strong approval and strong disapproval in the current survey produces a "hard" or "committed" vote, pro and con together, of 57%, representing those persons who presumably would be slow to switch from approval to disapproval, or the reverse. In contrast, President Jimmy Carter, who at a similar point in time had virtually the same overall approval rating as Reagan, had a hard or committed vote of only 39%. In fact, the pattern of intensity of approval for Reagan's job performance differs from that of his four predecessors. In the case of Carter, Gerald Ford, Richard Nixon, and Lyndon Johnson, moderate approval consistently outweighed strong approval by as much as 2 to 1. In the case of

Reagan, however, strong approval virtually matches moderate approval.

A difference also is recorded in terms of the intensity of disapproval between the ratings given Reagan and those given his four predecessors. In the case of Carter, Ford, Nixon, and Johnson, disapproval was about evenly divided between strong and moderate. In the case of Reagan, strong disapproval far outweighs moderate disapproval.

Another factor explaining the remarkable stability in Reagan's job performance ratings is that opinion divides strongly on the basis of the sex, racial background, and socioeconomic background of survey respondents.

The president's current lack of support among women is almost the exact reverse of that among men. Women disapprove of Reagan's job performance by the margin of 52% to 39%, while men approve by almost the same percentages, 51% to 39%. This is even more dramatically revealed when the ratings given him by women and men are compared with those given his predecessors.

In the case of the four earlier chief executives, women and men alternately rated the president higher in terms of approval, with the difference in ratings never great. In the case of Reagan, however, women have consistently rated him lower than have men and by wide margins.

Up to now, Reagan's average approval figure has been 9 points lower among women than men. In contrast, Nixon's rating among women was, on the average, 4½ points lower among women than men, and in the case of the other presidents, the difference between the ratings given by the sexes was only 1 or 2 percentage points.

The following table shows how the approval ratings for the presidents have differed between men and women at a comparable point (18 months after taking office):

Job Approval Ratings

(After 18 Months in Office)

	National	Men	Women
Reagan	45%	51%	39%
Carter	43	43	42
Nixon	56	57	54
Kennedy	74	74	74
Eisenhower	61	62	61

In addition to these divisions of men and women, differences also may be found between whites and nonwhites. President Reagan's approval rating (12%) among nonwhites today is the lowest recorded for any president at any point in his term. The one exception is the rating given Nixon at the time of his resignation, when his rating among nonwhites was also at 12%. But Nixon's approval then among whites was only 24%, while Reagan currently wins the approval of 50% of whites.

Similarly, at this point in time, Reagan's approval among nonwhites is by far the lowest of any of the elected presidents, as shown in the following table:

Job Approval Ratings

(After 18 Months in Office)

	National	White	Nonwhite
Reagan	45%	50%	12%
Carter	43	41	54
Nixon	59	63	27
Kennedy	74	72	90
Eisenhower	61	63	38

JULY 11
ECONOMIC SITUATION

Interviewing Date: 6/11–14/82
Survey #196-G

Do you approve or disapprove of the way Reagan is handling economic conditions in this country?

Approve...........................35%
Disapprove 58
No opinion 7

By Sex

Male

Approve...........................41%
Disapprove 53
No opinion 6

Female

Approve...........................31%
Disapprove 62
No opinion 7

By Race
White

Approve...........................40%
Disapprove 53
No opinion 7

Nonwhite

Approve........................... 8%
Disapprove 87
No opinion 5

By Education
College

Approve...........................43%
Disapprove 54
No opinion 3

High School

Approve...........................33%
Disapprove 60
No opinion 7

Grade School

Approve...........................28%
Disapprove 59
No opinion 13

By Region
East

Approve...........................29%
Disapprove 62
No opinion 9

Midwest

Approve...........................35%
Disapprove 58
No opinion 7

South

Approve...........................41%
Disapprove 53
No opinion 6

West

Approve...........................36%
Disapprove 59
No opinion 5

By Age
18–24 Years

Approve...........................32%
Disapprove 62
No opinion 6

25–29 Years

Approve...........................35%
Disapprove 64
No opinion 1

30–49 Years

Approve...........................39%
Disapprove 54
No opinion 7

50–64 Years

Approve...........................33%
Disapprove 61
No opinion 6

65 Years and Over

Approve...........................37%
Disapprove 51
No opinion 12

By Income
$25,000 and Over

Approve...........................47%
Disapprove 51
No opinion 2

$15,000 and Over

Approve.............................42%
Disapprove 53
No opinion 5

Under $15,000

Approve.............................27%
Disapprove 64
No opinion 9

By Politics
Republicans

Approve.............................65%
Disapprove 29
No opinion 6

Democrats

Approve.............................16%
Disapprove 78
No opinion 6

Independents

Approve.............................38%
Disapprove 55
No opinion 7

By Occupation
Professional and Business

Approve.............................45%
Disapprove 52
No opinion 3

Clerical and Sales

Approve.............................28%
Disapprove 66
No opinion 6

Manual Workers

Approve.............................30%
Disapprove 65
No opinion 5

Nonlabor Force

Approve.............................36%
Disapprove 54
No opinion 10

Labor Union Families Only

Approve.............................25%
Disapprove 70
No opinion 5

Nonlabor Union Families Only

Approve.............................38%
Disapprove 55
No opinion 7

Do you approve or disapprove of the way Reagan is handling inflation?

Approve.............................37%
Disapprove 58
No opinion 5

By Sex
Male

Approve.............................46%
Disapprove 50
No opinion 4

Female

Approve.............................29%
Disapprove 65
No opinion 6

By Race
White

Approve.............................41%
Disapprove 54
No opinion 5

Nonwhite

Approve.............................13%
Disapprove 80
No opinion 7

By Education
College
Approve......................48%
Disapprove 48
No opinion 4

High School
Approve......................33%
Disapprove 62
No opinion 5

Grade School
Approve......................27%
Disapprove 62
No opinion 11

By Region
East
Approve......................31%
Disapprove 63
No opinion 6

Midwest
Approve......................38%
Disapprove 55
No opinion 7

South
Approve......................40%
Disapprove 55
No opinion 5

West
Approve......................40%
Disapprove 57
No opinion 3

By Age
18–24 Years
Approve......................32%
Disapprove 63
No opinion 5

25–29 Years
Approve......................34%
Disapprove 63
No opinion 3

30–49 Years
Approve......................41%
Disapprove 55
No opinion 4

50–64 Years
Approve......................35%
Disapprove 58
No opinion 7

65 Years and Over
Approve......................37%
Disapprove 55
No opinion 8

By Income
$25,000 and Over
Approve......................52%
Disapprove 45
No opinion 3

$15,000 and Over
Approve......................45%
Disapprove 51
No opinion 4

Under $15,000
Approve......................27%
Disapprove 67
No opinion 6

By Politics
Republicans
Approve......................61%
Disapprove 33
No opinion 6

Democrats

Approve...........................21%
Disapprove 75
No opinion 4

Independents

Approve...........................38%
Disapprove 56
No opinion 6

By Occupation
Professional and Business

Approve...........................48%
Disapprove 47
No opinion 5

Clerical and Sales

Approve...........................24%
Disapprove 75
No opinion 1

Manual Workers

Approve...........................31%
Disapprove 65
No opinion 4

Nonlabor Force

Approve...........................37%
Disapprove 54
No opinion 9

Labor Union Families Only

Approve...........................28%
Disapprove 68
No opinion 4

Nonlabor Union Families Only

Approve...........................39%
Disapprove 55
No opinion 6

Do you approve or disapprove of the way Reagan is handling unemployment?

Approve...........................22%
Disapprove 70
No opinion 8

By Sex
Male

Approve...........................25%
Disapprove 68
No opinion 7

Female

Approve...........................20%
Disapprove 71
No opinion 9

By Race
White

Approve...........................25%
Disapprove 67
No opinion 8

Nonwhite

Approve........................... 6%
Disapprove 90
No opinion 4

By Education
College

Approve...........................29%
Disapprove 64
No opinion 7

High School

Approve...........................20%
Disapprove 72
No opinion 8

Grade School

Approve...........................21%
Disapprove 72
No opinion 7

By Region

East

Approve...........................20%
Disapprove 73
No opinion 7

Midwest

Approve...........................22%
Disapprove 70
No opinion 8

South

Approve...........................26%
Disapprove 65
No opinion 9

West

Approve...........................21%
Disapprove 71
No opinion 8

By Age

18–24 Years

Approve...........................16%
Disapprove 75
No opinion 9

25–29 Years

Approve...........................22%
Disapprove 73
No opinion 5

30–49 Years

Approve...........................26%
Disapprove 67
No opinion 7

50–64 Years

Approve...........................20%
Disapprove 72
No opinion 8

65 Years and Over

Approve...........................26%
Disapprove 65
No opinion 9

By Income

$25,000 and Over

Approve...........................32%
Disapprove 61
No opinion 7

$15,000 and Over

Approve...........................28%
Disapprove 64
No opinion 8

Under $15,000

Approve...........................16%
Disapprove 77
No opinion 7

By Politics

Republicans

Approve...........................42%
Disapprove 47
No opinion 11

Democrats

Approve...........................10%
Disapprove 84
No opinion 6

Independents

Approve...........................24%
Disapprove 69
No opinion 7

By Occupation

Professional and Business

Approve...........................31%
Disapprove 62
No opinion 7

Clerical and Sales

Approve.............................13%
Disapprove 76
No opinion 11

Manual Workers

Approve.............................18%
Disapprove 76
No opinion 6

Nonlabor Force

Approve.............................23%
Disapprove 68
No opinion 9

Labor Union Families Only

Approve.............................17%
Disapprove 78
No opinion 9

Nonlabor Union Families Only

Approve.............................24%
Disapprove 67
No opinion 9

The inflation rate is now running at about 7%. By the end of 1982, what do you think the inflation rate will be?

15% or more........................ 3%
14% 1
13% 1
12% 3
11% 2
10% 15
9% or less 64
No opinion 12
    Median estimate: 7.9%

National Trend

January 1982

15% or more........................11%
14% 1
13% 3
12% 12
11% 12

10% 14
9% or less 36
No opinion 11
    Median estimate: 10.2%

*March 1981**

15% or more........................35%
14% 10
13% 6
12% 15
11% 4
10% 12
9% or less 7
No opinion 11
    Median estimate: 13.5%

*November 1980**

15% or more........................35%
14% 6
13% 13
12% 5
11% 4
10% 11
9% or less 8
No opinion 18
    Median estimate: 13.6%

*By end of 1981.

The current unemployment rate is 9.5%. By the end of 1982, what do you think the unemployment rate will be?

10% or more........................63%
9% 12
8% 9
7% 5
6% 1
5% or less 1
No opinion 9
    Median estimate: 10.1%

National Trend

January 1982

10% or more........................44%
9% 18
8% 11
7% 9

6% 7
5% or less 2
No opinion 9

Median estimate: 9.4%

March 1981*

10% or more........................ 28%
9% 13
8% 17
7% 15
6% 11
5% or less 7
No opinion 9

Median estimate: 8.2%

November 1980*

10% or more........................ 15%
9% 9
8% 12
7% 17
6% 17
5% or less 15
No opinion 15

Median estimate: 7.1%

*By end of 1981.

Note: President Ronald Reagan continues to run afoul of the "misery index," an economic yardstick he used effectively during the 1980 presidential campaign to point up the failings of Jimmy Carter's economic policies. The index—a combination of the public's median estimates of the inflation (7.9%) and unemployment (10.1%) rates by year-end—now stands at 18%, statistically indistinguishable from the 20% observed in a January survey. Although the index itself has not changed appreciably, its two components are dramatically different from those recorded six months ago, with a substantially poorer outlook for unemployment offset by improved expectations for inflation.

In January, 36% of Americans forecast an inflation rate of 9% or less by the end of 1982; today almost twice as many (64%) predict the rate of inflation will be that low. In Gallup surveys conducted in March 1981 and November 1980, the comparable figures were only 7% and 8%, respectively. For the twelve months ending in May, the government's estimate of the inflation rate was 6.7%. When Reagan took office in 1981, the inflation rate for the preceding twelve months was 12.4%, or almost twice the present figure.

On the other hand, the public's estimates of the unemployment rate have grown steadily more pessimistic. In January, 44% told Gallup interviewers they thought the jobless rate by the end of the year would be 10% or higher. In the current survey, 63% offer the same gloomy forecast. In the 1981 and 1980 studies, 28% and 15% believed the unemployment rate might be 10% or higher by the end of 1981. The government's recently released unemployment estimate for June was 9.5%, unchanged from May. Many economists think that the unemployment rate has not yet peaked and that joblessness will get worse before it gets better. Judging from their estimates, the public agrees with this assessment.

Perhaps because the present high jobless rate is such bitter medicine, even if it helps cure the nation of double-digit inflation, the public has not credited the Reagan administration with reducing the inflation rate, although they have done so indirectly in their inflation estimates. As shown in the table below, there has been no improvement since January in the proportion of Americans approving of the president's handling of inflation and a slow but steady erosion in favorable attitudes about Reagan's handling of unemployment and economic conditions in general:

	Economic conditions	Inflation	Unemployment
April–May 1982	37%	36%	23%
April 1982	38	38	23
March 1982	38	37	25
February 1982	38	37	27
January 1982	41	37	26

As might be expected, there is a strong political cast to predictions about the inflation and unemployment rates, with Republicans much more likely than Democrats and independents to anticipate both lower inflation and unemployment rates by the end of 1982. Similarly, the component population groups with strong Republican leanings have a more sanguine outlook toward these economic barometers than do demographic groups with a traditionally Democratic bent:

Estimates of Inflation and Unemployment Rates by Year-End

	Inflation 9% or less	Unemployment 9% or less
National	64%	29%

By Sex

White	67%	32%
Nonwhite	41	13

By Race

College	74%	35%
High school or less	60	27

By Income

Family income of $15,000 and over	71%	34%
Family income of under $15,000	55	23

By Politics

Republicans	79%	51%
Democrats	55	16
Independents	67	29

JULY 15
REAGANOMICS

Interviewing Date: 6/11–14/82
Survey #196-G

Now let's talk about the Reagan administration's economic policies. What effect do you think these policies will have on your own and your family's financial situation? Do you feel your financial situation will be much better, somewhat better, somewhat worse, or much worse as a result of the Reagan economic policies?

Much better	4%
Somewhat better	25
Somewhat worse	33
Much worse	18
Same (volunteered)	15
No opinion	5

National Trend

	Better	Worse	Same	No opinion
March 1982	28%	51%	15%	6%
February 1982	31	44	17	8
November 1981	35	49	12	4
October 1981	42	39	13	6
August 1981	48	36	*	16
May 1981	48	37	*	15

*Volunteered "same" response not recorded.

Thinking about a year from now, do you feel your financial situation will be much better, somewhat better, somewhat worse, or much worse as a result of the Reagan economic policies?

Much better	5%
Somewhat better	31
Somewhat worse	27
Much worse	13
Same (volunteered)	19
No opinion	5

How about over the long run? In the long run, do you feel your economic situation will be better or worse because of the Reagan economic policies?

Better	43%
Worse	34
Same (volunteered)	13
No opinion	10

By Sex
Male

Better	49%
Worse	28

Same (volunteered) 14
No opinion 9

Female

Better.............................. 39%
Worse............................... 39
Same (volunteered) 11
No opinion 11

By Race
White

Better.............................. 47%
Worse............................... 31
Same (volunteered) 13
No opinion 9

Nonwhite

Better.............................. 21%
Worse............................... 50
Same (volunteered) 11
No opinion 18

By Education
College

Better.............................. 53%
Worse............................... 30
Same (volunteered) 10
No opinion 7

High School

Better.............................. 41%
Worse............................... 35
Same (volunteered) 14
No opinion 10

Grade School

Better.............................. 34%
Worse............................... 35
Same (volunteered) 17
No opinion 14

By Income
$25,000 and Over

Better.............................. 58%
Worse............................... 24

Same (volunteered) 12
No opinion 6

$15,000 and Over

Better.............................. 52%
Worse............................... 29
Same (volunteered) 11
No opinion 8

Under $15,000

Better.............................. 32%
Worse............................... 41
Same (volunteered) 15
No opinion 12

By Politics
Republicans

Better.............................. 67%
Worse............................... 13
Same (volunteered) 14
No opinion 6

Democrats

Better.............................. 28%
Worse............................... 48
Same (volunteered) 12
No opinion 12

Independents

Better.............................. 46%
Worse............................... 32
Same (volunteered) 13
No opinion 9

Those Who Approve of Reagan

Better.............................. 70%
Worse............................... 10
Same (volunteered) 13
No opinion 7

Those Who Disapprove of Reagan

Better.............................. 18%
Worse............................... 58
Same (volunteered) 13
No opinion 11

Note: The American people are deeply skeptical that President Ronald Reagan's program for economic recovery will improve their family finances, but the steady downward trend in optimism about Reaganomics appears to have leveled off. In a survey conducted shortly before the 10% personal tax cut and 7.4% increase in Social Security benefits went into effect on July 1, 29% of the public told Gallup interviewers they thought Reaganomics would improve their own and their families' financial condition. In contrast, 51% believed their finances would be worsened and 15% did not think the Reagan program would have any effect one way or the other.

The current figures are virtually the same as those recorded in a March survey, when 28% voiced optimism and 51% pessimism about the program. However, there are far fewer optimists now than were found in surveys conducted last year, when as many as half the public (48%) said Reaganomics would work.

Some political analysts now claim that Reagan needs prompt, unequivocal evidence of an economic recovery if the Republican party is to avoid stunning losses in November's elections. The survey results reported today give no indication that the public anticipates an economic turnaround any time soon.

Since the program was announced, the public consistently has been more sanguine about Reaganomics as the time reference is extended into the future. Thus, in the latest survey, 36% see their family finances improving one year from now and 43% are positive over the long run, as shown in the table below:

Effect of Reaganomics on Personal Finances

	Better	Worse	Same	No opinion
Now	29%	51%	15%	5%
One year from now	36	40	19	5
In the long run	43	34	13	10

Major differences of opinion are found among various population groups. More than twice the proportion of whites (47%) as nonwhites (21%) believe Reaganomics will improve their financial situation in the long run. Other groups with a more positive outlook include men, persons who attended college, those with family incomes over $15,000 per year, and Republicans. On the other hand, those with a more negative outlook toward the eventual success of Reaganomics include women, those with no college training, persons with family incomes under $15,000, Democrats, and nonwhites.

There is a strong correlation between approval of Reagan's job performance and assessments of the economic consequences of Reaganomics. Fully 70% of those who approve of the way Reagan is handling his presidential duties are bullish about the effect of Reaganomics on their family finances over the long run, compared to only 18% of those whose overall evaluation of Reagan is negative.

JULY 18
DEMOCRATIC PRESIDENTIAL CANDIDATES/PRESIDENTIAL TRIAL HEATS

Interviewing Date: 6/25–28/82
Survey #197-G

Asked of Democrats and independents: Suppose the choice for president in the Democratic convention in 1984 narrows down to Edward Kennedy and Walter Mondale. Which one would you prefer to have the Democratic convention select?

Democrats

Kennedy	58%
Mondale	30
Other; undecided	12

Independents

Kennedy	36%
Mondale	44
Other; undecided	20

Democrats and Independents

Kennedy 50%
Mondale. 35
Other; undecided 15

Asked of registered voters: Suppose the presidential election were being held today. If President Ronald Reagan were the Republican candidate and Senator Edward Kennedy were the Democratic candidate, which would you like to see win? [Those who named another person or who were undecided were asked: As of today, do you lean more to Reagan, the Republican, or to Kennedy, the Democrat?]

Reagan. 45%
Kennedy 48
Other; undecided 7

By Sex
Male

Reagan. 48%
Kennedy 46
Other; undecided 6

Female

Reagan. 43%
Kennedy 50
Other; undecided 7

By Race
White

Reagan. 51%
Kennedy 42
Other; undecided 7

Nonwhite

Reagan. 6%
Kennedy 88
Other; undecided 6

By Education
College

Reagan. 54%
Kennedy 40
Other; undecided 6

High School

Reagan. 40%
Kennedy 53
Other; undecided 7

Grade School

Reagan. 47%
Kennedy 49
Other; undecided 4

By Region
East

Reagan. 46%
Kennedy 51
Other; undecided 3

Midwest

Reagan. 45%
Kennedy 47
Other; undecided 8

South

Reagan. 42%
Kennedy 48
Other; undecided 10

West

Reagan. 48%
Kennedy 47
Other; undecided 5

By Age
18–29 Years

Reagan. 39%
Kennedy 54
Other; undecided 7

30–49 Years

Reagan. 45%
Kennedy 49
Other; undecided 6

50 Years and Over

Reagan.............................48%
Kennedy 45
Other; undecided 7

By Income
$25,000 and Over

Reagan.............................59%
Kennedy 36
Other; undecided 5

$15,000 and Over

Reagan.............................54%
Kennedy 40
Other; undecided 6

Under $15,000

Reagan.............................32%
Kennedy 62
Other; undecided 6

By Politics
Republicans

Reagan.............................86%
Kennedy 12
Other; undecided 2

Democrats

Reagan.............................16%
Kennedy 78
Other; undecided 6

Independents

Reagan.............................54%
Kennedy 34
Other; undecided 12

By Religion
Protestants

Reagan.............................49%
Kennedy 44
Other; undecided 7

Catholics

Reagan.............................42%
Kennedy 53
Other; undecided 5

National Trend

	Reagan	Kennedy	Other; undecided
June 1982	45%	48%	7%
April 1982	45	51	4
November 1981	56	35	9

Asked of registered voters: Suppose the presidential election were being held today. If President Ronald Reagan were the Republican candidate and former Vice-President Walter Mondale were the Democratic candidate, which would you like to see win? [Those who named another person or who were undecided were asked: As of today, do you lean more to Reagan, the Republican, or to Mondale, the Democrat?]

Reagan.............................43%
Mondale............................49
Other; undecided 8

By Sex
Male

Reagan.............................46%
Mondale............................46
Other; undecided 8

Female

Reagan.............................40%
Mondale............................51
Other; undecided 9

By Race
White

Reagan.............................48%
Mondale............................44
Other; undecided 8

Nonwhite

Reagan............................12%
Mondale...........................76
Other; undecided 12

By Education
College

Reagan............................50%
Mondale...........................43
Other; undecided 7

High School

Reagan............................39%
Mondale...........................51
Other; undecided 10

Grade School

Reagan............................41%
Mondale...........................50
Other; undecided 9

By Region
East

Reagan............................40%
Mondale...........................53
Other; undecided 7

Midwest

Reagan............................46%
Mondale...........................46
Other; undecided 8

South

Reagan............................40%
Mondale...........................50
Other; undecided 10

West

Reagan............................46%
Mondale...........................45
Other; undecided 9

By Age
18–29 Years

Reagan............................45%
Mondale...........................48
Other; undecided 7

30–49 Years

Reagan............................42%
Mondale...........................48
Other; undecided 10

50 Years and Over

Reagan............................42%
Mondale...........................50
Other; undecided 8

By Income
$25,000 and Over

Reagan............................52%
Mondale...........................41
Other; undecided 7

$15,000 and Over

Reagan............................49%
Mondale...........................43
Other; undecided 8

Under $15,000

Reagan............................32%
Mondale...........................59
Other; undecided 9

By Politics
Republicans

Reagan............................85%
Mondale...........................12
Other; undecided 3

Democrats

Reagan............................15%
Mondale...........................75
Other; undecided 10

Independents

Reagan............................48%
Mondale............................43
Other; undecided 9

By Religion

Protestants

Reagan............................46%
Mondale............................46
Other; undecided 8

Catholics

Reagan............................40%
Mondale............................52
Other; undecided 8

National Trend

	Reagan	Mondale	Other; undecided
June 1982	43%	49%	8%
April 1982	46	46	8
November 1981	54	37	9

Note: Senator Edward Kennedy is the 2-to-1 choice of Democrats over former Vice-President Walter Mondale to be their party's presidential nominee, but the two Democratic front-runners fare about equally well when pitted against President Ronald Reagan in Gallup test elections for 1984.

Among registered voters nationwide, Mondale beats Reagan by a narrow 49% to 43% margin, and Kennedy tops the president by an even slimmer edge, 48% to 45%. In similar contests conducted in April, the Massachusetts senator led Reagan 51% to 45%, while Mondale and the president each received 46% of the vote.

In a head-to-head match for the nomination, Democratic voters pick Kennedy over Mondale by a convincing 2-to-1 ratio, 58% to 30%. Independents, however, side with the former vice-president over Kennedy by 44% to 36%.

These survey results suggest that the road to the 1984 election will be paved with uncertainty for the Democratic contenders as well as for Reagan if he decides to run:

1) Kennedy enjoys his greatest strength among younger adults (under 30), nonwhites, less well-educated persons, and those in the lower income strata. Persons in these categories tend to cast their ballots less often than do their older, more affluent counterparts.

2) Kennedy is the certain leader for the Democratic nomination among hard-core, traditionally Democratic groups, but he has relatively little support among independents and Republicans who are or might become disenchanted with the president.

3) Mondale's constituency, the survey shows, is broader than Kennedy's and includes more independents. At the same time, it is less committed and could be more susceptible to defection to the Republican nominee.

4) Reagan could be a strong contender for reelection in 1984 if he chooses to run. He makes a strong showing in the test elections reported today, given the minority status of the Republican party, the recession, and the voter groups he has alienated through his programs and policies.

JULY 22
UNITED NATIONS

Interviewing Date: 6/25–28/82
Survey #197-G

In general, do you feel the United Nations is doing a good job or a poor job in trying to solve the problems it has had to face?

Good job............................36%
Poor job............................49
No opinion 15

By Education
College

Good job............................35%
Poor job............................53
No opinion 12

High School

Good job 37%
Poor job 49
No opinion 14

Grade School

Good job 32%
Poor job 40
No opinion 28

By Age
18–24 Years

Good job 38%
Poor job 48
No opinion 14

25–29 Years

Good job 39%
Poor job 50
No opinion 11

30–49 Years

Good job 38%
Poor job 50
No opinion 12

50–64 Years

Good job 33%
Poor job 53
No opinion 14

65 Years and Over

Good job 29%
Poor job 44
No opinion 27

By Politics
Republicans

Good job 38%
Poor job 47
No opinion 15

Democrats

Good job 34%
Poor job 49
No opinion 17

Independents

Good job 35%
Poor job 54
No opinion 11

National Trend

	Good job	Poor job	No opinion
1982	36%	49%	15%
1980	31	53	16
1975	33	51	16
1971	35	43	22
1970	44	40	16
1967	49	35	16
1956	51	37	12

Do you think the United States should give up its membership in the United Nations, or not?

Should 12%
Should not 79
No opinion 9

By Education
College

Should 12%
Should not 84
No opinion 4

High School

Should 12%
Should not 79
No opinion 9

Grade School

Should 9%
Should not 68
No opinion 23

By Age

18–24 Years

Should 6%
Should not 83
No opinion 11

25–29 Years

Should 8%
Should not 84
No opinion 8

30–49 Years

Should 13%
Should not 80
No opinion 7

50–64 Years

Should 15%
Should not 79
No opinion 6

65 Years and Over

Should 13%
Should not 69
No opinion 18

By Politics

Republicans

Should 13%
Should not 80
No opinion 7

Democrats

Should 10%
Should not 79
No opinion 11

Independents

Should 13%
Should not 81
No opinion 6

National Trend

	Should	Should not	No opinion
June 1982	12%	79%	9%
November 1975	16	74	10
February 1975	11	75	14
July 1967	10	85	5
November 1963	8	79	13
January 1962	9	86	5
January 1951	14	72	14

Note: Against a depressing background of crises in many parts of the world, the U.S. public holds a somewhat negative view of the performance of the United Nations Organization, but at the same time overwhelmingly favors the United States retaining membership in the world body.

In the latest survey, 36% believe the United Nations is doing a good job in trying to solve the problems it has had to face, while 49% say it is doing a poor job. Although the current figure represents a slight increase since 1980 in those saying good, this figure falls below the findings recorded prior to 1971.

The high point in favorable attitudes toward the United Nations (as determined by surveys since 1956) was in the year 1956, when 51% said the United Nations was doing a good job and 37% a poor job. The low point to date was recorded in 1980, when the comparable figures were 31% and 53%.

Only one person in eight (12%) thinks the United States should give up its membership in the United Nations. The highest figure recorded since the surveys were undertaken was the 16% recorded in 1975, while the lowest percentage of persons in favor of withdrawing was 8%, in 1963.

JULY 24

AMERICANS GIVE LEGAL SYSTEM VERY LOW MARKS*

Anger and frustration about last month's verdict in the case of would-be presidential assassin

*This Gallup analysis was written by Andrew Kohut, president of the Gallup Organization Inc.

John Hinckley probably will not alter public attitudes toward the judicial system in any significant way. Americans already hold the courts in such low regard that finding Hinckley not guilty by reason of insanity will only serve to confirm their worst fears about the judicial system.

For some time now, the polls have shown deep-seated public dissatisfaction with American criminal justice. Sizable majorities disapprove of the courts in general, believe that they do not treat criminals severely enough, and have little faith in the courts' willingness to convict criminals and mete out sentences they consider appropriate.

The results of a recently released sixteen-nation opinion survey provide a perspective on just how critical Americans are of their legal system. The survey was designed to compare the values and beliefs of Americans with people in other industrialized nations. Generally, it found that U.S. citizens hold their social, economic, and political institutions in higher esteem than do citizens of other countries—with the major exception of the court system. Sponsored in the United States by the CARA organization and conducted by Gallup, the multinational poll showed only 51% of Americans had a great deal of faith in their legal system. In Japan, Great Britain, West Germany, and other European countries, significantly larger percentages voiced confidence in the courts. This was virtually the only area in an hour-long survey in which Americans had a more negative view of one of its political, economic, or social systems than did citizens of the other participating countries.

Confidence in Institutions

	Courts	Average seven institutions
Japan	68%	38%
Great Britain	66	52
West Germany	67	45
Ireland	57	60
France	55	45
United States	51	60
Spain	48	45
Italy	43	45

Since the late 1960s, when substantial changes in the laws were made regarding the rights of those accused of crimes, the polls have indicated public disillusionment with the courts. In 1967 the Harris Poll found a majority (56%) who believed that the American law enforcement system did not deter people from committing crimes. Every year since then, a larger percentage has subscribed to this view, with 79% expressing that opinion in the most recent survey.

Public criticism of the courts is directed at several perceived shortcomings. Leniency is viewed as the principal element in the rising crime rate. A 1981 *Newsweek* Poll by Gallup found survey respondents citing the courts' leniency as often as any other factor as causal to the rise of violent crime. The same poll also showed that more severe sentencing tops the public's list of things that can be done to stem the national crime wave.

By overwhelming margins, Americans say too much emphasis is placed on the rights of the accused. Gallup, for *Newsweek,* found only 16% worrying that the constitutional rights of accused persons are not being upheld, while 78% were more worried about criminals being let off too easily.

As the crime rate has soared in recent years, opinion surveys have shown greater support for the punishment of criminals and sentencing, which protects society from criminals. Approval of the death penalty is at an all-time high in the Gallup Poll. A recent Gallup survey found as many as 30% of the public believing it is more important to punish criminals while in prison than to "get them started on the right road" (59%). Similarly, Harris finds a sharp decline since 1970 in the percentage who feel the main emphasis of the prison system should be on rehabilitation.

Large percentages of the American population are frightened by crime, and many are plagued by it to such an extent that they have changed their life-styles to cope with it. The passage of Proposition 8 in California calling for legal changes that make it easier to convict criminals and keep them in jail longer may well signal the focusing of public discontent with the criminal justice system.

JULY 25
PARTY BETTER FOR PEACE AND PROSPERITY

Interviewing Date: 6/25–28/82
Survey #197-G

Which political party—the Republican party or the Democratic party—do you think will do a better job of keeping the country prosperous?

Republican 33%
Democratic 43
No difference (volunteered) 13
No opinion 11

By Sex
Male

Republican 36%
Democratic 44
No difference (volunteered) 12
No opinion 8

Female

Republican 29%
Democratic 42
No difference (volunteered) 15
No opinion 14

By Race
White

Republican 36%
Democratic 38
No difference (volunteered) 15
No opinion 11

Nonwhite

Republican 11%
Democratic 72

No difference (volunteered) 8
No opinion 9

By Education
College

Republican 43%
Democratic 37
No difference (volunteered) 12
No opinion 8

High School

Republican 30%
Democratic 46
No difference (volunteered) 13
No opinion 11

Grade School

Republican 22%
Democratic 44
No difference (volunteered) 16
No opinion 18

By Region
East

Republican 33%
Democratic 43
No difference (volunteered) 13
No opinion 11

Midwest

Republican 33%
Democratic 40
No difference (volunteered) 15
No opinion 12

South

Republican 33%
Democratic 44
No difference (volunteered) 12
No opinion 11

West

Republican 31%
Democratic 45

No difference (volunteered) 13
No opinion 11

By Age
18–29 Years
Republican 37%
Democratic 41
No difference (volunteered) 12
No opinion 10

30–49 Years
Republican 34%
Democratic 42
No difference (volunteered) 15
No opinion 9

50 Years and Over
Republican 29%
Democratic 45
No difference (volunteered) 13
No opinion 13

By Income
$25,000 and Over
Republican 44%
Democratic 32
No difference (volunteered) 15
No opinion 9

$15,000 and Over
Republican 40%
Democratic 37
No difference (volunteered) 14
No opinion 9

Under $15,000
Republican 23%
Democratic 50
No difference (volunteered) 13
No opinion 14

By Politics
Republicans
Republican 73%
Democratic 9

No difference (volunteered) 9
No opinion 9

Democrats
Republican 9%
Democratic 70
No difference (volunteered) 11
No opinion 10

Independents
Republican 35%
Democratic 29
No difference (volunteered) 23
No opinion 13

By Occupation
Professional and Business
Republican 44%
Democratic 34
No difference (volunteered) 11
No opinion 11

Clerical and Sales
Republican 35%
Democratic 42
No difference (volunteered) 18
No opinion 5

Manual Workers
Republican 29%
Democratic 47
No difference (volunteered) 15
No opinion 9

Nonlabor Force
Republican 27%
Democratic 46
No difference (volunteered) 12
No opinion 15

Labor Union Families Only
Republican 29%
Democratic 48
No difference (volunteered) 13
No opinion 10

Nonlabor Union Families Only

Republican 27%
Democratic 51
No difference (volunteered) 7
No opinion 15

National Trend

	Republican	Democratic	No opinion*
June 1982	33%	43%	24%
Feb. 1982	32	42	26
1978	23	41	36
1974	19	49	32
1970	25	40	35
1966	26	38	36
1962	25	48	27
1958	23	44	33

*Includes "no difference."

Which political party do you think would be more likely to keep the United States out of World War III—the Republican party or the Democratic party?

Republican 26%
Democratic 42
No difference (volunteered) 19
No opinion 13

By Sex
Male

Republican 28%
Democratic 40
No difference (volunteered) 20
No opinion 12

Female

Republican 23%
Democratic 44
No difference (volunteered) 19
No opinion 14

By Race
White

Republican 29%
Democratic 37

No difference (volunteered) 21
No opinion 13

Nonwhite

Republican 9%
Democratic 70
No difference (volunteered) 8
No opinion 13

By Education
College

Republican 30%
Democratic 41
No difference (volunteered) 19
No opinion 10

High School

Republican 24%
Democratic 45
No difference (volunteered) 19
No opinion 12

Grade School

Republican 22%
Democratic 36
No difference (volunteered) 23
No opinion 19

By Region
East

Republican 26%
Democratic 44
No difference (volunteered) 20
No opinion 10

Midwest

Republican 27%
Democratic 39
No difference (volunteered) 21
No opinion 13

South

Republican 27%
Democratic 43

No difference (volunteered) 16
No opinion 14

West

Republican 22%
Democratic 42
No difference (volunteered) 20
No opinion 16

By Age
18–24 Years

Republican 22%
Democratic 48
No difference (volunteered) 12
No opinion 18

25–29 Years

Republican 26%
Democratic 46
No difference (volunteered) 16
No opinion 12

30–49 Years

Republican 26%
Democratic 44
No difference (volunteered) 20
No opinion 10

50–64 Years

Republican 30%
Democratic 38
No difference (volunteered) 22
No opinion 10

65 Years and Over

Republican 24%
Democratic 36
No difference (volunteered) 23
No opinion 17

By Income
$25,000 and Over

Republican 30%
Democratic 36
No difference (volunteered) 22
No opinion 12

$15,000 and Over

Republican 29%
Democratic 39
No difference (volunteered) 21
No opinion 11

Under $15,000

Republican 20%
Democratic 46
No difference (volunteered) 18
No opinion 16

By Politics
Republicans

Republican 61%
Democratic 10
No difference (volunteered) 16
No opinion 13

Democrats

Republican 7%
Democratic 65
No difference (volunteered) 17
No opinion 11

Independents

Republican 25%
Democratic 33
No difference (volunteered) 28
No opinion 14

National Trend

	Republican	Democratic	No opinion*
June 1982	26%	42%	32%
Feb. 1982	24	41	35
1978	25	31	44
1974	21	29	50
1970	28	22	50
1966	30	22	48
1962	30	30	40
1958	29	23	48
1954	26	18	56

*Includes "no difference."

Note: With election day less than four months away, Republican efforts to make headway with the nation's voters on the long-term issues of peace and prosperity have yet to materialize. These twin issues historically have been the key ones in national elections, with the party on top on both having a distinct advantage at election time.

By the ratio of 43% to 33%, voters credit the Democrats as better able to keep the country prosperous, and by a vote of 42% to 26% as more likely to keep the nation at peace. These findings are almost a duplicate of those recorded in February.

In fact, the Republican party actually has lost ground on both issues since last fall. At that time, the GOP held a 40% to 31% advantage on the prosperity issue (an all-time high for the Republicans) and narrowly trailed the Democrats on the peace issue, 29% to 34%.

JULY 29

REAGAN ADMINISTRATION POLICIES

Interviewing Date: 6/11–14/82
Survey #196-G

I am going to read off some foreign and domestic problems that the Reagan administration has been faced with since taking office. As I read off each problem, one at a time, would you tell me whether you feel it has gotten much better, somewhat better, somewhat worse, or much worse as a result of the Reagan policies:

Ability of the nation to defend itself militarily?

Better............................... 54%
Worse............................... 13
Same (volunteered) 26
No opinion 7

By Politics

Republicans

Better............................... 65%
Worse............................. 8

Same (volunteered) 20
No opinion 7

Democrats

Better............................... 45%
Worse............................... 15
Same (volunteered) 31
No opinion 9

Independents

Better............................... 58%
Worse............................... 14
Same (volunteered) 23
No opinion 5

Chances for reducing the size of the federal government?

Better............................... 43%
Worse............................... 26
Same (volunteered) 19
No opinion 12

By Politics

Republicans

Better............................... 62%
Worse............................... 18
Same (volunteered) 14
No opinion 6

Democrats

Better............................... 31%
Worse............................... 31
Same (volunteered) 21
No opinion 17

Independents

Better............................... 45%
Worse............................... 26
Same (volunteered) 19
No opinion 10

Chances for reducing the federal taxes of the average citizen?

Better............................... 39%
Worse............................... 36

Same (volunteered) 17
No opinion 8

By Politics
Republicans

Better 61%
Worse 22
Same (volunteered) 13
No opinion 4

Democrats

Better 25%
Worse 46
Same (volunteered) 20
No opinion 9

Independents

Better 40%
Worse 36
Same (volunteered) 16
No opinion 8

Inflation?

Better 37%
Worse 48
Same (volunteered) 13
No opinion 2

By Politics
Republicans

Better 46%
Worse 30
Same (volunteered) 14
No opinion .... *

Democrats

Better 23%
Worse 64
Same (volunteered) 11
No opinion 2

*Less than 1%

Independents

Better 39%
Worse 45
Same (volunteered) 13
No opinion 3

Increasing respect for the United States abroad?

Better 35%
Worse 39
Same (volunteered) 19
No opinion 7

By Politics
Republicans

Better 51%
Worse 26
Same (volunteered) 18
No opinion 5

Democrats

Better 26%
Worse 45
Same (volunteered) 21
No opinion 8

Independents

Better 36%
Worse 42
Same (volunteered) 17
No opinion 5

Chances for balancing the national budget?

Better 31%
Worse 44
Same (volunteered) 17
No opinion 8

By Politics
Republicans

Better 50%
Worse 28
Same (volunteered) 19
No opinion 3

Democrats

Better............................20%
Worse..............................55
Same (volunteered) 15
No opinion 10

Independents

Better............................30%
Worse..............................43
Same (volunteered) 20
No opinion 7

Energy situation?

Better............................25%
Worse..............................39
Same (volunteered) 28
No opinion 8

By Politics
Republicans

Better............................37%
Worse..............................23
Same (volunteered) 33
No opinion 7

Democrats

Better............................16%
Worse..............................50
Same (volunteered) 25
No opinion 9

Independents

Better............................28%
Worse..............................35
Same (volunteered) 29
No opinion 8

Chances for world peace?

Better............................24%
Worse..............................44
Same (volunteered) 26
No opinion 6

By Politics
Republicans

Better............................41%
Worse..............................29
Same (volunteered) 26
No opinion 4

Democrats

Better............................16%
Worse..............................51
Same (volunteered) 26
No opinion 7

Independents

Better............................22%
Worse..............................44
Same (volunteered) 26
No opinion 8

Environmental situation?

Better............................20%
Worse..............................35
Same (volunteered) 32
No opinion 13

By Politics
Republicans

Better............................31%
Worse..............................23
Same (volunteered) 35
No opinion 11

Democrats

Better............................15%
Worse..............................40
Same (volunteered) 30
No opinion 15

Independents

Better............................17%
Worse..............................37
Same (volunteered) 34
No opinion 12

Unemployment?

Better	8%
Worse	81
Same (volunteered)	9
No opinion	2

By Politics

Republicans

Better	15%
Worse	67
Same (volunteered)	15
No opinion	3

Democrats

Better	4%
Worse	88
Same (volunteered)	6
No opinion	2

Independents

Better	5%
Worse	85
Same (volunteered)	7
No opinion	3

Note: As President Ronald Reagan completes a year and one-half in office, U.S. voters give his administration positive ratings on its record of achievement in handling only three of ten key problems. Not only is the administration given poor marks in dealing with areas where it is most vulnerable (unemployment) but also, to some extent, in those that have been the focus of Reagan's policies (reducing taxes and dampening inflation, among others).

On the international front, the administration gets its highest marks on national defense, with 54% saying the nation is better off militarily today than in the past and only 13% saying worse. This advantage, however, is vitiated by the 44% to 24% negative view regarding the administration's progress in bringing about world peace. Similarly, Reagan receives a 39% to 35% negative assessment for achieving respect for the United States abroad.

After defense, the administration receives the most favorable appraisal for reducing the

size of the federal government (43% say better, 26% worse), and for reducing the federal taxes of the average citizen (39% to 36% positive).

On the minus side, the assessment is 48% to 37% negative on inflation; 44% to 31% negative on chances for balancing the national budget; 39% to 25% negative on the energy situation; 44% to 24% negative on chances for world peace; 35% to 20% on the environmental situation; and finally, a whopping 81% to 8% negative on unemployment.

AUGUST 1
CONGRESS

Interviewing Date: 6/11–14/82
Survey #196-G

Do you approve or disapprove of the way Congress is handling its job?

Approve	29%
Disapprove	54
No opinion	17

By Sex

Male

Approve	26%
Disapprove	60
No opinion	14

Female

Approve	31%
Disapprove	49
No opinion	20

By Race

White

Approve	30%
Disapprove	54
No opinion	16

Nonwhite

Approve	21%
Disapprove	50
No opinion	29

By Education
College

Approve. 27%
Disapprove 62
No opinion 11

High School

Approve. 30%
Disapprove 52
No opinion 18

Grade School

Approve. 27%
Disapprove 44
No opinion 29

By Region
East

Approve. 30%
Disapprove 53
No opinion 17

Midwest

Approve. 29%
Disapprove 53
No opinion 18

South

Approve. 30%
Disapprove 54
No opinion 16

West

Approve. 24%
Disapprove 56
No opinion 20

By Age
18–24 Years

Approve. 37%
Disapprove 48
No opinion 15

25–29 Years

Approve. 31%
Disapprove 49
No opinion 20

30–49 Years

Approve. 26%
Disapprove 61
No opinion 13

50–64 Years

Approve. 29%
Disapprove 55
No opinion 16

65 Years and Over

Approve. 23%
Disapprove 49
No opinion 28

By Politics
Republicans

Approve. 29%
Disapprove 57
No opinion 14

Democrats

Approve. 30%
Disapprove 53
No opinion 17

Independents

Approve. 27%
Disapprove 55
No opinion 18

Registered Voters Only

Approve. 27%
Disapprove 59
No opinion 14

Nonregistered Voters Only

Approve. 32%
Disapprove 43
No opinion 25

National Trend

	Approve	Disapprove	No opinion
1982	29%	54%	17%
1981	38	40	22
1979	19	61	20
1977	34	42	24
1975	29	54	17

Do you happen to know the name of the representative in Congress from your district? What is his/her name?

Correct. 46%
Incorrect; don't know. 54

By Sex
Male

Correct. 50%
Incorrect; don't know. 50

Female

Correct. 43%
Incorrect; don't know. 57

By Race
White

Correct. 49%
Incorrect; don't know. 51

Nonwhite

Correct. 25%
Incorrect; don't know. 75

By Education
College

Correct. 52%
Incorrect; don't know. 48

High School

Correct. 45%
Incorrect; don't know. 55

Grade School

Correct. 40%
Incorrect; don't know. 60

By Region
East

Correct. 47%
Incorrect; don't know. 53

Midwest

Correct. 50%
Incorrect; don't know. 50

South

Correct. 52%
Incorrect; don't know. 48

West

Correct. 33%
Incorrect; don't know. 67

By Age
18–24 Years

Correct. 26%
Incorrect; don't know. 74

25–29 Years

Correct. 34%
Incorrect; don't know. 66

30–49 Years

Correct. 52%
Incorrect; don't know. 48

50–64 Years

Correct. 54%
Incorrect; don't know. 46

65 Years and Over

Correct. 56%
Incorrect; don't know. 44

By Politics
Republicans

Correct. 50%
Incorrect; don't know. 50

Democrats

Correct............................47%
Incorrect; don't know..................53

Independents

Correct............................44%
Incorrect; don't know..................56

Registered Voters Only

Correct............................55%
Incorrect; don't know..................45

Nonregistered Voters Only

Correct............................26%
Incorrect; don't know..................74

Asked of those who were able to name their congressman (46% nationally): Do you happen to know what political party he/she belongs to? Which party is that?

Democratic........................50%
Republican 39
Don't know 11

Also asked of those who were able to name their congressman: Do you approve or disapprove of the way the representative from your congressional district is handling his/her job?

Approve............................69%
Disapprove 15
No opinion 16

By Sex
Male

Approve............................69%
Disapprove 17
No opinion 14

Female

Approve............................69%
Disapprove 12
No opinion 19

By Race
White

Approve............................49%
Disapprove 39
No opinion 12

Nonwhite

Approve............................54%
Disapprove 40
No opinion 6

By Education
College

Approve............................69%
Disapprove 17
No opinion 14

High School

Approve............................70%
Disapprove 14
No opinion 16

Grade School

Approve............................66%
Disapprove 11
No opinion 23

By Region
East

Approve............................74%
Disapprove 9
No opinion 17

Midwest

Approve............................69%
Disapprove 13
No opinion 18

South

Approve............................68%
Disapprove 18
No opinion 14

West

Approve............................64%
Disapprove 21
No opinion 15

By Age
18–24 Years

Approve............................66%
Disapprove 17
No opinion 17

25–29 Years

Approve............................73%
Disapprove 12
No opinion 15

30–49 Years

Approve............................68%
Disapprove 13
No opinion 19

50–64 Years

Approve............................68%
Disapprove 16
No opinion 16

65 Years and Over

Approve............................72%
Disapprove 16
No opinion 12

By Politics
Republicans

Approve............................76%
Disapprove 13
No opinion 11

Democrats

Approve............................68%
Disapprove 15
No opinion 17

Independents

Approve............................65%
Disapprove 15
No opinion 20

Those Who Identified Congressman as Democrat (50%)

Approve............................70%
Disapprove 16
No opinion 14

Those Who Identified Congressman as Republican (39%)

Approve............................69%
Disapprove 14
No opinion 17

Note: With only three months remaining before the congressional elections, more than half the nation's eligible voters are unable to name the U.S. congressman or congresswoman representing their district. This finding, together with the problem that voter registration is no higher now than it was in July 1978—70% in each case—suggests that turnout will be as poor this year as it has been in earlier off-year congressional elections.

Among the 46% of the public able to identify their representative in a recent Gallup survey, the weight of opinion is more than 4 to 1 (69% to 15%) that he or she is doing a good job. In sharp contrast, only 29% of the public approves of the way the Congress, collectively, is handling its duties, while 54% disapprove.

The survey found wide variations in the ability of persons from different population groups to name their congressman, one of the most disturbing being the fact that only 30% of eighteen to twenty-nine year olds can identify their representative, compared to 52% of those thirty to forty-nine years old and 55% of those fifty and older.

A similar disparity is found on the part of persons now registered to vote: 55% can name their congressman compared to only 26% of the nonregistered. However, there is surprisingly little difference on the basis of political affiliation, with roughly equal proportions of Republicans, Democrats, and independents able to identify their congressman. The importance of name recognition is accented by the fact that in none of the demographic groups studied does approval of their congressman fall below a majority, and in most groups it greatly exceeds 50%. Conversely, in no group (except race) is disapproval more than 25%, and for most groups the figure is well below that level.

The public's evaluation of Congress as a body—as differentiated from its individual members—has proved to be highly volatile and dependent on the legislation at hand. The latest figures, for example, were recorded when Congress was being widely criticized for not having approved a budget for fiscal 1983. In June 1979, the low point in these ratings, President Jimmy Carter was at loggerheads with Congress for its refusal to enact his energy legislation.

AUGUST 5
EMPLOYMENT

Interviewing Date: 6/11–14/82
Survey #196-G

Are you now employed full time, part time, or not employed?

Full time 44%
Part time 10
Not employed 45
No answer 1

By Sex
Male

Full time 58%
Part time 8
Not employed 32
No answer 2

Female

Full time 31%
Part time 12

Not employed 56
No answer 1

By Race
White

Full time 45%
Part time 10
Not employed 44
No answer 1

Nonwhite

Full time 39%
Part time 10
Not employed 48
No answer 3

By Education
College

Full time 57%
Part time 13
Not employed 29
No answer 1

High School

Full time 43%
Part time 9
Not employed 47
No answer 1

Grade School

Full time 18%
Part time 8
Not employed 72
No answer 2

By Region
East

Full time 41%
Part time 11
Not employed 47
No answer 1

Midwest

Full time 43%
Part time 11

Not employed 45
No answer 1

South

Full time 46%
Part time 9
Not employed 43
No answer 2

West

Full time 45%
Part time 8
Not employed 46
No answer 1

By Age

18–24 Years

Full time 38%
Part time 18
Not employed 42
No answer 2

25–29 Years

Full time 58%
Part time 10
Not employed 31
No answer 1

30–49 Years

Full time 63%
Part time 8
Not employed 28
No answer 1

50–64 Years

Full time 40%
Part time 9
Not employed 50
No answer 1

65 Years and Over

Full time 5%
Part time 5
Not employed 88
No answer 2

Asked of working people: Thinking about the next twelve months, how likely do you think it is that you will lose your job or be laid off—very likely, fairly likely, not too likely, or not at all likely?

Very likely 8%
Fairly likely 7
Not too likely 27
Not at all likely 54
No opinion 4

By Sex

Male

Very likely 9%
Fairly likely 8
Not too likely 27
Not at all likely 52
No opinion 4

Female

Very likely 6%
Fairly likely 7
Not too likely 28
Not at all likely 55
No opinion 4

By Race

White

Very likely 6%
Fairly likely 7
Not too likely 28
Not at all likely 55
No opinion 4

Nonwhite

Very likely 15%
Fairly likely 10
Not too likely 23
Not at all likely 46
No opinion 6

By Education

College

Very likely 5%
Fairly likely 6

Not too likely 27
Not at all likely. 59
No opinion 3

High School

Very likely. 9%
Fairly likely. 7
Not too likely 27
Not at all likely. 53
No opinion 4

Grade School

Very likely. 12%
Fairly likely. 11
Not too likely 29
Not at all likely. 34
No opinion 14

By Region
East

Very likely. 5%
Fairly likely. 7
Not too likely 25
Not at all likely. 58
No opinion 5

Midwest

Very likely. 9%
Fairly likely. 4
Not too likely 29
Not at all likely. 52
No opinion 6

South

Very likely. 9%
Fairly likely. 11
Not too likely 26
Not at all likely. 50
No opinion 4

West

Very likely. 8%
Fairly likely. 6
Not too likely 28
Not at all likely. 55
No opinion 3

By Age
18–24 Years

Very likely. 10%
Fairly likely. 4
Not too likely 26
Not at all likely. 55
No opinion 5

25–29 Years

Very likely. 14%
Fairly likely. 10
Not too likely 30
Not at all likely. 44
No opinion 2

30–49 Years

Very likely. 5%
Fairly likely. 9
Not too likely 28
Not at all likely. 55
No opinion 3

50–64 Years

Very likely. 5%
Fairly likely. 6
Not too likely 28
Not at all likely. 53
No opinion 8

65 Years and Over

Very likely. 10%
Fairly likely. 2
Not too likely 10
Not at all likely. 73
No opinion 5

Asked of nonworking people: At the present time, are you actively looking for a job, or not?

Looking 17%
Not looking 72
Gave up looking (volunteered). 3
No answer. 8

By Sex

Male

Looking 28%
Not looking 59
Gave up looking (volunteered) 4
No answer 9

Female

Looking 12%
Not looking 78
Gave up looking (volunteered) 3
No answer 7

By Race

White

Looking 14%
Not looking 76
Gave up looking (volunteered) 3
No answer 7

Nonwhite

Looking 36%
Not looking 48
Gave up looking (volunteered) 4
No answer 12

By Education

College

Looking 22%
Not looking 70
Gave up looking (volunteered) 2
No answer 6

High School

Looking 20%
Not looking 70
Gave up looking (volunteered) 4
No answer 6

Grade School

Looking 6%
Not looking 77
Gave up looking (volunteered) 3
No answer 14

By Region

East

Looking 19%
Not looking 72
Gave up looking (volunteered) 4
No answer 5

Midwest

Looking 18%
Not looking 69
Gave up looking (volunteered) 3
No answer 10

South

Looking 14%
Not looking 76
Gave up looking (volunteered) 3
No answer 7

West

Looking 19%
Not looking 69
Gave up looking (volunteered) 2
No answer 10

By Age

18–24 Years

Looking 50%
Not looking 46
Gave up looking (volunteered) 4
No answer . . . . *

25–29 Years

Looking 30%
Not looking 60
Gave up looking (volunteered) 6
No answer 4

30–49 Years

Looking 23%
Not looking 71
Gave up looking (volunteered) 1
No answer 5

50–64 Years

Looking 9%
Not looking 78
Gave up looking (volunteered) 4
No answer 9

65 Years and Over

Looking . . . . *%
Not looking 83
Gave up looking (volunteered) 3
No answer 14

*Less than 1%

Note: At least one adult American in every six (17%) currently is either unemployed or fearful of losing his or her job. According to the latest Gallup survey, 8% of adults are not presently employed but are actively looking for work. Another 1% volunteered the information that they were unemployed but had given up looking. In addition, 8% said they were now employed but thought they were at least fairly likely to lose their jobs or be laid off within the next twelve months.

Fear of unemployment is highest among black workers, 14% of whom say it is very (8%) or fairly (6%) likely they will be laid off. In a January survey, 11% of blacks reported believing their jobs were in jeopardy. The comparable figures for employed whites were 8% in January and 8% in June.

There is a great deal of overlap between population groups with higher-than-average expectations of losing their jobs; in addition to blacks, these include blue-collar workers (17%), members of labor-union households (13%), Democrats (11%), and southerners (11%). Groups in which a high proportion of those not now employed are looking for jobs include blacks (16% compared to 6% of whites), and 18 to 29 year olds (17%). Twice the proportion of Democrats (9%) and independents (8%) is actively searching for employment, compared to only 4% of Republicans.

AUGUST 8
IDEAL LIFE-STYLE FOR WOMEN

Interviewing Date: 6/25–28/82
Survey #197-G

Asked of women: Let's talk about the ideal life for you personally. Which one of the alternatives on this card do you feel would provide the most interesting and satisfying life for you personally? [Respondents were handed a card listing five alternative life-styles.]

Married with children
  With full-time job 40%
  With no full-time job 39
Married with no children
  With full-time job 5
  With no full-time job 2
Unmarried with full-time job 6
No opinion 8

By Race
White

Married with children
  With full-time job 40%
  With no full-time job 42
Married with no children
  With full-time job 5
  With no full-time job 2
Unmarried with full-time job 5
No opinion 6

Nonwhite

Married with children
  With full-time job 42%
  With no full-time job 22
Married with no children
  With full-time job 5
  With no full-time job 2
Unmarried with full-time job 11
No opinion 18

By Education
College

Married with children
  With full-time job 46%

With no full-time job 31
Married with no children
   With full-time job 6
   With no full-time job 2
Unmarried with full-time job 9
No opinion 6

High School

Married with children
   With full-time job 40%
   With no full-time job 40
Married with no children
   With full-time job 5
   With no full-time job 2
Unmarried with full-time job 5
No opinion 8

Grade School

Married with children
   With full-time job 28%
   With no full-time job 48
Married with no children
   With full-time job 3
   With no full-time job 2
Unmarried with full-time job 3
No opinion 16

By Region

East

Married with children
   With full-time job 44%
   With no full-time job 41
Married with no children
   With full-time job 4
   With no full-time job. . . . . *
Unmarried with full-time job 5
No opinion 6

Midwest

Married with children
   With full-time job 35%
   With no full-time job 39
Married with no children
   With full-time job 7
   With no full-time job 3
Unmarried with full-time job 3
No opinion 13

South

Married with children
   With full-time job 38%
   With no full-time job 37
Married with no children
   With full-time job 4
   With no full-time job 3
Unmarried with full-time job 8
No opinion 10

West

Married with children
   With full-time job 43%
   With no full-time job 40
Married with no children
   With full-time job 5
   With no full-time job 1
Unmarried with full-time job 7
No opinion 4

By Age
18–24 Years

Married with children
   With full-time job 60%
   With no full-time job 20
Married with no children
   With full-time job 5
   With no full-time job. . . . . *
Unmarried with full-time job 11
No opinion 4

25–29 Years

Married with children
   With full-time job 44%
   With no full-time job 38
Married with no children
   With full-time job 5
   With no full-time job 1
Unmarried with full-time job 6
No opinion 6

30–49 Years

Married with children
   With full-time job 43%
   With no full-time job 31

Married with no children
    With full-time job 4
    With no full-time job 2
Unmarried with full-time job 5
No opinion 9

50–64 Years

Married with children
    With full-time job 25%
    With no full-time job 55
Married with no children
    With full-time job 5
    With no full-time job 2
Unmarried with full-time job 5
No opinion 8

65 Years and Over

Married with children
    With full-time job 29%
    With no full-time job 42
Married with no children
    With full-time job 6
    With no full-time job 3
Unmarried with full-time job 4
No opinion 16

By Income
$25,000 and Over

Married with children
    With full-time job 43%
    With no full-time job 36
Married with no children
    With full-time job 8
    With no full-time job 3
Unmarried with full-time job 4
No opinion 6

$15,000 and Over

Married with children
    With full-time job 41%
    With no full-time job 40
Married with no children
    With full-time job 6
    With no full-time job 2
Unmarried with full-time job 4
No opinion 7

Under $15,000

Married with children
    With full-time job 37%
    With no full-time job 39
Married with no children
    With full-time job 4
    With no full-time job 2
Unmarried with full-time job 7
No opinion 11

By Politics
Republicans

Married with children
    With full-time job 38%
    With no full-time job 44
Married with no children
    With full-time job 2
    With no full-time job 4
Unmarried with full-time job 6
No opinion 6

Democrats

Married with children
    With full-time job 39%
    With no full-time job 39
Married with no children
    With full-time job 6
    With no full-time job 1
Unmarried with full-time job 6
No opinion 9

Independents

Married with children
    With full-time job 45%
    With no full-time job 32
Married with no children
    With full-time job 5
    With no full-time job. . . . . *
Unmarried with full-time job 7
No opinion 11

By Religion
Protestants

Married with children
    With full-time job 37%
    With no full-time job 43

Married with no children
 With full-time job 4
 With no full-time job 2
Unmarried with full-time job 4
No opinion 10

Catholics

Married with children
 With full-time job 46%
 With no full-time job 35
Married with no children
 With full-time job 3
 With no full-time job 2
Unmarried with full-time job 8
No opinion 6

By Occupation

Professional and Business

Married with children
 With full-time job 58%
 With no full-time job 17
Married with no children
 With full-time job 5
 With no full-time job . . . . *
Unmarried with full-time job 10
No opinion 10

Clerical and Sales

Married with children
 With full-time job 50%
 With no full-time job 34
Married with no children
 With full-time job 7
 With no full-time job . . . . *
Unmarried with full-time job 5
No opinion 4

Manual Workers

Married with children
 With full-time job 47%
 With no full-time job 36
Married with no children
 With full-time job 1
 With no full-time job 1

*Less than 1%

Unmarried with full-time job 7
No opinion 8

Nonlabor Force

Married with children
 With full-time job 29%
 With no full-time job 50
Married with no children
 With full-time job 5
 With no full-time job 3
Unmarried with full-time job 3
No opinion 10

By Marital Status

Married

Married with children
 With full-time job 39%
 With no full-time job 46
Married with no children
 With full-time job 4
 With no full-time job 2
Unmarried with full-time job 2
No opinion 7

Single

Married with children
 With full-time job 54%
 With no full-time job 14
Married with no children
 With full-time job 5
 With no full-time job 1
Unmarried with full-time job 18
No opinion 8

Widowed

Married with children
 With full-time job 30%
 With no full-time job 42
Married with no children
 With full-time job 10
 With no full-time job 2
Unmarried with full-time job 1
No opinion 15

National Trend

1980

Married with children

    With full-time job 33%

    With no full-time job 41

Married with no children

    With full-time job 6

    With no full-time job 4

Unmarried with full-time job 8

No opinion 8

1975

Married with children

    With full-time job 32%

    With no full-time job 44

Married with no children

    With full-time job 6

    With no full-time job 3

Unmarried with full-time job 9

No opinion 6

Note: Although the traditional role of wife and mother is still perceived as the ideal life-style by the great majority of American women, there has been a sharp increase since 1975 in the percentage of women who regard a full-time job outside the home as an integral part of this ideal. Today as many women say they would like to be a wife and mother and hold a full-time job outside the home (40%) as would prefer being a stay-at-home wife and mother (39%). In 1975 the comparable figures were 32% and 44%.

There has been no increase in the small percentage who regard work but not children as their ideal. However, the desire for outside work among those who prefer a married life-style shows marriage and outside work actually ahead of marriage without work by a slim 45%-to-41% margin. In 1975 the overall figures were 38% and 47%.

The perception of outside work as part of women's ideal has grown at a faster rate than the percentage of women entering the work force, suggesting that the latter is likely to continue, perhaps at an even greater rate than at present. While the shift in preference has occurred among all groups of women, the most pronounced increase—and the key reason for the shift overall—has been the change in views among college-educated women and those under 30 years old.

In 1975 the ideal life-style of 18- to 29-year-old women was about evenly divided between marriage with children and working at a full-time job outside the home (40%) and being a wife and mother without a formal job (37%). In contrast, the ideal for women under 30 today is to be a wife and mother with an outside job, chosen by a 2-to-1 ratio (52% to 29%). Similarly, among college-educated women, the comparable percentages are now 46% to 31% in favor of marriage with children and outside work while in 1975 the figures were 37% to 34%.

Although a growing number hold jobs outside the home, women still prefer the traditional framework of marriage and parenthood. Only one woman in eight, 13%, would prefer not to have children and only about half this proportion, 6%, indicate a preference for staying single.

The stereotypical career-woman life-style—single, free, and in pursuit of a full-time career—has very little appeal to American women, at least as a permanent way of life. Only 6% in the current survey say they would prefer this type of existence.

AUGUST 9
VIEWS ON REAGAN DIVIDED, INTENSE, AND STALLED*

Despite lingering recession, President Ronald Reagan's standing in the opinion polls has been remarkably steady over the past five months. The president's approval rating in the Gallup Poll has not changed by more than 1 or 2 percentage points since early March and has been almost as steady in other opinion polls. At this time, it is hard to say whether that should be read

*This Gallup analysis was written by Andrew Kohut, president of the Gallup Organization Inc.

as good or bad news for the administration. A case can be made either way.

Certainly, the lack of movement in the polls reinforces the degree to which presidents' fortunes with the public are linked to the economic picture. As long as the economy shows no marked improvement or deterioration, neither does the public's appraisal of the president.

Uncharacteristically, Reagan's trip to Europe and the outbreak of war in the Middle East failed to increase his approval rating. Past presidents almost always could count on a boost in the polls when they took a foreign trip or when the public became anxious over the outbreak of war in some other part of the world. Not so with Reagan—he continues to be strictly a one-issue president. Analysis of Gallup approval ratings in 1981, early 1982, and again most recently all show that attitudes toward Reaganomics far overshadow opinion of the president in other performance areas.

Since early March, the public's overall evaluation of the president has been practically deadlocked, with about equal numbers of Americans approving and disapproving of the way he is carrying out his duties. A major political question is whether Reagan's public standing will revive if and when the economy recovers, or whether the current deadlock represents a permanent popularity plateau for him. Evidence to support either conclusion can be found in the public opinion polls.

Survey findings suggest that opinion of the president will improve dramatically when the recession ends. In the past, other presidents have regained lost support as the economy recovered; this was the case for Dwight Eisenhower after the 1958 recession, and Gerald Ford's popularity improved measurably after the 1974–75 slump, to the extent that Ford almost was reelected despite the severity of that recession.

Should the current recession end without a return to high inflation rates, Reagan would be in a position to take credit for successfully lowering the price spiral. Until now, the polls have shown that the public gives the administration little credit for ending double-digit inflation. A low inflation rate during a recession does not warrant public merit, but lower inflation during a recovery period might be a different matter altogether.

Despite the severe recession, there is still some reserve of long-term confidence in Reaganomics. To be sure, by a margin of almost 2 to 1, the public believes it has been hurt rather than helped by Reagan's economic program. But looking ahead a year, the public is divided on whether they will be helped or hurt and, in the long run, a plurality expects to be helped.

The most significant argument against a Reagan resurgence is the deep-seated feeling that many people have about him. The Gallup Poll has found that, compared to past presidents, the public holds more intensely positive and intensely negative opinions of Reagan. Consequently, his standing in the polls is less likely to fluctuate widely. In contrast, opinion of Jimmy Carter during his term in office rose and fell sharply, because the public did not have strongly held views of Carter. Reagan, on the other hand, is better defined to the public and evokes stronger opinions; therefore, his popularity may be extremely hard to challenge.

Given economic recovery, a Reagan climb in the polls may be inhibited by the extent of polarization in public opinion about his administration. The traditional Democratic coalition—lower-income groups, blacks, city dwellers, union members—is so anti-Reagan there may be little chance of any significant fence mending. In other words, the president would have to evince extraordinarily high approval among the rest of the population to overcome the collective antagonism of this bloc. To a degree, that is what the polls are showing now—strong approval for Reagan among upscale groups and equally strong (if not stronger) disapproval among downscale groups, with the middle class tilting against the president since the beginning of the year and the onset of the recession.

A strong recovery would almost certainly help the president, but given the steadfastness of public opinion, the recovery will have to be strong and unequivocal for it to have a big and immediate impact. The public opinion momentum of the Reagan administration in its first year probably cannot be reachieved, particularly if the Republicans sustain major losses in the congressional elections. However, should there be a demonstration of economic progress in coming months, there is a base of confidence in the administration's economic policies, albeit a shaky one, which can be built upon. It is not likely that Reagan and the Republicans can recover the ground they have lost among traditional Democrats, but with enough economic success, they can likely succeed without them.

If economic recovery is not just around the corner, the issue becomes how long Reagan's current modest level of support will be sustained. The experience of the past five months suggests that, given the intense character of Reagan's constituency, he has some staying power. However, that also has limits, which could be tested by prolonged or worsened recession.

AUGUST 12
MIDDLE EAST SITUATION

Interviewing Date: 7/23–26/82
Survey #198-G

Have you heard or read about the situation in the Middle East?

Yes 90%
No 10

Asked of those who replied in the affirmative: In the Middle East situation, are your sympathies more with Israel or more with the Arab nations?

Israel 41%
Arab nations 12
Neither (volunteered) 31
No opinion 16

By Sex
Male

Israel 46%
Arab nations 14

Neither (volunteered) 31
No opinion 9

Female

Israel 36%
Arab nations 11
Neither (volunteered) 31
No opinion 22

By Race
White

Israel 44%
Arab nations 11
Neither (volunteered) 30
No opinion 15

Nonwhite

Israel 23%
Arab nations 18
Neither (volunteered) 36
No opinion 23

By Education
College

Israel 46%
Arab nations 18
Neither (volunteered) 27
No opinion 9

High School

Israel 41%
Arab nations 10
Neither (volunteered) 32
No opinion 17

Grade School

Israel 28%
Arab nations 10
Neither (volunteered) 33
No opinion 29

By Region
East

Israel 34%
Arab nations 17

Neither (volunteered) 35
No opinion 14

Midwest

Israel 43%
Arab nations 10
Neither (volunteered) 33
No opinion 14

South

Israel 43%
Arab nations 10
Neither (volunteered) 29
No opinion 18

West

Israel 46%
Arab nations 14
Neither (volunteered) 24
No opinion 16

By Age
18–29 Years

Israel 45%
Arab nations 12
Neither (volunteered) 28
No opinion 15

30–49 Years

Israel 41%
Arab nations 15
Neither (volunteered) 31
No opinion 13

50 Years and Over

Israel 38%
Arab nations 10
Neither (volunteered) 32
No opinion 20

By Income
$25,000 and Over

Israel 48%
Arab nations 16

Neither (volunteered) 29
No opinion 7

$15,000 and Over

Israel 46%
Arab nations 13
Neither (volunteered) 30
No opinion 11

Under $15,000

Israel 34%
Arab nations 12
Neither (volunteered) 31
No opinion 23

By Politics
Republicans

Israel 52%
Arab nations 9
Neither (volunteered) 25
No opinion 14

Democrats

Israel 35%
Arab nations 14
Neither (volunteered) 32
No opinion 19

Independents

Israel 42%
Arab nations 12
Neither (volunteered) 32
No opinion 14

By Religion
Protestants

Israel 41%
Arab nations 12
Neither (volunteered) 30
No opinion 17

Catholics

Israel 41%
Arab nations 12
Neither (volunteered) 33
No opinion 14

National Trend

	Israel	Arab nations	Neither	No opinion
July 1982	41%	12%	31%	16%
June 1982	52	10	29	9
April–May 1982	51	12	26	11
January 1982	49	14	23	14

Also asked of the aware group: Do you approve or disapprove of the invasion of Lebanon by Israel to attack Palestine Liberation Organization (PLO) forces there?

Approve..............................23%
Disapprove 49
No opinion 28

By Sex
Male

Approve..............................34%
Disapprove 45
No opinion 21

Female

Approve..............................14%
Disapprove 52
No opinion 34

By Race
White

Approve..............................26%
Disapprove 48
No opinion 26

Nonwhite

Approve..............................10%
Disapprove 54
No opinion 36

By Education
College

Approve..............................29%
Disapprove 54
No opinion 17

High School

Approve..............................24%
Disapprove 46
No opinion 30

Grade School

Approve..............................11%
Disapprove 46
No opinion 43

By Region
East

Approve..............................23%
Disapprove 49
No opinion 28

Midwest

Approve..............................23%
Disapprove 54
No opinion 23

South

Approve..............................21%
Disapprove 43
No opinion 36

West

Approve..............................27%
Disapprove 49
No opinion 24

By Age
18–29 Years

Approve..............................24%
Disapprove 54
No opinion 12

30–49 Years

Approve..............................25%
Disapprove 47
No opinion 28

50 Years and Over

Approve...........................22%
Disapprove 47
No opinion 31

By Income
$25,000 and Over

Approve...........................31%
Disapprove 51
No opinion 18

$15,000 and Over

Approve...........................29%
Disapprove 48
No opinion 23

Under $15,000

Approve...........................16%
Disapprove 49
No opinion 35

By Politics
Republicans

Approve...........................31%
Disapprove 44
No opinion 25

Democrats

Approve...........................18%
Disapprove 53
No opinion 29

Independents

Approve...........................27%
Disapprove 46
No opinion 27

By Religion
Protestants

Approve...........................23%
Disapprove 47
No opinion 30

Catholics

Approve...........................20%
Disapprove 52
No opinion 28

*Also asked of the aware group: Some
people say the United States should require
that all weapons sent by the United States
to Israel should be used only for defensive
purposes. Other people say that Israel
should be able to use these weapons in any
way they feel is necessary. Which point of
view comes closer to your own?*

Defensive purposes only..............64%
Any way necessary 26
No opinion 10

By Sex
Male

Defensive purposes only..............59%
Any way necessary 32
No opinion 9

Female

Defensive purposes only..............69%
Any way necessary 19
No opinion 12

By Race
White

Defensive purposes only..............65%
Any way necessary 26
No opinion 9

Nonwhite

Defensive purposes only..............61%
Any way necessary 20
No opinion 19

By Education
College

Defensive purposes only..............64%
Any way necessary 28
No opinion 8

High School

Defensive purposes only 66%
Any way necessary 25
No opinion 9

Grade School

Defensive purposes only 59%
Any way necessary 22
No opinion 19

By Region
East

Defensive purposes only 68%
Any way necessary 23
No opinion 9

Midwest

Defensive purposes only 68%
Any way necessary 23
No opinion 9

South

Defensive purposes only 61%
Any way necessary 27
No opinion 12

West

Defensive purposes only 58%
Any way necessary 29
No opinion 13

By Age
18–29 Years

Defensive purposes only 64%
Any way necessary 25
No opinion 11

30–49 Years

Defensive purposes only 64%
Any way necessary 27
No opinion 9

50 Years and Over

Defensive purposes only 65%
Any way necessary 24
No opinion 11

By Income
$25,000 and Over

Defensive purposes only 63%
Any way necessary 30
No opinion 7

$15,000 and Over

Defensive purposes only 65%
Any way necessary 27
No opinion 8

Under $15,000

Defensive purposes only 62%
Any way necessary 24
No opinion 14

By Politics
Republicans

Defensive purposes only 59%
Any way necessary 35
No opinion 6

Democrats

Defensive purposes only 67%
Any way necessary 22
No opinion 11

Independents

Defensive purposes only 64%
Any way necessary 24
No opinion 12

By Religion
Protestants

Defensive purposes only 64%
Any way necessary 25
No opinion 11

Catholics

Defensive purposes only................66%
Any way necessary....................22
No opinion 12

Those Who Approve of Israel's Invasion of Lebanon

Defensive purposes only................46%
Any way necessary....................52
No opinion 2

Those Who Disapprove of Israel's Invasion of Lebanon

Defensive purposes only................77%
Any way necessary....................16
No opinion 7

Also asked of the aware group: As you know, one of the major questions in the Middle East situation concerns the Palestinian people. Do you think a separate, independent Palestinian nation should be established, or do you think the Palestinians should continue to live as they do now in Israel and the neighboring Arab nations?

Separate nation 46%
Continue as now 23
Other; no opinion...................31

By Sex
Male

Separate nation 52%
Continue as now 25
Other; no opinion...................23

Female

Separate nation 40%
Continue as now 22
Other; no opinion...................38

By Race
White

Separate nation 46%
Continue as now 24
Other; no opinion...................30

Nonwhite

Separate nation 42%
Continue as now 22
Other; no opinion...................36

By Education
College

Separate nation 53%
Continue as now 21
Other; no opinion...................26

High School

Separate nation 45%
Continue as now 24
Other; no opinion...................31

Grade School

Separate nation 34%
Continue as now 27
Other; no opinion...................39

By Region
East

Separate nation 54%
Continue as now 16
Other; no opinion...................30

Midwest

Separate nation 42%
Continue as now 26
Other; no opinion...................32

South

Separate nation 41%
Continue as now 26
Other; no opinion...................33

West

Separate nation 47%
Continue as now 26
Other; no opinion...................27

By Age

18–29 Years

Separate nation 49%
Continue as now 20
Other; no opinion. 31

30–49 Years

Separate nation 45%
Continue as now 27
Other; no opinion. 28

50 Years and Over

Separate nation 45%
Continue as now 22
Other; no opinion. 33

By Income

$25,000 and Over

Separate nation 51%
Continue as now 25
Other; no opinion. 24

$15,000 and Over

Separate nation 50%
Continue as now 23
Other; no opinion. 27

Under $15,000

Separate nation 40%
Continue as now 24
Other; no opinion. 36

By Politics

Republicans

Separate nation 47%
Continue as now 26
Other; no opinion. 27

Democrats

Separate nation 46%
Continue as now 21
Other; no opinion. 33

Independents

Separate nation 45%
Continue as now 24
Other; no opinion. 31

By Religion

Protestants

Separate nation 43%
Continue as now 25
Other; no opinion. 32

Catholics

Separate nation 48%
Continue as now 20
Other; no opinion. 32

Those Who Approve of Israel's Invasion of Lebanon

Separate nation 56%
Continue as now 26
Other; no opinion. 18

Those Who Disapprove of Israel's Invasion of Lebanon

Separate nation 52%
Continue as now 25
Other; no opinion. 23

Those Who Say That Israel Should Use U.S. Weapons for Defensive Purposes Only

Separate nation 49%
Continue as now 22
Other; no opinion. 29

Those Who Say That Israel Should Use U.S. Weapons in Any Way Necessary

Separate nation 48%
Continue as now 31
Other; no opinion. 21

Note: Sympathy among Americans for Israel in the Middle East conflict has shown a sharp decline in the past month, with 41% now siding with Israel over the Arab nations. In a mid-June survey, 52% took Israel's side. The decrease in sympathy for Israel has not been accompanied by a gain for the Arabs, however, since earlier supporters of the Israeli cause have moved into the ranks of the undecided. Twelve percent now side with the Arab nations, compared to 10% one month ago.

A major factor in the declining pro-Israel loyalties among Americans appears to be growing disapproval of Israel's invasion of Lebanon. In the early stages of its military operations to prevent Palestinian rocket attacks on Israeli settlements, American approval outweighed disapproval, 40% to 35%. But public support waned when the Israeli military operation grew into a massive assault on Beirut. The U.S. public today disapproves of the invasion by a 2-to-1 margin (49% to 23%).

Another question in the survey reveals that many Americans disapprove of the means used by Israel to gain its ends. A 64% majority believes the United States should require that all weapons sent to Israel be used only for defensive purposes.

One effect of the Middle East situation is an increase in the number of Americans who favor the establishment of a separate, independent Palestinian nation. At present, support for this outweighs opposition by 46% to 23%, among those familiar with the Middle East situation. When the same question was posed in 1975, 36% voted in favor, while 29% said the Palestinians should continue to live as they do now in Israel and the neighboring Arab nations.

AUGUST 15
JOB DISCRIMINATION AGAINST WOMEN

Interviewing Date: 6/25–28/82
Survey #197-G

Do you feel that women in this country have equal job opportunities with men, or not?

Have 43%
Have not 52
No opinion 5

By Sex
Male

Have 46%
Have not 50
No opinion 4

Female

Have 41%
Have not 54
No opinion 5

By Race
White

Have 43%
Have not 53
No opinion 4

Nonwhite

Have 47%
Have not 47
No opinion 6

By Education
College

Have 33%
Have not 63
No opinion 4

High School

Have 47%
Have not 49
No opinion 4

Grade School

Have 51%
Have not 40
No opinion 9

By Region
East

Have 42%
Have not 55
No opinion 3

Midwest

Have 41%
Have not 53
No opinion 6

South

Have 48%
Have not 45
No opinion 7

West

Have 41%
Have not 57
No opinion 2

By Age
18–24 Years

Have 45%
Have not 51
No opinion 4

25–29 Years

Have 37%
Have not 59
No opinion 4

30–49 Years

Have 42%
Have not 54
No opinion 4

50 Years and Over

Have 46%
Have not 48
No opinion 6

By Income
$25,000 and Over

Have 35%
Have not 62
No opinion 3

$15,000 and Over

Have 40%
Have not 56
No opinion 4

Under $15,000

Have 48%
Have not 46
No opinion 6

By Politics
Republicans

Have 48%
Have not 47
No opinion 5

Democrats

Have 44%
Have not 52
No opinion 4

Independents

Have 39%
Have not 59
No opinion 2

If you were taking a new job and had your choice of a boss, would you prefer to work for a man or for a woman?

Man 46%
Woman 12
Either (volunteered)...................38
No opinion 4

By Sex
Male

Man 40%
Woman 9
Either (volunteered)...................46
No opinion 5

Female

Man 52%
Woman 15

Either (volunteered)................... 30
No opinion 3

By Race
White

Man 46%
Woman 12
Either (volunteered)................... 38
No opinion 4

Nonwhite

Man 43%
Woman 14
Either (volunteered)................... 40
No opinion 3

By Education
College

Man 41%
Woman 13
Either (volunteered)................... 42
No opinion 4

High School

Man 47%
Woman 13
Either (volunteered)................... 37
No opinion 3

Grade School

Man 51%
Woman 7
Either (volunteered)................... 35
No opinion 7

By Region
East

Man 44%
Woman 10
Either (volunteered)................... 40
No opinion 6

Midwest

Man 46%
Woman 11

Either (volunteered)................... 39
No opinion 4

South

Man 49%
Woman 13
Either (volunteered)................... 35
No opinion 3

West

Man 45%
Woman 14
Either (volunteered)................... 38
No opinion 3

By Age
18–24 Years

Man 33%
Woman 21
Either (volunteered)................... 40
No opinion 6

25–29 Years

Man 41%
Woman 16
Either (volunteered)................... 38
No opinion 5

30–49 Years

Man 45%
Woman 12
Either (volunteered)................... 39
No opinion 4

50 Years and Over

Man 53%
Woman 7
Either (volunteered)................... 37
No opinion 3

By Income
$25,000 and Over

Man 47%
Woman 11

Either (volunteered)................... 39
No opinion 3

$15,000 and Over

Man 48%
Woman 11
Either (volunteered)................. 38
No opinion 3

Under $15,000

Man 43%
Woman 13
Either (volunteered)................. 38
No opinion 6

By Politics
Republicans

Man 50%
Woman 10
Either (volunteered)................. 37
No opinion 3

Democrats

Man 47%
Woman 12
Either (volunteered)................. 36
No opinion 5

Independents

Man 41%
Woman 14
Either (volunteered)................. 42
No opinion 3

National Trend

	Man	Woman	Either	No opinion
Views of Men				
1982	40%	9%	46%	5%
1975	63	4	32	1
1953	75	2	21	2
Views of Women				
1982	52	15	30	3
1975	60	10	27	3
1953	57	8	29	6

If a woman has the same ability as a man, does she have as good a chance to become the executive of a company, or not?

Yes................................42%
No.................................53
No opinion 5

By Sex
Male

Yes................................45%
No.................................49
No opinion 6

Female

Yes................................40%
No.................................56
No opinion 4

By Race
White

Yes................................40%
No.................................55
No opinion 5

Nonwhite

Yes................................55%
No.................................39
No opinion 6

By Education
College

Yes................................31%
No.................................66
No opinion 3

High School

Yes................................46%
No.................................50
No opinion 4

Grade School

Yes................................53%
No.................................37
No opinion 10

By Region

East

Yes................................46%
No.................................50
No opinion 4

Midwest

Yes................................42%
No.................................52
No opinion 6

South

Yes................................45%
No.................................49
No opinion 6

West

Yes................................33%
No.................................64
No opinion 3

By Age

18–24 Years

Yes................................48%
No.................................50
No opinion 2

25–29 Years

Yes................................42%
No.................................53
No opinion 5

30–49 Years

Yes................................38%
No.................................57
No opinion 5

50 Years and Over

Yes................................44%
No.................................50
No opinion 6

By Income

$25,000 and Over

Yes................................30%
No.................................65
No opinion 5

$15,000 and Over

Yes................................37%
No.................................59
No opinion 4

Under $15,000

Yes................................50%
No.................................45
No opinion 5

By Politics

Republicans

Yes................................47%
No.................................47
No opinion 6

Democrats

Yes................................43%
No.................................53
No opinion 4

Independents

Yes................................37%
No.................................60
No opinion 3

Note: Although women now comprise more than 40% of the U.S. labor force, the public sees little progress toward equal employment opportunities for men and women. Comparison of the results of a recent Gallup survey with one taken in 1975, in fact, reveals that fewer women now (41%) than in the earlier study (49%) perceive that equal job opportunities exist for the sexes, with a concomitant increase from 46% to 54% in the belief that women are discriminated against in employment. The attitudes of men toward female employment have not changed in the seven-year period between the two surveys.

In both polls, 46% believed that women have equal job opportunities and 50% thought that they do not.

This is not to say that job bias actually has grown during the seven-year interval. Instead, the figures probably reflect heightened awareness of sex discrimination in employment. As a case in point, 68% of college-educated women in the latest survey say their sex does not have equal job opportunities; the figure for women whose education ended at or before the high-school level is 49%.

Some change is noted in the proportions of men and women who believe the sex of their boss would be immaterial to them in a new job situation. Among men, however, there has been a sharp dropoff since 1975 (and an even greater decrease since 1953) in the proportion who say they would rather work for a male boss, from 75% in 1953 to 63% in 1975 to 40% today. There has been a less pronounced decline among women who prefer a male superior, but a 52% majority still would rather work for a man. There has been a marginal increase in the percentages of both sexes saying they would rather work for a woman: 15% of women and 9% of men would like to do so.

Finally, scant progress is recorded in the public's perception of the likelihood of women being promoted to executive positions, even if they have the same ability as men. In 1975 only 43% of men thought women had the chance to become executives, while 54% did not; in that same year, only 37% of women thought they could reach such positions, while 59% believed they could not. These figures are close to the present survey: men voted 45% to 49%, and women 40% to 56%.

Education plays a formative role in this perception, too, with 71% of college-educated women compared to 50% of the less well educated believing women do not have equal access to executive jobs. The comparable figures among men are 61% and 43%, respectively. Interestingly, women employed outside the home are far less likely than those without formal jobs to believe that women have equal job opportunities with men, or that they have an equal chance to achieve executive status. Among women with outside jobs, the weight of opinion is 2 to 1 (65% to 32%) that women do not have equal opportunities. And by a 67% to 30% margin, working women believe members of their sex do not have the same opportunity for advancement as men. Among nonworking women, opinion splits down the middle on both questions: 47% to 46% negative on equal job rights and 48% to 47% positive on women's chances of becoming executives.

AUGUST 19
PRESIDENT REAGAN

Interviewing Date: 7/30–8/2/82
Survey #199-G

Do you approve or disapprove of the way Ronald Reagan is handling his job as president?

Approve............................41%
Disapprove 47
No opinion 12

By Sex
Male

Approve............................45%
Disapprove 44
No opinion 11

Female

Approve............................37%
Disapprove 50
No opinion 13

By Race
White

Approve............................45%
Disapprove 43
No opinion 12

Nonwhite

Approve............................14%
Disapprove 73
No opinion 13

By Education
College
Approve......................49%
Disapprove 40
No opinion 11

High School
Approve......................38%
Disapprove 49
No opinion 13

Grade School
Approve......................35%
Disapprove 52
No opinion 13

By Region
East
Approve......................40%
Disapprove 49
No opinion 11

Midwest
Approve......................45%
Disapprove 45
No opinion 10

South
Approve......................38%
Disapprove 46
No opinion 16

West
Approve......................40%
Disapprove 48
No opinion 12

By Age
18–24 Years
Approve......................40%
Disapprove 49
No opinion 11

25–29 Years
Approve......................45%
Disapprove 41
No opinion 14

30–49 Years
Approve......................42%
Disapprove 45
No opinion 13

50–64 Years
Approve......................36%
Disapprove 51
No opinion 13

65 Years and Over
Approve......................45%
Disapprove 45
No opinion 10

By Income
$25,000 and Over
Approve......................51%
Disapprove 39
No opinion 10

$15,000 and Over
Approve......................47%
Disapprove 42
No opinion 11

Under $15,000
Approve......................33%
Disapprove 54
No opinion 13

By Politics
Republicans
Approve......................75%
Disapprove 18
No opinion 7

Democrats

Approve.............................21%
Disapprove 67
No opinion 12

Independents

Approve.............................44%
Disapprove 42
No opinion 14

*Now let me ask you about specific foreign
and domestic problems. As I read off each
problem, one at a time, would you tell me
whether you approve or disapprove of the
way President Reagan is handling that
problem:*

Economic conditions in this country?

Approve.............................31%
Disapprove 59
No opinion 10

By Politics
Republicans

Approve.............................62%
Disapprove 30
No opinion 8

Democrats

Approve.............................13%
Disapprove 79
No opinion 8

Independents

Approve.............................33%
Disapprove 55
No opinion 12

Inflation?

Approve.............................33%
Disapprove 58
No opinion 9

By Politics
Republicans

Approve.............................60%
Disapprove 32
No opinion 8

Democrats

Approve.............................16%
Disapprove 76
No opinion 8

Independents

Approve.............................39%
Disapprove 51
No opinion 10

Unemployment?

Approve.............................22%
Disapprove 66
No opinion 12

By Politics
Republicans

Approve.............................47%
Disapprove 43
No opinion 10

Democrats

Approve............................. 9%
Disapprove 81
No opinion 10

Independents

Approve.............................20%
Disapprove 65
No opinion 15

National defense?

Approve.............................47%
Disapprove 38
No opinion 15

By Politics

Republicans

Approve.............................63%
Disapprove 27
No opinion 10

Democrats

Approve.............................37%
Disapprove 45
No opinion 18

Independents

Approve.............................52%
Disapprove 34
No opinion 14

Environmental issues?

Approve.............................34%
Disapprove 41
No opinion 25

By Politics

Republicans

Approve.............................55%
Disapprove 26
No opinion 19

Democrats

Approve.............................24%
Disapprove 50
No opinion 26

Independents

Approve.............................35%
Disapprove 37
No opinion 28

Relations with the Soviet Union?

Approve.............................44%
Disapprove 34
No opinion 22

By Politics

Republicans

Approve.............................66%
Disapprove 19
No opinion 15

Democrats

Approve.............................31%
Disapprove 45
No opinion 24

Independents

Approve.............................47%
Disapprove 29
No opinion 24

Energy situation?

Approve.............................33%
Disapprove 48
No opinion 19

By Politics

Republicans

Approve.............................56%
Disapprove 32
No opinion 12

Democrats

Approve.............................21%
Disapprove 61
No opinion 18

Independents

Approve.............................33%
Disapprove 43
No opinion 24

Foreign policy?

Approve.............................36%
Disapprove 41
No opinion 23

By Politics
Republicans

Approve. 54%
Disapprove 29
No opinion 17

Democrats

Approve. 24%
Disapprove 51
No opinion 25

Independents

Approve. 41%
Disapprove 37
No opinion 22

National Trend of Attitudes Toward Foreign Policy

	Approve	Disapprove	No opinion
June 1982	45%	36%	19%
April–May 1982	43	37	20
April 1982	36	45	19
March 1982	36	44	20
February 1982	44	38	18
December 1981	49	36	15
October 1981	56	29	15
August 1981	52	26	22
March 1981	53	29	18
February 1981	51	16	33

Note: President Ronald Reagan generally has won higher marks from the American people for his conduct of foreign policy than for his handling of domestic affairs. The latest Gallup survey, however, shows an abrupt decline in the proportion approving of Reagan's efforts in foreign policy. A falloff also has been recorded in positive public assessments of two aspects of foreign affairs—the president's handling of the nation's defense and our relations with the Soviet Union.

Currently, 36% of the public approve of Reagan's handling of foreign policy, representing a 9-percentage point decrease from mid-June, when 45% held favorable opinions. By comparison, Reagan gets positive ratings from 31% and 35% of the American people for his handling of economic conditions in the latest and June surveys, a 4-point drop.

During only one other period in Reagan's term has he received as low an approval score for his handling of foreign policy as in the latest survey. In two Gallup surveys conducted in mid-March and early April of this year, when the El Salvador elections and labor unrest in Poland were in the headlines, only 36% rated Reagan's efforts in international affairs favorably.

Together with the pronounced decline in favorable public attitudes toward the administration's foreign policy, fewer people now (47%) than in June (56%) approve of Reagan's handling of national defense. There also has been a drop, from 49% to 44%, in those supporting Reagan's handling of our relations with the Soviet Union.

Although it is difficult to isolate the reasons underlying the public's growing disaffection with Reagan's foreign policy, some observers point to the administration's failure to resolve the Middle East crisis and to widespread public criticism of Israel's invasion of Lebanon. (A Gallup Poll conducted late last month showed more than 2-to-1 disapproval.) Others see Reagan's intransigence in the trans-Siberian natural gas pipeline deal with the Soviet Union, in the face of European disagreement, as one contribution to American dissatisfaction with foreign policy.

The president's overall popularity has been less vulnerable to shifts in public opinion on his conduct of foreign affairs than on economic matters. Last spring, for example, Reagan's overall approval rating fell merely 1 point while he was losing 8 points of support for his foreign policy. Currently, 41% of the public approve of the way Reagan is handling his presidential duties, while 47% disapprove.

AUGUST 22
NATURAL GAS PIPELINE

Interviewing Date: 7/30–8/2/82
Survey #199-G

Have you heard or read about the Reagan administration's attempts to prevent our allies from supplying U.S. equipment and technology to build a natural gas pipeline between the Soviet Union and Western Europe?

Yes.................................52%
No..................................48

Asked of those who replied in the affirmative: What do you see as the advantages of the administration's position on this matter? And what do you see as the disadvantages?

Sixty-three percent of the aware group, or 33% of the total sample, were able to name either an advantage or disadvantage.

Advantages of Administration's Position
(Based on Aware Group)

Forestalls European dependence on
  Soviet energy......................13%
Avoids helping Soviet Union.......... 7
Denies the Soviets Western currency.... 6
Strong position for United States........ 4
Shows disapproval of Soviet Union 4
Will save U.S. taxpayers money........ 2
Other 2
None; no advantages..................23
Don't know..........................41
                                    102%*

Disadvantages of Administration's Position
(Based on Aware Group)

Creates bad relations with our allies..... 21%
Poor, shortsighted, inconsistent
  foreign policy...................... 9
Hurts American business, workers 8
Damages Europe's economy 6
If U.S. technology not used, others
  will provide it..................... 4
Benefits Soviets more than
  United States...................... 4
Other 7
None; no disadvantages 10
Don't know..........................37
                                    106%*

*Totals add to more than 100% due to multiple responses.

Asked of the aware group (52% of the total sample): Would you say you approve or disapprove of the administration's position on this matter?

Approve............................48%
Disapprove 42
No opinion 10

By Sex
Male

Approve............................51%
Disapprove 42
No opinion 7

Female

Approve............................43%
Disapprove 42
No opinion 15

By Race
White

Approve............................50%
Disapprove 40
No opinion 10

Nonwhite

Approve............................30%
Disapprove 56
No opinion 14

By Education
College

Approve............................47%
Disapprove 45
No opinion 8

High School

Approve............................49%
Disapprove 40
No opinion 11

Grade School

Approve............................44%
Disapprove 41
No opinion 15

By Region

East

Approve.............................47%
Disapprove 38
No opinion 15

Midwest

Approve.............................54%
Disapprove 37
No opinion 9

South

Approve.............................50%
Disapprove 42
No opinion 8

West

Approve.............................38%
Disapprove 54
No opinion 8

By Age

18–29 Years

Approve.............................51%
Disapprove 38
No opinion 11

30–49 Years

Approve.............................50%
Disapprove 42
No opinion 8

50 Years and Over

Approve.............................45%
Disapprove 43
No opinion 12

By Politics

Republicans

Approve.............................67%
Disapprove 27
No opinion 6

Democrats

Approve.............................34%
Disapprove 53
No opinion 13

Independents

Approve.............................49%
Disapprove 40
No opinion 11

Those Who Approve of Reagan

Approve.............................66%
Disapprove 26
No opinion 8

Those Who Disapprove of Reagan

Approve.............................29%
Disapprove 62
No opinion 9

Note: The Reagan administration's attempts to block construction of a natural gas pipeline between Western Europe and the Soviet Union are endorsed by 48% of those Americans familiar with the situation and opposed by 42%. However, only about half the public (52%) in a recent Gallup survey say they have heard or read of the president's stand on the pipeline project, and still fewer (33%) can describe it. There is a strong partisan cast to public opinion on the issue, with "aware" Republicans backing the Reagan position by a 67% to 27% margin and Democrats voting against it, 53% to 34%.

The most frequently mentioned disadvantage of the Reagan position on the pipeline is the harm it has caused in our relations with our Western European allies, cited by 21% of the aware group. No other reason is mentioned by as many as 10%. There is even less consensus on the perceived advantages of the embargo, with only 13% of those aware stating that the U.S. stand would prevent Europe from becoming dependent on Soviet gas. Almost two in three in the aware group (64%), in fact, are unable to name any advantages (41%) or say there are none (23%).

President Ronald Reagan thus far has refused

to allow our European allies to use U.S.-licensed technical equipment in building a natural gas pipeline between Western Europe and the Soviet Union, as a protest against Soviet-directed repression in Poland. The U.S. position is that the pipeline eventually would make the West dependent on energy from the USSR and, further, that it would provide the Soviets with large sums of Western currency with which to advance its military and political interests. Reagan's obstruction of the project has caused severe strains in the Atlantic Alliance, and Germany, France, Italy, and Great Britain have refused to join in the U.S. embargo. The Europeans see an apparent strategic inconsistency in our continuing to sell grain to the Soviets in face of the boycott of the pipeline project.

AUGUST 26
DEMOCRATIC PRESIDENTIAL CANDIDATES

Interviewing Date: 7/30–8/2/82
Survey #199-G

Asked of Democrats: Will you please look over the list and tell me which of these persons you have heard of? [Respondents were handed a card listing fifteen possible nominees.] Now will you please tell me which of these persons you know something about?

	Heard of	Know something about
Jimmy Carter	93%	82%
Edward Kennedy	92	77
Walter Mondale	83	61
Edmund (Jerry) Brown	76	55
John Glenn	69	50
Jay Rockefeller	52	24
Daniel (Pat) Moynihan	43	20
Robert Strauss	38	14
Alan Cranston	34	17
John Y. Brown	31	13
Bill Bradley	30	14
Reubin Askew	24	9
Gary Hart	23	10

Ernest Hollings	15	6
Bruce Babbitt	14	5

Asked of Democrats: Which one of these persons would you like to see nominated as the Democratic party's candidate for president in 1984? And who would be your second choice? And who would be your third choice?

First Choice of Democrats

Kennedy	43%
Mondale	13
Carter	8
Glenn	7
Brown (Jerry)	4
Others on list	6
No opinion	19

First, Second, and Third Choices of Democrats Combined

Kennedy	64%
Mondale	39
Glenn	26
Carter	25
Brown (Jerry)	23
Rockefeller	5
Cranston	5
Moynihan	5
Others on list	*

*All others received less than 5% of the votes each.

Note: Edward Kennedy continues to enjoy a large lead over fourteen other possible contenders for the Democratic party's presidential nominee in 1984. The Massachusetts senator wins more than three times the vote as the runner-up, former Vice-President Walter Mondale, 43% to 13%. At this point in each of the last four presidential campaigns (two years prior to the election), Kennedy has led all other Democratic contenders or has been in a virtual tie for the lead.

Other front-runners are former President Jimmy Carter (8%), Ohio Senator John Glenn

(7%), and California Governor Jerry Brown (4%). The ten others on the list each receives less than 2% of Democrats' votes. The findings reported today are not significantly different from those recorded in an April survey when Kennedy led Mondale, 45% to 12%, among Democrats.

To a considerable extent, the current choices for the Democratic nomination are a result of name awareness. A majority of survey respondents has heard of only six of the fifteen persons tested and claims to know something about only four of the fifteen. As the table above indicates, the choices closely parallel awareness levels at this early stage and clearly show the importance of candidates making themselves known to the public. An obvious exception is Carter, who, though the best known, is thought not to be a candidate for a second term and has publicly endorsed Mondale for the nomination.

Although the current figures show that many Democratic hopefuls have a long way to go before they are well known to the electorate, they can take encouragement from the dramatic example of Carter, who was recognized by few people outside his native Georgia two years before the 1976 primaries. In fact, it was not until mid-1975 that as many as one Democrat in four had heard of Carter. At that point, he was the choice of merely 1% of Democrats to be their party's standard-bearer in the 1976 presidential race.

AUGUST 29
EVOLUTIONISTS VS. CREATIONISTS

Interviewing Date: 7/23–26/82
Survey #198-G

Which of the statements on this card comes closest to describing your views about the origin and development of man?

God created man pretty much in his present form at one time during the last 10,000 years 44%
Man has developed over millions of years from less advanced forms of life. God had no part in this process 9

Man has developed over millions of years from less advanced forms of life, but God guided this process, including man's creation 38
Other; don't know 9

By Sex
Male

Creationism 41%
Evolution without God 12
Evolution with God 38
Other; don't know 9

Female

Creationism 47%
Evolution without God 6
Evolution with God 38
Other; don't know 9

By Race
White

Creationism 44%
Evolution without God 10
Evolution with God 38
Other; don't know 8

Nonwhite

Creationism 46%
Evolution without God 7
Evolution with God 36
Other; don't know 11

By Education
College

Creationism 30%
Evolution without God 15
Evolution with God 50
Other; don't know 5

College (Graduates)

Creationism 24%
Evolution without God 17
Evolution with God 53
Other; don't know 6

College (Nongraduates)

Creationism 36%
Evolution without God 12
Evolution with God 47
Other; don't know 5

High School

Creationism 49%
Evolution without God 7
Evolution with God 35
Other; don't know 9

Grade School

Creationism 52%
Evolution without God 5
Evolution with God 26
Other; don't know 17

By Region
East

Creationism 40%
Evolution without God 9
Evolution with God 38
Other; don't know 13

Midwest

Creationism 46%
Evolution without God 6
Evolution with God 39
Other; don't know 9

South

Creationism 49%
Evolution without God 6
Evolution with God 34
Other; don't know 11

West

Creationism 40%
Evolution without God 17
Evolution with God 40
Other; don't know 3

By Age
18–24 Years

Creationism 35%
Evolution without God 9
Evolution with God 45
Other; don't know 11

25–29 Years

Creationism 41%
Evolution without God 12
Evolution with God 42
Other; don't know 5

30–49 Years

Creationism 40%
Evolution without God 10
Evolution with God 42
Other; don't know 8

50–64 Years

Creationism 54%
Evolution without God 8
Evolution with God 30
Other; don't know 8

65 Years and Over

Creationism 51%
Evolution without God 6
Evolution with God 29
Other; don't know 14

By Income
$25,000 and Over

Creationism 39%
Evolution without God 12
Evolution with God 45
Other; don't know 4

$15,000 and Over

Creationism 40%
Evolution without God 11
Evolution with God 42
Other; don't know 7

Under $15,000

Creationism 50%
Evolution without God 6
Evolution with God.................32
Other; don't know 12

By Religion
Protestants

Creationism 49%
Evolution without God 7
Evolution with God.................36
Other; don't know 8

Catholics

Creationism 38%
Evolution without God 8
Evolution with God.................47
Other; don't know 7

By Community Size
One Million and Over

Creationism 39%
Evolution without God 10
Evolution with God.................36
Other; don't know 15

500,000–999,999

Creationism 33%
Evolution without God 12
Evolution with God.................51
Other; don't know 4

50,000–499,999

Creationism 43%
Evolution without God 10
Evolution with God.................40
Other; don't know 7

2,500–49,999

Creationism 48%
Evolution without God 8
Evolution with God.................32
Other; don't know 12

Under 2,500; Rural

Creationism 51%
Evolution without God 8
Evolution with God.................34
Other; don't know 7

Which of these do you think should be taught in the public schools?

Creationism 38%
Evolution without God 9
Evolution with God.................33
All three (volunteered) 4
None (volunteered) 4
Other; don't know 13

101%*

By Sex
Male

Creationism 34%
Evolution without God 11
Evolution with God.................34
All three (volunteered) 5
None (volunteered) 4
Other; don't know 14

102%*

Female

Creationism 42%
Evolution without God 8
Evolution with God.................32
All three (volunteered) 3
None (volunteered) 5
Other; don't know 11

101%*

By Race
White

Creationism 37%
Evolution without God 9
Evolution with God.................34
All three (volunteered) 4
None (volunteered) 4
Other; don't know 13

101%*

Nonwhite

Creationism 45%
Evolution without God 8
Evolution with God...................28
All three (volunteered) 3
None (volunteered) 3
Other; don't know 14

101%*

By Education
College

Creationism 23%
Evolution without God 17
Evolution with God...................41
All three (volunteered) 6
None (volunteered) 6
Other; don't know 8

101%*

High School

Creationism 43%
Evolution without God 7
Evolution with God...................32
All three (volunteered) 3
None (volunteered) 3
Other; don't know 12

Grade School

Creationism 47%
Evolution without God 2
Evolution with God...................21
All three (volunteered) 2
None (volunteered) 5
Other; don't know 23

By Region
East

Creationism 32%
Evolution without God 9
Evolution with God...................36
All three (volunteered) 3
None (volunteered) 4
Other; don't know 16

Midwest

Creationism 38%
Evolution without God 7
Evolution with God...................36
All three (volunteered) 3
None (volunteered) 5
Other; don't know 13

102%*

South

Creationism 48%
Evolution without God 7
Evolution with God...................27
All three (volunteered) 4
None (volunteered) 2
Other; don't know 13

101%*

West

Creationism 31%
Evolution without God 14
Evolution with God...................33
All three (volunteered) 6
None (volunteered) 8
Other; don't know 10

102%*

By Age
18–24 Years

Creationism 28%
Evolution without God 11
Evolution with God...................36
All three (volunteered) 7
None (volunteered) 2
Other; don't know 18

102%*

25–29 Years

Creationism 35%
Evolution without God 17
Evolution with God...................37
All three (volunteered) 5
None (volunteered) 4
Other; don't know 5

103%*

30–49 Years

Creationism	36%
Evolution without God	9
Evolution with God	38
All three (volunteered)	4
None (volunteered)	4
Other; don't know	10
	101%*

50–64 Years

Creationism	46%
Evolution without God	6
Evolution with God	28
All three (volunteered)	3
None (volunteered)	4
Other; don't know	14
	101%*

65 Years and Over

Creationism	44%
Evolution without God	5
Evolution with God	24
All three (volunteered)	2
None (volunteered)	8
Other; don't know	18
	101%*

By Income
$25,000 and Over

Creationism	31%
Evolution without God	13
Evolution with God	40
All three (volunteered)	5
None (volunteered)	7
Other; don't know	6
	102%*

$15,000 and Over

Creationism	33%
Evolution without God	11
Evolution with God	38
All three (volunteered)	4

None (volunteered)	5
Other; don't know	10
	101%*

Under $15,000

Creationism	44%
Evolution without God	7
Evolution with God	27
All three (volunteered)	4
None (volunteered)	3
Other; don't know	17
	102%*

By Religion
Protestants

Creationism	43%
Evolution without God	8
Evolution with God	31
All three (volunteered)	3
None (volunteered)	4
Other; don't know	12
	101%*

Catholics

Creationism	32%
Evolution without God	7
Evolution with God	39
All three (volunteered)	4
None (volunteered)	4
Other; don't know	14

By Community Size
One Million and Over

Creationism	35%
Evolution without God	11
Evolution with God	33
All three (volunteered)	1
None (volunteered)	2
Other; don't know	18

500,000–999,999

Creationism	25%
Evolution without God	11
Evolution with God	45

All three (volunteered) 8
None (volunteered) 6
Other; don't know 7
                                102%*

50,000–499,999

Creationism 39%
Evolution without God 11
Evolution with God 32
All three (volunteered) 4
None (volunteered) 5
Other; don't know 10
                                101%*

2,500–49,999

Creationism 45%
Evolution without God 6
Evolution with God 28
All three (volunteered) 4
None (volunteered) 3
Other; don't know 15
                                101%*

Under 2,500; Rural

Creationism 41%
Evolution without God 7
Evolution with God 31
All three (volunteered) 3
None (volunteered) 5
Other; don't know 13

*Totals add to more than 100% due to multiple responses.

Teaching vs. Own Belief

Among those who believe in	Schools should teach only
Creationism	78%
Evolution without God	57
Evolution with God	74

Note: Debate over the origin of man is as alive today as it was at the time of the famous trial of Tennessee teacher John T. Scopes in 1925, with the public now about evenly divided between those who believe in the biblical account of creation and those who believe either in a strict interpretation of evolution or in an evolutionary process directed by God.

In a recent Gallup survey, 44% say they believe that God created man in his present form within the last 10,000 years, while 9% believe in the theory of evolution with God as creator, and 38% believe that man evolved from less advanced forms of life in a process guided by God.

Evolution theorists believe the earth is billions of years old, and that life forms developed gradually over millions of years. To support their views they cite evidence gathered during the last two centuries from geology, paleontology, molecular biology, and other scientific disciplines. Those believing in creationism, on the other hand, hold that the earth and most life forms came into existence suddenly at some time within the last 10,000 years, as an act of God.

Analysis of the survey brings the following to light:

1) Persons with college training lean 2 to 1 in favor of evolution, but nearly one third of the college segment believes the biblical account of creation. A difference, however, is found between college graduates and those who did not finish college. Graduates are more apt than nongraduates to believe in evolution, with or without God, and less apt to believe in biblical creationism.

2) Adults under 30 years old are about as likely to believe in the biblical account of creation as are persons 30 to 49 years old. Those 50 and over, however, are more likely to do so.

3) Southerners and midwesterners are slightly more likely to accept creationism than are persons from other regions of the nation.

4) The views of Protestants and Catholics differ rather sharply, with Protestants leaning toward the biblical account of creation, 49% to 43%, but Catholics siding with the evolutionary theories, 55% to 38%.

5) Most respondents would like to see their own view taught in the public schools. Those who believe in evolution without intervention by

God are the least likely to insist that only their view be taught.

Earlier this year a federal judge ruled that an Arkansas law requiring schools to balance their teaching of evolution and creationism violates constitutional guarantees of separation between church and state. U.S. District Judge William Overton held that what Arkansas called "creation science" met none of the essential characteristics of science. Instead, he wrote, it was an effort "to introduce the biblical version of creation into the public schools of the state."

SEPTEMBER 2
MIDDLE EAST SITUATION

Interviewing Date: 8/13–16/82
Survey #200-G

You notice that the ten boxes on this card go from the highest position of +5 for a country you have a very favorable opinion of all the way down to the lowest position of −5 for a country you have a very unfavorable opinion of. How far up the scale or how far down the scale would you rate Israel?

	1982	1981
Highly favorable (+5, +4)	18%	21%
Moderately favorable (+3, +2, +1)	37	54
Moderately unfavorable (−1, −2, −3)	25	15
Highly unfavorable (−4, −5)	12	4
No opinion	8	6

By Sex
Male

Favorable	61%
Unfavorable	33
No opinion	6

Female

Favorable	51%
Unfavorable	40
No opinion	9

By Race
White

Favorable	56%
Unfavorable	37
No opinion	7

Nonwhite

Favorable	48%
Unfavorable	37
No opinion	15

By Education
College

Favorable	63%
Unfavorable	34
No opinion	3

High School

Favorable	52%
Unfavorable	40
No opinion	8

Grade School

Favorable	54%
Unfavorable	29
No opinion	17

By Region
East

Favorable	60%
Unfavorable	36
No opinion	4

Midwest

Favorable	50%
Unfavorable	31
No opinion	9

South

Favorable	55%
Unfavorable	33
No opinion	12

West

Favorable 58%
Unfavorable 37
No opinion 5

By Age
18–24 Years

Favorable 56%
Unfavorable 40
No opinion 4

25–29 Years

Favorable 54%
Unfavorable 42
No opinion 4

30–49 Years

Favorable 57%
Unfavorable 35
No opinion 8

50 Years and Over

Favorable 54%
Unfavorable 36
No opinion 10

By Income
$25,000 and Over

Favorable 58%
Unfavorable 38
No opinion 4

$15,000 and Over

Favorable 59%
Unfavorable 36
No opinion 5

Under $15,000

Favorable 52%
Unfavorable 37
No opinion 11

By Politics
Republicans

Favorable 62%
Unfavorable 32
No opinion 6

Democrats

Favorable 55%
Unfavorable 37
No opinion 8

Independents

Favorable 52%
Unfavorable 41
No opinion 7

By Religion
Protestants

Favorable 55%
Unfavorable 37
No opinion 8

Catholics

Favorable 56%
Unfavorable 38
No opinion 6

National Trend

	Favorable	Unfavorable	No opinion
August 1982*	56%	36%	8%
1981	75	19	6
1980	74	21	5
September 1979	68	22	10
February 1979**	68	24	8
April 1978	59	28	13
July 1976	60	24	16
June 1976***	65	25	10
1967	74	19	7
1966	64	20	16
1956	49	25	26

*Invasion of Lebanon, June 1982
**Camp David summit, September 1978
***Yom Kippur War, October 1973; Six-Day War, June 1967

You notice that the ten boxes on this card go from the highest position of +5 for a person you have a very favorable opinion of all the way down to the lowest position of −5 for a person you have a very unfavorable opinion of. How far up the scale or how far down the scale would you rate Menachem Begin?

Highly favorable (+5, +4)............10%
Moderately favorable (+3, +2, +1).....37
Moderately unfavorable (−1, −2, −3)...26
Highly unfavorable (−4, −5)..........18
No opinion 9

National Trend

	Favorable	Unfavor- able	No opinion
August 1982	47%	44%	9%
June 1982	52	34	14
1981..............	54	30	16
December 1978	59	20	21
April 1978.........	39	23	38

The Palestinian people?

Highly favorable (+5, +4)............12%
Moderately favorable (+3, +2, +1).....45
Moderately unfavorable (−1, −2, −3)...23
Highly unfavorable (−4, −5).......... 7
No opinion 13

The Palestine Liberation Organization (PLO)?

Highly favorable (+5, +4)............ 2%
Moderately favorable (+3, +2, +1)..... 9
Moderately unfavorable (−1, −2, −3)...28
Highly unfavorable (−4, −5)..........49
No opinion 12

By Sex

Male

Highly favorable (+5, +4)............ 1%
Moderately favorable (+3, +2, +1).....11
Moderately unfavorable (−1, −2, −3)...27
Highly unfavorable (−4, −5)..........51
No opinion 10

Female

Highly favorable (+5, +4)............ 2%
Moderately favorable (+3, +2, +1)..... 9
Moderately unfavorable (−1, −2, −3)...29
Highly unfavorable (−4, −5)..........47
No opinion 13

By Race

White

Highly favorable (+5, +4)............ 2%
Moderately favorable (+3, +2, +1)..... 9
Moderately unfavorable (−1, −2, −3)...28
Highly unfavorable (−4, −5)..........51
No opinion 10

Nonwhite

Highly favorable (+5, +4)............ 4%
Moderately favorable (+3, +2, +1).....12
Moderately unfavorable (−1, −2, −3)...30
Highly unfavorable (−4, −5)..........33
No opinion 21

By Education

College

Highly favorable (+5, +4)............ 1%
Moderately favorable (+3, +2, +1)..... 8
Moderately unfavorable (−1, −2, −3)...34
Highly unfavorable (−4, −5)..........52
No opinion 5

High School

Highly favorable (+5, +4)............ 2%
Moderately favorable (+3, +2, +1)..... 9
Moderately unfavorable (−1, −2, −3)...27
Highly unfavorable (−4, −5)..........51
No opinion 11

Grade School

Highly favorable (+5, +4)............ 3%
Moderately favorable (+3, +2, +1).....12
Moderately unfavorable (−1, −2, −3)...22
Highly unfavorable (−4, −5)..........35
No opinion 28

By Region

East

Highly favorable (+5, +4)............. 2%
Moderately favorable (+3, +2, +1)..... 11
Moderately unfavorable (−1, −2, −3)... 27
Highly unfavorable (−4, −5).......... 53
No opinion 7

Midwest

Highly favorable (+5, +4)............. 2%
Moderately favorable (+3, +2, +1)..... 10
Moderately unfavorable (−1, −2, −3)... 29
Highly unfavorable (−4, −5).......... 44
No opinion 15

South

Highly favorable (+5, +4)............. 2%
Moderately favorable (+3, +2, +1)..... 10
Moderately unfavorable (−1, −2, −3)... 27
Highly unfavorable (−4, −5).......... 45
No opinion 16

West

Highly favorable (+5, +4)............. 2%
Moderately favorable (+3, +2, +1)..... 8
Moderately unfavorable (−1, −2, −3)... 27
Highly unfavorable (−4, −5).......... 56
No opinion 7

By Age

18–24 Years

Highly favorable (+5, +4)............. 2%
Moderately favorable (+3, +2, +1)..... 11
Moderately unfavorable (−1, −2, −3)... 34
Highly unfavorable (−4, −5).......... 44
No opinion 9

25–29 Years

Highly favorable (+5, +4)............. *%
Moderately favorable (+3, +2, +1)..... 10
Moderately unfavorable (−1, −2, −3)... 39
Highly unfavorable (−4, −5).......... 46
No opinion 5

30–49 Years

Highly favorable (+5, +4)............. 2%
Moderately favorable (+3, +2, +1)..... 9
Moderately unfavorable (−1, −2, −3)... 30
Highly unfavorable (−4, −5).......... 48
No opinion 11

50–64 Years

Highly favorable (+5, +4)............. 1%
Moderately favorable (+3, +2, +1)..... 11
Moderately unfavorable (−1, −2, −3)... 21
Highly unfavorable (−4, −5).......... 56
No opinion 11

65 Years and Over

Highly favorable (+5, +4)............. 2%
Moderately favorable (+3, +2, +1)..... 9
Moderately unfavorable (−1, −2, −3)... 19
Highly unfavorable (−4, −5).......... 49
No opinion 21

By Income

$25,000 and Over

Highly favorable (+5, +4)............. *%
Moderately favorable (+3, +2, +1)..... 7
Moderately unfavorable (−1, −2, −3)... 30
Highly unfavorable (−4, −5).......... 57
No opinion 6

$15,000 and Over

Highly favorable (+5, +4)............. 1%
Moderately favorable (+3, +2, +1)..... 8
Moderately unfavorable (−1, −2, −3)... 30
Highly unfavorable (−4, −5).......... 53
No opinion 8

Under $15,000

Highly favorable (+5, +4)............. 2%
Moderately favorable (+3, +2, +1)..... 11
Moderately unfavorable (−1, −2, −3)... 25
Highly unfavorable (−4, −5).......... 46
No opinion 16

By Politics

Republicans

Highly favorable (+5, +4). 2%
Moderately favorable (+3, +2, +1). 8
Moderately unfavorable (−1, −2, −3). . . 25
Highly unfavorable (−4, −5). 56
No opinion 9

Democrats

Highly favorable (+5, +4). 1%
Moderately favorable (+3, +2, +1). 11
Moderately unfavorable (−1, −2, −3). . . 37
Highly unfavorable (−4, −5). 49
No opinion 12

Independents

Highly favorable (+5, +4). 3%
Moderately favorable (+3, +2, +1). 8
Moderately unfavorable (−1, −2, −3). . . 34
Highly unfavorable (−4, −5). 44
No opinion 11

By Religion

Protestants

Highly favorable (+5, +4). 2%
Moderately favorable (+3, +2, +1). 11
Moderately unfavorable (−1, −2, −3). . . 26
Highly unfavorable (−4, −5). 47
No opinion 14

Catholics

Highly favorable (+5, +4). 2%
Moderately favorable (+3, +2, +1). 9
Moderately unfavorable (−1, −2, −3). . . 30
Highly unfavorable (−4, −5). 52
No opinion 7

*Less than 1%

Note: The number of Americans who hold an unfavorable view of the nation of Israel has risen sharply in the aftermath of recent events and is at the highest point since these Gallup measurements started in 1956. In the current survey, completed before the evacuation of the Palestine Liberation Organization (PLO) from Beirut, 55% of Americans give Israel a favorable rating, while 37% of Americans give it an unfavorable rating. In a 1981 survey, the comparable figures were 75% to 19%, respectively.

Despite the increase in unfavorable attitudes toward Israel, however, the ratings remain very much on the positive side. In fact, the percentage of those with a highly favorable opinion is virtually the same as that recorded in the 1981 survey. The sharpest decline in favorable opinion between the 1981 and 1982 surveys has occurred among women, a decline of 23 points compared to 16 points among men.

Unfavorable opinion of Israeli Prime Minister Menachem Begin also has grown since the invasion of Lebanon and is currently at an all-time high, with the public now evenly divided in their views of the Israeli leader. In the previous survey (June) conducted in the early stages of the invasion, public opinion in the United States toward Begin leaned heavily to the favorable side, 52% to 34%.

The overall favorable rating (both highly and moderately favorable) given the Palestinian people, 57%, exactly parallels the rating currently given Israel. The proportion of Israel enthusiasts (those giving that nation a highly favorable rating) is twice that for the Palestinian people.

One effect of the Middle East situation, as reported earlier, is an increase in the number of Americans who favor the establishment of a separate, independent Palestinian nation. A late July survey showed support for this outweighing opposition, 46% to 23%, among those familiar with the Middle East situation. When the same question was posed in 1975, 36% voted in favor, while 29% believed the Palestinians should continue to live as they do now in Israel and the neighboring Arab nations.

The American people draw a sharp distinction between the Palestinian people and the PLO. Whereas 57% give the Palestinian people a favorable rating, only 11% rated the PLO favorably.

SEPTEMBER 5
SEAT BELTS

Interviewing Date: 7/23–26/82
Survey #198-G

Thinking about the last time you got into a car, did you use a seat belt?

	1982 Yes	1973 Yes
National	17%	28%

By Sex

Male	18%	29%
Female	17	26

By Education

College	28%	40%
High school	13	26
Grade school	9	17

By Region

East	17%	27%
Midwest	16	29
South	14	21
West	24	38

By Age

18–29 years	17%	27%
30–49 years	17	30
50 years and over	17	27

By Occupation

Professional and business	25%	41%
Clerical and sales	17	33
Manual workers	12	22

What percentage comes closest to your best estimate of the number of persons whose lives would have been saved if they had used seat belts?

	Average estimate of lives
National	40%

Used seat belt last time	47%
Did not use seat belt	38

Favor $25 fine	50%
Oppose $25 fine	37

Drivers	40%
Nondrivers	40

Would you favor or oppose a law that would fine a person $25 if he or she did not wear a seat belt when riding in an automobile?

Favor	19%
Oppose	75
No opinion	6

National Trend

	Favor	Oppose	No opinion
1977	17%	78%	5%
1973	23	71	6

Note: This weekend 500 Americans may lose their lives in auto accidents and another 20,000 may be seriously injured. According to some estimates, as many as half these deaths and injuries could be avoided if motorists wore their seat belts.

The public is well aware of the lifesaving potential of seat belts, with the average estimate in the latest Gallup survey that 40% of auto fatalities could be prevented through the regular use of these safety restraints. Yet according to the survey, only one adult in six (17%) buckled up the last time he rose in a car, the lowest proportion recorded since this measurement began in 1973. In that year, 28% of survey participants were regular seat belt users.

As in the earlier surveys, persons living in the Far West and those from up-scale population groups—persons employed in business or the professions, the college educated, and those from upper-income families—are more likely to use their seat belts regularly. As a case in point, 28% of persons who attended college report they buckled up the last time they rode in a car. The comparable figure is 13% for those whose education ended at the high-school level and 9% for persons with only a grade-school education. However, the substantial decline in seat belt use in the decade between the 1973 and 1982 surveys—11 percentage points nationally—has been experienced among all major population groups and to about the same extent.

Given the present low level of seat belt use, it is not surprising that the public rejects, by a 75% to 19% margin, a proposal to fine a person $25 for not wearing a seat belt when riding in a car; these figures are consistent with earlier findings. Even among the 17% in the current survey who use their seat belts regularly, the weight of opinion is almost 2 to 1 (63% to 33%) against the fine.

A federal court recently announced that 1984 model cars must be equipped with passive safety restraints. From the start, the issue has been controversial. Last October President Ronald Reagan rescinded a federal regulation established in 1977 by the Carter administration, requiring all cars sold in this country after 1983 to have either an airbag or an automatic seat belt. Passive restraints, critics thought, were not worth the considerable added expense and represented unwarranted interference in citizens' lives. A better way, they said, was to mount an extensive public relations campaign to get people to voluntarily use the seat belts they already have.

Auto manufacturers balk at the ruling on economic grounds—automatic belts could add $150 to the cost of a new car and airbags from $300 to $1,000—and point to General Motors' unsuccessful 1975–76 effort to market airbags as an option.

SEPTEMBER 6
AUTOMOBILE SAFETY

Interviewing Date: 7/23–26/82
Survey #198-G

Have you ever been in a car accident in which someone was hurt?

	Yes
National	25%

The respondent was wearing a seat belt in 17% of these situations, while in 78% seat belts were not used.

Were you driving? Did you happen to be wearing a seat belt at the time, or not?

In accident situations where the respondent was driving the car, 23% were wearing seat belts, while in situations where the respondent was a passenger, only 11% said they were buckled up.

Do you favor or oppose keeping the present 55-mile-per-hour speed limit on the highways of the nation?

Favor	76%
Oppose	21
No opinion	3

By Sex
Male

Favor	67%
Oppose	30
No opinion	3

Female

Favor	84%
Oppose	13
No opinion	3

By Education
College

Favor	75%
Oppose	24
No opinion	1

High School

Favor	75%
Oppose	21
No opinion	4

Grade School

Favor..............................81%
Oppose............................18
No opinion 1

By Region
East

Favor..............................81%
Oppose............................16
No opinion 3

Midwest

Favor..............................76%
Oppose............................22
No opinion 2

South

Favor..............................72%
Oppose............................25
No opinion 3

West

Favor..............................74%
Oppose............................23
No opinion 3

By Age
18–29 Years

Favor..............................74%
Oppose............................24
No opinion 2

30–49 Years

Favor..............................72%
Oppose............................24
No opinion 4

50 Years and Over

Favor..............................81%
Oppose............................17
No opinion 2

Drivers Only

Favor..............................74%
Oppose............................24
No opinion 2

Nondrivers Only

Favor..............................83%
Oppose............................10
No opinion 7

Those Who Have Been Stopped for Speeding

Favor..............................63%
Oppose............................35
No opinion 2

Those Who Have Not Been Stopped for Speeding

Favor..............................79%
Oppose............................19
No opinion 2

Asked of drivers: Have you ever been stopped by the police for exceeding the 55-mile-per-hour speed limit?

                                    Yes

National 29%

By Sex

Male.................................39%
Female............................17

By Education

College.............................33%
High school......................27
Grade school....................21

By Region

East 26%
Midwest..........................25
South 32
West...............................32

By Age

18–29 years 35%
30–49 years........................ 29
50 years and over.................... 22

Note: Despite mounting pressure on Congress to repeal the national 55-mile-per-hour speed limit, the public votes overwhelmingly to retain it. In the latest Gallup survey, 76% favor keeping the 55-mph limit, while 21% would like to see it abolished. Public opinion on the issue has been remarkably stable since the law was enacted in 1974 as an energy-saving measure. In six national studies, support for the 55-mph limit has never fallen below 71%, and opposition has not topped 26% (both from the 1979 survey).

In addition to contributing to the lower rate of consumption of petroleum products, the 55-mph limit has reduced auto accidents by forcing motorists to drive more slowly. Now that there is an oversupply of oil and lower gas prices, critics of the legal speed limit have increased their demands for its repeal. Criticism of the national limit has been particularly intense in the western and southern states, where long stretches of uncrowded, open highways are common. However, public support in these states for keeping the 55-mph limit is only marginally lower than in other areas of the nation.

A 1978 federal law requires that at least 50% of the motorists in each state comply with the law. Failure to meet this requirement could cause noncomplying states to lose 5% of their federal funds for highway construction and repair. Nevertheless, some states are finding ways to circumvent the law. Nevada, for example, imposes only a $5 fine for motorists driving between 55 and 70 mph.

Despite evidence that many states and localities are relaxing their efforts to enforce the 55-mph limit, three drivers in 10 (29%), by their own testimony, have been stopped by the police for exceeding it. Most likely to say they have disobeyed the national speed limit are men, young adults of both sexes, and the college educated.

The legal 55-mph maximum speed is credited with having saved 50,000 lives since it was enacted in 1974. By some estimates, as many as a quarter-million barrels of oil per day are conserved because of the lower speed limit.

SEPTEMBER 12
MOST IMPORTANT PROBLEM

Interviewing Date: 8/13–16/82
Survey #200-G

What do you think is the most important problem facing this country today?

	August 1982	June 1982
Unemployment; recession	48%	41%
Inflation; high cost of living...	23	25
Economy (general)	16	11
High interest rates..........	8	10
Fear of war................	6	10
Excessive government spending	5	6
Reagan budget cuts..........	5	5
Moral decline in society......	4	4
International problems	3	3
Crime	3	3
All other responses	6	8
No opinion	3	3
	130%*	129%*

By Region**
East

Unemployment; recession 49%
Inflation; high cost of living 21
Economy (general)..................... 17
High interest rates 6

Midwest

Unemployment; recession 53%
Inflation; high cost of living 22
Economy (general)..................... 18
High interest rates 9

South

Unemployment; recession	40%
Inflation; high cost of living	29
Economy (general).	12
High interest rates	9

West

Unemployment; recession	51%
Inflation; high cost of living	19
Economy (general).	20
High interest rates	8

*Totals add to more than 100% due to multiple responses.
**Top four problems named

Asked of those who named a problem: Which political party do you think can do a better job of handling the problem you have just mentioned—the Republican party or the Democratic party?

Republican	26%
Democratic.	35
No difference (volunteered)	27
No opinion	12

Note: With the congressional elections now less than two months away, nearly half of U.S. voters (48%) name unemployment as the most important problem facing the country, while 23% cite inflation or the high cost of living. In mid-June these figures were 41% and 25%, respectively. Another 16% say the economy in general, and 8% say high interest rates. Next are fear of war (6%), excessive government spending (5%), and the Reagan administration's budget cuts (5%).

In the latest survey, 35% of all voters nationwide believe the Democratic party is better able to deal with the problem, while 26% name the Republican party. Another 39% perceive no difference between the parties in their ability to handle the nation's top problems or do not express an opinion.

The political significance of these findings stems from the fact that the views of voters on the relative ability of the parties to deal with the top problems has proved to be an accurate barometer of the division of the popular vote in congressional elections. For example, the Democratic-Republican division was 55% to 45% in an October survey in the previous (1978) off-year congressional election, foreshadowing the 54% to 46% two-party split in the popular vote for Congress that November. In 1974 an October test found the Democrats leading 61% to 39% on this barometer, closely comparable to the 59% to 41% vote in the congressional races that November. The two-party split in the current survey is 55% Democratic, 45% Republican.

SEPTEMBER 16
REPUBLICAN PRESIDENTIAL CANDIDATES

Interviewing Date: 8/13–16/82
Survey #200-G

Asked of Republicans: Will you please look over this list and tell me which of these persons you have heard of? [Respondents were handed a card listing fifteen possible nominees.] Now will you please tell me which of these persons you know something about?

	Heard of	Know something about
George Bush.	93%	76%
John Connally	83	56
Howard Baker	81	55
Robert Dole	69	43
Jesse Helms	55	28
Jack Kemp	46	25
Philip Crane	37	16
Orrin Hatch	35	14
Lowell Weicker	34	19
William Armstrong.	31	8
Paul Laxalt.	24	12
John Danforth	21	7
Robert Packwood	21	9
Richard Lugar	20	10
David Durenberger	12	5

Asked of Republicans and independents: If Ronald Reagan decides not to stand for reelection, which one would you like to see nominated as the Republican party's candidate for president in 1984? And who would be your second and third choices?

First Choices of Republicans

Bush	32%
Baker	15
Connally	7
Kemp	4
Dole	4
Helms	2
Others on list*	5
No opinion	31

First Choices of Independents

Bush	21%
Baker	15
Connally	9
Kemp	5
Dole	2
Helms	2
Weicker	2
Others on list*	6
No opinion	38

First, Second, and Third Choices of Republicans

Bush	50%
Baker	39
Connally	20
Dole	19
Kemp	13
Crane	5
Armstrong	5
Helms	5
Weicker	3
Lugar	3
Others on list*	**

First, Second, and Third Choices of Independents

Baker	23%
Bush	19

Dole	14
Connally	8
Kemp	8
Crane	5
Armstrong	4
Helms	4
Weicker	4
Lugar	2
Others on list*	**

*All others received 1% or less. Write-in candidates, none of whom received as much as 1%, included John Anderson, Gerald Ford, Barry Goldwater, Alexander Haig, Richard Nixon, and Charles Percy.

**Two percent or less of the votes of Republicans and independents.

Asked of the entire sample: Would you like to see Ronald Reagan run for president in 1984, or not?

Would	36%
Would not	51
No opinion	13

By Politics
Republicans

Would	65%
Would not	24
No opinion	11

Democrats

Would	19%
Would not	72
No opinion	9

Independents

Would	35%
Would not	48
No opinion	17

Also asked of the entire sample: Regardless of whether you would like to see him run, do you think Reagan will run for president in 1984, or not?

Will 67%
Will not 21
No opinion 12

By Politics

Republicans

Will 68%
Will not 21
No opinion 11

Democrats

Will 68%
Will not 23
No opinion 9

Independents

Will 69%
Will not 19
No opinion 12

Note: Vice-President George Bush is the early first choice of Republicans to be their party's 1984 presidential nominee if President Ronald Reagan decides not to run again. In the latest Gallup survey, Bush receives twice as many first-place votes from Republicans (32%) as does the runner-up, Senator Howard Baker (15%).

Only about one-third of all voters (36%) say they would like to see Reagan run for reelection in 1984, virtually unchanged from a March survey, when 35% expressed the same opinion. However, 67% currently say they think Reagan will run, up substantially from the 59% recorded in March.

Predictably, the public's expressed desire to see Reagan run follows party lines, with far more Republicans (65%) than either independents (35%) or Democrats (19%) saying the president should stand for reelection. Two in three from each political background now hold the view that Reagan will again be the GOP standard-bearer in 1984. If he runs, the survey results suggest he will find strong Republican support.

SEPTEMBER 19
CONGRESSIONAL ELECTIONS

Interviewing Date: 8/13–16, 27–30/82
Survey #200-G; 201-G

Asked of registered voters: If the elections for Congress were being held today, which party would you like to see win in this congressional district—the Republican party or the Democratic party? [Those who said they were undecided or who voted for a different party were asked: As of today, do you lean more to the Republican party or to the Democratic party?]

Republican 44%*
Democratic 56

By Region

Nonsouth

Republican 44%
Democratic 56

South

Republican 44%
Democratic 56

*The undecided vote has been eliminated.

Note: With the congressional elections only seven weeks away, the Democratic party enjoys a solid lead over the Republican party in the popular vote for seats in the U.S. House of Representatives. The Democrats are currently the choice of 56% of likely voters to 44% for the Republicans. In the 1978 congressional elections, Democratic candidates won about 55% of the popular vote, resulting in a seat division of 276 for the Democrats and 157 for the Republicans.

While the current findings do not look hopeful for the Republicans this fall in terms of the overall division of House seats, GOP strength has remained constant in recent months after a steady decline between June of 1981 and February of the current year. At this point, however, the GOP appears headed for at least the normal seat loss for the party in control of the White House—a loss that has averaged about 30 seats in the nine off-year elections since 1946.

Historically, little change has been recorded in Gallup findings from September—when campaigns unofficially begin—and the final preelection survey figures, as shown in the table below. Events and other factors could change this pattern.

Vote for Democratic Candidates
(Based on Registered Voters)

	September survey	Final Preelection survey	Election results
1978	56%	55%	54.6%
1974	60	60	58.9
1970	54	53	54.3
1966*	52	52.5	51.9
1962	57	55.5	52.7
1958	58	57	56.5
1954	52	51.5	52.7

*October survey

A key reason for the Democrats' continuing wide lead in the congressional race thus far is the fact that the Republicans have yet to persuade the electorate they can do a better job on the issues considered most important by voters. A recent Gallup report indicated that, by a 55%-to-45% margin among those who make a choice, voters hold the view that the Democratic party is better able than the GOP to handle the problem they consider most vital to the nation.

SEPTEMBER 20
PLO FAILS TO BENEFIT FROM WANING SYMPATHY FOR ISRAEL*

For the first time since its creation as a nation, Israel is viewed unfavorably by a sizable pro-

*This Gallup analysis was written by Andrew Kohut, president of the Gallup Organization Inc.

portion of Americans. However, the Palestine Liberation Organization (PLO) has failed to gain support in the United States as a consequence of increasing American disaffection with Israel. The PLO's diplomatic successes and respectability in Western Europe stand in sharp contrast to the American public's view.

Throughout the war in Lebanon, opinion polls in the United States have monitored American attitudes toward the conflict and the larger issues of the Middle East dispute. The first polls in early June showed no immediate loss of support for Israel as a result of the war, but as the fighting escalated and Beirut itself became a battleground, public reaction changed.

In June, two weeks after Israel sent its forces into Lebanon, 52% of the Gallup sample aware of the situation reported that its sympathies were with Israel, a level of support almost exactly equal to that recorded by Gallup a month before the invasion. The CBS/*New York Times* Poll also showed no general falloff in support for Israel at the time, but a June NBC/AP Poll found a 41% plurality condemning the specific actions taken by Israel in Lebanon.

When Gallup repeated its basic sympathies question in late July as the siege of Beirut continued, American opinion of Israel showed a marked decline: only 41% reported their sympathies were with the Israelis. The NBC/AP Poll found a 10-percentage point increase in disapproval of Israel's actions in Lebanon. A mid-August Gallup Poll found even more dramatic changes in opinion. The percentage of Americans who held an unfavorable view of Israel rose from 19% in 1981 to 36%, the largest to express an unfavorable opinion of Israel in nearly twenty years of Gallup ratings. Commensurately, favorable opinion declined from 75% to 56%.

As longstanding feelings of friendship for Israel initially inhibited a loss of support over the war, longstanding American antipathy toward the PLO appears to have forestalled, if not precluded, gains in American sympathy. The polls of the past month have shown that the PLO has failed to achieve respectability in the eyes of the American public.

Since 1978 the percentage who rate Menachem Begin poorly for his efforts to achieve peace in the Middle East has steadily grown, yet opinion of Yasir Arafat has not improved. A 1981 *Newsweek* Poll had 5% giving the PLO chief good marks for his peace efforts. Last month, *Newsweek* repeated the question and still found only about one in 20 Americans having a favorable opinion of Arafat. Similarly, the *Los Angeles Times* Poll showed only 9% holding a positive impression of the PLO. The NBC/AP Poll showed no significant change in American attitudes toward diplomatic recognition of the PLO: 60% were opposed in 1981 and 57% in August of 1982.

These polls and others suggest that American views of the PLO and its leadership have changed little despite Israel's fall from favor. To a plurality of Americans, the PLO continues to be defined in terrorist terms; 49% in the August *Newsweek* Poll felt that the principal purpose of the PLO is the destruction of Israel, compared to the 29% who saw the purpose of the organization as the establishment of a Palestinian homeland.

The war in Lebanon has unsettled American views of the Middle East situation. On balance, basic sympathies continue to rest with the Israelis, but significant numbers of Americans now have reservations about Israel's policies. A plurality sees Israel relying too much on force, and polls also have shown increased support for a homeland for the Palestinians. But the siege of West Beirut has not accorded instant legitimacy to the PLO. The polls suggest that Americans are taking a more pro-Palestinian view of the issues without raising their opinion of the PLO itself.

SEPTEMBER 23
REAGANOMICS

Interviewing Date: 8/13–16/82
Survey #200-G

What effect do you think the Reagan administration's economic policies will have on your own and your family's financial situation? Do you feel your financial situation will be much better, somewhat better, somewhat worse, or much worse as a result of the Reagan economic policies?

Better.............................23%
Worse..............................56
Same (volunteered)...................15
No opinion.......................... 6

By Sex
Male

Better.............................26%
Worse..............................53
Same (volunteered)...................15
No opinion.......................... 6

Female

Better.............................20%
Worse..............................58
Same (volunteered)...................15
No opinion.......................... 7

By Race
White

Better.............................27%
Worse..............................53
Same (volunteered)...................15
No opinion.......................... 5

Nonwhite

Better............................. 6%
Worse..............................73
Same (volunteered)...................11
No opinion..........................10

By Education
College

Better.............................29%
Worse..............................50
Same (volunteered)...................17
No opinion.......................... 4

High School

Better.............................22%
Worse.............................59
Same (volunteered)................13
No opinion........................ 6

Grade School

Better.............................17%
Worse.............................59
Same (volunteered)................15
No opinion........................ 9

By Region
East

Better.............................23%
Worse.............................57
Same (volunteered)................15
No opinion........................ 5

Midwest

Better.............................21%
Worse.............................56
Same (volunteered)................16
No opinion........................ 7

South

Better.............................23%
Worse.............................54
Same (volunteered)................17
No opinion........................ 6

West

Better.............................25%
Worse.............................61
Same (volunteered)................10
No opinion........................ 4

By Age
18–24 Years

Better.............................22%
Worse.............................55
Same (volunteered)................14
No opinion........................ 9

25–29 Years

Better.............................27%
Worse.............................57
Same (volunteered)................12
No opinion........................ 4

30–49 Years

Better.............................26%
Worse.............................55
Same (volunteered)................14
No opinion........................ 5

50 Years and Over

Better.............................20%
Worse.............................58
Same (volunteered)................16
No opinion........................ 6

By Income
$25,000 and Over

Better.............................32%
Worse.............................51
Same (volunteered)................14
No opinion........................ 3

$15,000 and Over

Better.............................28%
Worse.............................51
Same (volunteered)................15
No opinion........................ 6

Under $15,000

Better.............................17%
Worse.............................62
Same (volunteered)................14
No opinion........................ 7

By Politics
Republicans

Better.............................46%
Worse.............................31
Same (volunteered)................19
No opinion........................ 4

Democrats

Better.............................11%
Worse.............................73
Same (volunteered) 12
No opinion 4

Independents

Better.............................22%
Worse.............................56
Same (volunteered) 14
No opinion 8

National Trend

	Better	Worse	Same	No opinion
August 1982	23%	56%	15%	6%
June 1982	29	51	15	5
February 1982	31	44	17	8
November 1981	35	49	12	4
May 1981	48	37	15*	

*Volunteered "same" response recorded with "no opinion."

How about the nation? What effect do you think the Reagan administration's economic policies will have on the nation's economic situation? Do you feel the nation's economic situation will be much better, somewhat better, somewhat worse, or much worse as a result of the Reagan economic policies?

Better.............................32%
Worse.............................54
Same (volunteered) 7
No opinion 7

By Politics
Republicans

Better.............................59%
Worse.............................28
Same (volunteered) 8
No opinion 5

Democrats

Better.............................16%
Worse.............................71
Same (volunteered) 7
No opinion 6

Independents

Better.............................33%
Worse.............................52
Same (volunteered) 7
No opinion 8

National Trend

	Better	Worse	Same	No opinion
August 1982	32%	54%	7%	7%
June 1982	39	48	8	5
February 1982	40	44	7	9
October 1981	53	37	4	6

How about a year from now? Do you feel the nation's economic situation will be better or worse as a result of the Reagan economic policies?

Better.............................40%
Worse.............................40
Same (volunteered) 12
No opinion 8

By Politics
Republicans

Better.............................67%
Worse.............................15
Same (volunteered) 12
No opinion 6

Democrats

Better.............................23%
Worse.............................57
Same (volunteered) 12
No opinion 8

Independents

Better.............................41%
Worse.............................35

Same (volunteered) 14
No opinion 10

How about over the long run? In the long run, do you feel the nation's economic situation will be better or worse because of the Reagan economic policies?

Better 46%
Worse 33
Same (volunteered) 9
No opinion 12

By Politics

Republicans

Better 75%
Worse 10
Same (volunteered) 7
No opinion 8

Democrats

Better 29%
Worse 49
Same (volunteered) 9
No opinion 13

Independents

Better 47%
Worse 31
Same (volunteered) 10
No opinion 12

Note: With the November elections widely considered to be a referendum on Reaganomics, the latest Gallup survey shows voter pessimism on the impact of the Reagan administration's economic policies to be greater than at any time since measurements began last year. At the same time, a substantial number of Americans remain relatively optimistic about the long-term effects of Reaganomics. A major thrust of the GOP campaign strategy has been a plea for patience on the part of voters.

Specifically, the current survey shows that 23% believe their own financial situation will improve as a result of Reagan's economic policies, while twice as many (56%) say it will

become worse. In May 1981, when this measurement was started early in Reagan's administration, 48% said better and 37% worse.

Growing pessimism also is recorded over the impact of Reaganomics on the nation as a whole, with 32% at present maintaining that the nation's economy will improve as a result of these policies and 54% saying it will be worse. In October 1981, when this question was first asked, 53% believed the economy would improve and 37% thought it would not.

When voters are asked what they think will be the impact of Reaganomics on the nation's economic situation one year from now, their views are more hopeful than their current outlook, with 40% saying better and 40% worse. Last March these figures were 42% and 40%, respectively. And when voters are asked to predict the result of the Reagan economic policies over the long run, opinion comes down clearly on the positive side, with 46% saying the nation's economic situation will be better and 33% holding the opposite opinion; again, these are very close to March's figures of 49% and 34%.

While a 7-point downtrend since June is noted in positive views on the immediate impact of Reaganomics on the nation, relatively little change has come about in the public's projections about the future outcome of the president's economic policies.

SEPTEMBER 23
MIDDLE EAST SITUATION

Interviewing Date: 9/7–12/82
Special Telephone Survey

Have you heard or read about President Reagan's plan for the Middle East?

Yes 45%
No 55

Asked of those who replied in the affirmative: Would you say you have followed the discussions about the plan very closely, fairly closely, or not closely?

Very, fairly closely................... 26%
Not closely; no opinion............... 74

Asked of the entire sample: In brief, President Reagan's plan calls for no further Israeli settlements on the West Bank and the Gaza Strip, and a homeland for the Palestinians in these territories, which were occupied by Israel in the 1967 war. In general, do you favor or oppose this plan?

Total Sample

Favor............................... 39%
Oppose............................. 27
No opinion 34

Heard/Read and Have Followed Closely

Favor............................... 62%
Oppose............................. 25
No opinion 13

Heard/Read But Not Followed Closely

Favor............................... 53%
Oppose............................. 25
No opinion 22

SEPTEMBER 26
BALANCED BUDGET AMENDMENT

Interviewing Date: 8/13–16/82
Survey #200-G

Have you heard or read about the proposal for a constitutional amendment which would require the federal government to balance the national budget each year?

Yes................................. 69%
No.................................. 31

Asked of those who replied in the affirmative: A proposed amendment to the Constitution would require Congress to approve a balanced federal budget each year. Government spending would have to be limited to no more than expected revenues, unless a three-fifths majority of Congress

voted to spend more than expected revenue. Would you favor or oppose this amendment to the Constitution?

Favor............................... 63%
Oppose............................. 23
No opinion 14

By Politics
Republicans

Favor............................... 74%
Oppose............................. 17
No opinion 9

Democrats

Favor............................... 57%
Oppose............................. 28
No opinion 15

Independents

Favor............................... 63%
Oppose............................. 22
No opinion 15

National Trend

	Favor	Oppose	No opinion
May 1982...........	74%	17%	9%
September 1981......	73	19	8
April 1981	70	22	8

Note: Although support for an amendment to the U.S. Constitution which would mandate a balanced federal budget has declined since May, a solid majority continues to favor such an amendment. In the latest Gallup survey, 63% of Americans who are familiar with the proposal favor a constitutional amendment requiring Congress to spend no more than expected revenues, unless overridden by a three-fifths majority of its members. In May, 74% of the aware group backed the amendment. The decline in support since May has occurred about equally among Republicans (down 9 percentage points), Democrats (down 10 points), and independents (down 13 points).

If the amendment is passed by Congress, it

would need the approval of thirty-eight state legislatures before becoming law. Public interest in the amendment has been heightened by a projected 1983 federal budget deficit of more than $100 billion.

SEPTEMBER 30
ALCOHOLIC BEVERAGES

Interviewing Date: 8/13–16/82
Survey #200-G

Do you have occasion to use alcoholic beverages such as liquor, wine, or beer, or are you a total abstainer?

	Those who drink
National	65%

By Sex

Male	69%
Female	61

By Education

College	79%
High school	66
Grade school	29

By Region

East	72%
Midwest	69
South	52
West	69

By Age

18–29 years	77%
30–49 years	71
50 years and over	52

By Income

$15,000 and over	77%
Under $15,000	51

By Religion

Protestants	58%
Catholics	76

National Trend

	Those who drink
1982	65%
1981	70
1979	69
1978	71
1976	71
1974	68
1969	64
1966	65
1964	63
1960	62
1958	55
1957	58
1951	59
1949	58
1947	63
1945	67
1939	58

Note: The percentage of Americans who drink alcoholic beverages declined from 70% in 1981 to 65% in the latest survey, and now represents the lowest level of alcohol use since 1969. The decline is more pronounced among older Americans (fifty and over), persons whose formal education ended at the grade-school level, and those whose annual family income is less than $15,000. These findings suggest that the current recession may be causing some people to curtail spending on alcoholic drinks in favor of household necessities.

The trend in alcohol use since 1939 offers further evidence that times of economic hardship are often associated with decreases in drinking. For example, the lowest percentage of drinkers was recorded during the recession year of 1958, when 55% said they used alcoholic beverages. The proportion of drinkers also dropped in 1949 when the nation was in another economic slump. The drinking data for the

1974–75 recession are inconclusive, because no figures are available for the years immediately prior to this period.

OCTOBER 3
CONGRESSIONAL ELECTIONS

Interviewing Date: 8/13–16, 27–30/82
Survey #200-G, 201-G

Asked of registered voters: If the elections for Congress were being held today, which party would you like to see win in this congressional district—the Democratic party or the Republican party? [Those who said they were undecided or who voted for a different party were asked: As of today do you lean more to the Democratic party or to the Republican party?]

South Only

Democratic..........................56%
Republican 44

Interviewing Date: 3/12–15/82
Survey #191-G

People who are conservative in their political views are referred to as being right of center and people who are liberal in their political views are referred to as being left of center. [Survey respondents were given a card listing eight categories.] Which one of these categories best describes your own political position?

	National	South only
Right of center	34%	40%
Center	41	36
Left of center	15	11
No opinion	10	13

Note: For the first time in the forty-seven year history of the Gallup Poll, Republican party preference at the congressional level is as high in the South as outside the South. The latest nationwide Gallup survey on congressional preferences shows the GOP winning 44% of the popular vote in the thirteen-state southern region to 56% for the Democratic party, the same division found outside the South. This development does not mean that proportionately as many Republicans and Democrats will be elected in and outside the South, but it does point to a dramatic change in the nation's political geography.

The current survey figures for the South—which match the actual division of the vote in the 1980 congressional elections there—represent the culmination of a fifty-year trend which has shown steady gains there in the popular vote for Republican congressional candidates. During this period, GOP strength has been as low as 18.5%, in the 1940 elections. The party's rising fortunes in the South have been occasioned in considerable measure by rapid industrialization, greater prosperity, and an influx of northerners. However, it is important to bear in mind that Republican gains in popular support have not always translated into seat gains. In the 1980 elections, for example, the GOP won 44% of the congressional vote in the South but only 43 out of 121 House seats, or 53%.

Historically, the GOP has been confronted with the virtually impossible task of winning enough seats outside the South to offset the Democrats' advantage there. This has meant that the GOP has had to win two-thirds, or about 200, of the approximately 300 seats outside the South to win a majority in the House of Representatives, or 218 out of 435. The Democratic party, on the other hand, has had to win only about 100 out of the 300 seats outside the South to have a working majority in the House.

Even in today's more evenly balanced political climate, if Southern Republicans were able to retain the 43 House seats they now hold, the GOP would have to capture well over half the seats outside the South to win a simple majority in November's elections. Compounding the Republican party's problem of winning this massive number is the fact that many congressional districts in the large cities of the North are considered "safe" for Democratic candidates.

The great advantage which the Democratic party has had in past congressional elections has resulted in its almost complete domination of the House during the last half century. In the fifty years beginning in 1930, the Republicans have had a majority in the House for only four years, 1947–48 and 1953–54.

Although, historically, Republicans have had a hard time winning seats in the House, the picture has brightened somewhat in regard to the long-term trend in seat gains. In the period between 1930 and 1950, the GOP won no more than nine seats in the South in any given election. But throughout the 1950s, 1960s, and 1970s the GOP steadily improved its totals, capped by the 43 seats won by Republicans in the South in the 1980 election, the high point to date.

Some political observers view this trend as a logical development, since Southern Democrats tend to be more closely aligned with Republicans than with Northern Democrats. They view the South, in one sense, as natural turf for Republican candidates in terms of basic political philosophy.

Another opportunity for the GOP to make further inroads in the South is presented by the reapportionment of House seats necessitated by the 1980 census. Beginning with this November's election, the South will pick up eight additional seats—four in Florida, three in Texas, and one in Tennessee. To a great extent, the population increases in these states which made reapportionment necessary represent influxes of northerners who may be less susceptible to single-party politics than native southerners have been.

Although Republican candidates in presidential elections fared well in the South in recent decades, the appeal of the Republican party has not been transferred to the southern electorate at the congressional level, in large measure because many southern seats have been uncontested and popular Republican candidates unavailable. The disparity between the southerners' preference for Republican presidential and congressional candidates is apparent in the following table, which shows the trend from 1952, when Dwight Eisenhower became the first Republican in two decades to win the White House:

National Trend of Southern Voters
(Percent Voting Republican)

	Presidential	Congressional
1980	50.8%	43.7%
1976	50.0	36.6
1972	61.8	40.2
1968	43.5	37.0
1964	61.3	32.6
1960	49.1	24.5
1956	51.4	26.6
1952	48.9	20.4

The following tables show the division in the South of the popular vote and seats in the House of Representatives:

	Congressional Vote in Elections in South		Congressional Seat Division in South	
	Demo-crats	Repub-licans	Demo-crats	Repub-licans
1980	56.3%	43.7%	78	43
1978	59.4	40.6	86	35
1976	63.4	36.6	91	30
1974	65.5	34.5	92	29
1972	59.8	40.2	84	37
1970	65.4	34.6	87	32
1968	63.0	37.0	88	31
1966	64.9	35.1	91	28
1964	67.4	32.6	101	18
1962	67.5	32.5	109	10
1960	65.5	24.5	110	10
1958	79.9	20.1	111	9
1956	73.4	26.6	110	10
1954	77.7	22.3	110	10
1952	79.6	20.4	111	9
1950	79.5	20.5	116	6
1948	79.1	20.9	118	4
1946	71.2	28.8	115	7
1944	77.7	22.3	117	5
1942	77.3	22.7	118	4
1940	81.5	18.5	116	4
1938	78.2	21.8	117	3
1936	78.8	21.2	117	3
1934	78.1	21.9	117	3
1932	79.8	20.2	118	2
1930	71.7	28.3	112	4

Interviewing Date: 8/13–16/82*
Survey #200-G

As I read off the names of some recently released movies, please tell me whether you, yourself, have seen that movie:

As I read off these movies [ones not seen], please tell me whether or not you would like to see that movie:

*The teen-age findings are based on telephone interviews with a representative national cross section of boys and girls ages 13–18, conducted during July 1982.

E.T.?

	Have seen or want to see
National	69%
Teen-agers	83
Adults	65

By Sex

Adults	
Men	63%
Women	66

By Education

College	77%
High school or less	59

By Region

East	73%
Midwest	60
South	60
West	66

By Age

18–29 years	79%
30–49 years	72
50 years and over	45

Teen-agers Only

Boys	81%
Girls	84

Rocky III?

	Have seen or want to see
National	51%
Teen-agers	87
Adults	42

By Sex

Adults	
Men	48%
Women	37

By Education

College	44%
High school or less	41

By Region

East	53%
Midwest	36
South	44
West	33

By Age

18–29 years	63%
30–49 years	43
50 years and over	23

Teen-agers Only

Boys	88%
Girls	85

Annie?

	Have seen or want to see
National	46%
Teen-agers	52
Adults	44

By Sex

Adults	
Men	32%
Women	54

By Education

College. 46%
High school or less. 43

By Region

East 47%
Midwest. 41
South 47
West. 38

By Age

18–29 years 38%
30–49 years. 50
50 years and over. 42

Teen-agers Only

Boys. 39%
Girls. 65

Star Trek II?

	Have seen or want to see
National	41%
Teen-agers	61
Adults	36

By Sex

Adults
Men. 43%
Women 30

By Education

College. 46%
High school or less. 32

By Region

East 41%
Midwest. 30
South 36
West. 39

By Age

18–29 years 45%
30–49 years. 44
50 years and over. 21

Teen-agers Only

Boys. 72%
Girls. 49

Poltergeist?

	Have seen or want to see
National	36%
Teen-agers	67
Adults	28

By Sex

Adults
Men. 32%
Women 25

By Education

College. 39%
High school or less. 33

By Region

East 38%
Midwest. 23
South 29
West. 22

By Age

18–29 years 42%
30–49 years. 31
50 years and over. 14

Teen-agers Only

Boys. 68%
Girls. 66

Asked of those who had seen the movie: As I read off each of the movies you've seen, would you tell me how much you liked or disliked it by using a number from 0 to 10, with 0 for a movie you disliked a great deal and 10 for a movie you liked a great deal:

E.T.?

	Highly favorable (9, 10)	Highest rating of 10
National	71%	54%
Teen-agers	77	
Adults	67	

Rocky III?

National	59	45
Teen-agers	74	
Adults	42	

Annie?

National	28	22
Teen-agers	25	
Adults	29	

Star Trek II?

National	28	20
Teen-agers	27	
Adults	29	

Poltergeist?

National	45	26
Teen-agers	47	
Adults	41	

Note: The extraordinary popularity of the movie *E.T.* is attested to by its earning the highest favorable rating recorded in more than four decades of Gallup movie assessments. Not only do almost nine in ten (87%) of those who have seen the film rate it favorably (giving it a rating of 6 through 10 on an 11-point scale), but also an unprecedented 54% award *E.T.* the highest rating—a perfect 10. In contrast, another popular current movie, *Rocky III,* enjoys a 77% overall favorable rating, but substantially fewer in its audience, 45%, give it a 10.

Another dimension of the exceptional drawing power of *E.T.* is that seven in ten Americans aged thirteen and over (69%) have either seen the film or say they would like to. The compa-rable figures for the other movies tested are: *Rocky III,* 51%; *Annie,* 46%; *Star Trek II,* 41%; and *Poltergeist,* 36%.

E.T. has a broad appeal to moviegoers of all ages. Among teen-agers, who play a dispro-portionately large role in determining a movie's success, more than eight in ten (83%) have seen or would like to see this film. A comparable percentage of teens, 87%, would like to see *Rocky III* or already have seen it. Sixty-five percent of adults, eighteen and older, have seen or want to see *E.T.* compared to 42% for *Rocky III* and 44% for *Annie.* The net result is that almost half again as many have seen or wish to see *E.T.* as either *Rocky III* or *Annie.*

The following are other distinguishing char-acteristics of the five movies included in the survey:

1) *E.T.* appeals about equally to moviegoers of both sexes; *Star Trek II* and *Rocky III* are strongly male-oriented, while *Annie* appeals more to women. *Poltergeist* comes closest to matching *E.T.* in its balanced attraction for men and women, boys and girls.

2) In terms of age, *Annie* fares less well than the others among young adults (eighteen to twenty-nine year olds), while *E.T.* enjoys its greatest popularity among this adult group.

3) Fewer persons fifty and older wish to see the movies tested. Within this group, the per-centages of those having seen or wanting to see each of the films range from 45% for *E.T.* down to 14% for *Poltergeist.*

4) College-educated adults are more likely than those whose education ended at the high-school level or earlier to have seen or to say they want to see each of the five movies. This is particularly true of *E.T.*, which has a score of 77% among college-educated persons, com-pared to 59% among the less well-educated group. *Star Trek II* also has a substantially greater potential audience among the college educated.

5) Easterners are more apt to have seen or want to see the five films than are those living in other parts of the country. On average, the scores are 50% for the East, 43% for the South, 40% for the West, and 38% for the Midwest.

OCTOBER 7
NATIONAL SERVICE

Interviewing Date: 7/30–8/2/82
Survey #199-G

Would you favor or oppose a system of voluntary national service in which young people (both men and women) after high school or college would be given opportunities to serve for one year, either in the military forces or in nonmilitary work here or abroad, such as VISTA or the Peace Corps?

Favor.............................77%
Oppose............................15
No opinion 8

By Sex
Male

Favor.............................78%
Oppose............................15
No opinion 7

Female

Favor.............................77%
Oppose............................14
No opinion 9

By Race
White

Favor.............................78%
Oppose............................15
No opinion 7

Nonwhite

Favor.............................72%
Oppose............................16
No opinion 12

By Education
College

Favor.............................78%
Oppose............................16
No opinion 6

High School

Favor.............................77%
Oppose............................15
No opinion 8

Grade School

Favor.............................74%
Oppose............................12
No opinion 14

By Region
East

Favor.............................80%
Oppose............................16
No opinion 4

Midwest

Favor.............................79%
Oppose............................14
No opinion 7

South

Favor.............................73%
Oppose............................14
No opinion 13

West

Favor.............................78%
Oppose............................15
No opinion 7

By Age
18–24 Years

Favor.............................80%
Oppose............................15
No opinion 5

25–29 Years

Favor.............................80%
Oppose............................10
No opinion 10

30–49 Years

Favor 79%
Oppose 14
No opinion 7

50 Years and Over

Favor 74%
Oppose 17
No opinion 9

Asked of those aged 18–29 years: Do you think you, yourself, would be interested in volunteering for such a program, or not?

Yes, definitely 23%
Yes, might be 20
No 54
No opinion 3

By Sex
Male

Yes, definitely 25%
Yes, might be 19
No 54
No opinion 2

Female

Yes, definitely 19%
Yes, might be 23
No 55
No opinion 3

Asked of those young adults who replied that they either definitely would or might volunteer: Would you volunteer for military or nonmilitary service?

Military 40%
Nonmilitary 56
No opinion 4

By Sex
Male

Military 54%
Nonmilitary 42
No opinion 4

Female

Military 25%
Nonmilitary 71
No opinion 4

Note: Evidence that young people today continue to have a powerful social conscience is seen from survey findings that almost one-fourth of young adults, ages eighteen through twenty-nine, indicate a strong interest in serving the nation for one year in some form of volunteer work. A total of 23% of this age group (an estimated 10 million people) say they definitely would be interested in participating in a voluntary national service program, either in the armed forces or in nonmilitary work here or abroad. Young men (25%) and women (19%) show about equal willingness to serve.

Earlier surveys have shown that the following areas are among those that potential volunteers would find of greatest interest: conservation work in national forests and parks, tutoring low achievers in school, day care for young children, assistance for the elderly, help in floods and national disasters, hospital work, and repairing and painting run-down houses.

OCTOBER 10
PRESIDENT REAGAN

Interviewing Date: 9/17–20/82
Survey #202-G

Do you approve or disapprove of the way Ronald Reagan is handling his job as president?

Approve 42%
Disapprove 48
No opinion 10

By Sex
Male

Approve 47%
Disapprove 43
No opinion 10

Female

Approve	37%
Disapprove	53
No opinion	10

By Race
White

Approve	47%
Disapprove	43
No opinion	10

Nonwhite

Approve	13%
Disapprove	75
No opinion	12

By Education
College

Approve	51%
Disapprove	43
No opinion	6

High School

Approve	39%
Disapprove	49
No opinion	12

Grade School

Approve	34%
Disapprove	56
No opinion	10

By Region
East

Approve	43%
Disapprove	50
No opinion	7

Midwest

Approve	43%
Disapprove	46
No opinion	11

South

Approve	40%
Disapprove	48
No opinion	12

West

Approve	44%
Disapprove	47
No opinion	9

By Age
18–29 Years

Approve	41%
Disapprove	47
No opinion	12

30–49 Years

Approve	46%
Disapprove	44
No opinion	10

50 Years and Over

Approve	39%
Disapprove	52
No opinion	9

By Income
$25,000 and Over

Approve	58%
Disapprove	37
No opinion	5

$15,000 and Over

Approve	52%
Disapprove	40
No opinion	8

Under $15,000

Approve	31%
Disapprove	57
No opinion	12

By Politics

Republicans

Approve..............................77%
Disapprove 17
No opinion 6

Democrats

Approve..............................21%
Disapprove 69
No opinion 10

Independents

Approve..............................44%
Disapprove 44
No opinion 12

By Occupation

Professional and Business

Approve..............................54%
Disapprove 41
No opinion 5

Clerical and Sales

Approve..............................39%
Disapprove 50
No opinion 11

Manual Workers

Approve..............................38%
Disapprove 49
No opinion 13

Nonlabor Force

Approve..............................43%
Disapprove 48
No opinion 9

Labor Union Families Only

Approve..............................36%
Disapprove 53
No opinion 11

Nonlabor Union Families Only

Approve..............................44%
Disapprove 46
No opinion 10

National Trend

	Approve	Dis-approve	No opinion
August 27–30, 1982	42%	46%	12%
August 13–16, 1982	41	49	10
July 30–August 2, 1982	41	47	12
July 23–26, 1982	42	46	12

Interviewing Date: 8/13–16/82
Survey #200-G

You will notice that the ten boxes on this scale go from the highest position of +5 for someone you have a very favorable opinion of all the way to the lowest position of −5 for someone you have a very unfavorable opinion of. How far up the scale or how far down the scale would you rate Ronald Reagan?

Very favorable (+5, +4) 21%
Favorable (+3, +2, +1)...............39
Unfavorable (−1, −2, −3).............17
Very unfavorable (−4, −5) 19
No opinion 4

By Sex

Male

Very favorable 23%
Favorable 39
Unfavorable 17
Very unfavorable 17
No opinion 4

Female

Very favorable 21%
Favorable 38
Unfavorable 16
Very unfavorable 20
No opinion 5

By Race

White

Very favorable 25%
Favorable 41
Unfavorable 16
Very unfavorable 15
No opinion 3

Nonwhite

Very favorable 4%
Favorable 21
Unfavorable 22
Very unfavorable 40
No opinion 13

By Education

College

Very favorable 25%
Favorable 44
Unfavorable 16
Very unfavorable 13
No opinion 2

High School

Very favorable 20%
Favorable 38
Unfavorable 17
Very unfavorable 21
No opinion 4

Grade School

Very favorable 22%
Favorable 29
Unfavorable 15
Very unfavorable 24
No opinion 10

By Region

East

Very favorable 24%
Favorable 33
Unfavorable 19
Very unfavorable 21
No opinion 3

Midwest

Very favorable 19%
Favorable 43
Unfavorable 14
Very unfavorable 19
No opinion 5

South

Very favorable 26%
Favorable 34
Unfavorable 16
Very unfavorable 18
No opinion 6

West

Very favorable 19%
Favorable 47
Unfavorable 16
Very unfavorable 16
No opinion 2

By Age

18–29 Years

Very favorable 17%
Favorable 46
Unfavorable 18
Very unfavorable 16
No opinion 3

30–49 Years

Very favorable 21%
Favorable 41
Unfavorable 17
Very unfavorable 17
No opinion 4

50 Years and Over

Very favorable 26%
Favorable 34
Unfavorable 13
Very unfavorable 23
No opinion 4

By Income

$25,000 and Over

Very favorable 26%
Favorable 45
Unfavorable 14
Very unfavorable 14
No opinion 1

$15,000 and Over

Very favorable 24%
Favorable 45
Unfavorable 15
Very unfavorable 14
No opinion 2

Under $15,000

Very favorable 19%
Favorable 32
Unfavorable 18
Very unfavorable 24
No opinion 7

By Politics

Republicans

Very favorable 50%
Favorable 38
Unfavorable 7
Very unfavorable 4
No opinion 1

Democrats

Very favorable 10%
Favorable 32
Unfavorable 22
Very unfavorable 32
No opinion 4

Independents

Very favorable 16%
Favorable 49
Unfavorable 16
Very unfavorable 14
No opinion 5

Note: President Ronald Reagan's job performance ratings have remained remarkably stable in recent months, with disapproval outweighing approval, 48% to 42%, in the latest nationwide survey. His approval ratings have varied by no more than one percentage point in five national surveys conducted since mid-July. In the previous (late August) survey, 42% of Americans approved of Reagan's performance in office while 46% disapproved.

By comparison, President Jimmy Carter's approval rating at this point in 1978 was only marginally more favorable than Reagan's is today. In mid-September 1978, 45% of the public approved of the way Carter was handling his presidential duties while 40% disapproved.

Although Reagan's personal appeal rating (60% favorable) is considerably higher than his current job performance rating (42% approval), his personal popularity—despite a widely held belief—is not disproportionately greater than that of his predecessors.

The following table shows that the president's personal approval rating is actually lower than the ratings for Presidents Carter, Ford, and Johnson when their performance ratings were at or near 40%:

National Trend
(Personal vs. Performance Ratings)

President	Personal appeal	Job performance
Reagan, Aug. 1982	60%	41%
Carter, April 1980........	66	40
Ford, Oct. 1975..........	69	44
Nixon, Aug. 1973	56	36
Johnson, July 1968	76	40

Low presidential approval ratings during off-year congressional campaigns have tended to be associated with larger than normal seat losses for the party holding the White House, particularly during an incumbent president's second term. Striking examples of the negative effect a president's popularity can have on his party's congressional strength can be seen in the 1974, 1966, and 1946 elections.

In 1974, although President Gerald Ford had taken office in August, the political downfall of President Richard Nixon cast a pall over his party in the fall elections. In 1966, President Johnson's slumping popularity hurt his party in that midterm election, while in 1946, President Harry Truman's low approval score seriously hurt the Democratic chances that year.

There are, however, exceptions to this pattern. Carter's relatively low popularity rating of 42% at the beginning of the 1978 congressional campaign apparently had little adverse effect on his party in terms of seat losses in November. The Democrats lost 16 seats, fewer than normal for the party in power. This may have been due, in part, to the fact that losses in seats tend to be fewer in the first midterm elections held after an elected president takes office.

The following table compares the presidents' early September popularity ratings for the last nine off-year congressional elections with the seat losses in November:

National Trend

(Presidential Popularity/Congressional Election Outcome)

Election year	President	Early campaign approval rating	Congressional seat loss
1978	Carter	42%	16
1974*	Ford	50	48
1970	Nixon	56	12
1966	Johnson	48	48
1962	Kennedy	67	5
1958	Eisenhower	56	47
1954	Eisenhower	65	18
1950	Truman	43	29
1946	Truman	32	54

The latest Gallup survey on congressional preferences showed the Democratic party with a solid lead over the Republican party in the popular vote for seats in the House of Representatives. The Democrats were the choice of

*This survey was conducted in late September, following President Ford's pardon of President Nixon.

56% of likely voters to 44% for the Republicans. In the 1978 congressional elections, Democratic candidates won about 55% of the popular vote, resulting in a seat division of 276 for the Democrats and 159 for the Republicans. The current seat division in the House is 243 Democrats and 192 Republicans.

OCTOBER 14
CONGRESSIONAL ELECTIONS

Interviewing Date: 8/13–16; 27–30/82
Survey #200-G; 201-G

Is your name now recorded in the registration book of the precinct or election district where you live?

	Yes
National	71%

By Age

18–24 years	50%
25–29 years	58
30–49 years	73
50 years and over	83

Interviewing Date: 9/17–20/82
Survey #202-G

How much thought have you given to the coming November elections—quite a lot, or only a little?

	A lot/ some interest
National	44%

By Age

18–24 years	28%
25–29 years	36
30–49 years	44
50 years and over	54

National Trend

	A lot/ some interest
September 22–25, 1978	39%
September 27–30, 1974	42
September 25–28, 1970	49

Note: Voter interest in the coming congressional elections, now less than three weeks away, is running higher at this time than it was in the last off-year elections in 1978. Currently 44% of the adult population say they have given quite a lot or some thought to the November 2 elections, compared to 39% at this time four years ago. The upturn in interest may be due in part to the fact that in many states this year the public will be voting not only on candidates but also on issues as well, including such controversial topics as gun laws, abortion, and a nuclear freeze.

A Gallup survey last year found that if Americans could vote on major issues facing the nation as well as on candidates, voter turnout in national elections—now the worst of any major democracy in the world—might improve substantially. When nonvoters in the 1980 presidential election were asked if they would be more or less likely to vote in national elections if they could vote on important national issues as well as on candidates, almost half (48%) said they would be more likely to go to the polls.

Although the current voter-interest figure suggests that the downtrend in voter turnout during the 1970s may be leveling off, it should be noted that the level of voter registration has shown no statistical change since 1978. In the latest surveys, 71% say they are registered to vote; four years ago, the figure was 70%. In 1978, 35.5% of the eligible population voted for candidates for the House of Representatives.

If the level of voter turnout does increase this year, it would likely benefit Democratic candidates since Democratic voter groups, such as blacks and blue-collar workers, historically have been less likely to go to the polls. For example, in Gallup measurements of the nationwide vote for Congress based on the total sample (both voters and nonvoters), the results are 60% for the Democrats and 40% for the Republicans. However, in test elections based only on those who are most likely to vote, the race is considerably closer. The latest (semifinal) Gallup Poll congressional figures show the Democrats leading 56% to 44%.

OCTOBER 17
MOST IMPORTANT PROBLEM

Interviewing Date: 9/17–20/82
Survey #202-G

What do you think is the most important problem facing this congressional district?

Unemployment	47%
Inflation; high cost of living	11
Economy (general)	9
Local problems	8
Taxes	7
Crime	7
High interest rates	3
All others	15
Don't know	11
	118%*

*Total adds to more than 100% due to multiple responses.

Those Who Named Unemployment as the Most Important Problem
(By Region)

East	14%
Midwest	58
South	45
West	36

Asked of those who named unemployment as the most important problem: Which political party do you think can do a better job of handling the problem you have just mentioned—the Republican party or the Democratic party?

Republican	25%
Democratic	45
No difference	19
No opinion	11

Note: With the congressional elections only two weeks away, nearly half of U.S. voters and equal proportions of supporters of Democratic and Republican candidates name unemployment as the most important problem facing their congressional districts. Nationally, 47% name unemployment as the worst problem facing their districts, with the percentage climbing to 58% among midwesterners. Named next often, but far behind unemployment, are inflation (11%), the economy in general (9%), local problems (8%), taxes (7%), and crime (7%).

When persons who named any problem were asked which party is better able to handle the problem cited, the Democratic party again emerged with an advantage of 38% to 25%, with 37% saying no difference or not expressing an opinion.

OCTOBER 21
JURY TRIALS IN DAMAGE SUITS

Interviewing Date: 8/27–30/82
Survey #201-G

In cases of civil suits for medical malpractice, car accidents, and the like, where the amount of damages sought exceeds $20,000, do you think it would be a good idea or a poor idea if the person or company being sued were to have the right to ask that the case be decided by a panel of three judges rather than by a jury?

Good idea............................46%
Poor idea............................38
No opinion 16

Would you favor or oppose placing a top limit on each type of injury; that is, so much for a broken arm, etc., with an upper limit of $100,000 for any kind of accident or treatment?

Favor...............................51%
Oppose..............................38
No opinion 11

When juries award huge sums of money against doctors or hospitals for what they claim is wrong treatment, who eventually bears the cost of these large jury awards—

the insurance companies, the doctors or hospitals, or persons who use doctors and hospitals?

Insurance companies..................19%
Doctors/hospitals....................5
Persons who use doctors/hospitals 69
No opinion 6

Note: The majority of opinion among Americans is that in damage suits where the amount sought exceeds $20,000, the person or company being sued should have the right to ask that the case be decided by a panel of three judges rather than by a jury. In addition, survey respondents, by a five-to-four ratio, favor placing a top limit on each type of injury, with a maximum award of $100,000 for any kind of accident or treatment. These attitudes have developed from an awareness on the part of seven in ten survey respondents that the public itself, rather than doctors, hospitals, or insurance companies, eventually bears the cost of large jury awards.

Critics of the present jury system argue that jurors tend to become involved emotionally in a case and therefore overcompensate victims. They also maintain that jurors have no objective criteria for deciding the size of punitive awards.

The large sums often awarded in medical malpractice suits have sparked renewed debate about the present jury system. Yet while these awards make the headlines, a report issued earlier this year by the Rand Institute for Civil Justice noted that half the plaintiffs who took their cases before a jury did not win. And of those who did, half took home less than $7,900. The conclusions of the institute were based on a tabulation of verdicts and awards by civil juries in Cook County, Illinois, over a 19-year period ending in 1979. But the report also notes that those people who filed and won product-liability and professional malpractice suits were awarded more money than those who filed other types of suits, pushing the awards up to a much higher figure—an average of $82,000 in 1978.

Indicative of a nationwide trend, results from a study in New York City show the sharply rising cost of injury claims. As reported recently by the *New York Times,* damage and injury awards paid by the city have increased more than tenfold since 1968. Large settlements, the article noted, are becoming increasingly common, especially in malpractice and other personal injury cases decided by jury trials. And while less than 1% of all cases last year were for more than $250,000, they accounted for nearly a third of the total cost.

OCTOBER 24

CONGRESSIONAL ELECTIONS— A GALLUP ANALYSIS

The closing days of the 1982 elections for the U.S. House of Representatives are characterized by six key factors, including some that are unique to this year's contests:

1) Economic concerns—unemployment in particular—dominate the worries of the electorate to a greater extent than in any off-year election since the 1930s, according to Gallup Poll experience. Nearly seven in ten voters now name economic problems as the most important facing the nation. Although the Democrats currently hold almost a 3-to-2 advantage as the party perceived to be better able to handle the nation's top problems, their margin over the GOP is somewhat less than at this point in previous off-year congressional elections, as seen in the following table:

Party Better Able To Handle Most Important Problem

	Democratic	Republican	No difference; no opinion
Aug. 13–16, 1982	35%	26%	39%
1978	34	19	47
1974	39	13	48
1970	30	21	49
1966	28	21	51
1962	33	17	50

2) The problems named by voters in their own congressional districts mirror national concerns, with seven in ten citing economic problems (mainly unemployment) as the chief local ones.

3) The long downtrend in interest in the elections appears to be leveling off, with 45% of survey respondents currently saying they have given a lot or some thought to the elections. In 1978 at this time, the comparable figure was 39%. Here is the trend since 1970:

National Trend Toward Interest in Coming Elections

	A lot; some interest
September 17–20, 1982	45%
1978	39
1974	42
1970	49

4) Low presidential approval ratings during off-year congressional campaigns usually result in larger-than-normal seat losses for the party holding the White House. Examples of the negative effect a president's low popularity can have on his party's strength in Congress are seen in the 1974, 1966, and 1946 elections. In 1974, Richard Nixon's resignation cast a pall over Republican efforts in the fall, even though Gerald Ford had assumed the presidential office in August. In 1966, Lyndon Johnson's plummeting popularity hurt his party in the midterm election, while in 1946 Democratic chances in Congress were hurt by Harry Truman's low approval rating.

Jimmy Carter may be the exception to this pattern. His relatively low approval rating of 42% at the beginning of the 1978 congressional campaign had little adverse effect on his party in terms of seat losses. By comparison, Ronald Reagan's recent job performance ratings range in the low-to-mid 40s.

5) For the first time in the forty-seven-year history of the Gallup Poll, Republican party preference at the congressional level is virtually as high in the South as outside it. The latest nationwide (semi-final) Gallup survey on congressional preferences shows the GOP winning 44% of the popular vote in the thirteen-state

southern region to 56% for the Democratic party, the same division found outside the South. This development does not mean that proportionately as many Republicans and Democrats will be elected outside the South, but it does point to a dramatic change in the nation's political geography.

The survey figures for the South, which match the actual division of the vote in the 1980 congressional elections there, represent the culmination of a fifty-year trend of steady gains in the South in the popular vote for Republican congressional candidates. During this period GOP strength has been as low as 18.5% in the 1940 elections.

6) Despite dramatic developments on the domestic and international fronts, the proportion of voters who claim affiliation with either major party is almost the same today as in 1978:

Party Affiliation

	1982	1978
Democrats	45%	46%
Republicans	27	23
Independents	28	31

In addition, relatively little change has come about in terms of the self-described political philosophy of Americans:

Party Philosophy*

	1982	1978
Left of center	21%	25%
Center	43	42
Right of center	36	33

*Responses based on those expressing an opinion.

OCTOBER 28
CONGRESSIONAL ELECTIONS—FINAL POLL

Interviewing Date: 9/17–20, 10/15–18/82
Survey #202-G; 203-G

Asked of likely voters: Here is your Gallup Poll ballot. Now suppose the election were being held today. Please mark that ballot for the party whose candidate you would like to see win, just as you would in a real election; then fold the ballot and drop it into the box. [If the respondent handed back the ballot without marking it, he or she was asked: Would you please mark the ballot for the party whose candidate you lean toward as of today?]

Democratic House candidates	53%
Republican House candidates	43
Other House candidates	1
Undecided	3

When the undecided vote is allocated, the division of the major party vote is:

Final Poll Results

Democrats	55%
Republicans	45

While percentages cannot be translated directly into House seats, the following table can serve as a guide to the general relationship between percentages and House seats:

Popular Vote for House

	1978	1974
Democrats		
Seats won	276	291
Popular vote	54.6%	58.9%
Republicans		
Seats won	159	144
Popular vote	45.4%	41.1%

In the 1980 presidential and congressional elections, many persons from traditionally Democratic groups including blue-collar workers, labor union members, and persons whose education ended at the high-school level or earlier abandoned their usual election behavior to vote for Ronald Reagan.* The survey results now

*In the 1980 elections, Democrats won 51.3% of the two-party vote and 243 seats in the House of Representatives, to 48.7% of the vote and 192 seats for the Republicans.

show that many of these voters intend to return to their political roots and vote for Democrats for Congress.

The following table shows the division of the 1982 congressional vote by key voter groups:

Vote for Congress**
(Choices of Likely Voters)

Democrats..........................52%
Republicans........................42
Other; undecided 6

By Sex
Male

Democrats..........................50%
Republicans........................44
Other; undecided 6

Female

Democrats..........................55%
Republicans........................40
Other; undecided 5

By Race
White

Democrats..........................48%
Republicans........................46
Other; undecided 6

Nonwhite

Democrats..........................85%
Republicans........................10
Other; undecided 5

By Education
College

Democrats..........................43%
Republicans........................52
Other; undecided 5

**Based on four surveys conducted August 13–16, 27–30; September 17–20; and October 15–18, 1982.

High School

Democrats..........................56%
Republicans........................38
Other; undecided 6

Grade School

Democrats..........................62%
Republicans........................33
Other; undecided 5

By Age
18–29 Years

Democrats..........................54%
Republicans........................39
Other; undecided 7

30–49 Years

Democrats..........................52%
Republicans........................41
Other; undecided 7

50 Years and Over

Democrats..........................53%
Republicans........................42
Other; undecided 5

By Income
$20,000 and Over

Democrats..........................47%
Republicans........................48
Other; undecided 5

$10,000–$19,999

Democrats..........................53%
Republicans........................41
Other; undecided 6

Under $10,000

Democrats..........................65%
Republicans........................30
Other; undecided 5

By Politics

Republicans

Democrats........................... 9%
Republicans......................... 88
Other; undecided 3

Democrats

Democrats...........................89%
Republicans......................... 9
Other; undecided 2

Independents

Democrats...........................43%
Republicans......................... 43
Other; undecided 14

By Occupation

Professional and Business

Democrats...........................44%
Republicans......................... 51
Other; undecided 5

Clerical and Sales

Democrats...........................58%
Republicans......................... 36
Other; undecided 6

Manual Workers

Democrats...........................60%
Republicans......................... 33
Other; undecided 7

Labor Union Households Only

Democrats...........................63%
Republicans......................... 33
Other; undecided 4

Nonlabor Union Households Only

Democrats...........................50%
Republicans......................... 44
Other; undecided 6

Note: Today's final survey figures are confined solely to races for the U.S. House of Representatives. Since senatorial elections are not held in all states in any one election year, the House contests constitute the only nationwide test of party strength.

Congressional elections pose major problems in relating voter opinion to the election results. To accurately anticipate the seat change in the election, a full-scale survey would have to be conducted in each of the nation's 435 congressional districts. Thus, a nationwide sampling is substituted to produce an estimate of how the total popular vote cast for members of Congress divides between the two major parties. This provides a picture of party strength at the national level and a truer measurement of party strength nationwide than does the distribution of House seats.

A series of questions designed to ascertain the likelihood of each survey participant actually going to the polls on November 2 was included in the final surveys. Since voter turnout in off-year congressional elections has been steadily declining—only 36% of eligible voters cast their ballots in the 1978 elections—identifying likely voters represents the pollster's greatest challenge.

OCTOBER 31
PUBLIC OPINION REFERENDUM

Interviewing Date: 9/17–20/82
Survey #202-G

> Suppose that on election day, November 2, you could vote on key issues as well as on candidates. Please tell me how you would vote on each of these propositions:*

*The results reported here not only are national in scope but also reflect the views of all adults, both those who will and those who will not participate in the November 2 elections. The survey findings, therefore, may not reflect the election results of individual state referendums on given issues.

Proposition 1: Balancing Budget

Favor a constitutional amendment
to balance the federal budget 75%
Oppose a constitutional amendment
to balance the federal budget 25

Proposition 2: Ban on Handguns

Favor a ban on possession of
handguns except by the police and
other authorized persons. 45%
Oppose a ban on possession of
handguns except by the police and
other authorized persons. 55

Proposition 3: Equal Rights Amendment

Favor the Equal Rights Amendment 61%
Oppose the Equal Rights Amendment . . . 39

Proposition 4: Unilateral Nuclear Freeze

Favor a freeze on the production
of nuclear weapons whether or not the
Soviet Union agrees to do the same 45%
Oppose a freeze on the production
of nuclear weapons whether or not the
Soviet Union agrees to do the same 55

Proposition 5: Busing

Favor busing children to achieve
better racial balance in the public
schools. 28%
Oppose busing children to achieve
better racial balance in the public
schools. 72

Proposition 6: New Federalism

Favor turning over more financial
responsibility for social programs
from the federal government to the
state governments 62%
Oppose turning over more financial
responsibility for social programs
from the federal government to the
state governments. 38

Proposition 7: Tuition Tax Credits

Favor a reduction in a family's
federal income tax of $100 for
each child attending a private or
parochial school. 50%
Oppose a reduction in a family's
federal income tax of $100 for
each child attending a private or
parochial school. 50

Proposition 8: Legalization of Marijuana

Favor legalizing the possession of
small amounts of marijuana for
personal use 30%
Oppose legalizing the possession of
small amounts of marijuana for
personal use 70

Proposition 9: Death Penalty

Favor the death penalty for persons
convicted of murder. 72%
Oppose the death penalty for persons
convicted of murder. 28

Proposition 10: Environmental Regulations

Favor reducing environmental
regulations if needed to improve
business conditions 45%
Oppose reducing environmental
regulations if needed to improve
business conditions 55

Proposition 11: Hiring Illegal Immigrants

Favor a law making it illegal to hire
an immigrant who has come into the
United States without proper papers. . . . 65%
Oppose a law making it illegal to hire
an immigrant who has come into the
United States without proper papers. . . . 35

Proposition 12: Spending for Social Programs

Favor a decrease in government
spending for social programs such as
health, education, welfare, etc. 34%

Oppose a decrease in government
spending for social programs such as
health, education, welfare, etc.........66

Proposition 13: Military Spending

Favor an increase in federal spending
for military and defense purposes 42%
Oppose an increase in federal spending
for military and defense purposes 58

**Proposition 14:
Prayer in Public Schools**

Favor a constitutional amendment
to permit prayer in public schools 73%
Oppose a constitutional amendment
to permit prayer in public schools 27

**Proposition 15:
Federal Financing of Abortions**

Favor a ban on federal financing
of abortions.......................44%
Oppose a ban on federal financing
of abortions.......................56

Proposition 16: Reaganomics

Favor the Reagan administration's
economic program and policies 44%
Oppose the Reagan administration's
economic program and policies 56

Note: Despite a Democratic tide in the congressional races, the results of a just-completed Public Opinion Referendum show Americans to be conservative on at least half of the sixteen issues tested. Through the Gallup Poll, it is possible to simulate a national referendum on issues, reflecting within a few percentage points the views of all U.S. adults, not just the fewer than half who will actually go to the polls on election day.

   The results of this referendum, conducted during the final stages of the 1982 campaign, help define the election mandate in a year when many issues have been overshadowed by the economy. The survey findings indicate that a strong Democratic showing in the U.S. House

races should not be interpreted as across-the-board support for liberal programs. While the public takes a liberal position on certain of the sixteen issues, such as the ERA and government spending for social programs, conservative sentiment is recorded on issues of busing, legalization of marijuana, and prayer in public schools.

   This year's Gallup referendum was conducted at a time of rising interest among voters in voicing their opinions on both issues and on candidates. Not only are there a greater number of statewide ballot propositions this year than at any time in the last half-century, but also Americans, by a 2-to-1 margin, want the opportunity to express themselves about issues as well as candidates.

NOVEMBER 4
FEDERAL FUNDING OF ELECTION CAMPAIGNS

Interviewing Date: 8/13–16/82
Survey #200-G

It has been suggested that the federal government provide a fixed amount of money for the election campaigns of candidates for Congress and that all private contributions from other sources be prohibited. Do you think this is a good idea or a poor idea?

Good idea..........................55%
Poor idea..........................31
No opinion 14

By Politics
Republicans

Good idea..........................54%
Poor idea..........................33
No opinion 13

Democrats

Good idea..........................54%
Poor idea..........................34
No opinion 12

Independents

Good idea............................61%
Poor idea............................26
No opinion 13

National Trend

	Good idea	Poor idea	No opinion
1979	57%	30%	13%
1977	57	32	11
September 1973 ..	65	24	11
June 1973........	58	29	13

Note: With spending for U.S. House and Senate races in the recent campaign at record levels, a solid majority of Americans (55%) would like to see the federal government provide a fixed amount of money for the election campaigns of candidates for Congress. All other contributions would be prohibited. The latest vote on this plan is consistent with the findings recorded in four earlier surveys conducted over the last decade. Majorities of Republicans, Democrats, and independents in the latest survey favor having the government set spending limits on the campaigns of congressional candidates.

The cost of running for Congress has sky-rocketed in recent years, with the spending in many congressional districts this year exceeding one million dollars. At the start of this year's campaign in September, Herbert E. Alexander, director of the Citizens' Research Foundation, estimated that spending for these races alone could surpass $300 million, compared with $239 million in 1980.

A key factor in this vast increase has been the escalation in contributions from political action committees (PACs). These committees reportedly pumped $88 million into this year's congressional races—60% more than they spent in 1980—which represents at least 30% of all funds raised by congressional candidates. Under the terms of the plan, contributions by PACs would be prohibited.

Some political observers, alarmed by the enormous increases in campaign spending, express concern that elections will be decided more on the basis of the amount of money spent than on issues, party loyalties, or the candidates themselves.

Although the public favors the current plan by a wide margin, Americans in the past have voted against federal financing of political campaigns. In 1938 and again in 1940, the Gallup Poll asked the following question:

Instead of the Republicans and Democrats getting their money from private contributions, would you favor having Congress appropriate $6 million each to the Republican and Democratic parties once every four years for campaign purposes, with proportionate amounts to minor parties?

	1940	1938
Favor...................	32%	25%
Oppose	54	58
No opinion	14	17

NOVEMBER 7
HOMOSEXUALITY—PART I

Interviewing Date: 6/25–28/82
Survey #197-G

Do you think homosexual relations between consenting adults should or should not be legal?

Should..............................45%
Should not..........................39
No opinion 16

By Sex
Male

Should..............................45%
Should not..........................40
No opinion 15

Female

Should..............................45%
Should not..........................38
No opinion 17

By Race
White
Should 45%
Should not. 39
No opinion 16

Nonwhite
Should 42%
Should not. 40
No opinion 18

By Education
College
Should 61%
Should not. 25
No opinion 14

High School
Should 43%
Should not. 41
No opinion 16

Grade School
Should 22%
Should not. 61
No opinion 17

By Region
East
Should 49%
Should not. 37
No opinion 16

Midwest
Should 43%
Should not. 39
No opinion 18

South
Should 35%
Should not. 47
No opinion 18

West
Should 57%
Should not. 30
No opinion 13

By Age
18–24 Years
Should 56%
Should not. 28
No opinion 16

25–29 Years
Should 56%
Should not. 29
No opinion 15

30–49 Years
Should 49%
Should not. 35
No opinion 16

50 Years and Over
Should 33%
Should not. 51
No opinion 16

By Income
$25,000 and Over
Should 56%
Should not. 26
No opinion 18

$15,000 and Over
Should 51%
Should not. 34
No opinion 15

Under $15,000
Should 37%
Should not. 46
No opinion 17

By Politics

Republicans

Should 43%
Should not 43
No opinion 14

Democrats

Should 43%
Should not 42
No opinion 15

Independents

Should 54%
Should not 30
No opinion 16

By Religion

Protestants

Should 40%
Should not 45
No opinion 15

Catholics

Should 46%
Should not 37
No opinion 17

By Occupation

Professional and Business

Should 58%
Should not 25
No opinion 17

Clerical and Sales

Should 54%
Should not 30
No opinion 16

Manual Workers

Should 47%
Should not 39
No opinion 14

Nonlabor Force

Should 34%
Should not 50
No opinion 16

National Trend

	Should	Should not	No opinion
1982	45%	39%	16%
1977	43	43	14

In your opinion, can a homosexual be a good Christian or a good Jew, or not?

Can 53%
Cannot 32
No opinion 15

By Sex

Male

Can 49%
Cannot 35
No opinion 16

Female

Can 57%
Cannot 29
No opinion 14

By Race

White

Can 54%
Cannot 32
No opinion 14

Nonwhite

Can 50%
Cannot 30
No opinion 20

By Education

College

Can 63%
Cannot 25
No opinion 12

High School

Can.................................54%
Cannot............................31
No opinion 15

Grade School

Can.................................32%
Cannot............................47
No opinion 21

By Region
East

Can.................................68%
Cannot............................21
No opinion 11

Midwest

Can.................................55%
Cannot............................30
No opinion 15

South

Can.................................36%
Cannot............................43
No opinion 21

West

Can.................................54%
Cannot............................32
No opinion 14

By Age
18–24 Years

Can.................................55%
Cannot............................27
No opinion 18

25–29 Years

Can.................................56%
Cannot............................31
No opinion 13

30–49 Years

Can.................................59%
Cannot............................29
No opinion 12

50 Years and Over

Can.................................47%
Cannot............................36
No opinion 17

By Income
$25,000 and Over

Can.................................60%
Cannot............................26
No opinion 14

$15,000 and Over

Can.................................56%
Cannot............................30
No opinion 14

Under $15,000

Can.................................49%
Cannot............................35
No opinion 16

By Politics
Republicans

Can.................................49%
Cannot............................38
No opinion 13

Democrats

Can.................................53%
Cannot............................32
No opinion 15

Independents

Can.................................58%
Cannot............................24
No opinion 18

By Religion

Protestants

Can. 44%
Cannot. 40
No opinion 16

Catholics

Can. 67%
Cannot. 23
No opinion 10

By Occupation

Professional and Business

Can. 64%
Cannot. 24
No opinion 12

Clerical and Sales

Can. 66%
Cannot. 24
No opinion 10

Manual Workers

Can. 53%
Cannot. 32
No opinion 15

Nonlabor Force

Can. 46%
Cannot. 37
No opinion 17

Those Who Think Homosexual Relations Between Consenting Adults Should Be Legal

Can. 75%
Cannot. 16
No opinion 9

Those Who Think Homosexual Relations Between Consenting Adults Should Not Be Legal

Can. 31%
Cannot. 56
No opinion 13

National Trend

	Can	Cannot	No opinion
1982	53%	32%	15%
1977	53	33	14

Do you think that homosexuality should be considered an acceptable alternative life-style or not?

Yes. 34%
No. 51
No opinion 15

By Sex

Male

Yes. 31%
No. 54
No opinion 15

Female

Yes. 36%
No. 49
No opinion 15

By Race

White

Yes. 34%
No. 52
No opinion 14

Nonwhite

Yes. 31%
No. 47
No opinion 22

By Education

College

Yes. 44%
No. 46
No opinion 10

High School

Yes. 32%
No. 52
No opinion 16

Grade School

Yes...............................17%
No................................59
No opinion.......................24

By Region
East

Yes...............................41%
No................................45
No opinion.......................14

Midwest

Yes...............................33%
No................................52
No opinion.......................15

South

Yes...............................24%
No................................58
No opinion.......................18

West

Yes...............................37%
No................................50
No opinion.......................13

By Age
18–24 Years

Yes...............................40%
No................................44
No opinion.......................16

25–29 Years

Yes...............................41%
No................................48
No opinion.......................11

30–49 Years

Yes...............................37%
No................................50
No opinion.......................13

50 Years and Over

Yes...............................25%
No................................57
No opinion.......................18

By Income
$25,000 and Over

Yes...............................40%
No................................48
No opinion.......................12

$15,000 and Over

Yes...............................37%
No................................50
No opinion.......................13

Under $15,000

Yes...............................30%
No................................53
No opinion.......................17

By Politics
Republicans

Yes...............................27%
No................................60
No opinion.......................13

Democrats

Yes...............................34%
No................................49
No opinion.......................17

Independents

Yes...............................40%
No................................49
No opinion.......................11

By Religion
Protestants

Yes...............................28%
No................................58
No opinion.......................14

Catholics

Yes.............................39%
No..............................46
No opinion 15

By Occupation

Professional and Business

Yes.............................46%
No..............................44
No opinion 10

Clerical and Sales

Yes.............................40%
No..............................45
No opinion 15

Manual Workers

Yes.............................34%
No..............................52
No opinion 14

Nonlabor Force

Yes.............................25%
No..............................57
No opinion 18

Those Who Think Homosexual Relations Between Consenting Adults Should Be Legal

Yes.............................59%
No..............................31
No opinion 10

Those Who Think Homosexual Relations Between Consenting Adults Should Not Be Legal

Yes............................. 9%
No..............................81
No opinion 10

Those Who Think Homosexuals Can Be Good Christians/Jews

Yes.............................53%
No..............................33
No opinion 14

Those Who Think Homosexuals Cannot Be Good Christians/Jews

Yes............................. 8%
No..............................86
No opinion 6

Those who responded in the affirmative
to the above three questions...........23%
Those who responded in the negative
to the above three questions..........21

Note: Although some legal barriers to homosexual rights have fallen, there has been little change in the last five years in the American public's tolerance of gays or gay life-styles. On the issue of homosexual conduct, a recent Gallup survey found 45% of the public saying homosexual relations between consenting adults should be legal while 39% said they should not. Public opinion was deadlocked in a 1977 survey, with 43% each saying homosexual relations should and should not be legal.

Somewhat greater acceptance of what might be called the moral aspect of homosexuality was found. In the latest survey, a 53% majority says a homosexual can be a good Christian or a good Jew compared to 32% who think otherwise. These beliefs are unchanged from those recorded five years ago. However, in response to a question asked for the first time this year, the public rejects by a 51%-to-34% margin the thesis that homosexuality should be considered a socially acceptable alternative life-style.

Based on their tolerance of gays on these three criteria, Americans divide roughly into three groups:

1) About one-quarter of the public is most tolerant of gays and most accepting of them on legal, moral, and social grounds. This group includes a preponderance of the college-educated, younger Americans (eighteen to twenty-nine), Catholics, residents of the East and Far West and, to a slightly lesser degree, women.

2) Another one-quarter of the adult population is least tolerant of gays; heavily represented in this group are those aged fifty and

older, persons with only a grade-school education, Protestants, and southerners.

3) The remaining one-half of Americans tends to have mixed opinions about homosexuality. The largest portion of this group—about one-fourth of the public—finds homosexuality morally and legally acceptable but votes against it as a socially acceptable alternative life-style.

NOVEMBER 8
HOMOSEXUALITY—PART II

Interviewing Date: 6/25–28/82
Survey #197-G

Just your opinion: Is homosexuality something a person is born with, or is homosexuality due to other factors such as upbringing or environment?

Born with....................................17%
Other factors..............................52
Both (volunteered)....................13
Neither (volunteered)................ 2
No opinion 16

By Education
College

Born with....................................17%
Other factors..............................51
Both (volunteered)....................17
Neither (volunteered)................ 3
No opinion 12

High School

Born with....................................16%
Other factors..............................55
Both (volunteered)....................12
Neither (volunteered)................ 2
No opinion 15

Grade School

Born with....................................19%
Other factors..............................41
Both (volunteered)....................10
Neither (volunteered)................ 1
No opinion 29

By Region
East

Born with....................................22%
Other factors..............................47
Both (volunteered)....................15
Neither (volunteered) 2
No opinion 14

Midwest

Born with....................................16%
Other factors..............................54
Both (volunteered)....................11
Neither (volunteered) 1
No opinion 18

South

Born with....................................15%
Other factors..............................51
Both (volunteered)....................12
Neither (volunteered) 2
No opinion 20

West

Born with....................................13%
Other factors..............................57
Both (volunteered)....................14
Neither (volunteered) 3
No opinion 13

By Age
18–24 Years

Born with....................................11%
Other factors..............................65
Both (volunteered)....................8
Neither (volunteered) 2
No opinion 14

25–29 Years

Born with....................................12%
Other factors..............................59
Both (volunteered)....................16
Neither (volunteered) 4
No opinion 9

30–49 Years

Born with. 18%
Other factors. 52
Both (volunteered). 14
Neither (volunteered) 2
No opinion 14

50 Years and Over

Born with. 21%
Other factors. 43
Both (volunteered). 13
Neither (volunteered) 1
No opinion 22

Those Who Think Homosexual Relations Between Consenting Adults Should Be Legal

Born with. 21%
Other factors. 51
Both (volunteered). 16
Neither (volunteered) 2
No opinion 10

Those Who Think Homosexual Relations Between Consenting Adults Should Not Be Legal

Born with. 14%
Other factors. 60
Both (volunteered). 8
Neither (volunteered) 3
No opinion 15

Those Who Think Homosexuals Can Be Good Christians/Jews

Born with. 22%
Other factors. 49
Both (volunteered). 15
Neither (volunteered) 1
No opinion 13

Those Who Think Homosexuals Cannot Be Good Christians/Jews

Born with. 12%
Other factors. 63
Both (volunteered). 9

Neither (volunteered) 3
No opinion 13

Those Who Think Homosexuality Should Be Considered an Acceptable Alternative Life-Style

Born with. 25%
Other factors. 46
Both (volunteered). 16
Neither (volunteered) 2
No opinion 11

Those Who Think Homosexuality Should Not Be Considered an Acceptable Alternative Life-Style

Born with. 13%
Other factors. 62
Both (volunteered). 10
Neither (volunteered) 3
No opinion 12

National Trend

	Born with	Other factors	Both/ neither	No opinion
1982 ...	17%	52%	15%	16%
1977 ...	12	56	17	15

Compared to nonhomosexuals, do you think that homosexuals are more likely or less likely to:

Lead happy well-adjusted lives?

More likely 13%
Less likely 66
Same; don't know. 21

By Education
College

More likely 9%
Less likely 74
Same; don't know. 17

High School

More likely 16%
Less likely 64
Same; don't know. 20

Grade School

More likely 13%
Less likely 56
Same; don't know 31

By Region
East

More likely 17%
Less likely 61
Same; don't know 22

Midwest

More likely 13%
Less likely 67
Same; don't know 20

South

More likely 11%
Less likely 68
Same; don't know 21

West

More likely 11%
Less likely 67
Same; don't know 22

By Age
18–24 Years

More likely 17%
Less likely 60
Same; don't know 23

25–29 Years

More likely 15%
Less likely 66
Same; don't know 19

30–49 Years

More likely 11%
Less likely 69
Same; don't know 20

50 Years and Over

More likely 12%
Less likely 66
Same; don't know 22

Have problems with alcohol?

More likely 41%
Less likely 21
Same; don't know 38

By Education
College

More likely 44%
Less likely 16
Same; don't know 40

High School

More likely 40%
Less likely 24
Same; don't know 36

Grade School

More likely 38%
Less likely 19
Same; don't know 43

By Region
East

More likely 36%
Less likely 24
Same; don't know 40

Midwest

More likely 40%
Less likely 23
Same; don't know 37

South

More likely 48%
Less likely 16
Same; don't know 36

West

More likely 40%
Less likely 18
Same; don't know.................... 42

By Age
18–24 Years

More likely 41%
Less likely 25
Same; don't know.................... 34

25–29 Years

More likely 41%
Less likely 22
Same; don't know.................... 37

30–49 Years

More likely 43%
Less likely 17
Same; don't know.................... 40

50 Years and Over

More likely 40%
Less likely 21
Same; don't know.................... 39

Have problems with drugs?

More likely 44%
Less likely 18
Same; don't know.................... 38

By Education
College

More likely 44%
Less likely 16
Same; don't know.................... 40

High School

More likely 44%
Less likely 20
Same, don't know.................... 36

Grade School

More likely 42%
Less likely 15
Same; don't know.................... 43

By Region
East

More likely 39%
Less likely 20
Same; don't know.................... 41

Midwest

More likely 44%
Less likely 20
Same; don't know.................... 36

South

More likely 48%
Less likely 15
Same; don't know.................... 37

West

More likely 44%
Less likely 16
Same; don't know.................... 40

By Age
18–24 Years

More likely 40%
Less likely 22
Same; don't know.................... 38

25–29 Years

More likely 42%
Less likely 20
Same; don't know.................... 38

30–49 Years

More likely 45%
Less likely 16
Same; don't know.................... 39

50 Years and Over

More likely 45%
Less likely 17
Same; don't know 38

Be involved in crime?

More likely 23%
Less likely 36
Same; don't know 41

By Education
College

More likely 22%
Less likely 37
Same; don't know 41

High School

More likely 22%
Less likely 38
Same; don't know 40

Grade School

More likely 31%
Less likely 26
Same; don't know 43

By Region
East

More likely 17%
Less likely 40
Same; don't know 43

Midwest

More likely 22%
Less likely 40
Same; don't know 38

South

More likely 31%
Less likely 29
Same; don't know 40

West

More likely 24%
Less likely 34
Same; don't know 42

By Age
18–24 Years

More likely 18%
Less likely 42
Same; don't know 40

25–29 Years

More likely 21%
Less likely 37
Same; don't know 42

30–49 Years

More likely 22%
Less likely 37
Same; don't know 41

50 Years and Over

More likely 28%
Less likely 32
Same; don't know 40

Do you think that, given the choice, most homosexuals would rather be homosexual or that most would rather not be homosexual?

Would be 33%
Would not be 37
No opinion 30

By Education
College

Would be 36%
Would not be 36
No opinion 28

High School

Would be 33%
Would not be 38
No opinion 29

Grade School

Would be.............................25%
Would not be 34
No opinion 41

By Region

East

Would be.............................34%
Would not be 37
No opinion 29

Midwest

Would be.............................30%
Would not be 37
No opinion 33

South

Would be.............................31%
Would not be 38
No opinion 31

West

Would be.............................40%
Would not be 34
No opinion 26

By Age

18–24 Years

Would be.............................42%
Would not be 32
No opinion 26

25–29 Years

Would be.............................42%
Would not be 31
No opinion 27

30–49 Years

Would be.............................31%
Would not be 38
No opinion 31

50 Years and Over

Would be.............................29%
Would not be 39
No opinion 32

Note: Homosexuals in the United States continue to be thought of by the public as leading unhappy, insecure lives despite their efforts to dispel this stereotype. In addition, according to a recent Gallup survey, the notion of "gay pride" that homosexual activist groups have tried to foster is largely unacknowledged by the public. Indeed, marginally fewer believe that, given the choice, most gays would opt for the gay life-style (33%) rather than a straight (nonhomosexual) existence (37%).

The majority of public opinion holds that homosexuality is caused by environmental factors, such as infant or early childhood influences, rather than by heredity. However, the Kinsey Institute for Sex Research reported last year that about 10% of all children apparently are born with a strong gender nonconformity—a failure to like the things other boys and girls like—that has nothing to do with upbringing and that inevitably causes many of them to be homosexuals. This view is reflected in a comparison of the latest survey results with those from a 1977 study, which shows an increase in the proportion of the public believing homosexuality is an inherited rather than an environmental trait. Still, the latter view prevails by a 3-to-1 ratio.

By a 5-to-1 margin, the public thinks gays are less likely than straights to lead happy, well-adjusted lives. By 2 to 1, gays are thought to have more drug and alcohol problems than straights. And Americans believe homosexuals are less apt than nonhomosexuals to be involved in crime, 36% to 23%.

A markedly greater tolerance of gays and gay life-styles is found among the college-educated, younger Americans (eighteen to twenty-nine), Catholics, women, and persons living in the East and Far West. There is less unanimity within this group, however, in perceptions of the homosexual as an individual. Roughly equal proportions of men and women, for instance, believe that gays are less happy than straights and that they are less involved with drugs, alcohol, or crime. Women are more likely than men, though, to think that gays are unhappy with their situation and that it is an inborn condition.

Similarly, the views of college-educated survey participants are not much different from those with less formal education on any of these questions, except that a smaller proportion of the college group believes gays are more apt than straights to lead happy, well-adjusted lives.

NOVEMBER 9
HOMOSEXUALITY—PART III

Interviewing Date: 6/25–28/82
Survey #197-G

As you know, there has been considerable discussion in the news lately regarding the rights of homosexual men and women. In general, do you think homosexuals should or should not have equal rights in terms of job opportunities?

Should 59%
Should not 28
No opinion 13

By Sex
Male

Should 56%
Should not 31
No opinion 13

Female

Should 63%
Should not 25
No opinion 12

By Race
White

Should 59%
Should not 29
No opinion 12

Nonwhite

Should 64%
Should not 24
No opinion 12

By Education
College

Should 70%
Should not 23
No opinion 7

High School

Should 60%
Should not 28
No opinion 12

Grade School

Should 38%
Should not 38
No opinion 24

By Region
East

Should 67%
Should not 24
No opinion 9

Midwest

Should 62%
Should not 26
No opinion 12

South

Should 48%
Should not 36
No opinion 16

West

Should 60%
Should not 27
No opinion 13

By Age

18–24 Years

Should 70%
Should not.........................19
No opinion 11

25–29 Years

Should 73%
Should not.........................19
No opinion 8

30–49 Years

Should 63%
Should not.........................28
No opinion 9

50 Years and Over

Should 47%
Should not.........................36
No opinion 17

By Religion

Protestants

Should 53%
Should not.........................33
No opinion 14

Catholics

Should 67%
Should not.........................24
No opinion 9

National Trend

	Should	Should not	No opinion
1982	59%	28%	13%
1977	56	33	11

Now, I'd like to ask you about the hiring of homosexuals in specific occupations. Do you think homosexuals should or should not be hired for the following occupations:

Salespersons?

Should 70%
Should not.........................18
No opinion 12

By Education

College

Should 80%
Should not.........................11
No opinion 9

High School

Should 71%
Should not.........................18
No opinion 11

Grade School

Should 48%
Should not.........................32
No opinion 20

By Age

18–24 Years

Should 75%
Should not.........................15
No opinion 10

25–29 Years

Should 78%
Should not.........................14
No opinion 8

30–49 Years

Should 77%
Should not.........................14
No opinion 9

50 Years and Over

Should 60%
Should not.........................24
No opinion 16

National Trend

	Should	Should not	No opinion
1982	70%	18%	12%
1977	68	22	10

The armed forces?

Should	52%
Should not	36
No opinion	12

By Education
College

Should	63%
Should not	30
No opinion	7

High School

Should	51%
Should not	36
No opinion	13

Grade School

Should	38%
Should not	45
No opinion	17

By Age
18–24 Years

Should	54%
Should not	34
No opinion	12

25–29 Years

Should	63%
Should not	30
No opinion	7

30–49 Years

Should	56%
Should not	34
No opinion	10

50 Years and Over

Should	45%
Should not	40
No opinion	15

National Trend

	Should	Should not	No opinion
1982	52%	36%	12%
1977	51	38	11

Doctors?

Should	50%
Should not	38
No opinion	12

By Education
College

Should	65%
Should not	26
No opinion	9

High School

Should	48%
Should not	39
No opinion	13

Grade School

Should	27%
Should not	58
No opinion	15

By Age
18–24 Years

Should	51%
Should not	37
No opinion	12

25–29 Years

Should	58%
Should not	32
No opinion	10

30–49 Years

Should	59%
Should not	31
No opinion	10

50 Years and Over

Should	39%
Should not	46
No opinion	15

National Trend

	Should	Should not	No opinion
1982	50%	38%	12%
1977	44	44	12

The clergy?

Should	38%
Should not	51
No opinion	11

By Education
College

Should	49%
Should not	44
No opinion	7

High School

Should	38%
Should not	51
No opinion	11

Grade School

Should	19%
Should not	68
No opinion	13

By Age
18–24 Years

Should	45%
Should not	46
No opinion	9

25–29 Years

Should	49%
Should not	42
No opinion	9

30–49 Years

Should	43%
Should not	48
No opinion	9

50 Years and Over

Should	27%
Should not	60
No opinion	13

National Trend

	Should	Should not	No opinion
1982	38%	51%	11%
1977	36	54	10

Elementary school teachers?

Should	32%
Should not	59
No opinion	9

By Education
College

Should	41%
Should not	53
No opinion	6

High School

Should	31%
Should not	59
No opinion	10

Grade School

Should	17%
Should not	71
No opinion	12

By Age

18-24 Years

Should 37%
Should not 54
No opinion 9

25-29 Years

Should 50%
Should not 42
No opinion 8

30-49 Years

Should 35%
Should not 57
No opinion 8

50 Years and Over

Should 22%
Should not 67
No opinion 11

National Trend

	Should	Should not	No opinion
1982	32%	59%	9%
1977	27	65	8

Those who replied "should" to all
of the above occupations 22%
Those who replied "should not" to all
of the above occupations 11

Note: The American people by a 2-to-1 margin believe that homosexuals should have the same job opportunities as nonhomosexuals. At the same time, however, a substantial proportion of the public would withhold this privilege from homosexuals seeking employment as clergy or elementary school teachers. There has been a small but significant increase since 1977 in public support of the principle of equal job opportunities for gays—one of the key objectives of the gay rights movement. Gains are also recorded in the percentages backing equal rights for certain occupations, including elementary school teachers and medical doctors.

A recent Gallup Poll found that 59% of persons nationwide believe that homosexuals should have equal rights in terms of job opportunities, with 28% opposed and 13% undecided. However, 59% are opposed to hiring homosexuals as elementary school teachers and 51% as clergy. There is less opposition to homosexuals serving in the armed forces (36%), as doctors (38%), or as salespersons (18%). These findings suggest that the issue of equal job rights for gays is situation-specific in much the same way as the issue of abortion.

Consistent with the findings reported recently on the public's tolerance of homosexuality, gay life-styles, and the image of gays in the United States, the principle of equal job opportunities has much greater support among women, the college-educated, young adults (eighteen to twenty-nine), Catholics, and easterners than among their counterparts. Most of the shifts since 1977 in opinion favorable to equal job rights for gays also have occurred among these population segments.

NOVEMBER 9
CONGRESSIONAL ELECTIONS—
THE RESULTS

On the basis of unofficial election returns, the Gallup Poll's final preelection report of the division of the national popular vote for U.S. House of Representatives candidates is within 1 percentage point of the actual vote division in the election of November 2.

On October 28 the Gallup Poll reported, on the basis of its final survey, that the popular vote for House candidates divided into 55% for the Democrats and 45% for the Republicans. According to a preliminary report of *Congressional Quarterly,* the national two-party popular vote for the House divides into 55.8% for the Democrats and 44.2% for the Republicans.

In its final report, the Gallup Poll stated that "the Democratic party is certain to add substantially to its present House majority in next

Tuesday's election." The Democrats picked up 26 seats, giving them a 269- to 166-seat advantage over the GOP.

The average deviation of Gallup Poll findings from the actual election results for the twelve off-year congressional elections since 1935 has been less than 2 percentage points. For the five congressional elections since and including 1966, the average deviation has been less than 1 percentage point.

NOVEMBER 9
AMBIVALENT ELECTION RESULTS MIRROR EQUIVOCAL OPINION OF REAGAN'S PROGRAM*

The results of last week's congressional election should give some comfort to pollsters. The election, heralded as a referendum on Reaganomics, has provided a somewhat ambivalent view of how voters reacted to the president and his economic program in much the same way polls have over recent months.

A loss of twenty-five or so Republican seats in the House and no change in the party division in the Senate cannot be read as a Democratic landslide nor as a public endorsement of Ronald Reagan's policies. The administration lost more seats in the House than first-term presidents usually do, but fewer than it might have considering the current depth of the recession. All in all, the Democrats came away with more than the Republicans, but still each party legitimately could claim some success.

The significant gains made by the Democrats in the House reflect the intense disillusionment of traditional Democratic voter groups with Reaganomics. Over the past two years the polls have shown blacks, manual workers, low-income

*This Gallup analysis was written by Andrew Kohut, president of the Gallup Organization Inc.

families, and union members coalescing in opposition to the administration. The Democratic party owes its strong showing in the House and in gubernatorial races to the solid support and turnout of old-line Democrats.

Beyond a return to the fold on the part of traditional Democrats, the election becomes a little harder to read; but this also has been the case with interpreting polls on Reaganomics in the past few months. The polls show many conflicting, if not contradictory, views of the president's economic programs.

Throughout the year a solid majority of Gallup's respondents have taken the position that Reaganomics will worsen, rather than improve, their own financial situation. Yet, Gallup consistently has found somewhat more public faith that Reaganomics will help the nation as a whole and even more faith in the president's program when the question is posed with regard to the long run. Surveys also indicate that the public has more confidence in Reagan than approval ratings of his performance would suggest. While only one third approve of the way he is handling the economy, close to half express some degree of confidence that he will do the right thing with regard to the economy.

Another likely reason the Democrats made only moderate gains is that, although the public thought the president's policies had hurt the economy, the Democratic party had no acceptable alternative to the Reagan plan. In fact, the September *Washington Post*/ABC Poll found as many who blamed the Democrats as blamed the Republicans for economic conditions. Along these same lines, the Gallup Poll showed the Democrats holding a numerical advantage over the Republicans as the party better able to handle the most important problems of the nation, but by a reduced margin over previous off-year measurements.

Indeed, much in the polls suggests that the Democratic victory on November 2 was a consequence of negative voting. According to the CBS/*New York Times* Poll only 24% thought that a big Democratic victory in the election would make much difference to the economy while 48% believed it would not. Similarly, the

Newsweek Poll found those who intended to vote against Republican incumbents were critical of Republican economic policies without having a favorable opinion of Democratic economic policies.

In many respects, the Democrats had the best of all possible worlds in which to have a congressional election. Between June and October concern for unemployment had soared as the most important national problem in almost all the polls. Unemployment is the only economic issue on which the Democratic party holds a decided advantage over the Republican party. Had inflation, controlling government spending, or holding down taxes been more at issue, Democrats likely would have been hard pressed to achieve the success they did.

Although casting ballots against Reaganomics on the part of many traditional Democrats who have been hard hit by the recession appeared instrumental to the Democratic gain, the election cannot be read as a total repudiation of Reaganomics and the president. A sufficient reserve of confidence in Reagan exists for an upturn in the economy to cause revival of support, to some extent, for the administration.

As it was when he took office, the president's future success with the voters will depend on what he produces over the next two years and not on his personal popularity or image. One of the most consistent myths about his administration is that the president receives public support because of his unusually high personal popularity. Historical Gallup comparisons show that this is not the case. Reagan is a popular man, as are most presidents or they never would be elected; but he is not personally more popular than his predecessors. The reserve of confidence in Reaganomics is the belief or perhaps the hope that the president's program will work despite its failures to date. There has been ample evidence in the polls, now confirmed by the congressional election results, that voters have not decisively rejected Reagan's new economic approach. Those who have been hurt the most by the program have registered their discontent, while others who have been less directly affected continue to take a wait-and-see attitude.

NOVEMBER 14
PRESIDENTIAL TRIAL HEATS

Interviewing Date: 10/15–18/82
Survey #203-G

Asked of registered voters: Suppose the presidential election were being held today. If President Ronald Reagan were the Republican candidate and Senator Edward Kennedy were the Democratic candidate, which would you like to see win? [Those who named another person or who were undecided were asked: As of today, do you lean more to Reagan, the Republican, or to Kennedy, the Democrat?]

Reagan. 47%
Kennedy 42
Other; undecided 11

National Trend

	Reagan	Kennedy	Other; undecided
June 25–28, 1982	45%	48%	7%
April 23–26, 1982	45	51	4
October 1981	56	35	9

Asked of registered voters: Suppose the presidential election were being held today. If President Ronald Reagan were the Republican candidate and former Vice-President Walter Mondale were the Democratic candidate, which would you like to see win? [Those who named another person or who were undecided were asked: As of today, do you lean more to Reagan, the Republican, or to Mondale, the Democrat?]

Reagan. 46%
Mondale. 44
Other; undecided 10

National Trend

	Reagan	Mondale	Other; undecided
June 25–28, 1982	43%	49%	8%
April 23–26, 1982	46	46	8
October 1981	54	37	9

Note: With the race for the presidency traditionally beginning immediately after the midterm congresional elections, in a recent Gallup test election nationwide for 1984 President Ronald Reagan won narrow victories over two of his most likely Democratic opponents. Reagan beat Senator Edward Kennedy, 47% to 42%, and former Vice-President Walter Mondale, 46% to 44%. In the same survey, Democratic candidates won 55% of the national popular vote for the U.S. House of Representatives to 45% for Republican candidates; these results are remarkably close to the 55.8% to 44.2% split of the actual two-party vote for the nation as a whole, as reported by *Congressional Quarterly*.

Reagan's slender margins over Kennedy and Mondale in the test elections represent a reversal of similar surveys conducted in June and April. In those tests, Reagan was beaten twice by Kennedy—48% to 45% in June and 51% to 45% in April. In the same surveys, Mondale won the June contest with 49% of the vote to 43% for Reagan, and the two men tied the April vote with 46% each.

When the latest trial-heat results are compared to intentions of voting for Democratic or Republican candidates for the House, 26% of registered voters who said they planned to vote for a Democrat in their congressional contest crossed over to vote for Reagan rather than for Kennedy. Conversely, 18% of those who backed a Republican for the House chose Kennedy in the presidential test election. The same crossover pattern was found with regard to the Reagan-Mondale trial heat.

The tables below show the crossover vote between the congressional and presidential trial heats based on the choices of registered voters:

Vote for Congress vs. Presidential Trial Heats

	National	Democratic candidates	Republican candidates
Reagan	47%	26%	76%
Kennedy	42	60	18
Other; undecided	11	14	6

Reagan	46%	26%	75%
Mondale	44	61	20
Other; undecided	10	12	5

NOVEMBER 15
ALCOHOLIC BEVERAGES—PART I

Interviewing Date: 8/3–30/82
Special telephone survey conducted in cooperation with the Care Unit Program.

Has drinking ever been a cause of trouble in your family?

By Age

	Yes
18–24 years	40%
25–29 years	37
30–49 years	35
50 years and over	26

In your opinion, would you say alcohol abuse is a major national problem, a minor national problem, or not a problem at all?

Major national problem	81%
Minor national problem	15
Not a problem at all	2
No opinion	2

Note: High proportions of both those who report a drinking problem in their families—and those who do not—believe alcohol abuse to be a major national problem. A total of 89% of the former and 77% of the latter group believe this to be the case. As many as one American in every three says a drinking-related problem has caused trouble in his family, according to a recent nationwide Gallup survey. The survey also reveals that an overwhelming eight in ten Americans believe that alcohol abuse is a major national problem.

When asked whether heavy drinking can lead to the use of other drugs, survey respondents were evenly divided, with 47% saying yes and 45% perceiving no connection.

Interviewing Date: 8/3–30/82
Special telephone survey conducted in cooperation with the Care Unit Program.

> Do you generally agree or generally disagree with this statement: Alcoholism is a disease and should be treated as such in a hospital?

	Agree
National	79%

National Trend

	Agree
1982	79%
1966	75
1955	63

> If a family member or a close friend had a serious long-term alcoholism problem, where would you advise him to go for help?

Hospital treatment program	42%
Self-help group or meetings	41
Halfway house,	4
Publicly funded treatment program	7
Other	6
Don't know	5
	105%*

*Total adds to more than 100% due to multiple responses.

> Do you generally agree or generally disagree with the following statement: Alcoholism treatment should be covered by medical insurance the same as any other disease?

Agree	59%
Disagree	33
Don't know	8

Note: A large and growing majority of Americans believes that alcoholism is a disease and should be treated as such in a hospital. The 79% holding this view is the largest figure recorded for this question since it was first posed in 1955.

Alcoholism was officially classified as a disease in that year by the American Medical Association.

Significantly more women than men agree that alcoholism is a disease to be treated in a hospital, by 83% as opposed to 76%. Income levels were an accurate predictor of the response to this question, with those in the lower-income brackets (under $10,000) at 74%, and those in the higher-income brackets (over $25,000) at 85%, with a corresponding gradual rise at the income levels in between.

When respondents were asked where they would advise treatment if a member of their own family or a close friend were ill with chronic alcoholism, most chose either a hospital treatment program or a self-help group or meetings. The remainder of responses split among halfway houses, publicly funded treatment programs, and other.

Currently most states have mandatory insurance coverage for alcoholism and treat it as a disease like all others. The difference in opinion on this question is also fairly wide between men and women, with men favoring insurance coverage at a significantly lower rate (52%) than women (64%). Once again, the percentage favoring coverage rises with income, with lower-income persons at 49% and rising to 66% in the highest bracket. Regionally, the lowest percentage favoring coverage is in the South (50%), with the West being highest (66%).

NOVEMBER 25
NATIONAL SERVICE

Special survey*

> Would you favor or oppose requiring all young men to give one year of service to the nation—either in the military forces or in

*Asked of a random selection of names from the latest edition of Who's Who in America. This survey was conducted by mail.

nonmilitary work here or abroad, such as work in hospitals or with elderly people?

Favor 78%
Oppose 17
No opinion 5

Note: With the urgent problem of unemployment facing the new Congress when it convenes in January, its members may wish to consider a program which wins the enthusiastic support of both the general public and the nation's opinion leaders: a program of mandatory military or nonmilitary service for young men.

Eight in ten opinion leaders—prominent in business, the sciences, the arts, politics, religion, and many other fields—say they would favor requiring all young men to give one year of service to the nation, either in the military forces or in nonmilitary activities such as work in hospitals or with elderly people. A solid seven in ten among the general public agree.

Proponents of national service believe that such a program should be part of the educational process, enabling young persons to experience the real world. Others favor it as a way to provide special training to young people who do not plan to go to college. Still others like the concept because they think it would give all young people a better and more realistic view of social problems, while offering them an opportunity to do something about them. And national service could meet head-on one of the most basic and intractable problems of U.S. society: youth unemployment.

Earlier surveys have shown that the following areas are among those in nonmilitary service of greatest interest to potential volunteers: conservation work in national forests and parks, tutoring low-achieving students in school, day-care for young children, assistance to the elderly, help in floods and natural disasters, hospital work, and repairing and painting run-down houses.

Some persons who support a compulsory national-service law qualify their opinion by noting that women should be included, that the program should apply to everyone, or that the program should last more than one year.

NOVEMBER 28
NATIONAL DEFENSE

Interviewing Date: 11/5–8/82
Survey #204-G

At the present time which nation do you feel is stronger in terms of nuclear weapons, the United States or the Soviet Union—or do you think they are about equal in nuclear strength?

United States 22%
Soviet Union 30
About equal 33
No opinion 15

By Education
College

United States 22%
Soviet Union 27
About equal 39
No opinion 12

High School

United States 20%
Soviet Union 34
About equal 32
No opinion 14

Grade School

United States 26%
Soviet Union 23
About equal 26
No opinion 25

By Region
East

United States 23%
Soviet Union 32
About equal 28
No opinion 17

Midwest

United States 21%
Soviet Union 29

About equal 39
No opinion 11

South

United States 23%
Soviet Union 30
About equal 32
No opinion 15

West

United States 18%
Soviet Union 27
About equal 37
No opinion 18

By Age
18–24 Years

United States 19%
Soviet Union 34
About equal 35
No opinion 12

25–29 Years

United States 22%
Soviet Union 31
About equal 36
No opinion 11

30–49 Years

United States 23%
Soviet Union 29
About equal 35
No opinion 13

50 Years and Over

United States 22%
Soviet Union 28
About equal 31
No opinion 19

By Politics
Republicans

United States 19%
Soviet Union 36

About equal 34
No opinion 11

Democrats

United States 25%
Soviet Union 24
About equal 35
No opinion 16

Independents

United States 17%
Soviet Union 34
About equal 32
No opinion 17

There is much discussion as to the amount of money the government in Washington should spend for national defense and military purposes. How do you feel about this? Do you think we are spending too little, too much, or about the right amount?

Too much 41%
Too little 16
About right 31
No opinion 12

By Education
College

Too much 50%
Too little 15
About right 29
No opinion 6

High School

Too much 38%
Too little 18
About right 32
No opinion 12

Grade School

Too much 30%
Too little 16
About right 32
No opinion 22

By Region

East

Too much	48%
Too little	12
About right	31
No opinion	9

Midwest

Too much	43%
Too little	16
About right	30
No opinion	11

South

Too much	31%
Too little	18
About right	36
No opinion	15

West

Too much	41%
Too little	20
About right	26
No opinion	13

By Age

18–24 Years

Too much	49%
Too little	15
About right	25
No opinion	11

25–29 Years

Too much	45%
Too little	19
About right	29
No opinion	7

30–49 Years

Too much	41%
Too little	16
About right	32
No opinion	11

50 Years and Over

Too much	35%
Too little	17
About right	34
No opinion	14

By Politics

Republicans

Too much	29%
Too little	20
About right	41
No opinion	10

Democrats

Too much	46%
Too little	14
About right	28
No opinion	12

Independents

Too much	43%
Too little	19
About right	27
No opinion	11

Note: President Ronald Reagan's proposal for greatly increasing the nation's nuclear strength comes at a time of growing public perception that the nuclear gap between the United States and the Soviet Union has narrowed. In this same period, Americans are more favorably disposed toward a reduction in defense spending than in almost a decade.

In the latest Gallup survey, 30% of the public say the USSR has a nuclear advantage, 22% say the United States has the edge, while 33% believe the two superpowers are about equal in nuclear arms. In a survey last spring, 40% thought the Soviet Union enjoyed nuclear superiority compared to 17% who cited the United States. Thus, the 23 percentage-point swing in favor of the Soviets recorded in the earlier survey has narrowed to an 8-point difference at present. Details are shown below:

Nuclear Superiority

	November 1982	April–May 1982	Point difference
United States	22%	17%	+ 5
Soviet Union	30	40	−10
About equal	33	32	+ 1
No opinion	15	11	+ 4

The weight of public opinion has swung to the view that the United States is spending too much for defense (41%) rather than about the right amount (31%), or too little (16%). In a March survey, the figures were: too much, 36%; about right, 36%; too little, 19%. Comparison of the March and November survey results shows a significant shift toward a softer defense posture undoubtedly stemming, at least in part, from growing public concern over the proportion of the federal budget earmarked for defense rather than for social programs. These relatively modest shifts, however, are dwarfed by a comparison of the latest findings with those recorded at the outset of the Reagan administration.

In a January–February 1981 survey, 51% of Americans said they believed too little was being spent on defense, while 22% thought the budget was adequate and only 15% thought that too much was budgeted for military purposes. One must go back to 1973 to find survey results comparable to those reported today, as shown in the following table:

National Trend

	Too much	Too little	About right	No opinion
1982	36%	19%	36%	9%
1981	15	51	22	12
1976	36	22	32	10
1973	46	13	30	11
1971	50	11	31	8
1969	52	8	31	9
1960	18	21	45	16

In a nationally televised address on November 22, Reagan proposed that an MX intercontinental missile system be deployed to modernize American nuclear forces, at an initial cost of $26 billion. The president said that his administration would aggressively pursue a mutual reduction in nuclear arms and that his plan would serve as an incentive to the Soviet Union to agree to an arms reduction. Critics of the president's plan maintain that American nuclear forces, though fewer in number than the Soviets, are superior in quality and flexibility.

As might be expected, the public's perceptions of whether the United States or the Soviet Union has a nuclear advantage are closely linked to its attitudes about U.S. defense spending. Among the 41% plurality who believe we are spending too much on defense, the weight of opinion is that the United States and the USSR are about equal in nuclear strength. On the other hand, among the 16% who think we are not budgeting enough for military purposes, the Soviet Union, by a 5-to-2 margin, is considered to have a nuclear edge over the United States.

There is a strong political coloration to public opinion on both nuclear superiority and the adequacy of U.S. defense expenditures. Equal proportions of Democrats, for example, believe the United States (25%) and the Soviet Union (24%) are stronger in nuclear arms, while 35% think there is nuclear parity between the two nations. Republicans, on the other hand, are about twice as likely to say the Soviet Union is stronger (36%) than the United States (19%). Independents are more apt to agree with the Republicans than with the Democrats. Similarly, a preponderance of Democrats thinks the United States is spending too much for defense, while Republicans lean to the view that our spending is about right.

DECEMBER 2
JOB SECURITY

Interviewing Date: 11/5–8/82
Survey #204-G

> Asked of employed persons: Thinking about the next twelve months, how likely do you think it is that you will lose your job or be laid off—very likely, fairly likely, not too likely, or not at all likely?

Very likely	5%
Fairly likely	5
Not too likely	15
Not at all likely	26
No opinion	2
Total employed:	53%

Loss of Jobs by Employed Persons

By Sex

	Very likely or fairly likely
Male	11%
Female	10

By Race

White	9%
Black	17

By Region

East	10%
Midwest	14
South	9
West	6

By Age

18–29 years	14%
30–49 years	13
50 years and over	5

By Income

$15,000 and over	9%
Under $15,000	12

By Politics

Republicans	6%
Democrats	11
Independents	13

By Occupation

Professional and business	7%
Clerical and sales	17
Manual workers	18
Skilled workers	11
Unskilled workers	23

Labor union families	17
Nonlabor union families	9

National Trend

	June 1982	January 1982
Very likely	4%	3%
Fairly likely	4	6
Not too likely	15	14
Not at all likely	29	31
No opinion	2	1
Total employed:	54%	55%

Asked of nonworking people: At the present time, are you actively looking for a job, or not?

Looking	9%
Not looking	27
Gave up looking (volunteered)	2
No answer	9
Total not employed:	47%

National Trend

	1982
Looking	8%
Not looking	32
Gave up looking (volunteered)	1
No answer	4
Total not employed:	45%

Note: As Congress reconvened this week, unemployment affected at least one adult American in five (21%). This represents a small but significant increase from the 17% recorded in a June survey. The latest Gallup Poll found 11% of the public either unemployed and actively looking for jobs or so discouraged they have given up looking. In addition, 10% of persons who now hold either full-time or part-time jobs say they are either very likely (5%) or fairly likely (5%) to lose their jobs or be laid off within the next twelve months.

One of the most pressing matters on the agenda of the Congress is consideration of a public works bill, which would provide 320,000 jobs to make necessary repairs to the nation's highways and bridges and would be financed mainly by a 5-cent federal tax on gasoline.

Fear of unemployment is higher among black workers, of whom 17% say it is very likely or fairly likely they will be laid off. In sharp contrast, only 9% of employed whites think it is at least fairly likely they will lose their jobs within the next twelve months.

Other worker groups with greater-than-average apprehension about the security of their jobs include eighteen to twenty-nine year olds (14%), unskilled blue-collar workers (23%), persons whose family income is less than $15,000 per year (12%), members of labor union households (17%), and midwesterners (14%). In addition, about twice the proportion of Democrats (11%) and independents (13%) as Republicans (6%) are afraid of losing their jobs.

Comparison of the latest findings with the June survey shows fear of joblessness to have grown in most major worker groups, a notable exception being men. In June, 11% of male workers and 6% of females thought it was very or fairly likely they would be terminated within twelve months. In the latest survey, 11% of men believe their jobs are in jeopardy, but the proportion of working women sharing this fear grew by 4 percentage points to 10%, so that women are now as apprehensive as men about their job security.

DECEMBER 5
NUCLEAR FREEZE

Interviewing Date: 11/5–8/82
Survey #204-G

Would you favor or oppose an agreement between the United States and the Soviet Union for an immediate, verifiable freeze on the testing, production, and deployment of nuclear weapons?

Favor.............................71%
Oppose............................20
No opinion 9

By Sex
Male

Favor.............................71%
Oppose............................23
No opinion 6

Female

Favor.............................72%
Oppose............................16
No opinion 12

By Race
White

Favor.............................71%
Oppose............................20
No opinion 9

Nonwhite

Favor.............................72%
Oppose............................16
No opinion 12

By Education
College

Favor.............................75%
Oppose............................22
No opinion 3

High School

Favor.............................72%
Oppose............................18
No opinion 10

Grade School

Favor.............................59%
Oppose............................19
No opinion 22

By Region
East

Favor.............................75%
Oppose............................18
No opinion 7

Midwest

Favor...................................75%
Oppose..................................16
No opinion 9

South

Favor...................................65%
Oppose..................................23
No opinion 12

West

Favor...................................70%
Oppose..................................20
No opinion 10

By Age
18–29 Years

Favor...................................75%
Oppose..................................17
No opinion 8

30–49 Years

Favor...................................73%
Oppose..................................19
No opinion 8

50 Years and Over

Favor...................................67%
Oppose..................................22
No opinion 11

By Politics
Republicans

Favor...................................67%
Oppose..................................28
No opinion 5

Democrats

Favor...................................73%
Oppose..................................17
No opinion 10

Independents

Favor...................................74%
Oppose..................................17
No opinion 9

By Religion
Protestants

Favor...................................71%
Oppose..................................19
No opinion 10

Catholics

Favor...................................72%
Oppose..................................20
No opinion 8

Those Who Think It Would Be Possible To Verify Whether the Soviet Union Is Conforming to a Nuclear Freeze Agreement

Favor...................................85%
Oppose..................................11
No opinion 4

Those Who Think It Would Not Be Possible To Verify Whether the Soviet Union Is Conforming to a Nuclear Freeze Agreement

Favor...................................65%
Oppose..................................30
No opinion 5

Those Who Think the United States Is Stronger in Nuclear Arms

Favor...................................68%
Oppose..................................24
No opinion 8

Those Who Think the Soviet Union Is Stronger in Nuclear Arms

Favor...................................68%
Oppose..................................29
No opinion 3

Those Who Think the United States and the Soviet Union Are About Equal in Nuclear Arms

Favor...............................81%
Oppose.............................13
No opinion 6

Do you think it would or would not be possible to set up a system for verifying or checking whether the Soviet Union is living up to the terms of a nuclear freeze agreement?

Possible............................39%
Not possible 47
No opinion 14

By Sex
Male

Possible............................40%
Not possible 49
No opinion 11

Female

Possible............................40%
Not possible 44
No opinion 16

By Race
White

Possible............................38%
Not possible 49
No opinion 13

Nonwhite

Possible............................46%
Not possible 34
No opinion 20

By Education
College

Possible............................43%
Not possible 52
No opinion 5

High School

Possible............................38%
Not possible 47
No opinion 15

Grade School

Possible............................38%
Not possible 35
No opinion 27

By Region
East

Possible............................41%
Not possible 47
No opinion 12

Midwest

Possible............................37%
Not possible 49
No opinion 14

South

Possible............................40%
Not possible 44
No opinion 16

West

Possible............................41%
Not possible 47
No opinion 12

By Age
18–29 Years

Possible............................42%
Not possible 47
No opinion 11

30–49 Years

Possible............................37%
Not possible 49
No opinion 14

50 Years and Over

Possible 39%
Not possible 45
No opinion 16

By Politics

Republicans

Possible 34%
Not possible 58
No opinion 8

Democrats

Possible 44%
Not possible 39
No opinion 17

Independents

Possible 40%
Not possible 49
No opinion 11

By Religion

Protestants

Possible 38%
Not possible 48
No opinion 14

Catholics

Possible 41%
Not possible 47
No opinion 12

Note: If the American people, including both those who did and did not vote in November on state and local referendums, were voting in a national referendum on a bilateral nuclear freeze, it would pass by a wide margin. The latest Gallup survey shows 71% of adults in favor of an agreement between the United States and the Soviet Union for an immediate, verifiable freeze on the testing, production, and deployment of nuclear weapons.

A bilateral freeze wins across-the-board support, with relatively little difference of opinion found on the basis of region, political affiliation, education, religion, sex, or age. While backing a freeze, the public nevertheless has serious doubts about the basis for an effective agreement—that is, a system for verifying or checking whether the Soviet Union is living up to the terms. By a narrow 5-to-4 margin, Americans believe it would not be possible to set up such a system.

The desire to cast a vote for peace is so strong that even those who think it would not be possible to monitor Soviet compliance vote 2 to 1 in favor of a bilateral nuclear freeze. Those who believe it is possible vote overwhelmingly (85% to 11%) in favor of a freeze.

The survey also sought views on how the relative nuclear strength of the two nations relates to opinion on a bilateral nuclear freeze. Equal proportions (68%) of both those who think the United States is stronger and those who believe the Soviet Union is ahead express support for a bilateral freeze. Among those who think the two nations are about equal in nuclear strength, 81% back a freeze.

The same survey reveals a growing public perception that the nuclear gap between the United States and the Soviet Union has narrowed. As reported recently, 30% of the public thinks the USSR has a nuclear advantage, 22% says the United States, while 33% believes the two superpowers are about equal in strength. In a survey last spring, 40% thought the Soviet Union enjoyed nuclear superiority compared to 17% who said the United States. This trend is paralleled by an increase in those favoring a reduction in U.S. defense spending. More Americans today want cuts than at any other time in almost a decade.

DECEMBER 9
UNITED STATES–SOVIET UNION RELATIONS

Interviewing Date: 11/19–22/82
Survey #205-G

Have you heard or read about the death of President Leonid Brezhnev and the election of Yuri Andropov as the new Soviet president?

	Yes
National	94%

Asked of those who replied in the affirmative: Would you favor or oppose the United States going further than it has so far in trying to develop better relations with the Soviet Union?

Favor	70%
Oppose	21
No opinion	9

By Education
College

Favor	75%
Oppose	20
No opinion	5

High School

Favor	66%
Oppose	21
No opinion	13

Grade School

Favor	58%
Oppose	24
No opinion	18

By Region
East

Favor	72%
Oppose	17
No opinion	11

Midwest

Favor	74%
Oppose	19
No opinion	7

South

Favor	59%
Oppose	29
No opinion	12

West

Favor	79%
Oppose	15
No opinion	6

By Politics
Republicans

Favor	67%
Oppose	24
No opinion	9

Democrats

Favor	67%
Oppose	21
No opinion	12

Independents

Favor	70%
Oppose	17
No opinion	13

Also asked of the aware group: As a result of the change in leadership in the Soviet Union, do you think relations between the United States and the Soviet Union will get better or worse during the next few years?

Better	31%
Worse	21
Same	30
No opinion	18

Asked of the entire sample: Have you heard or read about President Reagan's removing the sanctions against using U.S. supplies and technology to build the pipeline between the Soviet Union and Western Europe?

	Yes
National	60%

Asked of those who replied in the affirmative: Do you approve or disapprove of the president's removing these restrictions?

Approve. 53%
Disapprove 27
No opinion 20

Note: As the leadership in the Soviet Union changes, the American people express uncertainty about what to expect, but at the same time are in a mood to try to develop better relations with the USSR. A total of 70% of those adults aware of the change in Soviet leadership would like to see the United States go further than it has so far in developing better relations with the USSR. Only 21% express opposition to new American overtures.

The same survey shows 31% of Americans expressing the view that relations between the United States and the Soviet Union will get better as a result of the change in leadership, while 21% believe they will get worse. Another 30% foresee little change, and 18% do not express an opinion.

The proposal to further better relations has solid bipartisan appeal. Large majorities in all key population groups favor new efforts to improve relations between the two nations, although southerners and those with less than a college education are not as inclined to favor new overtures to the USSR.

DECEMBER 12
INFLATION AND UNEMPLOYMENT

Interviewing Date: 11/19–22/82
Survey #205-G

The inflation rate is now running at about 6%. By this time next year, what do you think the inflation rate will be?

10% or more. 18%
9% 6
8% 16
7% 9
6% 17
5% 10
4% or less 8
No opinion 16
 Median estimate: 7.3%

Comparison Table: June 1982*

10% or more. 24%
9% 15
8% 11
7% 16
6% 10
5% 9
4% or less 3
No opinion 12
 Median estimate: 7.9%

Comparison Table: January 1982*

10% or more. 54%
9% 13
8% 10
7% or less 12
No opinion 11
 Median estimate: 10.2%

*Question asked what inflation rate will be at the end of 1982.

The current unemployment rate is now 10.4%. By this time next year, what do you think the unemployment rate will be?

13% or more. 16%
12% 16
11% 12
10% 14
9% 12
8% or less 17
No opinion 13
 Median estimate: 10.6%

Comparison Table: June 1982*

13% or more. 10%
12% 12
11% 15
10% 26
9% 12
8% or less 16
No opinion 9
 Median estimate: 10.1%

Comparison Table: January 1982*

13% or more. 8%
12% 6

11%	6
10%	24
9%	18
8% or less	29
No opinion	9

Median estimate: 9.4%

*Question asked what inflation rate will be at the end of 1982.

As shown in the table below, Republicans, whites, and persons from the upper-income and college-educated strata are far more optimistic on both the inflation and unemployment fronts than are persons from groups with a Democratic orientation:

Inflation and Unemployment Rate Forecasts

	Inflation 7% or less	Unemployment 10% or less
National	44%	43%
By Race		
White	47%	45%
Black	22	22
By Education		
College	58%	52%
High school or less	38	38
By Income		
$15,000 and over	53%	50%
Under $15,000	33	31
By Politics		
Republicans	60%	61%
Democrats	37	34
Independents	42	41

Note: President Ronald Reagan is still haunted by the misery index, an economic barometer he effectively used against Jimmy Carter during the 1980 presidential campaign. The index—a combination of the public's estimates of the inflation and unemployment rates—now stands at 18%, identical to last June's assessment. Although the misery index itself remains unchanged, its two components continue to shift, as they have since the Gallup Poll began these measurements soon after the 1980 election.

On the one hand, reflecting the steady deterioration in employment, the public's estimate of the jobless rate has gone from 7.1% in the November 1980 survey to 10.1% last June to 10.6% at present, strikingly close to the 10.8% rate for November 1982 reported by the U.S. Department of Labor. On the other, the public's estimate of the inflation rate at this time next year now stands at 7.3%, down sharply from 13.6% in the benchmark 1980 survey, but somewhat higher than the current 6% rate reported by the federal government.

To a considerable extent, the public's views of the twin economic problems of inflation and unemployment are colored by their political allegiance, with 60% of Republicans, but only 37% of Democrats, predicting an inflation rate of 7% or less a year from now. The same pattern holds for unemployment, with Republicans far more sanguine about the jobless rate. Nationally, 43% of the public believes the unemployment rate will be 10% or less at this time next year. The same sentiment is expressed by 61% of Republicans but only 34% of Democrats.

DECEMBER 16
SOCIAL SECURITY

Interviewing Date: 11/19–22/82
Survey #205-G

As I read off some ways Social Security could help pay its way, please tell me whether you approve or disapprove of each one:

Have employees of the federal government—who are not now covered—included in and paying into the Social Security system?

Approve	75%
Disapprove	15
No opinion	10

By Age

18–29 Years

Approve............................75%
Disapprove 14
No opinion 11

30–49 Years

Approve............................79%
Disapprove 15
No opinion 6

50–64 Years

Approve............................68%
Disapprove 21
No opinion 11

65 Years and Over

Approve............................74%
Disapprove 12
No opinion 14

By Politics

Republicans

Approve............................76%
Disapprove 14
No opinion 10

Democrats

Approve............................77%
Disapprove 15
No opinion 8

Independents

Approve............................73%
Disapprove 17
No opinion 10

Have cost-of-living adjustments to Social Security benefits tied to wages rather than to prices, as at present?

Approve............................49%
Disapprove 32
No opinion 19

By Age

18–29 Years

Approve............................55%
Disapprove 24
No opinion 21

30–49 Years

Approve............................50%
Disapprove 34
No opinion 16

50–64 Years

Approve............................43%
Disapprove 40
No opinion 17

65 Years and Over

Approve............................43%
Disapprove 29
No opinion 18

By Politics

Republicans

Approve............................51%
Disapprove 31
No opinion 18

Democrats

Approve............................50%
Disapprove 32
No opinion 18

Independents

Approve............................49%
Disapprove 32
No opinion 19

Increase the amount employers and employees pay into the system each month?

Approve............................34%
Disapprove 59
No opinion 7

By Age
18–29 Years

Approve..............................33%
Disapprove 59
No opinion 8

30–49 Years

Approve..............................28%
Disapprove 68
No opinion 4

50–64 Years

Approve..............................39%
Disapprove 54
No opinion 7

65 Years and Over

Approve..............................40%
Disapprove 48
No opinion 12

By Politics
Republicans

Approve..............................31%
Disapprove 62
No opinion 7

Democrats

Approve..............................38%
Disapprove 55
No opinion 7

Independents

Approve..............................30%
Disapprove 63
No opinion 7

Gradually increase the age at which people become eligible to receive Social Security benefits?

Approve..............................30%
Disapprove 63
No opinion 7

By Age
18–29 Years

Approve..............................28%
Disapprove 65
No opinion 7

30–49 Years

Approve..............................29%
Disapprove 65
No opinion 6

50–64 Years

Approve..............................24%
Disapprove 70
No opinion 6

65 Years and Over

Approve..............................41%
Disapprove 47
No opinion 12

By Politics
Republicans

Approve..............................41%
Disapprove 51
No opinion 8

Democrats

Approve..............................28%
Disapprove 66
No opinion 6

Independents

Approve..............................25%
Disapprove 69
No opinion 6

Increase federal income taxes so that Social Security benefits could be paid out of general revenues?

Approve..............................24%
Disapprove 62
No opinion 14

By Age
18–29 Years

Approve. 26%
Disapprove 60
No opinion 14

30–49 Years

Approve. 22%
Disapprove 69
No opinion 9

50–64 Years

Approve. 23%
Disapprove . . . .,. . . .62
No opinion 15

65 Years and Over

Approve. 27%
Disapprove 53
No opinion 20

By Politics
Republicans

Approve. 18%
Disapprove 69
No opinion 13

Democrats

Approve. 28%
Disapprove 58
No opinion 14

Independents

Approve. 26%
Disapprove 63
No opinion 11

Make Social Security benefits subject to federal income tax, the same as any other income?

Approve. 19%
Disapprove 73
No opinion 8

By Age
18–29 Years

Approve. 28%
Disapprove 64
No opinion 8

30–49 Years

Approve. 14%
Disapprove 81
No opinion 5

50–64 Years

Approve. 17%
Disapprove 78
No opinion 5

65 Years and Over

Approve. 18%
Disapprove 69
No opinion 13

By Politics
Republicans

Approve. 22%
Disapprove 70
No opinion 8

Democrats

Approve. 18%
Disapprove 75
No opinion 7

Independents

Approve. 20%
Disapprove 74
No opinion 6

Note: Of six widely discussed proposals for preventing the collapse of the Social Security system, only one receives the public's clear endorsement. The proposal to include federal government employees, who are not now covered in the old-age benefits plan, has heavy (5-to-1) public backing, with 75% voting for this provision and 15% opposed.

Another proposal that would help bring the system back to solvency is to have cost-of-living benefit increases tied to national wage hikes rather than to prices, as at present. A 5-to-3 plurality of the public backs this plan, with greater support than opposition found in all age groups including persons sixty-five and older, most of whom are already receiving Social Security benefits and thus would be directly affected if this proposal became law.

By almost 2 to 1, the public disapproves of increasing the amount employers and employees pay into the Social Security fund each month. Greater opposition to this proposal is expressed by persons under age fifty than by those over this age. Among retirement-age survey respondents, most of whom would benefit if this proposal were adopted, disapproval only narrowly outweighs approval, 48% to 40%.

The public opposes by a full 2-to-1 ratio a gradually raising of the age at which those covered by Social Security become eligible to receive benefits. Understandably, opposition to this reform is particularly strong among persons on the threshold of retirement, ages fifty to sixty-four. Within this group, 70% disapprove of the proposal while 24% approve. As might be expected, only token opposition (41% to 47%) is expressed by the sixty-five and over age group.

The political dimension to these proposals is surprisingly muted, with similar proportions of Republicans, Democrats, and independents in general agreement. On the gradually rising age requirement, however, the opinions of persons of different political stripes are widely divergent. By a slim 5-to-4 edge, Republicans are against the proposal, while opposition from Democrats (66% to 28%) and independents (69% to 25%) is more than 2 to 1.

The fifth proposal, to fund Social Security out of general revenues by increasing federal income taxes for that purpose, is voted down 62% to 24%. Although the divergence on the basis of political affiliation is not as great as that noted above, Democrats (58% to 28%) and independents (63% to 26%) are more favorably disposed toward this proposal than are Republi-

cans, who oppose it by almost a 4-to-1 margin (69% to 18%).

The last proposal, to eliminate the current tax-free feature of Social Security benefits by making retirement payments subject to federal income tax, draws the public's greatest ire. Nationally, 73% disapprove while 19% approve. Although this idea would only affect relatively wealthy individuals, the extent of the public's disaffection with it is indicated by the fact that in only the youngest population group does approval exceed 25%.

DECEMBER 19
ELECTORAL REFORMS—PART I

Interviewing Date: Various dates during 1981 and 1982
Various surveys

Would you like to see any changes in the way political campaigns are conducted?

Yes 55%
No 31
No opinion 14

By Education
College

Yes 71%
No 24
No opinion 5

High School

Yes 49%
No 35
No opinion 16

Grade School

Yes 44%
No 29
No opinion 27

Do you believe we need to adopt a better way to select candidates for the presidency?

Yes............................... 40%
No................................ 45
No opinion 15

By Education
College

Yes............................... 43%
No................................ 47
No opinion 10

High School

Yes............................... 36%
No................................ 48
No opinion 16

Grade School

Yes............................... 46%
No................................ 31
No opinion 23

When a large business concern, a foundation, or a university needs a new president, the usual practice is to appoint a search committee to seek out the best candidates. Do you think that search committees should be used by the Republican and Democratic parties to find the best possible candidates and then let party members choose the one they prefer?

Yes............................... 54%
No................................ 33
No opinion 13

By Education
College

Yes............................... 54%
No................................ 39
No opinion 7

High School

Yes............................... 54%
No................................ 31
No opinion 15

Grade School

Yes............................... 56%
No................................ 24
No opinion 20

In 1980 presidential primaries were held in thirty-seven states. It has been proposed that four individual regional primaries be held in different weeks of June during a presidential year. Does this sound like a good idea or a poor idea?

General Public

Good idea......................... 44%
Poor idea......................... 34
No opinion 22

Opinion Leaders*

Good idea......................... 50%
Poor idea......................... 30
No opinion 20

It has been suggested that presidential candidates be chosen by the voters in a nationwide primary election instead of by the present system. Would you favor or oppose this?

General Public

Favor............................. 66%
Oppose............................ 24
No opinion 10

Opinion Leaders

Favor............................. 47%
Oppose............................ 42
No opinion 11

If a committee came to you and asked you to run on your party's ticket for the U.S. Senate and offered to pay all campaign expenses, do you think you would accept?

*Asked of a random selection of names from the latest edition of *Who's Who in America*. This survey was conducted by mail.

Opinion Leaders

Yes	29%
No; no opinion	71

Note: In the wake of the costliest congressional election in U.S. history and with the 1984 presidential campaign about to get under way, a majority of Americans favors major changes in political campaigns and far-reaching electoral reforms. When asked if they want changes in the way political campaigns are conducted, 55% replied affirmatively, with the proportion rising to 71% among persons with a college background. Leading the list of complaints are the enormous cost of the campaigns, mudslinging by candidates, and the length of the campaign period.

Fully half of the electorate with views on the matter think a better way is needed to select presidential candidates. And a majority of voters back a proposal to use search committees to seek out the most highly qualified candidates, following the procedure used by large corporations, foundations, and universities in filling vacancies. A total of 54% of survey respondents think this process should be followed by the Republican and Democratic parties as a way of finding exceptional candidates. Rank-and-file party members then could choose the one they prefer in the primaries.

The views of 1,346 opinion leaders on electoral reform also were sought in a special survey among the nation's most prominent citizens, including university presidents, scientists, statesmen, clergy, business and labor leaders, and generals. Results of this survey suggest that search committees would have a large pool of talent upon which to draw. As many as three in ten leaders say that if a committee were to come to them and ask them to run on their party's ticket for the U.S. Senate, while offering to pay all campaign expenses, they would accept such an offer.

Not only do the public and some opinion leaders favor the idea of search committees, but they also would support changes in other stages of the nomination procedure. A recent Gallup survey shows voters, by 44% to 34%, in favor of changing the present primary-election system to a regional one in which four individual regional primaries would be held in different weeks of June during a presidential election year.

A 1980 Gallup survey found an even larger proportion of the public (66%) in favor of a plan that would replace the many state nomination races with a single national primary, allowing voters in all fifty states to choose the nominees by direct popular vote. Opinion leaders vote 50% to 30% in favor of four regional primaries and 47% and 42% in favor of a nationwide primary election instead of the present system.

DECEMBER 20
ELECTORAL REFORMS—PART II

Interviewing Date: Various dates during 1981 and 1982
Various surveys

Would you favor changing the term of office of the president of the United States to one six-year term with no reelection?

Favor	49%
Oppose	47
No opinion	4

It has been suggested that the federal government provide a fixed amount of money for the election campaign of candidates for Congress and that all private contributions from other sources be prohibited. Do you think this is a good idea or a poor idea?

General Public

Good idea	55%
Poor idea	31
No opinion	14

Opinion Leaders*

Good idea	46%
Poor idea	46
No opinion	8

How would you feel about changing the term of members of the House of Representatives from two years to four years? Would you favor or oppose this?

General Public

Favor 51%
Oppose 37
No opinion 12

Opinion Leaders

Favor 58%
Oppose 36
No opinion 6

A law has been proposed which would limit a member of the House of Representatives to three terms of four years apiece, for a total of twelve years. Would you favor or oppose such a law?

General Public

Favor 59%
Oppose 32
No opinion 9

Opinion Leaders

Favor 43%
Oppose 51
No opinion 6

*Asked of a random selection of names from the latest edition of *Who's Who in America*. This survey was conducted by mail.

Note: If the two years between now and the 1984 election were to follow the public's script, this would be the sequence of events. Search committees set up by both major parties would help to select the best possible candidates, from whom voters would choose. A national primary, or regional primaries, would replace the present system of individual state primaries. Voters in each party would select a single candidate.

The conventions would be shortened and made more dignified, and the campaign would be shortened to a few weeks. The presidential election would be held in September instead of November, allowing incoming presidents more time to prepare legislation for the opening of Congress in early January. Nationally televised debates among the candidates would replace the traditional "whistle-stopping" approach. In addition, the federal government would provide a fixed amount of money for each candidate to spend.

The public would have the opportunity to vote on national issues as well as on candidates. Surveys have indicated that voter turnout might increase substantially if voters could express their opinions on national issues.

The Electoral College would be abolished; the president would be chosen by direct popular vote. He would be limited to a single six-year term, and limits would be set for the terms of office of U.S. senators and representatives.

DECEMBER 23
SATISFACTION INDEX

Interviewing Date: 9/17–20/82
Survey #202-G

In general are you satisfied or dissatisfied with the way things are going in the United States at this time?

Satisfied 24%
Dissatisfied 72
No opinion 4

National Trend

	Satisfied	Dis-satisfied	No opinion
April 1982	25%	71%	4%
December 1981 ..	27	67	6
June 1981	33	61	6
January 1981	17	78	5
November 1979 ..	19	77	4
August 1979	12	84	4
February 1979 ...	26	69	5

In general are you satisfied or dissatisfied with the way things are going in your own personal life?

Satisfied 75%
Dissatisfied 23
No opinion 2

National Trend

	Satisfied	Dis-satisfied	No opinion
April 1982	76%	22%	2%
December 1981 . .	81	17	2
June 1981	81	16	3
January 1981	81	17	2
November 1979 . .	79	19	2
August 1979	73	23	4
February 1979 . . .	77	21	2

Note: Despite widespread concern over the economy, the American public's overall mood is about the same today as it was last spring. Only 24% in the latest survey say they are satisfied with the way things are going in the country, while three times as many, 72%, say they are dissatisfied. In an April survey the percentages were virtually the same, 25% and 71%.

When survey respondents are asked about how things are going in their personal lives, the responses are almost exactly the reverse of their answers to the question about the nation: 75% say they are satisfied and 23% dissatisfied. On this measurement, too, little change is noted from the April findings, when 76% expressed satisfaction with their personal life and 22% dissatisfaction.

As might be expected, satisfaction levels differ sharply on the basis of respondents' assessment of their family's financial status. About one-third (35%) of persons who are optimistic about their financial situation express satisfaction with the way things are going in the nation, compared to only 10% among financial pessimists. As many as nine in ten optimists (88%) express satisfaction with the way things are going in their personal lives, compared to far fewer (58%) among those who are pessimistic

about their financial outlook, as seen in the following table:

Attitudes Toward Personal and National Financial Situation

	Optimists	Pessimists	Neutral
Satisfied with nation	35%	10%	24%
Dissatisfied with nation	60	88	71
No opinion	5	2	5
Satisfied with personal life	88%	58%	79%
Dissatisfied with personal life	11	40	19
No opinion	1	2	2

DECEMBER 26
OUTLOOK FOR WAR

Interviewing Date: 11/19–28/82 (U.S. only)
Special telephone survey

Asked in twenty-six countries: I'd like your opinion of the chances of a world war breaking out in the next ten years. If 0 means that there is no chance of a world war breaking out and if 10 means it is absolutely certain that a world war will break out, where on this scale of 0 to 10 would you rate the chances of world war breaking out in the next ten years?

The following are the results ranked from the most optimistic nation to the least:

	1982
Finland	73%
Italy	72
Japan	71
Greece	70
Chile	68
Norway	68
Sweden	68
Great Britain	65
Luxembourg	65

Argentina. 63
Peru 62
Switzerland 62
Denmark 61
France 60
Netherlands. 60
Uruguay. 60
Ireland 58
Germany 56
Brazil 55
Belgium 54
Canada. 54
Philippines. 49
Australia 43
United States 42
Colombia. 40

The consensus for the countries covered in the nationwide survey is as follows:*

Less than 50% 58%
About 50–50. 14
More than 50% 17
No opinion 11

Note: A rising tide of optimism about the chances for world peace is found in many nations around the globe, as determined by a recent Gallup International survey in which more than 25,000 representative citizens were interviewed. Optimists are defined as those who believe the chances of a world war in the next ten years are less than 50%. The balance of responses in each nation is grouped into the categories of about 50–50, more than 50%, and no opinion.

In virtually all of the twenty-six countries where nationwide surveys were conducted, the chances of an all-out conflict are less than 50%, with the proportion of optimists having increased over the last twelve months in the nineteen nations that participated in both the 1981 and 1982 surveys.

*The survey was also carried out in South Africa by the Gallup-affiliated organization. The results showed 42% of whites saying the chances of war are under 50%, with 24% of blacks sharing this opinion.

Optimism runs strongest in Finland (73% say chances of war are less than 50%), Italy (72%), Japan (71%), and Greece (70%). Least optimistic are Australians (43% think the chances of an all-out conflict are less than 50%), Americans (42%), and Colombians (40%).

In the United States, 42% say chances of a world war are less than 50%, 20% say about 50–50, and 29% believe there is more than a 50% likelihood of war. Most inclined to be optimistic are men, adults over the age of twenty-four, persons with a college background, Republicans, and westerners.

DECEMBER 30
MOVIE ATTENDANCE*

Interviewing Date: 8/13–16/82**
Survey #200-G

When was the last time you, yourself, went out to the movies? About how many times did you, yourself, go out to the movies within the last twelve months?

The following tables show the percentage of Americans who attended movies within the twelve-month test period, frequency of attendance during this period, and the percentage who attended within the last thirty days:

	Attended within last 12 months	Frequency within last 12 months	Attended within last 30 days
National	67%	5.1	46%

By Age

13–15	91%	6.9	75%
16–18	93	8.2	80

*This special analysis was written by Alec M. Gallup, vice-chairman of the Gallup Organization Inc.
**The teen-age findings are based on telephone interviews with a representative national cross section of boys and girls (thirteen to eighteen), conducted during July 1982.

19–24	92	7.2	69
25–29	79	5.1	51
30–49	70	3.9	48
50 years and over	38	1.4	20

By Age and Sex

13–15 boys......	89%	7.2	78%
13–15 girls	92	6.6	74
16–18 boys......	94	8.2	81
16–18 girls	93	8.1	78
19+ men........	62	3.8	42
19+ women	63	3.3	41

By Age and Race

13–18 whites	94%	7.7	79%
13–18 nonwhites .	84	5.7	66
19+ whites......	65	3.7	43
19+ nonwhites...	50	3.5	31

By Age and Education

13–18 above average	95%	7.8	81%
13–18 below average	90	7.3	74
19+ college	79	5.3	57
19+ high school ..	62	3.2	40
19+ grade school	28	.9	12

Two persons in every three over the age of 13 (67%) attended at least one movie within the last year, an increase of 10 percentage points from the 57% reported just one year ago. During this twelve-month period, Americans attended an average of five movies. Significantly, the increase in attendance for the last year occurred largely among persons over 25 (including even those 50 years and older) and not among the traditional movie audience, persons under 25. Among persons 13 to 24, for example, the increase was only about 3 percentage points, but among those 25 and over the gain was about 14 points.

A possible explanation for the increase in attendance among older Americans is the surprising popularity of such movies as *E.T.* Whether the uptrend in moviegoing among older persons is a harbinger of a major trend remains to be seen. Prior to the advent of the television era, movies tended to appeal to audiences of all ages. But with television and the movie industry's targeting of the youth market, many older people have stayed home.

While moviegoing among older Americans has shown a sharp rise, the traditional attendance patterns by age, as recorded by Gallup surveys dating back to the 1930s, are found in the latest measurement. Attendance is highest among persons under 24 years old, drops off steadily from 25 on, and drops precipitously among persons 50 years and older. The fall-off in attendance among older people, however, is not so marked as in previous years.

In terms of frequency of attendance, the key market segment continues to be 16- to 18-year-olds, who attended movies an average of eight times within the last twelve months. In contrast, persons over 50 attended an average of only one movie during this same twelve-month period.

The rate of attendance differs to some degree by educational background and race. Academically above-average teen-agers are slightly more likely to attend movies than are those below average in standing. College-educated adults are considerably more apt to attend movies, and more frequently, than those whose formal education ended at the high-school or grade-school level. Teen-agers from households in which both parents attended college also are more likely to attend movies, and to attend more frequently. And whites—both teen-agers and adults—are somewhat more likely to have attended movies in the last year than nonwhites.

Index

Budget (federal) (*continued*)
  reduce deficit by postponing tax cuts, 127
  reduce deficit by reducing military spending, 126
  reduce deficit by reducing spending for social programs, 126-27
Burglary
  incidence of, 79-81
  reported to police, 81
Bush, George
  approval rating as vice-president, 128-29
  as nominee for Republican presidential candidate, 223-24
  in trial heats vs. Kennedy, 103
  in trial heats vs. Mondale, 103
Busing
  of children to achieve racial balance (vote on Proposition 5), 251

C

Canada
  outlook for war, 295
Car
  importance of, 28
  incidence of theft of, 79-81
Carter, Jimmy
  approval rating vs. Reagan, 7, 41, 57, 107, 117, 148, 243
  as nominee for Democratic presidential candidate, 104, 104, 207
  popularity and congressional seat change, 30, 244
  as presidential candidate vs. Kennedy, 37-38
  in trial heats vs. Reagan, 102
Catholics
  not wanted as neighbors, 20-22
  religious preference, 37
Children
  satisfaction with relations with, 16
Chile
  outlook for war, 294
Church
  importance of, 27-28
Cigarettes
  reduce budget deficit by increasing tax on, 127-28
Clergy
  homosexuals hired as, 269
Colombia
  outlook for war, 295
Community
  satisfaction with, 18
Congress
  approval rating, 173-74
    national trend, 175
  approval rating of your district representative in, 176-77
  name of your district representative in, 175-76
  party of your district representative in, 176

see also Electoral reforms
Congressional elections
  analysis by A. Kohut, 29-30
  appropriate money to Republican and Democratic parties for, 253
  federal funding of candidates in, 252-53, 292
    national trend, 253
  final poll, 248-50
  Gallup analysis, 247-48
  interest in coming elections
    national trend, 247
  most important problem facing this district, 245
  party preference in, 52, 92-93, 132-34, 225, 233, 248
    national trend, 93, 134, 234
  results, 270-71
  run for Senate if party pays campaign expenses, 291-92
  seat change and presidential popularity, 30, 244
  thought you have given to, 244
    national trend, 244
  your name recorded in registration book, 244
Connally, John
  as nominee for Republican presidential candidate, 223-24
Conservatives
  and your political position, 233
Constitutional amendments see Budget (federal); Equal Rights Amendment (ERA); Prayer in public schools
Cosell, Howard
  approval rating, 3
Cost of living
  amount needed each week by your family, 51
  amount needed each week for family of four, 50
    national trend, 50-51
  amount spent on food each week, 49-50
    national trend, 50
  as most important problem, 32, 96, 136-37, 222-23, 245
Crane, Philip
  as nominee for Republican presidential candidate, 223-24
Cranston, Alan
  as nominee for Democratic presidential candidate, 104, 207
Creationism
  and origin of man, 208-10
  taught in public schools, 210-13
Crime
  afraid to walk alone at night, 46, 81
    national trend, 81
  and crime-watch program, 46-47
  happened to you in last twelve months, 79-81
    national trend, 81
  homosexuals involved in, 264
  as most important problem, 32, 96, 136-37, 222, 245
  relation between rising crime rate and violence on television, 107-08
  reported to police, 81

Cuban refugees
not wanted as neighbors, 20-22

D

Damage suits
case decided by panel of three judges, 246
top limit on each type of injury, 246
who bears cost of large jury awards, 246
Danforth, John
as nominee for Republican presidential candidate, 223
Dawson, Len
approval rating, 3
Death penalty
for persons convicted of murder (vote on Proposition 9), 251
Democratic party
appropriate money to, for campaign purposes, 253
better for dealing with national problems, 51-52
better for handling most important problem, 32, 136-37, 223, 245
national trend, 247
convention choice for president between Carter and Kennedy, 37-38
convention choice for president between Mondale and Kennedy, 38, 158-59
and inflation and unemployment, 33
and keeping country prosperous, 45, 166-68
national trend, 45, 168
and keeping United States out of war, 45, 168-69
national trend, 45, 169
nominees for presidential candidate, 104-05, 207
preference for, in congressional elections, 52, 92-93, 132-34, 225, 233, 248
national trend, 93, 134, 226, 234
search committees for best candidates for, 291
Denmark
outlook for war, 295
Doctors
bearing cost of jury awards, 246
homosexuals hired as, 268-69
Dole, Robert
as nominee for Republican presidential candidate, 223-24
Draft registration
approval of, 40
national trend, 40
Drinking age
now eighteen or nineteen, 95
now twenty or twenty-one, 95-96
Drinking and driving
mandatory jail sentence for first offenders, 91
police stopping motorists at random, 91-92
stricter laws regarding, 90-91
Drugs
problems of homosexuals with, 263-64

see also Marijuana
Durenberger, David
as nominee for Republican presidential candidate, 223

E

E.T. (movie)
approval rating, 237
seen/would like to see, 235
Eastern Orthodox churches
religious preference, 37
Economic conditions
handled by Reagan, 30, 42, 57-58, 114, 148-50, 202
national trend, 31, 116
political party better for dealing with, 51
see also Reaganomics
Economy
during next three months, 97-98
as most important problem, 96, 136-37, 222-23, 245
Ecuador
opinions in, on Falkland Islands crisis, 86-88
Eisenhower, Dwight
approval rating vs. Reagan, 7, 41, 57, 107, 148
popularity and congressional seat change, 30, 244
Elderly people
work with, as nonmilitary service, 40, 274-75
Electoral reforms
better way to select candidates for presidency, 290-91
changes in way political campaigns are conducted, 290
four regional presidential primaries, 291
limit member of House to three terms of four years apiece, 293
money provided by government for campaign of candidates for Congress, 292
presidential candidates chosen in nationwide primary, 291
run for Senate if party pays campaign expenses, 291-92
search committees for Republican and Democratic candidates, 291
term of members of House changed from two years to four years, 293
term of office of president changed to one six-year, 292
Elementary school teachers
homosexuals hired as, 269-70
El Salvador
public opinion on (analysis by A. Kohut), 53-54
situation handled by Reagan, 66-67
Employment and job security
accept less money or status to get another job, 99
actively looking for a job, 180-82, 279
national trend, 279
easy to get another job as good, 98-99
emphasis on working hard, 13-14
equal rights for homosexuals in, 266-67
importance of interesting job, 26

Employment and job security (*continued*)
   likely to lose job, 39, 179-80, 278-79
      national trend, 279
   losing job or taking pay cut, 99
   now employed, 178-79
   require employers to hire young people, 100-01
   satisfaction with job, 18
   see also Job discrimination
Enberg, Dick
   approval rating, 2
Energy situation
   handled by Reagan, 203
   political party better for dealing with, 51
   and Reagan administration policies, 172
Environmental issues/situation
   handled by Reagan, 203
   political party better for dealing with, 51-52
   and Reagan administration policies, 172
   reducing regulations to improve business (vote on Proposition 10), 251
Equal Rights Amendment (ERA)
   approval of (vote on Proposition 3), 251
   approval rating, 138-40
      national trend, 140
   chance of passage if reoffered, 142
   reoffer after deadline, 140-42
Evolution
   and origin of man, 208-10
   taught in public schools, 210-13

F

Falkland Islands crisis
   attacking Argentine ships and troops, 85-86
   attacking mainland Argentina, 86
   criticism of government justified, 85
   cutting off trade with Argentina, 86
   fight by Argentina if Great Britain takes islands, 87
   force or negotiations by Great Britain, 87
   government's action, following invasion, 85
   military procedure or peaceful negotiations by Argentina, 86
   occupation by Argentina political or historic, 88
   owned by Argentina or Great Britain, 86
   Reagan as mediator in, 88
   removal of its troops by Argentina, 86-87
   sending British fleet to, 85
   United States should help Argentina or Great Britain, 99
   war will be won by Great Britain or Argentina, 87
   your sympathies with Argentina or Great Britain, 99
   your town on side of Argentina or Great Britain, 87-88
Falwell, Jerry
   approval rating, 25
Family life
   importance of, 25
   satisfaction with, 16-17
Family ties
   emphasis on traditional, 9-10

Finances *see* Personal finances
Finland
   outlook for war, 294
Football
   watched on television, 1-2
Football sportscasters
   commentary rated, 2-3
Ford, Gerald
   approval rating vs. Reagan, 107, 117, 243
   popularity and congressional seat change, 244
Foreign policy/affairs
   handled by Reagan, 42, 63-64, 115, 203-04
      national trend, 116, 204
   political party better for dealing with, 51
France
   outlook for war, 295
   public confidence in courts and institutions, 165
Freedom of choice
   importance of, 26
Friends
   importance of, 27

G

Gasoline
   reduce budget deficit by increasing tax on, 127
Gifford, Frank
   approval rating, 2
Glenn, John
   as nominee for Democratic presidential candidate, 104, 105, 207
Government size
   reducing, and Reagan administration policies, 170
Government spending
   as most important problem, 32, 96, 136-37, 222
   see also National defense; Social programs
Great Britain
   outlook for war, 294
   public confidence in courts and institutions, 165
   see also Falkland Islands crisis
Greece
   outlook for war, 294
Gumbel, Bryant
   approval rating, 2

H

Haig, Alexander
   approval rating, 130
Handguns
   ban on possession of (vote on Proposition 2), 251
   law forbidding possession of, 135
   laws covering sale of, 135
   registration of, 134-35
Hart, Gary
   as nominee for Democratic presidential candidate, 105, 207

Jews (*continued*)
  religious preference, 37
Job discrimination
  chance of woman to become the executive, 198-99
  choice of man or woman as boss, 196-98
    national trend, 198
  women have equal job opportunities with men, 195-96
Job security *see* Employment and job security
Johnson, Lyndon
  approval rating vs. Reagan, 107, 243
  popularity and congressional seat change, 30, 244
Jury trials
  case decided by panel of three judges, 246
  top limit on each type of injury, 246
  who bears cost of large jury awards, 246

K

Kemp, Jack
  as nominee for Republican presidential candidate, 223-24
Kennedy, Edward
  as nominee for Democratic presidential candidate, 104, 105, 207
  as presidential candidate vs. Carter, 37-38
  as presidential candidate vs. Mondale, 38, 158-59
  in trial heats vs. Bush, 103
  in trial heats vs. Reagan, 103, 159-60, 272
    national trend, 160, 272
Kennedy, John
  approval rating vs. Reagan, 7, 41, 57, 107, 148
  popularity and congressional seat change, 30, 244
Kohut, Andrew, analyses by
  ambivalent election results mirror equivocal opinion of Reagan's program, 271-72
  Americans give legal system very low marks, 164-66
  congressional elections, 29-30
  nuclear freeze movement, 94-95
  PLO fails to benefit from waning sympathy for Israel, 226-27
  political differences between men and women, 35-36
  sharp distinctions found in public opinion on El Salvador and Vietnam, 53-54
  views on Reagan divided, intense, and stalled, 186-88

L

Laxalt, Paul
  as nominee for Republican presidential candidate, 223
Lebanon
  and Israel's invasion of, 190-91
  and Israel's military operations in, 145-47
Legal system
  given very low marks (analysis by A. Kohut), 164-66
  public confidence in courts and institutions, 165
Leisure time
  importance of, 28

satisfaction with free time, 19
Liberals
  and your political position, 233
Lugar, Richard
  as nominee for Republican presidential candidate, 223-24
Luxembourg
  outlook for war, 294

M

Madden, John
  approval rating, 2
Malvinas Islands *see* Falkland Islands crisis
Marijuana
  legalizing possession of (vote on Proposition 8), 251
Marriage
  satisfaction with, 17
Material possessions
  importance of, 25-28
Meredith, Don
  approval rating, 2
Mexicans
  not wanted as neighbors, 20-22
Middle East situation *see* Arab nations; Israel
Military spending
  increase in federal spending for military and defense (vote on Proposition 13), 252
  reduce budget deficit by reducing, 126
Mondale, Walter
  as nominee for Democratic presidential candidate, 104, 105, 207
  as presidential candidate vs. Kennedy, 38, 158-59
  in trial heats vs. Bush, 103
  in trial heats vs. Reagan, 102, 160-62, 272
    national trend, 162, 272
Money
  emphasis on, 12-13
Moral code
  importance of, 27
Moral decline
  as most important problem, 32, 96, 136-37, 222
Moral Majority
  approval rating, 22-24
  willing to belong to, 25
Movies
  attendance, 295-96
  those seen/would like to see, 235-37
Moynihan, Daniel (Pat)
  as nominee for Democratic presidential candidate, 104, 105, 207

N

National defense
  amount spent by government for, 77-78, 276-77
    national trend, 78, 278

handled by Reagan, 42, 61-63, 115, 202-03
  national trend, 116
as most important problem, 96
political party better for dealing with, 51
and Reagan administration policies, 170
United States or Soviet Union stronger in military
  power, 76-77
United States or Soviet Union stronger in nuclear
  weapons, 275-76
see also Military spending
National security
as most important problem, 96
National service
and adoption of European plan, 39-40
interested in volunteering for, 239
military or nonmilitary, 40, 238-39, 274-75
  national trend, 40
volunteer for military or nonmilitary, 239
Natural gas pipeline
advantages of Reagan administration's position on
  Soviet, 205
approval of administration's position on Soviet, 205-06
removing sanctions against using U.S. supplies to build,
  284-85
Netherlands
outlook for war, 295
New Federalism
approval rating, 48-49
more responsibility to state governments (vote on Proposition 6), 251
states' care vs. federal, 49
and taxes paid by your family, 49
Nixon, Richard
approval rating vs. Reagan, 7, 41, 57, 107, 117, 148,
  243
popularity and congressional seat change, 30, 244
Norway
outlook for war, 294
Nuclear freeze
agreement between United States and Soviet Union for
  immediate freeze, 280-82
system for verifying whether Soviet Union is living up
  to terms, 282-83
unilateral freeze on production of nuclear weapons (vote
  on Proposition 4), 251
Nuclear freeze movement
analysis by A. Kohut, 94-95
Nuclear weapons
United States or Soviet Union stronger in, 275-76

P

Packwood, Robert
as nominee for Republican presidential candidate, 223
Palestine Liberation Organization (PLO)
approval rating, 216-18
fails to benefit from waning sympathy for Israel
  (analysis by A. Kohut), 226-27

invasion of Lebanon by Israel to attack, 190-91
Palestinians
approval rating, 216
independent nation for, 193-94
Israel's operations in Lebanon to stop attacks by, 145-47
Reagan's plan for homeland for, 231
Peace
chances for world, and Reagan administration policies,
  172
keeping United States out of war *see* Democratic party;
  Republican party
Peace Corps
nonmilitary service in, 238-39
Personal assets
importance of, 25-28
Personal finances
better next year than now, 44, 156
  national trend, 44
better now than a year ago, 43-44
  national trend, 44
better over the long run, 156-57
effect of Reaganomics on, 42, 83-85, 156, 227-29
  national trend, 42, 85, 156, 229
Personal satisfaction *see* Satisfaction
Peru
opinions in, on Falkland Islands crisis, 86-88
outlook for war, 295
Philippines
outlook for war, 295
Poland
situation in, dealt with by Reagan, 31
Political differences between men and women
analysis by A. Kohut, 35-36
Poltergeist (movie)
approval rating, 237
seen/would like to see, 236
Potential
living up to, importance of, 26
Prayer in public schools
approval of proposed amendment for, 121-23
arguments against amendment for, 121
arguments in favor of amendment for, 121
amendment to permit (vote on Proposition 14), 252
home, school, or church in religious development of
  child, 123-24
Presidential candidates
see Democratic party; Electoral reforms; Republican
  party
Presidential term of office
change to one six-year term, 292
Presidential trial heats
Bush vs. Kennedy, 103
Bush vs. Mondale, 103
Reagan vs. Carter, 102
Reagan vs. Kennedy, 103, 159-60, 272
  national trend, 160, 272
Reagan vs. Mondale, 102, 160-62, 272
  national trend, 162, 272

Prison reform
    appoint more judges to reduce time between arrest and
        trial, 75
    convert army bases into prisons, 70
    need for more state prisons, 68-69
    pay prisoners with return to victims or state, 73-74
    permit wives some weekends with prisoner husbands,
        74-75
    prisoner required to read and write before release, 73
    prisons for first offenders as well as for committers of
        serious crimes, 70-71
    punish men in prison or start them on right road, 71-72
    refuse parole to prisoner paroled before committing
        crime, 75
    services performed by prisoners for state, 73
    skill or job for prisoner before release, 72-73
    willing to pay more taxes to build prisons, 69-70
Problems
    most important, 32-33, 96-97, 136-37, 222-23, 245
Prosperity
    see Democratic party; Republican party
Protestants
    not wanted as neighbors, 20-22
    religious preference, 37
Public opinion referendum
    on sixteen propositions, 250-52
Puerto Ricans
    not wanted as neighbors, 20–22
Puerto Rico
    independence for, 9
    statehood for, 8

R

Reagan, Ronald
    advantages of his position on Soviet natural gas pipeline,
        205
    analysis of approval rating, 147-48
    approval of his position on Soviet natural gas pipeline,
        205-06
    approval rating, 6-7, 30, 41, 55-57, 105, 114, 200-02,
        239-41
        national trend, 8, 30, 116, 241
    approval rating as person, 41, 107
    approval rating by degree, 105-07, 241-43
    approval rating vs. predecessors, 7, 41, 57, 107, 117,
        148, 243
    and economic conditions, 30, 42, 57-58, 114, 148-50,
        202
        national trend, 31, 116
    election results mirror opinion of Reagan's program
        (analysis by A. Kohut), 271-72
    and energy situation, 203
    and environmental issues, 203
    and foreign policy/affairs, 42, 63-64, 115, 203-04
        national trend, 116, 204

    and inflation, 31, 42, 58–60, 115, 150–52, 202
        national trend, 31, 116
    like to see run for president in 1984, 89, 224
    as mediator in Malvinas Islands conflict, 88
    and national defense, 42, 61-63, 115, 202-03
        national trend, 116
    perceived concern for different population groups of,
        120
    perceived job-related characteristics of, 120
    perceived personal characteristics of, 119-20
    plan for West Bank and Gaza Strip and homeland for
        Palestinians, 230-31
    and policies for foreign and domestic problems, 170-73
    and relations with Soviet Union, 31, 42, 64-66, 115-16,
        203
        national trend, 31, 116
    removing sanctions against natural gas pipeline, 284-85
    and situation in El Salvador, 66-67
    and situation in Poland, 31
    in trial heats vs. Carter, 102
    in trial heats vs. Kennedy, 103, 159-60, 272
        national trend, 160, 272
    in trial heats vs. Mondale, 102, 160-62, 272
        national trend, 162, 272
    and unemployment, 31, 42, 60-61, 115, 152-54, 202
        national trend, 31, 116
    views on, divided, intense, and stalled (analysis by A.
        Kohut), 186–88
    will run for president in 1984, 90, 224
    see also Budget (federal)
Reaganomics
    administration's economic program and policies (vote
        on Proposition 16), 252
    effect on nation's economic situation, 42-43, 82-83, 229
        national trend, 43, 83, 229
    effect on nation's economic situation over the long run,
        83, 230
    effect on nation's economic situation a year from now,
        83, 229-30
    effect on your financial situation, 42, 83-85, 156, 227-
        29
        national trend, 42, 85, 156, 229
    effect on your financial situation over the long run,
        156-57
    effect on your financial situation a year from now, 44,
        156
        national trend, 44
Recession
    during next three months, 97-98
    as most important problem, 32, 96, 136-37, 222-23
Regan, Donald
    approval rating, 130
Religion
    church or synagogue attendance, 36
        national trend, 36
    church or synagogue membership, 36
        national trend, 37
    importance of church or synagogue, 27-28

S

Strauss, Robert
    as nominee for Democratic presidential candidate, 104, 207
Summerall, Pat
    approval rating, 2
Sweden
    outlook for war, 294
Switzerland
    outlook for war, 295
Synagogue
    importance of, 27-28

T

Tarkenton, Fran
    approval rating, 2
Taxes
    as most important problem, 245
    paid by your family under New Federalism, 49
    reducing, and Reagan administration policies, 170-71
    tuition tax credits, 251
    willing to pay more, to build prisons, 69–70
    see also Budget (federal); Social Security
Television violence
    relation between violence on television and rising crime rate, 107-08
    shown only after 10 o'clock at night, 108-09
    taken off television entirely, 109-10
Theft of car
    incidence of, 79-81
    reported to police, 81
Theft of money or property
    incidence of, 79-81
    reported to police, 81
Truman, Harry
    popularity and congressional seat change, 30, 244
Tuition tax credits
    reduction in federal tax for each child (vote on Proposition 7), 251

U

Unemployment
    handled by Reagan, 31, 42, 60-61, 115, 152-54, 202
        national trend, 3, 116
    handled by Republican or Democratic party, 33
    as most important problem, 32, 96-97, 136-37, 222-23, 245
    political party better for dealing with, 51
    and Reagan administration policies, 173
    reduced by government, 39
        national trend, 39
Unemployment rate
    by end of next year, 285-86

by end of 1982, 34, 154
    national trend, 154-55
United Nations
    approval rating, 162-63
        national trend, 163
    and Falkland Islands crisis, 86
    and U.S. membership in, 163–64
        national trend, 164
United States
    increasing respect abroad for, and Reagan administration policies, 171
    membership in United Nations, 163-64
        national trend, 164
    outlook for war, 295
    party keeping country prosperous, 45, 166-68
        national trend, 45, 168
    party likely to keep out of war, 45, 168-69
        national trend, 45, 169
    satisfaction with way things are going in, 3-4, 117-18
        national trend, 5, 6, 118
    and Soviet Union *see* Soviet Union
Uruguay
    opinions in, on Falkland Islands crisis, 86-88
    outlook for war, 295

V

Vandalism of property
    incidence of, 79-81
    reported to police, 81
Vietnam
    public opinion on (analysis by A. Kohut), 53-54
Vietnamese refugees
    not wanted as neighbors, 20-22
VISTA
    nonmilitary service in, 238-39

W

War
    chances of world war in next ten years, 294-95
    fear of, as most important problem, 32, 96, 136-37, 222
    party likely to keep United States out of, 45, 168-69
        national trend, 45, 169
Watt, James
    approval rating, 131
Weicker, Lowell
    as nominee for Republican presidential candidate, 223-24
Weinberger, Caspar
    approval rating, 129
West Germany
    outlook for war, 295

public confidence in courts and institutions, 165

Women

  chance to become the executive, 198-99

  choice of man or woman as boss, 196-98

    national trend, 198

  equal job opportunities with men, 195-96

  ideal life-style, 182-85

    national trend, 186

  political differences between men and (analysis by A. Kohut), 35-36

public confidence in courts and institutions, 165
Women
  chance to become the executive, 198-99
  choice of man or woman as boss, 196-98
    national trend, 198

equal job opportunities with men, 195-96
ideal life-style, 182-85
  national trend, 186
political differences between men and (analysis by A. Kohut), 35-36